Discussions in commodity-exporting emerg[...] ideas without empirical or analytical support. 1... .... g.... ....on to improving our understanding of those economies, based on rigorous research. It provides robust empirical evidence including a long-term perspective on commodity prices. It also contains very thoughtful policy analysis, with implications for resilience, macroeconomic policies, and development strategies. It will be a key reference for scholars as well as policy makers.

José De Gregorio
Dean of the School of Economics and Business
Universidad de Chile
Former Minister of Economy, Mining and Energy
and Former Governor of the Central Bank of Chile

Commodity Markets: Evolution, Challenges, and Policies is a broad-ranging analysis of just about everything you have ever wanted to know about commodity markets. It has a broad sweep of commodity prices and production (primarily energy, metals, and agricultural commodities) over the past century, carefully documenting and rigorously analyzing the important difference in experiences across different groups of commodities. It is comprehensive in its historical coverage but also addresses contemporary issues such as an insightful analysis of the impact of the COVID-19 pandemic and the Ukraine war on commodity prices. It draws out the impact of shocks, technology, and policy as drivers of demand and supply for a range of different commodities. This book is essential reading for anyone interested in the drivers of commodity prices and production over the last century and the implications for future trends.

Warwick McKibbin
Distinguished Professor of Economics and Public Policy
Director of the Centre for Applied Macroeconomic Analysis
Director of Policy Engagement
at the Australian Research Centre of Excellence in Population Ageing Research
Australian National University

A sound understanding of commodity markets is more essential than ever in light of the COVID-19 pandemic, the war in Ukraine, and the transition from fossil fuels to renewable energy commodities. This volume offers an excellent, comprehensive, and very timely analysis of the wide range of factors that affect commodity markets. It carefully surveys historical and future trends in commodity supply, demand, and prices and offers detailed policy proposals to avoid the havoc that turbulent commodity markets can cause on the economies of commodity exporters and importers.

Rick Van der Ploeg
Research Director of Oxford Centre for the Analysis of Resource-Rich Economies
University of Oxford

Commodity prices tend to be seen as an aggregate, especially when they periodically move upward together. While these aggregate movements are important, this excellent and well-researched volume emphasizes the heterogeneity of commodity markets and the differing economic forces that act upon them. Heterogeneity calls for differentiated and tailored policy tools that take into account the specificities of markets, a message that analysts and policy makers would do well to heed.

Ravi Kanbur
T. H. Lee Professor of World Affairs
International Professor of Applied Economics and Management
Cornell University

Commodity markets are complex and constantly evolving. This insightful and well-structured study of all the ins and outs of commodity markets is a valuable addition to the literature for understanding how these markets function and their impacts on the global economy. As the war in Ukraine and the COVID-19 pandemic continue to have substantial impacts on commodity prices and supply chains, this incredibly timely study offers analysts and policy makers a firm foundation for making better predictions and developing more effective policy responses.

Abdolreza Abbassian
Former FAO Senior Economist and G20-AMIS Secretary

I wish I had this book earlier in my career! *Commodity Markets: Evolution, Challenges, and Policies* provides an insightful analysis of the dynamics of commodity markets and their implications on the broader economy. A must-read for anyone interested in commodity markets.

Xiaoli Etienne
Associate Professor and Idaho Wheat Commission
Endowed Chair in Commodity Risk Management
University of Idaho

While many African countries were spared the ravages of the COVID-19 pandemic, their economies suffered because commodity prices collapsed. Since then, the war in Ukraine has affected developing countries thousands of miles away because oil, gas, and food prices have spiked. Commodity markets not only receive the impact of global shocks, but they transmit them to commodity-dependent countries around the world. This book lucidly explains how these shocks affect commodity markets and, in turn, how fluctuations in these markets affect developing economies. As the world deals with climate change and the energy transition, these findings will become even more important.

Shanta Devarajan
Professor of the Practice of International Development
Georgetown University

This book brings into one place otherwise scattered information on the evolution of commodity markets, causes and impacts of price shocks, and the drivers and implications of commodity demand. These are issues of great importance to policy makers, particularly in commodity-dependent developing countries. Three major events that have recently affected commodity markets, namely, the energy transition, the COVID-19 pandemic, and the war in Ukraine, highlight the vulnerability of commodity-dependent countries to price shocks. This book should be a source of inspiration for these countries as they attempt to move away from the commodity dependence trap that has afflicted them for so long. I strongly recommend this book to colleagues working on the topic.

Janvier Nkurunziza
Officer in Charge
Commodities Branch
United Nations Conference on Trade and Development

Commodity Markets: Evolution, Challenges, and Policies will provide the J.P. Morgan Center for Commodities with the comprehensive textbook we have always wanted to write. Currently, the vast majority of commodity-related textbooks are dominated by trading issues, with a limited focus on market fundamentals. As a result, our instructors typically rely on a wide mix of articles, book chapters, and case studies for their respective courses. By providing a comprehensive detailed coverage of these issues, this book fills a major gap in the literature.

Tom Brady
Executive Director
J.P. Morgan Center for Commodities
University of Colorado Denver

Commodity Markets

Commodity Markets

Evolution, Challenges, and Policies

Edited by
John Baffes and Peter Nagle

Summary of Contents

Contents

Figures

Tables

Foreword

Global economic development has long been propelled by the mass production and consumption of raw materials—for food, energy, shelter, and all the comforts of modern civilization. Even as the human population quadrupled over the past 100 years, global commodity markets kept the world well stocked and supported poverty reduction and better living standards.

Amid overlapping crises over the past two years and the ongoing transition to lower carbon intensity, commodity markets are being reshaped. COVID-19 highlighted the volatility of these markets: global shocks can boost or drop prices sharply and suddenly, with destabilizing consequences for developing economies. The war in Ukraine has made the security of energy and supply chains a more prominent goal, even if it entails higher costs. Efforts to reduce greenhouse gas emissions are shifting demand away from fossil fuels while increasing demand for the metals and materials needed to build solar and wind infrastructure and battery storage. The sudden disruption of natural gas markets, which have often provided electricity base load during peak demand, brought new concerns about grid stability, grid capacity when adding intermittent renewables, and a global return to coal and diesel electricity generation.

This book offers a comprehensive analysis of major commodity markets and analyzes how changes in these markets affect the economies of developing countries. Over the next three decades, the growth of global demand for commodities is likely to decelerate as population growth slows, with many developing economies maturing and shifting their demand mix more toward consumption and services. The energy transition is likely to bring a major boost to metal-producing economies because technologies related to renewable energy tend to be more metals-intensive.

The ongoing transformation of global commodity markets will have profound implications for countries that depend on commodity production for economic growth, exports, and fiscal revenues. Countries that depend on commodities account for half of the world's extreme poor. But the report suggests there may be differentiation among exporters: fossil fuel exporters could see a decline in revenues while metals exporters reap windfall gains as the energy transition proceeds.

The book sheds new light on the causes and consequences of commodity market volatility. It shows that commodity price shocks tend to have asymmetric effects, which could in part be driven by the nature of (often nontransparent) export contracts. Price increases do not materially boost the economic growth of commodity-exporting countries, but price declines significantly reduce their growth, sometimes for several years. As a result, policy solutions need to be tailored to each country's circumstances and characteristics. This finding highlights why policy makers should use upswings in commodity prices to prepare for the next downturn. Policy makers can choose from three sets of instruments to mitigate or manage commodity shocks:

1. *Better fiscal, monetary, and regulatory frameworks.* Commodity price swings often spur governments to adopt policies that aggravate boom-and-bust cycles, ramping up government spending when commodity prices rise and keeping spending high even when prices and government revenues fall. Governments should put in place a fiscal framework that builds rainy day funds that benefit from export surges and can be deployed quickly in an emergency. Doing so would add to the stability of currency and monetary systems, which are key ingredients in attracting investment and raising living standards. Regulators have to guard against the accumulation of excessive financial sector risks—especially those that accompany nontransparent capital inflows and foreign currency debt.

2. *Avoidance of subsidies and trade restraint.* Governments tend to resort to subsidies or trade protection to reduce the effects of commodity price movements on consumers. Commodity-exporting countries often try to mitigate market volatility by reaching agreements to regulate supply. History shows that such efforts are always costly and usually counterproductive. A better approach is to adopt market-based risk mechanisms to reduce exposure to price movements and to provide targeted safety nets to protect the poor.

3. *Economic diversification.* Commodity market risks are greatest for countries that depend on the exports of just a few commodities—especially fossil fuels. The risk of a climate-related secular decline in fossil fuel demand argues for diversification. Similarly, low-income countries that depend too heavily on exports of agricultural products would benefit from reforms that encourage diversification into other sectors. In both cases, the key first step is to avoid subsidizing exports, given the fiscal cost and volatility risk. A wide range of structural measures can help encourage economic diversification: building human capital, promoting competition, strengthening institutions, and reducing distorting subsidies. The record is clear: an economy's long-term growth prospects and resilience to external shocks usually improve as it allows diversification beyond commodities.

For sound global development, the next few years are critical in adopting policies that allow rapid growth in median income and the income of the world's poor. Inflation and commodity market volatility have contributed to the reversals in development in recent years, undermining poverty reduction and the energy transition. Over time, demand for commodities will have to be met by greater productive capacity—either through technological advances or the substitution of one commodity for another. A sound goal is for the shifts in commodity markets to encourage good outcomes for both development and environmental sustainability. All countries have a shared interest in acting promptly to defuse the risks of stagflation, slow growth, and environmental harm. This book provides some of the key information needed to act on that interest.

David Malpass
President
World Bank Group

Acknowledgments

This book is a product of the Prospects Group in the Equitable Growth, Finance and Institutions Vice Presidency. The project was managed by John Baffes and Peter Nagle, coeditors of the volume, under the guidance of M. Ayhan Kose and Franziska Ohnsorge. Ayhan and Franziska's advice, feedback, and support helped enrich and deepen the analysis and insights of the book.

The core team underlying the project consists of John Baffes (overview, chapters 1 and 2), Alain Kabundi (chapters 3 and 4), Wee Chian Koh (chapter 1), Peter Nagle (overview, chapters 1, 2, and 4), Franziska Ohnsorge (chapter 4), Garima Vasishtha (chapter 3), Takefumi Yamazaki (chapter 4), and Hamza Zahid (chapter 3).

We owe a particular debt of gratitude to Kevin Clinton, who painstakingly edited all the chapters, and Kaltrina Temaj, who managed the database and produced all of the graphics of the volume. We thank Shane Streifel for his contributions to individual sections and broader editorial guidance. We are also indebted to colleagues who supported us in the production process: Adriana Maximiliano, for designing and typesetting, and Graeme Littler, for editorial and website support.

The completion of the project would not have been possible without the help of numerous World Bank Group colleagues. Several colleagues reviewed various parts of the book: Ergys Islamaj, Alain Kabundi, Jeetendra Khadan, Csilla Lakatos, Shane Streifel, Garima Vasishtha, Dana Vorisek, and Shu Yu. Other colleagues commented on earlier drafts of chapters: Carlos Arteta, Madhur Gautam, Justin Damien Guenette, Sergiy Kasyanenko, Gene Kindberg-Hanlon, Patrick Kirby, Somik Lall, Hideaki Matsuoka, Franz Ulrich Ruch, Temel Taskin, Sameh Wahba, and Collette Wheeler. Excellent research assistance was provided by Lule Bahtiri, Hrisyana Doytchinova, Arika Kayastha, Maria Hazel Macadangdang, Muneeb Naseem, Ceylan Oymak, Vasiliki Papagianni, Lorez Qehaja, Juan Felipe Serrano Ariza, and Jinxin Wu.

Many outside experts—including Christiane Baumeister, Valery Charnavoki, Manmohan Kumar, Gert Peersman, James Rowe, Bent Sorensen, Martin Stuermer, John Tilton, Jian Yang, and Kei-Mu Yi—commented on early draft chapters of the book.

The team is also thankful to the organizers and participants at various seminars and conferences who provided valuable early feedback on analytical work included in the book. Events included the Center of Commodity Markets Research's third commodity market winter workshop (Hannover, Germany, February 2019); the Commodity and Energy Markets Association's annual meeting (Pittsburgh, June 2019); a seminar at Tongji University (Shanghai, July 2019); the Commodity and Energy Markets Association conference (virtual, June 2021), and the J.P. Morgan Center for Commodities Research Symposium (virtual, August 2021). Comments and suggestions from participants at seminars at the World Bank in the fall of 2021 are also gratefully acknowledged.

External affairs for the book were managed by Alejandra Viveros, Joseph Rebello, and Nandita Roy, supported by Paul Blake, Jose Carlos Ferreyra, Kavell Joseph, and Torie Smith.

The research in this book builds upon a large body of earlier work published by the Prospects Group: *Global Economic Prospects* reports (special focus section of the June 2018 edition and chapter 3 of the January 2022 edition); *Commodity Markets Outlook* reports (special focuses of October 2018, October 2019, October 2020, April 2021, and October 2021 editions); and *Global Commodity Markets* report (special focus of January 2000 edition). The analysis in this book also extends research published in several academic and working papers.

The Prospects Group gratefully acknowledges financial support from the Policy and Human Resources Development Fund provided by the Government of Japan.

Authors

John Baffes, Senior Economist, World Bank

Alain Kabundi, Senior Economist, World Bank

Wee Chian Koh, Researcher, Centre for Strategic and Policy Studies, Brunei Darussalam

Peter Nagle, Senior Economist, World Bank

Franziska Ohnsorge, Manager, World Bank

Garima Vasishtha, Senior Economist, World Bank

Takefumi Yamazaki, Senior Economist, World Bank

Hamza Zahid, Economist, World Bank

Executive Summary

Wars, pandemics, and global recessions have occurred frequently throughout history and have had major impacts on commodity markets. In the early 2020s, the COVID-19 pandemic and the war in Ukraine caused extensive disruptions to commodity markets and the global economy. In 2020, the pandemic triggered a sharp fall in global demand for commodities, especially crude oil; however, commodity prices rapidly recovered as demand rebounded and supply was slow to respond because of capacity constraints and supply bottlenecks. In 2022, the war in Ukraine disrupted the production and trade of commodities in which the Russian Federation and Ukraine are key players, leading to further price increases, especially for energy and food. These developments exacerbated inflationary pressures, weighed on economic growth, and contributed to food and energy insecurity.

Climate change and the transition from fossil fuels to zero-carbon sources of energy add another dimension to the uncertainties that roil commodity markets. Extreme weather events will become increasingly common and can affect the production of many commodities. The energy transition—intended to minimize the worst effects of climate change—is altering patterns of commodity production and consumption. Demand for fossil fuels is expected to be flat or decline over the next few decades, whereas demand for metals is likely to rise because of higher metal content of renewable energy infrastructure. On the policy front, COVID-19-related supply disruptions and the war in Ukraine could lead to increased protectionism on energy security and food self-sufficiency grounds, as well as fragmentation of trade, investment, and financial networks.

This study examines the factors that determine developments in commodity markets and analyzes how changes in these markets can affect the economies of commodity exporters and importers. The analysis is based on four broad approaches. First, it studies the evolution of commodity markets over the past century and identifies key drivers of supply, demand, and price movements across commodity groups. The drivers include income and population growth, industrialization and urbanization, technological innovations, and policy changes. Second, it quantifies the relative importance of these drivers for different commodity groups and concludes that income plays a crucial role in driving demand for industrial commodities over the long term, while agriculture is chiefly driven by population growth. Third, it takes a detailed look at the nature and drivers of commodity price fluctuations. Fourth, it assesses the impact of commodity price fluctuations on commodity exporters and importers.

The book offers a range of analytical findings, which can be grouped under four categories.

First, commodity markets are going through a major transformation, with large shifts in the magnitude and location of production and consumption. The relative importance of commodities has also evolved over time, as technological innovation has led to new uses for some materials and substitution among commodities. Commodity markets will continue to see large transformations in coming years. Demand from China, the largest consumer of many commodities, is likely to slow as its economy matures and shifts toward consumption and services. At the same time, the energy transition is likely to trigger substantial changes in patterns of demand, with a bigger role for the metals needed for low-carbon technologies and a smaller role for fossil fuels. Fragmentation of global value chains and reshoring could also alter patterns of commodity trade.

Second, the study establishes that commodity markets are highly heterogeneous in terms of their drivers and price behavior. Over the past century, agricultural prices have declined in real terms, energy prices have risen, and the performance of metal prices has been mixed. Further, the cyclical components of energy and metal prices follow the business and investment cycles more closely than do most agricultural prices. In part, this heterogeneity reflects differences in the drivers of demand for these commodities—demand for energy and metals is much more closely related to economic growth than is agricultural demand. The relationship between economic growth and commodity demand also varies widely across countries, depending on the country's stage of economic development. At low levels of income, commodity demand, especially for industrial commodities, rises rapidly with economic growth. As incomes rise, however, growth in demand for commodities starts to slow.

Third, commodity price shocks have asymmetric effects on commodity exporters, in part a reflection of the structure of their economies. Oil exporters tend to be less diversified and rely more on petroleum for export and fiscal revenues than metal and agricultural exporters do on their commodities. As a result, oil-exporting economies may be more vulnerable to fluctuations in oil prices than other commodity producers are to changes in the prices of the foods or metals they export. There are also significant variations in the size, duration, and impact of price fluctuations across commodities. Further, price shocks have asymmetric effects: large price declines hurt growth in commodity exporters much more, and in a more lasting manner, than large price increases benefit their growth. This asymmetric impact requires policy responses that, in the midst of upturns, carefully prepare for downturns.

Fourth, the study confirms that the heterogeneous nature of commodity markets requires policy tools tailored to the type of commodity produced (or consumed) and to the origin of the shock. Policy makers have used a variety of tools to address the challenges originating from commodity markets and especially those posed by commodity price fluctuations. For policy makers, these tools can be grouped into three categories: macroeconomic frameworks, measures to moderate boom-and-bust cycles in commodity prices, and structural policies to reduce vulnerabilities to price volatility, mostly relevant in the longer term.

Macroeconomic policy frameworks oriented toward longer-term sustainability offer the best protection against commodity price volatility. Key ingredients of this approach are

- Strong fiscal frameworks that encourage countercyclical fiscal policy, notably by building fiscal space during booms to support spending during slumps;

- Exchange rate flexibility linked to a monetary policy with credible low-inflation objectives; and

- A regulatory system for the financial sector that deters the accumulation of excessive risks, especially with respect to capital inflows and foreign currency debt.

In addition, policy makers can make use of risk management like futures and options contracts.

At the same time, commodity price booms and busts frequently lead to calls for additional actions to protect consumers or producers. Price spikes for food and energy can have a disproportionate effect on the poorest households and have often led to subsidies or trade measures. For example, the war in Ukraine led to significant energy price spikes and resulted in many governments reducing fuel taxes or increasing other energy subsidies, as well as releasing strategic oil inventories. At the international level, attempts to mitigate market volatility can take the form of coordinated supply measures to achieve price goals. Although such policies may be necessary as a short-term transitional tool, their use should be temporary. History suggests that the prolonged use of these policy instruments has generally led to undesirable consequences.

Exposure to commodity market risks is most pronounced for countries that depend on a narrow range of resource-based exports. The underlying vulnerability can be addressed through structural changes in the economy and well-designed macroeconomic policy frameworks. For example, whereas economic diversification is expected to reduce the risks of terms-of-trade shocks, direct government intervention to achieve diversification not only is seldom successful but also goes against the comparative advantage that countries may possess. A more promising approach is to create a business climate that favors innovation and investment throughout the economy. The establishment of sovereign wealth funds can enable wealth diversification, thus reducing vulnerability to commodity price volatility. Commodity exporters also face environmental risks and, for their future prosperity, must ensure that their resources are extracted in a sustainable way.

Abbreviations

AEs	advanced economies
bbl	barrel of crude oil
BCE	before Common Era
CAP	Common Agricultural Policy
CBOT	Chicago Board of Trade
CPI	Consumer Price Index
EEC	European Economic Community
EMDE	emerging market and developing economy
EU	European Union
EV	electric vehicle
FAVAR	factor-augmented vector autoregression
FEVD	forecast error variance decomposition
GDP	gross domestic product
GHG	greenhouse gas
IOCC	Interstate Oil Compact Commission
IRF	impulse-response function
LNG	liquefied natural gas
mb/d	million barrels per day
MMBtu	metric million British thermal units
Mmt	million metric tons
mt	metric ton
OECD	Organisation for Economic Co-operation and Development
OPEC	Organization of the Petroleum Exporting Countries
OPEC+	OPEC and 10 non-OPEC oil-exporting countries
PMI	Purchasing Managers' Index
PPP	purchasing power parity
RHS	right-hand side
RMSE	root mean square error
SVAR	structural vector autoregression
WTI	West Texas Intermediate
WWII	World War II

OVERVIEW

Motivation

Commodity markets are integral to the global economy. Developments in these markets have major effects on the global economy. In turn, changes in the global economy materially affect commodity markets. A deeper understanding of the determinants of the supply of and demand for commodities can help clarify the nature of commodity price movements and what drives them. Understanding those determinants would also help assess how commodity market developments, such as oil price shocks, affect commodity-exporting and commodity-importing countries. Such analysis is critical to the design of policy frameworks that facilitate the economic objectives of sustainable growth, inflation stability, poverty reduction, food security, and the mitigation of climate change.

Several major events since the beginning of the current decade highlight the complex and volatile relationship between commodity markets and economic activity. In 2020, the COVID-19 pandemic triggered a sharp fall in global demand for commodities—especially crude oil, which experienced its sharpest one-month price decline ever in April 2020. Prices subsequently rebounded, however, amid capacity constraints, supply bottlenecks, and a strong economic recovery. In 2022, the war in Ukraine led to further disruptions to commodity markets and more costly patterns of trade, with a major diversion of trade in energy as Ukraine could not export grains and some countries banned imports of Russian energy. The disruption also displayed how interrelated commodity markets are—high energy prices pushed up the production costs of other commodities (such as fertilizers), fueling a broad-based increase in commodity prices. The increase in prices had major economic and humanitarian impacts, especially for energy- and food-importing economies. In the longer term, the war may have accelerated the energy transition as countries seek to reduce their reliance on fossil fuels.

Shifts in commodity markets pose challenges for emerging market and developing economies (EMDEs). Commodities are critical sources of export and fiscal revenues for almost two-thirds of EMDEs, and more than half of the world's poor reside in commodity exporters (World Bank 2018a). The macroeconomic performance and progress on poverty reduction in commodity-exporting EMDEs historically has varied in line with commodity price cycles. This is especially so for low-income countries that rely on a narrow set of commodities (Richaud et al. 2019).

Commodity price movements may present large terms-of-trade shocks for economies that rely heavily on exports of a few commodities. For example, for an oil exporter, a fall in the price of oil causes a deterioration in the current account balance and puts downward pressure on its currency. Absorbing these shocks can be particularly challenging for economies with fixed exchange rates (Drechsel, McLeay, and Tenreyro 2019; Ha, Kose, and Ohnsorge 2019; World Bank 2020).

Commodity price cycles can lead to procyclical patterns in public spending. In other words, fiscal policy often amplifies the impact of the commodity price cycle on economic growth and increases the amplitude of cycles in economic activity (Mendes and Pennings 2020; Riera-Crichton, Végh, and Vuletin 2015).

Commodity price cycles have often created credit booms and busts in EMDEs, amplifying the macroeconomic effects. These cycles usually involve international capital flows and the supply of domestic credit. Commodity booms have frequently encouraged a surge in capital inflows and a buildup of foreign currency debt by domestic borrowers that proved excessive when the bust arrived (Masson 2014). Strong growth in domestic credit, frequently denominated in foreign currency, has often exacerbated the accumulation of risky debt (Koh et al. 2020). Capital inflows can cause a simultaneous real appreciation of the domestic currency—whether through nominal currency appreciation or domestic inflation—that reduces the competitiveness of the non-tradeable sector and holds back economic diversification (Ostry et al. 2010). Often, surges in capital inflows and undue risk tolerance by lenders during price booms lay the groundwork for systemic financial crises when commodity prices decline. Capital flight adds to the damaging economic impact of a commodities bust.

Commodity price shocks can intensify global inflationary pressures. The oil price shocks of the mid-1970s triggered a global increase in inflation that was brought under control only in the 1980s after central banks imposed steep increases in interest rates. Food price inflation can be an especially difficult challenge for low-income countries because food constitutes a large share of consumption and food insecurity is pervasive. Following the COVID-19 pandemic, reduced incomes and lost wages, combined with higher domestic food prices and supply constraints, exacerbated undernourishment. The number of people facing hunger globally increased from 650 million in 2019 to 768 million in 2020, undoing most of the progress achieved over the previous 15 years (FAO 2021).

Climate change and the transition to more climate-friendly sources of energy add another dimension to the uncertainties that roil commodity markets. Climate change and more frequent extreme weather events are likely to affect the production of all commodities. In what was perhaps a harbinger, in 2021 extreme weather disrupted the production of many commodities: droughts reduced hydroelectric generation in several countries including Brazil, China, and the United States; freezing weather and hurricanes disrupted crude oil and natural gas production in the United States; floods interrupted the production and transport of coal and some metals in Australia; and drought in Brazil reduced its coffee production to historic lows.

The energy transition—intended to minimize the worst impacts of climate change—will materially alter the production and consumption of commodities. Demand for fossil fuels is expected to be flat or to decline over the next 30 years, whereas demand for metals and minerals will be boosted by ramped-up investment in renewable energy infrastructure. The effects on agriculture are less certain and depend on the evolution of demand for biofuels. The energy transition will also have major economic and geopolitical consequences. Fossil fuel exporters may see a decline in export and fiscal revenues, whereas metal exporters could receive windfall revenues. Because metal reserves are much more geographically concentrated than other commodities, the global economy could be more at risk of supply disruptions. The energy transition could also lead to additional energy price volatility in the short run if investment in fossil fuels declines before there is sufficient alternative renewable energy capacity. Technological innovation is likely to generate inherently unpredictable shifts in commodity demand and supply. Thus, although the general nature of the energy transition may have a clear endpoint (that is, reduced reliance on fossil fuels), the speed at which it takes place and the implications for the demand for individual commodities are highly uncertain.

Main findings and policy challenges

This volume examines the channels by which developments in the global economy drive commodity markets, and how changes in commodity markets can affect commodity exporters and importers. The analysis in the following chapters encompasses four broad approaches. First, it studies the evolution of commodity markets over the past century and identifies similarities and differences among commodity groups. It shows that several factors—such as income and population growth, industrialization and urbanization, technology, and policy changes—frequently reappear as key drivers of supply, demand, and price movements both across commodity groups and over time. Second, it quantifies the relative importance of these drivers for different commodity groups using an econometric model and concludes that income elasticity plays a crucial role in driving the demand for industrial commodities over the long term. Third, it takes a detailed look at the nature and drivers of commodity price cycles. Fourth, it assesses the impact of commodity price fluctuations on commodity exporters and importers.

Main findings

The book offers a range of analytical findings.

The quantity of commodities consumed has risen enormously over the past century, driven by population and income growth (figure O.1). Demand for metals has risen tenfold, energy sixfold, and food fourfold. The center of commodity demand has shifted over the past half century from advanced economies toward EMDEs. China, in particular, has substantially increased its market share in both the production and consumption of commodities—especially energy and metals—over the past two decades.

The relative importance of commodities has shifted over time, as technological innovation created new uses for some materials and facilitated substitution among commodities. For example, crude oil products replaced coal in transportation in the first half of the 1900s. Later, natural gas emerged as a major fuel for electricity generation and heating. More recently, renewable sources such as solar and wind energy have

FIGURE O.1 Overview

Global consumption of metal commodities has grown in line with GDP while consumption of agricultural commodities resembles population growth. China dominates the consumption of most industrial commodities. Production has likewise seen a huge increase, assisted by technological developments that have boosted productivity. Commodity exporters, particularly oil exporters, rely on these commodities for export and fiscal revenue.

A. Commodity demand, GDP, and population

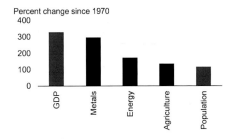

B. China's share of global consumption

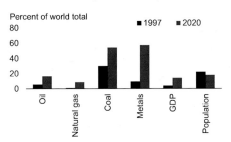

C. World metal ore production and GDP

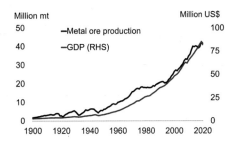

D. Maize yields, United States

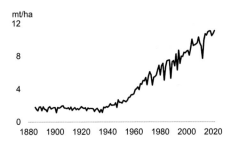

E. Share of oil or metal exports in total exports, oil and metal exporters

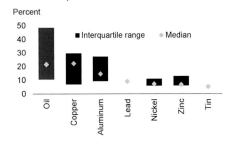

F. Share of resource revenues in total government revenues, oil and metal exporters

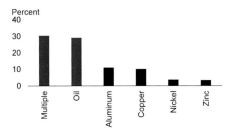

Sources: BP Statistical Review; UN Comtrade; United States Department of Agriculture; World Bureau of Metals Statistics; World Bank.
Note: EMDE = emerging market and developing economy; mt = metric ton; RHS = right-hand side.
A. Data show increase in global commodity consumption, GDP, and population between 1970 and 2019.
E.F. Charts show the median and interquartile range of the share of exports and share of fiscal revenues
accounted for by resource sectors for EMDE exporters of that commodity. Oil includes 62 EMDEs, copper 14, aluminum 10, zinc 5, nickel 3, and lead and tin each have 1. Export data are from 2019 depending on availability.
E. Because of small sample size, lead and tin do not have an interquartile range.
F. "Multiple" exporters include exporters who export both oil and copper.

accounted for a growing share of global energy demand as the world shifts toward zero-carbon energy. Among metals, aluminum's light weight, strength, and affordability have made it an attractive replacement for metals, such as steel, in such industries as packaging, auto manufacturing, and construction. Among agricultural commodities, substitution is common among some grains and especially different types of oilseeds. Shifts also have occurred on the demand side, including the ongoing increase in the consumption of animal products that require soybeans and maize for animal feed, and the increased use of biofuels that raises demand for maize, vegetable oils, and sugarcane.

Growth in China's demand for commodities is expected to slow, whereas other fast-growing EMDEs are likely to account for an increasing share of commodity demand. China's economic growth is projected to slow as its economy shifts from manufacturing and investment to services and domestic consumption. However, China's experience over the past half century is unlikely to be repeated, unless a group of other EMDEs collectively (or India) replicates China's growth performance. As some EMDEs mature, broader slowdowns in global economic and population growth will also contribute to slower growth in overall commodity demand. At the same time, as the energy transition gathers speed, fossil fuels will increasingly be replaced by metals, while climate change and changing weather patterns are likely to affect the production of many commodities. Technological innovations will further affect commodity demand—perhaps through better and cheaper materials, new methods of extracting or consuming resources, and increased energy efficiency of consumption.

Commodity markets are heterogeneous in terms of their drivers, price behavior, and macroeconomic impact on EMDEs. Policy makers often treat commodities as homogeneous, and as a result misinterpret the drivers of price changes and their impact, which can lead to inappropriate policy responses. To formulate appropriate policy, it is critical to understand differences among commodity markets.

The relationship between economic growth and commodity demand varies widely across countries, depending on their stage of economic development. At low levels of income, commodity demand rises rapidly with economic growth (that is, income elasticities of demand are high). But, as incomes rise, demand growth starts to slow as basic infrastructure and energy needs are fulfilled. For advanced economies, demand has actually decreased at the highest levels of income in response to conservation efforts and efficiency gains. Aggregate income growth is more important for metals and energy demand than for food commodities, which more closely track population growth.

Real commodity prices follow different paths in the long term. Adjusted for inflation, prices of agricultural commodities have been on a long-term downward path, reflecting the spectacular increase in productivity and low income elasticity of demand for these commodities (figure O.2). In contrast, energy prices have risen since the early twentieth century, as demand has risen in line with income and suppliers have had to turn to less accessible sources. The long-run trends in metal prices have been mixed because of their high income elasticities of demand, while extraction processes have benefited from technological improvements. Moreover, the cyclical components of energy and metal prices follow business and investment cycles more closely than agricultural prices.

FIGURE O.2 Real prices of key commodities

Energy prices, which were broadly stable before 1970, have experienced two cycles, one associated with the oil crises of the 1970s and the other with the emergence of EMDEs (and China) in the 2000s. Most agricultural commodity prices have followed a long-term downward path, consistent with the fact that demand grows in line with population. The evolution of metal prices has been mixed, with significant volatility in copper—a reflection of its close link with industrial activity— and a downward trend for aluminum resulting from its relative abundance.

A. Oil

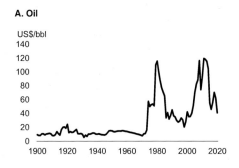

B. Coal

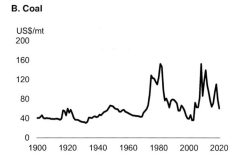

C. Maize

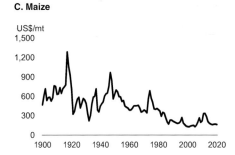

D. Wheat

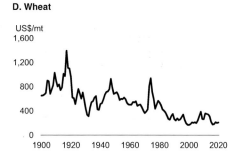

E. Copper

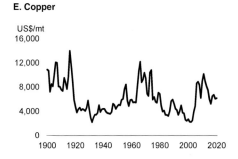

F. Aluminum

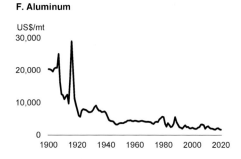

Source: World Bank.
Note: Prices have been deflated by the US Consumer Price Index (CPI); base year is 1990. bbl = barrel of crude oil; EMDE = emerging market and developing economy; mt = metric ton.

Global macroeconomic shocks have been the main source of short-term commodity price volatility over the past 25 years—particularly for metals. Global demand shocks have accounted for 50 percent of the variance of global commodity prices, and global supply shocks accounted for 20 percent. In contrast, during 1970–96, supply shocks specific to particular commodity markets—such as the 1970s and 1980s oil price volatility—were the main source of variability in global commodity prices.

Among commodity exporters, oil exporters tend to be less diversified than metal and agricultural exporters. They depend much more on oil for export and fiscal revenue than other commodity exporters depend on agricultural products or metals. As a result, oil-exporting economies are quite vulnerable to fluctuations in oil prices. However, there are significant variations in the size, duration, and impact of price fluctuations across commodities. Moreover, price shocks have asymmetric impacts, with large price declines having a bigger impact on commodity exporters than do large price increases.

Policy frameworks that enable countercyclical macroeconomic responses have become increasingly common—and beneficial. This is particularly true during the past two decades when the number of commodity-exporting EMDEs with fiscal rules and inflation-targeting central banks increased (figure O.3). These frameworks have helped moderate macroeconomic fluctuations and boost growth. Similarly, the use of sovereign wealth funds has helped countries diversify their national assets and may reduce the risks posed by the "resource curse," a term used to describe how resource-rich countries can perform more poorly than less-endowed developing economies.

Other policy tools have had mixed outcomes. Many countries use subsidies to mitigate the impact of price spikes on poorer households, particularly for food and energy. Trade interventions, such as export restrictions, have also been used to counter external shocks. At the international level, coordinated supply management efforts were used in many commodity markets over the past century to stabilize markets in response to short-term disruptions, or to raise or stabilize prices over the longer term. Despite some successes when these tools had short-run and targeted objectives, their prolonged use often led to unintended consequences—subsidies are very costly, regressive, and can encourage excess consumption; trade policies can exacerbate price spikes; and commodity agreements have almost always failed, leading to major price volatility. The mixed impact of these tools reflects, in part, the difficulty faced by policy makers in determining whether price shocks are permanent or transitory. The next section examines the reasons why policy tools are needed and considers the best approach for policy makers to respond to different challenges.

Policy challenges and responses

Policy tools should be tailored to the type of shock and the terms-of-trade effects faced by different types of commodity exporters and importers. For all economies, strong macroeconomic frameworks that provide countercyclical fiscal and monetary policies can help build buffers and allow authorities to better manage the negative economic effects of commodity price fluctuations. For longer-term trends, such as the energy

FIGURE O.3 **Policy improvements in recent years**

Policies in commodity exporters have shown marked improvement during the past two decades. A rising share of commodity-exporting EMDEs has adopted inflation targeting and fiscal rules, and central bank transparency has also improved. Both energy subsidies and agricultural subsidies (the latter among OECD countries) have been reduced. Historically, commodity markets have been subjected to supply management schemes. These have all ended (except oil), often followed by large price falls.

A. Commodity-exporting EMDEs with fiscal rules or inflation targeting

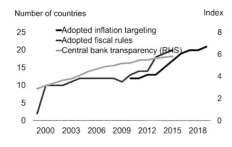

B. Agricultural subsidies

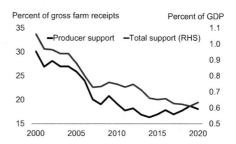

C. Energy subsidies

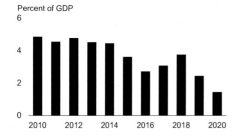

D. Change in price after agreements collapse

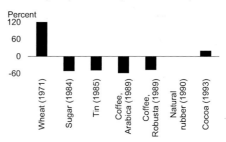

Sources: Cerutti, Claessens and Laeven 2017; Dincer, Eichengreen, and Geraats 2019; Ha, Kose, and Ohnsorge 2019; International Energy Agency; International Monetary Fund; Organisation for Economic Co-operation and Development; United States Department of Agriculture; World Bank.

Note: EMDE = emerging market and developing economy; OECD = Organisation for Economic Co-operation and Development; RHS = right-hand side.

A. An economy is considered to be implementing a fiscal rule if it has one or more fiscal rules on expenditures, revenues, balancing the budget, or limiting debt. Inflation targeting as classified in the International Monetary Fund's Annual Report of Exchange Arrangements and Exchange Restrictions.

B. Shows total support granted to the agricultural sector as percent of GDP. Producer support is measured at the farm gate level and comprises market price support, budgetary payments, and the cost of revenue forgone.

C. Sample includes 25 energy-exporting EMDEs and 14 energy-importing EMDEs.

D. The change is based on the three-year nominal average before and after the year of the collapse of the agreement. The year of collapse is noted in parentheses and is excluded from the comparison.

transition and climate change, policy makers in EMDEs can take steps now to prepare for and build resilience to potential shifts in commodity demand, even though the speed at which these shifts will occur is uncertain. In some countries, notably fossil fuel exporters, expected long-term trends require efforts to reduce their exposure to resource sectors over the medium to long term. For metals exporters, strong demand for certain metals arising from the energy transition may lead to windfall revenue, which will require policies to ensure that these revenues are used strategically and equitably.

Agricultural exporters are likely to experience differing effects of climate change and will need to build resilience to extreme weather shocks.

Policies to manage the macroeconomic impact of commodity price fluctuations

Robust macroeconomic policy frameworks oriented toward longer-term sustainability offer the best protection against commodity price volatility (Borensztein et al. 1994; World Bank 2009). Key ingredients are strong fiscal frameworks that encourage counter-cyclical fiscal policy, notably by building fiscal space during booms to support spending during slumps; exchange rate flexibility linked to a monetary policy with credible low-inflation objectives; and a regulatory system for the financial sector that deters the accumulation of excessive risks, especially from capital inflows and foreign currency debt. In addition, policy makers may use financial market-based risk-management instruments offered on commodity markets such as futures and options contracts.

Fiscal policies. Swings in commodity-based fiscal revenues in EMDEs often lead to procyclical fiscal policies: spending rises when commodity prices are high and falls when commodity prices decrease (Arezki, Hamilton, and Kazimov 2011; Frankel, Végh, and Vuletin 2013; Ilzetzki and Végh 2008). This procyclicality, however, tends to be asymmetric between booms and slumps. Spending typically rises faster during a resource boom than it falls during a slump, reducing net public savings (Gill et al. 2014). A sustainable and stability-oriented fiscal framework would build buffers during the boom phase of a cycle to prepare for a later bust. Fiscal rules can help in this regard by dampening the observed procyclicality of government spending among commodity exporters. Sovereign wealth funds can also be used to invest commodity revenue windfalls, thereby generating revenue for future generations.

Monetary policies. For commodity exporters subject to terms-of-trade volatility, a flexible exchange rate regime can be superior to a fixed exchange rate. Flexible exchange rates can act as a mechanism of adjustment to commodity price shocks (Berg, Goncalves and Portillo 2016; Broda 2004; Céspedes and Velasco 2012). For example, during the 2014 oil price plunge, oil exporters with a floating exchange rate had better macroeconomic outcomes than those with a fixed exchange rate (World Bank 2016). For a flexible exchange rate to work effectively, monetary policy has to provide a solid anchor to longer-term inflation expectations. Many central banks use flexible inflation targeting for this purpose, allowing inflation to vary in the short term but returning it to target over time. In contrast, for small open economies or countries with less developed financial markets, a fixed exchange rate regime can offer some advantages, especially if the central bank cannot commit credibly to an inflation target (Frankel 2017).

Macroprudential policies, capital flow management measures. Commodity price fluctuations often lead to substantial capital inflows, which can cause sharp movements in asset prices and credit markets and amplify business cycles in commodity-exporting countries (IMF 2012). Capital flows to developing countries tend to be procyclical (Kaminsky, Reinhart, and Végh 2004). Macroprudential policies can be used to address vulnerabilities that arise from excessive capital inflows. Such policies could include requiring countercyclical capital buffers by financial institutions, restricting foreign currency borrowing, limiting loan-to-value ratios in housing finance, and limiting the accumulation of short-term debt. Capital controls can also be used to limit the financial risks arising from short-term capital flows.

Market-based mechanisms. Governments exposed to commodity price fluctuations can use market-based risk mechanisms such as futures and options contracts to limit their exposure to price movements. Such instruments, however, have their own shortcomings. They can be costly (especially if they involve exchange rate contracts in which the commodity in question is traded in a different currency), and they can be subjected to large interest rate risk if hedges are mismatched. These instruments also apply only to the short term (with the exception of crude oil, few futures contracts extend much more than a year) and so cannot be used to address long-term changes in prices. Other options include state-contingent debt instruments, such as commodity-linked bonds, which fluctuate in value in line with commodity price movements and can thereby help governments manage public debt, although in practice these novel instruments are hard to use (Benford, Best, and Joy 2016).

Structural policies to reduce vulnerability to commodity price fluctuations

Exposure to commodity market risks is most pronounced for countries that depend on a narrow range of resource-based exports. The underlying vulnerability can be addressed only over the longer run, via structural changes in the economy and through macroeconomic policies discussed earlier. Economic diversification reduces the risks of terms-of-trade shocks, but direct government intervention to achieve it is seldom successful and may go against the country's comparative advantages. A more promising way forward is to establish an environment that favors innovation and investment generally. Commodity exporters also face environmental risks, and for their future prosperity they must ensure that their resources are extracted in a sustainable way.

Commodity importers face a different set of risks. They are less subject to terms-of-trade volatility from commodity price shocks than exporters because commodity concentration is much less on the import side. However, importers may face risks of accessibility to resources that commodity exporters do not. Accessibility has become a more pressing issue during the energy transition because some countries may find it harder to obtain the metals needed for renewable energy infrastructure in a similar way that some countries today have difficulties accessing energy resources.

Economic diversification. The prospect of a long-term decline in demand for fossil fuels gives hydrocarbon exporters an especially strong motive to diversify their economies. In addition, for countries that rely heavily on commodities that may be subject to downward price trends, structural policies may be needed to facilitate adjustments to new economic environments. For example, low-income countries that depend on exports of agricultural products as a source of revenue may benefit from reforms that facilitate the expansion of other sectors of their economy. There is strong evidence that diversifying exports and government revenues away from commodities strengthens an economy's long-term growth prospects and resilience to external shocks (Hesse 2008; Papageorgiou and Spatafora 2012; World Bank 2018a).

Diversification can take different forms. Policies can support vertical integration—which, in the case of an oil producer, could involve oil refining and petrochemicals. Governments could also encourage firms to diversify their output mix (horizontal diversification) with an emphasis on innovation and technological upgrading (Cherif and Hasanov 2014). Governments can also diversify their national asset portfolios—an economy's mix of natural resources, human and physical capital, and economic institutions (Gill et al. 2014; World Bank 2021, 2022). For example, reforms to enhance the economic value of the workforce (human capital accumulation) can promote export diversification partly by promoting innovation and the development of new products (Giri, Quayyum, and Yin 2019). More generally, education is a key driver of long-term economic growth and poverty reduction and can help boost innovation as well as lead to stronger institutions (World Bank 2018b).

Wealth diversification. Sovereign wealth funds have been used successfully by several countries to diversify wealth and provide stable long-term foreign income. These funds allow countries to invest windfall revenues rather than spending them, diversifying the country's wealth. For energy exporters anticipating a decline in future demand, building a rainy day fund while prices remain elevated becomes more pressing. For metal exporters that may benefit from future windfalls, creating frameworks and legislation to create sovereign wealth funds now can help preserve resource revenue for the future.

Resource security. The energy transition is expected to result in a sharp increase in demand for metals and minerals and will pose several challenges. First, policy makers must provide a conducive policy environment that ensures sufficient investment goes into metals production to avoid future shortfalls (Boer, Pescatori, and Stuermer 2021). Policy makers could remove obstacles that prevent businesses from rapidly increasing the production of a metal following the discovery of a reserve. Second, the resources required for the energy transition must be extracted in an equitable and environmentally friendly manner, while recycling rates will need to be stepped up (Hund et al. 2020). Third, to facilitate the smooth functioning of metal markets, greater availability of data and analysis is required, including robust forecasts of global supply and demand. The creation of an international institution focused on metals—similar to the International Energy Agency (which was established after the 1970 oil crises) and the Agricultural Marketing Information System (established after the 2010–11 food price spikes)—could provide a useful forum for cooperation.

Policies to moderate boom-and-bust cycles: Use cautiously

Commodity price booms and busts often lead to calls for policy measures to protect producers or consumers. For example, governments often use subsidies or trade measures to try to moderate the effects of commodity price movements on consumers. At the international level, attempts to mitigate market volatility can take the form of agreements among producers to manage supplies in order to achieve price goals.

However, history suggests that these policies may be effective only for achieving limited, short-term objectives. Prolonged use of these schemes has generally led to undesirable consequences, and such tools should be used cautiously.

Domestic policy initiatives. Commodity price spikes can hurt households, particularly poorer households, which spend a large portion of their disposable income on food. Consumer subsidies are frequently used to protect households from destabilizing shocks, especially for food and energy. For example, the energy price spikes of 2021–22 led both advanced economies and EMDEs to announce fuel subsidies or tax breaks. Policy makers have also often turned to trade measures such as restrictions and bans on the export of agricultural products to boost domestic supply and dampen inflation in food prices.

Although subsidies may be an effective tool to temporarily moderate the impact of shocks, they can have adverse effects if they remain in place for too long. Subsidies are very expensive and can erode fiscal space, diverting funds from potentially more productive spending in other sectors such as infrastructure, health, and education (Guenette 2020). Often, subsidies benefit wealthier households more than poorer households and, as a result, encourage excess consumption. In addition, trade policies that seem appropriate at the country level can have significant negative global consequences when applied simultaneously by many countries. For example, the combined use of trade restrictions during the 2010–11 food price spike amplified the increase in world prices and tipped millions of people into poverty, even though each country's policies dampened domestic price movements (Laborde, Lakatos, and Martin 2019; World Bank 2019). Instead of subsidies, policy makers should use social welfare policies where feasible to protect the most vulnerable households. These policies could include targeted safety net interventions such as cash transfers, food and in-kind transfers, school feeding programs, and public works programs (World Bank 2019).

International policy initiatives. Coordinated supply management efforts have been implemented in numerous commodity markets over the past century. The Organization of the Petroleum Exporting Countries is a well-known arrangement to coordinate supply and one of the longer-lived. Supply management schemes may appear attractive as a permanent facility to mitigate boom-and-bust cycles of commodity prices by controlling production. Indeed, internationally negotiated supply management schemes have often had the goal of long-term price stabilization. Experience has shown, however, that high and stable prices encourage new producers to enter the market and consumers to reduce their consumption. These market pressures often lead to the eventual collapse of such supply management schemes. At their worst, these mechanisms exacerbate commodity price cycles and harm producers by encouraging consumers to switch to alternatives, which may lead to a permanent reduction in demand for the commodity.

Synopsis

The remainder of this overview chapter summarizes the main messages of the subsequent chapters in this volume. For each chapter, the main theme, contributions to the literature, and analytical findings are presented. These summaries are followed by a discussion of future research directions.

Chapter 1. The Evolution of Commodity Markets over the Past Century

Commodity markets have undergone massive changes over the past century. Dramatic increases in productivity have led to a declining trend in commodity prices relative to manufactured goods and services. Technical innovations have affected patterns of consumption as well as production. Innovations in transportation have reduced costs and widened the opportunities for international trade in commodities, while innovations in communication have facilitated the development of price benchmarks and greater integration of commodity markets. The growing role of EMDEs in the global economy has shifted the location of demand, especially for energy and metals. In chapter 1, Baffes, Koh, and Nagle review developments during the past century for three key commodity groups: energy, metals, and agriculture.

Contribution. The chapter examines demand trends, technological progress, price fluctuations, and policy interventions. It makes three contributions to the literature. First, it analyzes all three main commodity markets—energy, metals (including precious metals), and agriculture—and highlights differences and similarities among commodity markets. Second, the discussion takes a longer-term perspective, including events and developments earlier in the twentieth century, such as World War I and the Great Depression, as well as recent events in the twenty-first century, such as the COVID-19 pandemic and the war in Ukraine. Third, in addition to price movements, it discusses three key aspects of commodity markets—preferences and demand shifts, technological progress, and policies. It also considers how the energy transition will affect commodity markets in the future.

Main findings. Four major themes emerge (figure O.4). First, commodity demand (and production) has increased enormously over the past century. The largest increases have been for energy and metals as population and per capita income have grown and technological change has encouraged the use of industrial commodities. Demand growth over the period has shifted from advanced economies toward EMDEs. There has also been significant substitution across groups of commodities. For example, in ocean shipping, oil replaced coal; in the package and container industry, aluminum and plastics replaced tin; and, more recently, biofuels (an agricultural product) have been used as a substitute for fossil fuel in gasoline. These changes mimic earlier historical shifts—such as steamers replacing sailing ships, diesel-powered ships replacing steamers, road vehicles and trains replacing animal power, and cotton and synthetic fibers substituting for wool and silk in clothing.

Second, technological advances have encouraged consumption by creating new products and new uses for commodities. They have also reduced the use of raw materials by improving efficiency in consumption and production. In addition, they have facilitated the discovery and development of new reserves and new commodities. Spectacular advances in agriculture took place after the development of hybrid varieties in the 1930s

FIGURE O.4 Evolution of commodity markets

The structure of energy markets has changed significantly over the past two centuries, with gradual transitions as new fuels have emerged. Periods of high prices have periodically led to the emergence of new producers, often via new discoveries or new technologies, such as in the Middle East after the Second World War, and in Alaska, Mexico, and the North Sea in the 1970s. Technology has also played a big role in the composition of production and consumption of commodities. For example, maize productivity increased almost tenfold during 1930-2020. Consumption of edible oils in particular has seen a massive increase, because of their many uses, including in food, animal feed, consumer products, and biofuels.

A. Level of global energy consumption, by source

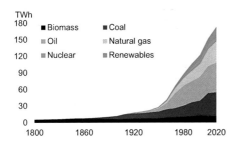

B. Global oil production, 1970-2019

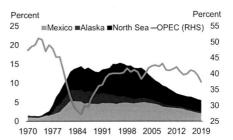

C. Metal demand since 1900

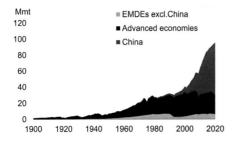

D. Copper use in electricity generation

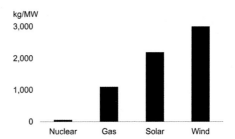

E. Grains and edible oils production

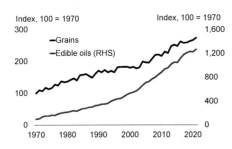

F. Output, population, and food consumption growth

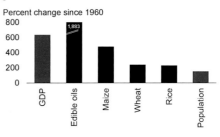

Sources: BP Statistical Review; Copper Alliance; Energy Information Administration; United States Department of Agriculture; World Bank.
Note: EMDE = emerging market and developing economy; kg/MW = kilogram per megawatt; Mmt = million metric tons; OPEC = Organization of the Petroleum Exporting Countries; RHS = right-hand side; TWh = terrawatt-hour.
A. Renewables include hydroelectric, solar, wind, geothermal, biomass, wave and tidal.
B. North Sea includes Norway and the United Kingdom.
C. Total metal consumption includes copper, aluminum, tin, lead, and zinc.
D. Chart shows the amount of copper required to generate one megawatt of electricity using different generation methods.
F. Edible oils include coconut, olive, palm, palm kernel, rapeseed, soybean, and sunflower seed oil. The base year is the average of 1964-65.

and again after the Green Revolution of the 1960s and 1970s. The development of communications and information technology has also had major effects on the structure of commodity markets. A notable feature of increased technical sophistication is the expansion of futures and options markets, and related hedging techniques.

Third, innovation in commodity markets has often occurred in response to periods of high prices. For example, technological improvements in aluminum and policy interventions in the tin market made aluminum the dominant commodity in packaging. Episodes of production restraint by the Organization of the Petroleum Exporting Countries stimulated the development of new sources of oil. The oil price shocks of the 1970s encouraged the development of off-shore oil in Mexico and the North Sea. High oil prices in the 2000s likewise spurred the development of shale oil production technology in the United States.

Fourth, various interventions have been used to mitigate commodity market volatility. Interventions have taken different forms, including subsidies, production quotas, trade measures, and internationally coordinated supply management schemes. Government intervention has been most prominent in agriculture. Policies have had large effects on commodity markets, but they have also had unintended consequences. Although supply schemes led to higher prices for a while, they also encouraged production by competitors outside of the agreement and stockpiling by consumers, which eventually resulted in increased downward pressures on prices.

Chapter 2. Commodity Demand: Drivers, Outlook, and Implications

Understanding the causes of variations in the long-term growth in commodity demand is critically important to the economic prospects of commodity-exporting EMDEs. Knowing how the key drivers—such as population growth, income growth, technology, and policies—shape long-term trends is a first step in making projections of future commodity demand growth. In chapter 2, Baffes and Nagle investigate the drivers of commodity demand over the past 50 years by looking at historical determinants, their evolution, and long-term prospects. They also discuss implications for policy makers.

Contribution. The chapter documents the channels through which population, income, technology, and policies affect commodity demand. It examines these relationships quantitatively by estimating income elasticities of demand for energy, metals, and agriculture, and uses these elasticities to build scenarios of future commodity demand, based on expectations for future population and income growth. The chapter makes two contributions to the literature. First, by estimating income elasticities of demand at the group level (for example, for aggregate metal demand, rather than for individual metals such as aluminum), it accounts for long-term substitution among commodities. Although a few studies have made this estimation for energy, none have used a common framework to compare income elasticities across commodity groups. Second, the methodology provides estimates of income-varying elasticities of demand, thus enabling an analysis of how commodity demand changes at different stages of economic development.

FIGURE O.5 **Commodity demand**

The relationship between income per capita and commodity consumption per capita shows signs of plateauing for most commodities as income rises. Although income elasticities decline as income increases across all commodity groups, the elasticities differ markedly at low-income levels: high for metals and low for food commodities, with energy in between. The energy transition will change the consumption landscape of some commodities, with an expected shift from energy to metals.

A. Energy consumption

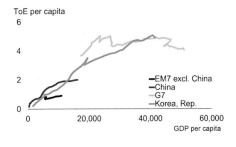

B. Metals consumption

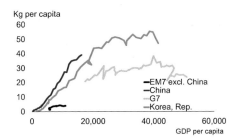

C. Shipping capacity in the United Kingdom

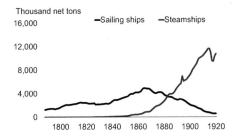

D. Aggregate elasticity estimates

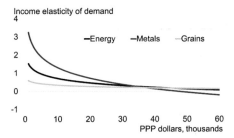

E. Income elasticity of demand for commodities, China and India

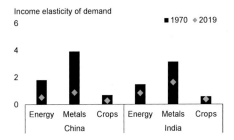

F. Copper use in autos

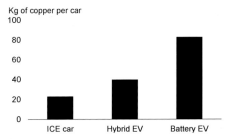

Sources: BP Statistical Review; World Bureau of Metal Statistics; World Bank.
A.B. GDP per capita in constant 2010 U.S. dollars. Lines show the evolution of income and commodity consumption per capita over the period 1965-2019. Each data point represents one country or group for one year. EM7 excl. China includes Brazil, India, Indonesia, Mexico, the Russian Federation, and Türkiye. kg = kilogram; ToE = tonnes of energy.
C. Denotes ocean transport capacity of ships registered in the United Kingdom.
D.E. Income elasticities calculated using elasticity coefficients in chapter 2. PPP = purchasing power parity.
F. Bars indicate the amount of copper used in different types of vehicles. EV = electric vehicle; ICE = internal combustion engine.

Main findings. The chapter offers three main findings (figure O.5). First, population and income growth are the two primary drivers of aggregate commodity demand in the long run. Whereas income is a key driver of growth for metals and energy, it is less important for food commodities, which tend to be driven more by population growth. Other factors—including relative prices, technology, substitutions from one commodity group to another, and government policies—are also important drivers of commodity demand growth. These factors can lead to changes in the intensity of commodity demand for a given level of per capita income, as well as to changes in the relative importance of individual commodities.

Second, per capita income elasticities of demand vary significantly among commodity groups. Base metals exhibit the highest income elasticity of demand, followed by energy. Food has the lowest income elasticity. Indeed, growth in metals consumption over the past 50 years has closely tracked growth in income, whereas growth in food consumption, particularly for grains, has more closely followed population growth. Income elasticities vary with per capita income levels as well. At low levels of income, demand elasticities are high (in some cases well above unity); but, as per capita income levels rise, demand elasticities fall, reflecting shifts in consumption patterns toward goods with high-value-added content, and toward services. At high income levels, elasticities may go to zero, or even turn negative.

Third, overall commodity demand is likely to continue to increase in the years ahead, but at a slower rate than over the past two decades. This slowdown is due to slower population and income growth, as well as economic changes, such as China's shift toward a more service- and consumer-based economy. Additionally, demand for individual commodities could be affected by transformative substitutions because of innovations and policy-driven initiatives to mitigate climate change. The energy transition is likely to induce large and potentially permanent changes in the demand for commodities. A shift to low-carbon sources of energy is expected to raise demand for metals used for clean energy (such as copper) and substantially reduce the consumption of fossil fuels.

Chapter 3. The Nature and Drivers of Commodity Price Cycles

During the past half century, there have been several episodes of synchronized commodity price booms and busts. Commodities in energy, metals, and agricultural markets experienced synchronized surges in prices in the 1970s and again in the 2000s. Fluctuations in commodity prices are common across commodity groups and have become more synchronized over time.

For EMDE commodity exporters, large fluctuations in commodity prices can pose significant policy challenges because macroeconomic performance has historically varied closely with commodity price cycles. This is especially true for EMDEs that rely on a narrow set of commodities for export and fiscal revenue. For policy makers, formulating the appropriate policy response depends on whether commodity price changes are expected to be permanent or temporary. To the extent that commodity price movements are temporary, they can be absorbed or smoothed by fiscal and monetary policies. For longer-lasting price shifts, however, structural changes may be needed. Understanding what is behind commodity price cycles is also critical for policy makers because the appropriate policy response depends on whether the changes in price were driven by global or commodity-specific factors, as well as whether they are predominantly demand or supply driven. In this chapter, Kabundi, Vasishtha, and Zahid investigate the nature and size of transitory and permanent components of commodity price cycles and the main drivers of common cycles in commodity prices.

Contribution. This chapter adds to the existing price cycle literature in two ways. First, whereas the existing literature analyzes price movements in the context of either super cycles or cyclical-versus-trend behavior, the analysis in this chapter focuses on business cycles and medium-term cycles, in line with the macroeconomic literature. Specifically, it separates the transitory component into two parts: the traditional 2-to-8-year cycle, which is associated with economic activity; and the medium-term cycle with a duration of 8 to 20 years. The contribution of these components has been studied extensively in the macroeconomic literature and, in the case of commodities, for metals. The medium-term cycle has not been studied as much in the literature but has received attention lately.

Second, the chapter examines both global and commodity-specific cycles for a large number of commodities, as well as the underlying drivers of these cycles. In contrast, earlier literature either focused on a small set of commodities (examining commodity demand and supply rather than aggregate demand and supply) or simply documented the existence of co-movement without identifying the underlying drivers. This chapter also provides an in-depth analysis of price cycles in key commodities since 1970 and compares the rebound in commodity prices after the COVID-19-induced global recession in 2020 with price recoveries after earlier recessions and slowdowns.

Main findings. The chapter offers three main findings (figure O.6). First, the long-term, or "permanent," component of commodity cycles accounts for nearly half of price variability, on average, across all commodities. The permanent component dominates agricultural prices and has a downward trend, while the transitory component is larger for industrial commodities. The analysis identifies three medium-term cycles. The first (from the early 1970s to mid-1980s) and third (from the early 2000s to 2020 onward) exhibited similar duration and involved all commodities, whereas the smaller second cycle (spanning the 1990s) applied mostly to metals and less so to agriculture.

Second, the chapter finds that global macroeconomic shocks have been the main source of short-term commodity price volatility over the past 25 years—particularly for metals. Global demand shocks have accounted for 50 percent of the variance in global commodity prices, and global supply shocks accounted for 20 percent. In contrast, during 1970–96, supply shocks specific to particular commodity markets—such as the oil shocks of the 1970s—were the main source of variability in global commodity prices. These results suggest that developments specific to commodity markets may have played a diminishing role over time in driving commodity price volatility.

FIGURE O.6 Evolution of commodity price cycles

Industrial commodity prices went through two large medium-term cycles in the 1970s and 2000s. Over the long term, energy prices are on an upward trend, and agricultural prices are on a downward trend. The response of industrial commodities to the recession triggered by COVID-19 has been larger than in previous recessions. Over time, the importance of global shocks for commodity prices has risen, whereas that of commodity-specific shocks has decreased.

A. Medium-term component, energy and metals

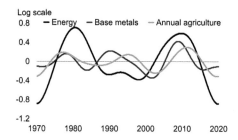

B. Permanent component, energy and metals

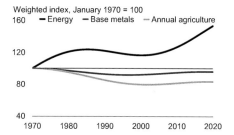

C. Energy

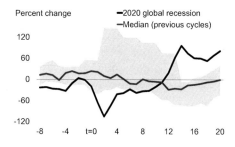

D. Base metals

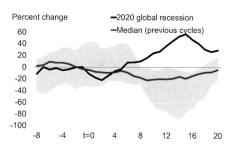

E. Response of global commodity prices to 1 percent increase in global demand and supply

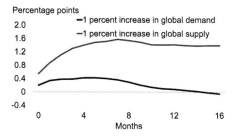

F. Drivers of global commodity price shocks

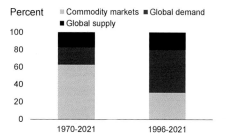

Sources: Baffes and Kabundi 2021; World Bank.

A.B. Charts show the medium-term cycle component (8-10 years frequency) and permanent component (above 20 years frequency) of the commodity price indexes. Decomposed using a frequency domain approach (see Baffes and Kabundi 2021 for more details).

C.D. The horizontal axis represent months, where t=0 denotes the peak of global industrial production before global recessions and downturns. The vertical axis measures the percent change in the commodity price series from a year earlier. The blue line shows the trajectory of the current commodity cycle around the COVID-19 recession, and the red line is the median of previous cycles around a global recession or downturn (Kose, Sugawara, and Terrones 2020). Gray shaded areas represent the range of observed values in previous cycles. Data from January 1970 to October 2021.

E. Cumulative median response of global commodity price growth to a 1 standard deviation (about 1 percent) increase in global demand and global supply.

F. Contribution of global demand, supply, and commodity market shocks to variance of month-on-month growth in commodity prices, based on samples covering 1970-2021 and 1996-2021.

Third, using an event study, the chapter finds that the shock to commodity prices caused by the COVID-19 pandemic varied compared with previous recessions. The collapse in energy prices in early 2020 was steeper than during any other global recession in the past five decades, and the subsequent recovery was likewise the steepest. For metals and agriculture, the fall in prices was not unusual by historical standards, but their recovery was much larger compared to recoveries from previous recessions.

Chapter 4. Causes and Consequences of Industrial Commodity Price Shocks

In chapter 4, Kabundi, Nagle, Ohnsorge, and Yamazaki build on the analysis in chapter 3 by focusing on shocks to the prices of energy and metals. The chapter examines the importance of energy and metals for the global economy and for EMDEs; it looks at the drivers of swings in energy and metals prices over the past seven decades, and it discusses the implications of such price swings for economic activity in EMDEs.

Contribution. Whereas the literature on the impact of oil price shocks is extensive, the literature on the impact of metal price shocks is scarce. This chapter adds to the relevant literature in four ways. First, it compares the structure of global energy and metals markets, including the extent to which producers of energy and metal commodities rely on commodities for export and fiscal revenue and for overall economic activity. Second, through comparable estimates for multiple commodities, the chapter allows a cross-commodity comparison that previous studies have not offered. In particular, it illustrates how different market structures have different implications for the behavior and impact of individual commodity markets.

Third, the chapter joins a few recent econometric studies in cross-checking the identified drivers of swings in metal prices against historical narratives. The approach used expands on previous studies by using monthly data, adding aluminum and nickel to the sample, and explicitly comparing results for metal prices with those for oil prices in a consistent framework. Fourth, using a local projections model, the chapter presents estimates of how output in metal exporters and importers responds to metal price shocks.

Main findings. The chapter offers three main findings (figure O.7). First, metal exporters are much less dependent on metal sectors than oil exporters are on oil sectors. Global metal production and consumption are considerably more concentrated geographically than oil production. China, in particular, is the single largest consumer and producer of all refined base metals. It accounts for roughly 50 percent of global consumption of metals, but it consumes just 15 percent of global crude oil output.

Second, except for nickel and zinc, demand shocks are the largest source of variability for almost all commodity prices, including oil. Collapses in demand during global recessions were the main drivers of sharp declines in energy and metal prices, and subsequent economic recoveries caused rebounds in commodity prices.

FIGURE O.7 Causes and consequences of industrial commodity price shocks

Industrial commodity price shocks are common, driven by demand and supply shocks in almost equal measure (except for aluminum). Oil and metal price shocks have asymmetric effects on economic activity in energy and metal producers: price increases are associated with small, temporary growth accelerations; price collapses are associated with pronounced and lasting slowdowns.

A. Forecast error variance decomposition of metal and oil prices

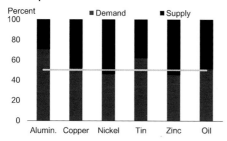

B. Number of large commodity price shocks

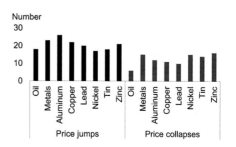

C. EMDE energy exporters: Impact of 10-percentage-point higher oil price growth

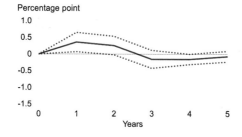

D. EMDE energy exporters: Impact of 10-percentage-point lower oil price growth

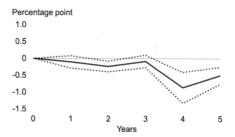

E. EMDE metal exporters: Impact of 10-percentage-point higher metal price growth

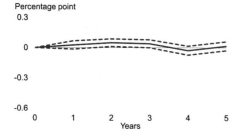

F. EMDE metal exporters: Impact of 10-percentage-point lower metal price growth

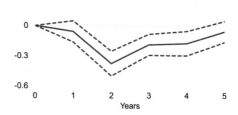

Source: World Bank.

Note: EMDE = emerging market and developing economy.

B. Large commodity price shocks are defined as price increases or decreases of 1 standard deviation over a six-month period.

C.-F. Cumulative impulse responses of output growth for 153 EMDEs, of which 34 are energy exporters and 28 are metal exporters, from a local projection estimation. Dependent variable is output growth after impact of a 10-percentage-point change in oil or metal price growth. Solid lines are coefficient estimates and dotted lines are 95 percent confidence bands based on heteroscedasticity consistent standard errors and Driscoll-Kraay standard errors. Estimation accounts for asymmetric effects of price increases and price declines.

Third, both oil and metal price shocks appear to have asymmetric impacts on output growth in energy and metal exporters: Price increases have been associated with small, temporary accelerations in output growth; price declines have been associated with more pronounced or longer-lasting growth slowdowns. Output growth among oil and copper exporters, in particular, declined significantly for several years following a fall in oil or copper prices. In contrast, there is no evidence of statistically significant output gains or losses in aluminum exporters after increases or decreases in prices. Among commodity importers, changes in metal or oil prices had negligible effects on output, reflecting the relatively low proportion of these industrial materials in the total inputs to their gross domestic product.

Future research directions

The study suggests several avenues for further research.

Implication of the energy transition. The analysis in this book focuses on the main energy, metals, and agricultural commodities. However, the ongoing transition from fossil fuels to zero-carbon sources of energy will increasingly require the use of commodities such as rare earth and precious metals. Gaining a deeper knowledge of the structure of the respective markets (as is done for base metals in chapter 4), as well as price behavior and drivers (along the lines of chapter 3), will enhance our understanding of the energy transition in terms of resource requirements, substitutability among commodities, and price drivers.

Broadening the econometric analysis. Chapter 3 focuses mostly on the business cycle component of prices. However, for some commodities, longer-term trends and super cycles account for a significant part of price behavior; for others, short-term price movements are important. Further research could analyze these components in greater detail; it could also examine the drivers of price movements as well as the correlation among prices at various time frequencies. Chapter 4 focuses on the sources and consequences of shocks to the prices of energy and metals. Future research could include agricultural commodities and fertilizers (an important input to the production of food). Results from such analysis, if complemented by the drivers of domestic food price inflation, would help shed light on the causes and consequences of food insecurity.

Deepening the policy discussion. The policy conclusions outlined in this volume reflect the implications of its analysis and econometric results. However, the policy issues relevant to commodity markets, especially for EMDEs, are complex, with far-reaching implications. Further research could focus on the relative importance of different policy frameworks for different types of commodity exporters to go beyond one-size-fits-all recommendations. It could also investigate in more detail the potential for risk sharing among commodity exporters—covering issues such as exchange rate management of commodity-exporting EMDEs, commodity price-linked debt, energy subsidies, agricultural trade policies, and the role of sovereign wealth funds.

References

Arezki, R., K. Hamilton, and K. Kazimov. 2011. "Resource Windfalls, Macroeconomic Stability and Growth: The Role of Political Institutions." IMF Working Paper 142, International Monetary Fund, Washington, DC.

Baffes, J., and A. Kabundi. 2021. "Commodity Price Shocks: Order within Chaos?" Policy Research Working Paper 9792, World Bank, Washington, DC.

Benford, J., T. Best, and M. Joy. 2016. "Sovereign GDP-Linked Bonds." Financial Stability Paper 39, Bank of England.

Berg, A., C. Goncalves, and R. Portillo. 2016. "Another Disconnect Puzzle: Should Floaters Fix and Fixers Float?" International Monetary Fund, Washington, DC.

Boer, P., A. Pescatori, and M. Stuermer. 2021. "Energy Transition Metals." IMF Working Paper 243, International Monetary Fund, Washington, DC.

Borensztein, E., P. Wickham, M. Khan, and C. Reinhart. 1994. *The Behavior of Non-Oil Commodity Prices.* Washington, DC: International Monetary Fund.

Broda, C. 2004. "Terms of Trade and Exchange Rate Regimes in Developing Countries." *Journal of International Economics* 63 (1): 31-58.

Cerutti, E., S. Claessens, and L. Laeven. 2017. "The Use and Effectiveness of Macroprudential Policies: New Evidence." *Journal of Financial Stability* 28 (February): 203-24. (Data set updated in 2018 and available at https://www.eugeniocerutti.com/datasets.)

Céspedes, L., and A. Velasco. 2012. "Macroeconomic Performance during Commodity Price Booms and Busts." *IMF Economic Review* 60 (4): 570-99.

Cherif, R., and F. Hasanov. 2014. "Soaring of the Gulf Falcons: Diversification in the GCC Oil Exporters in Seven Propositions." IMF Working Paper 177, International Monetary Fund, Washington, DC.

Dincer, N. N., B. Eichengreen, and P. Geraats. 2019. "Transparency of Monetary Policy in the Postcrisis World." In *The Oxford Handbook of the Economics of Central Banking*, edited by D. G. Mayes, P. L. Siklos, and J.-E. Sturm. Oxford, U.K.: Oxford University Press. Data set available at https://eml.berkeley.edu/~eichengr/data.shtml.

Drechsel, T., M. McLeay, and S. Tenreyro. 2019. "Monetary Policy for Commodity Booms and Busts." Paper presented at the Federal Reserve Bank of Kansas City Jackson Hole Economic Policy Symposium, Jackson Hole, Wyoming, August 22-24.

FAO (Food and Agriculture Organization of the United Nations). 2021. "The State of Food Security and Nutrition in the World." Food and Agriculture Organization, Rome.

Frankel, J. 2017. "How to Cope with Volatile Commodity Export Prices: Four Proposals." CID Faculty Working Paper 335, Center for International Development at Harvard University, Cambridge, MA.

Frankel, J. A., C. A. Végh, and G. Vuletin. 2013. "On Graduation from Fiscal Procyclicality." *Journal of Development Economics* 100 (1): 32-47.

Gill, I. S., I. Izvorski, W. van Eeghen, and D. De Rosa. 2014. *Diversified Development: Making the Most of Natural Resources in Eurasia.* Washington, DC: World Bank.

Giri, R., S. N. Quayyum, and R. J. Yin. 2019. "Understanding Export Diversification: Key Drivers and Policy Implications." IMF Working Paper 105, International Monetary Fund, Washington, DC.

Guenette, J. D. 2020. "Price Controls: Good Intentions, Bad Outcomes." Policy Research Working Paper 9212, World Bank, Washington, DC.

Ha, J., M. A. Kose, and F. Ohnsorge, eds. 2019. *Inflation in Emerging and Developing Economies: Evolution, Drivers, and Policies.* Washington, DC: World Bank.

Hesse. H. 2008. "Export Diversification and Economic Growth." Commission on Growth and Development Working Paper 21, World Bank, Washington, DC.

Hund, K., D. La Porta, T. Fabregas, T. Laing, and J Drexhage. 2020. *Minerals for Climate Action: The Mineral Intensity of the Clean Energy Transition.* Washington, DC: World Bank.

Ilzetzki, E., and C. A. Végh. 2008. "Procyclical Fiscal Policy in Developing Countries: Truth or Fiction?" NBER Working Paper 14191, National Bureau of Economic Research, Cambridge, MA.

IMF (International Monetary Fund). 2012. *World Economic Outlook: Coping with High Debt and Sluggish Growth.* October. Washington, DC: International Monetary Fund.

Kaminsky, G. L., C. M. Reinhart, and C. A. Végh. 2004. "When It Rains, It Pours: Procyclical Capital Flows and Macroeconomic Policies." In *NBER Macroeconomics Annual 19,* edited by M. Gertler and K. Rogoff, 11-53. Cambridge, MA: MIT Press.

Koh, W. C., M. A. Kose, P. S. O. Nagle, F. Ohnsorge, and N. Sugawara. 2020. "Debt and Financial Crises." CEPR Discussion Paper 14442, Centre for Economic Policy Research, London.

Kose, M. A., N. Sugawara, and M. E. Terrones. 2020. "Global Recessions." Policy Research Working Paper 9172, World Bank, Washington, DC.

Laborde, D., C. Lakatos, and W. Martin. 2019. "Poverty Impact of Food Price Shocks and Policies." In *Inflation in Emerging and Developing Economies: Evolution, Drivers, and Policies,* edited by J. Ha, M. A. Kose, and F. Ohnsorge, 371-401. Washington, DC: World Bank Group.

Masson, P. R. 2014. "Macroprudential Policies, Commodity Prices and Capital Inflows." BIS Paper 76, Bank for International Settlements, Basel.

Mendes, A., and S. Pennings. 2020. "One Rule Fits All? Heterogenous Fiscal Rules for Commodity Exporters when Price Shocks Can Be Persistent: Theory and Evidence." Policy Research Working Paper 9400, World Bank, Washington, DC.

Ostry, J., A. Ghosh, K. Habermeier, M. Chamon, M. Qureshi, and D. Reinhardt. 2010. "Capital Inflows: The Role of Controls." IMF Staff Position Note 04, International Monetary Fund, Washington, DC.

Papageorgiou, C., and N. Spatafora. 2012. "Economic Diversification in LICs: Stylized Facts and Macroeconomic Implications." IMF Staff Discussion Note 13, International Monetary Fund, Washington, DC.

Richaud, C., A. G. M. Galego, F. Ayivodji, S. Matta, and S. Essl. 2019. "Fiscal Vulnerabilities in Commodity Exporting Countries and the Role of Fiscal Policy." Discussion Paper 15, World Bank, Washington, DC.

Riera-Crichton, D., C. Végh, and G. Vuletin. 2015. "Procyclical and Countercyclical Fiscal Multipliers: Evidence from OECD Countries." *Journal of International Money and Finance* 52 (C): 15-31.

World Bank. 2009. *Global Economic Prospects: Commodities at the Crossroads*. Washington, DC: World Bank.

World Bank. 2016. "Resource Development in an Era of Cheap Commodities." *Commodity Markets Outlook*. April. Washington, DC: World Bank.

World Bank. 2018a. *Global Economic Prospects: The Turning of the Tide?* June. Washington, DC: World Bank.

World Bank. 2018b. *World Development Report 2018: Learning to Realize Education's Promise.* Washington, DC: World Bank.

World Bank. 2019. *Commodity Markets Outlook: The Role of Substitution in Commodity Demand.* October. Washington, DC: World Bank.

World Bank. 2020. *Global Economic Prospects: Slow Growth, Policy Challenges.* January. Washington, DC: World Bank.

World Bank. 2021. *The Changing Wealth of Nations 2021: Managing Assets for the Future.* Washington, DC: World Bank.

World Bank. 2022. *Global Economic Prospects.* January. Washington, DC: World Bank.

CHAPTER 1

The Evolution of Commodity Markets over the Past Century

John Baffes, Wee Chian Koh, and Peter Nagle

Commodity markets have evolved dramatically over the past century. Consumption has soared, particularly for energy and metals, with a shift toward emerging market and developing economies. Significant technological developments, combined with the opening of new sources of raw materials, have led to a large expansion of supply. This chapter discusses the evolution of three commodity sectors: energy, metals, and agriculture. The composition of demand has evolved under the impetus of technical innovation, relative prices, and government policies. Although commodity prices often move together in the short run, in real, inflation-adjusted terms, energy prices have trended upward and agriculture prices downward in the long run. Various policies have been used to stabilize commodity markets at the national level, and agreements have been signed with the same objective at the international level. These agreements have tended to break down, however, under the pressure of competition from new sources. In the years ahead, climate change poses a risk to agricultural output and rural communities. The ongoing energy transition from fossil fuels to zero-carbon energy sources has major implications for the composition of commodity demand, and new technological innovations will likely be required.

Introduction

Commodity markets have undergone seismic changes over the past century. Dramatic increases in productivity have resulted in a declining trend in prices relative to manufactured goods and services. Technical innovations have affected patterns of consumption and production. Innovations in transportation have reduced costs and widened the opportunities for international trade in commodities. The growing role of emerging market and developing economies (EMDEs) in the global economy has dramatically shifted the composition of demand for commodities, especially for energy and metals.

Economic expansion after World War II (WWII), and more recently the emergence of EMDEs as important players in the global economy, has increased commodity demand, especially for energy commodities and metals and minerals. Even though the world's population rose from 2 billion in 1920 to 8 billion in 2020, the production of commodities to feed, clothe, and support the rising population has more than kept pace. Expanding production was possible because of technological innovations, the discovery of new reserves of commodities, and more intensive agricultural production.

On the energy front, crude oil became the most important commodity, replacing coal. Known reserves of crude oil and natural gas have increased substantially even as production has risen. For example, the development of shale technology during the early

2000s enabled producers to exploit deposits that had previously been considered unprofitable; as a result, the United States became once again the largest producer of crude oil. Mineral resource development expanded because of advances in technology and new discoveries.

Metal production has become more efficient as innovations and productivity improvements became widespread in mining, smelting, and refining. Improved fabrication and new alloys have allowed less metal to be used without loss of strength. Despite radical changes in supply and consumption, metals prices, in real terms, have seen cycles around a quite flat trend over the past century. The major price fluctuations of metals (perhaps more so than of other commodities) have been mainly driven by global demand shocks, such as wars, the Great Depression of the 1930s, and the rapid industrialization of China in the 2000s.

Food production has increased faster than population, and most of the world's consumers have better access to adequate food supplies today than they did a century ago. This improvement is due to technological advances in the 1900s, especially the Green Revolution.[1] In large part because of increasing productivity, prices of agricultural commodities have experienced a downward trend over the past 100 years. During the Great Depression, however, weak demand and falling prices caused widespread hardship in rural communities. This situation led to numerous efforts by governments to protect domestic farmers and stabilize prices at a level that would allow agricultural workers to earn incomes in line with those of urban workers. More generally, large fluctuations in prices for a range of commodities have resulted in periodic efforts to reduce their volatility. At the international level, governments have negotiated agreements to stabilize prices for various products, but these agreements have caused distortions in world markets and have usually broken down.

The objective of this chapter is to review historical developments for three commodity groups: energy, metals (including precious metals), and agriculture. The chapter discusses demand trends, technological progress, price fluctuations, and policy interventions.

Several themes emerge:

- *Changes in demand.* Commodity demand has increased substantially over the past century. The largest increases have been for energy and metals—as population and per capita income have grown, and technical change has leaned toward the use of metal inputs. The location of demand growth has changed, with a shift from advanced economies (AEs) toward EMDEs. There has been significant cross-

---

[1] The Green Revolution was initiated by Norman Ernest Borlaug, an American agronomist and recipient of the 1970 Nobel Peace Prize. He developed and promoted the use of new wheat varieties with short sturdy stems, high tilling ability, drought resistance, and responsiveness to fertilizers. The early maturity of these varieties allowed two (and sometimes three) crops to be grown each year.

commodity evolution. For example, in ocean shipping, oil replaced coal, and, more recently, biofuels (an agricultural product) have been used as a substitute for fossil fuel-derived gasoline.

- *Technology.* Technological advances have encouraged consumption of some commodities via the creation of new products and new uses of commodities. They have also reduced the use of some raw materials by improving efficiency in consumption and production. In addition, technological advances have facilitated the discovery and development of new reserves and new commodities. Spectacular advances in agricultural production took place after the development of hybrid varieties in the 1930s and the Green Revolution of the 1960s-70s. The development of information and communication technology has had major impacts on the structure of commodity markets. A notable feature of the increased technical sophistication has been the expansion of futures and options markets and related hedging techniques.

- *Induced innovation.* Innovation in commodity markets has often occurred in response to periods of high prices. For crude oil, episodes of production restraint by the Organization of Petroleum Exporting Countries (OPEC) have stimulated the development of new sources of oil. The oil price shocks of the 1970s encouraged the development of offshore oil in the Gulf of Mexico and the North Sea. High oil prices in the 2000s likewise spurred the development of shale oil production technology.

- *Policies.* Both domestic and international policies have been used to mitigate commodity price volatility. Intervention has taken varied forms at national levels, including subsidies, production quotas, and trade controls, as well as commodity agreements at the international level. Interventions have been most prominent in agriculture. Efforts to support prices, although potentially effective in the short term, often have unintended consequences: higher prices dampen demand and attract new suppliers. Downward pressure on prices often follows.

This chapter proceeds as follows. The next section covers energy markets, notably crude oil, coal, natural gas, nuclear, and renewable energy. The third section examines the markets of iron ore, aluminum, copper, other base metals, and precious metals. The fourth section assesses the evolution of agriculture through the lenses of technology and demand, with a fifth section covering agricultural policies. The sixth section concludes.

Energy

Overview

Although the demand for energy has long tracked economic growth, its consumption accelerated after WWII (figure 1.1). At the start of the 1900s, coal was the dominant fuel, but by 1920 oil was already making inroads—for road and sea transportation, and for heating. Global crude oil production increased from just over 1 million barrels per

FIGURE 1.1 **Energy markets**

The structure of energy markets has changed significantly over the past two centuries, with gradual transitions as new fuels have emerged. Crude oil is the largest of the energy commodities in terms of value and is mainly used for transportation. Natural gas and coal are used for electricity generation, heating, and industrial uses such as fertilizers (gas) and metal smelting (coal).

A. Level of global energy consumption, by source

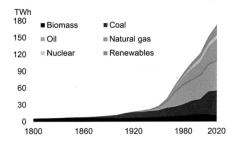

B. Share of global energy consumption, by source

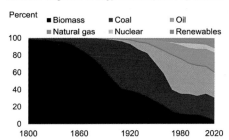

C. Relative size of the three main fuels

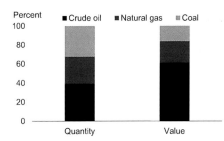

D. Energy use, by sector

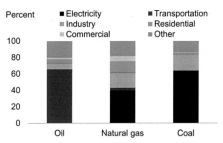

Sources: BP Statistical Review of World Energy 2021; International Energy Agency; OurWorldinData; UN Comtrade Database; World Bank.
A. TWh = terrawatt-hour.
A.B. Renewables include hydroelectric, solar, wind, geothermal, wave, and tidal.
C. Quantity refers to total consumption of the three fuels measured in exajoules. Value of consumption estimated as the sum of total consumption (quantity) and prices of crude oil, natural gas, and coal, using average nominal prices from the World Bank's Commodity Markets (Pink Sheet) database. Data for 2019.
D. Use of oil shows total final consumption of oil products, derived from crude oil. Natural gas and coal show total consumption, including use in electricity production. Electricity also includes use in heating. Data are for 2019.

day (mb/d) in 1920 to nearly 100 mb/d in 2019. Crude oil's share of global energy rose from less than 5 percent in 1920 to a peak of 43 percent in 1973, when price shocks dented demand. Consumption of natural gas began to rise alongside crude oil in the 1900s, but initially at a much slower pace. However, the increasing use of natural gas in electricity generation, as well as heating and cooking, resulted in natural gas rising from 1 percent of global energy consumption in 1920 to 22 percent in 2019.

Among the non-fossil fuel sources of energy, nuclear power emerged as an important source of electricity in the 1970s, peaking in 2000 at about 6 percent of total energy consumption. The share of renewable energy gradually increased in the late 1900s before accelerating in the 2010s, reaching 10 percent of energy consumption in 2019.

Because of the ever-expanding demand for energy, new sources of energy have not replaced existing sources. Consumption of coal, for example, has risen in every decade, even though its share of total energy demand has fallen since 1920.

Today, the three main fossil fuels—oil, coal, and natural gas—account for 83 percent of total energy consumption, down from 94 percent in 1970. Crude oil is dominant among the fossil fuels, accounting for 61 percent of the value of fossil fuels and 39 percent of the quantity. The larger share of crude oil reflects its wide range of uses, limited substitutes for air and sea transportation, readily available reserves, low cost of production, and ease of transportation. For an equivalent energy output, coal is the cheapest of the three fuels, in part because of lower costs and plentiful reserves— estimated at about 140 years of current production compared to less than 60 years for crude oil and 50 years for natural gas.

Of the main uses of the three primary fuels, about two-thirds of crude oil is used for transportation, with the remainder primarily used for petrochemicals. There are currently few substitutes for crude oil in transportation. In contrast, the primary use of natural gas and coal is in electricity generation, accounting for about 40 percent and 60 percent of their consumption, respectively. Numerous substitute fuels can be used to generate electricity, although adoption can take time. Some plants are equipped to switch quickly between oil and gas, depending on relative costs. In the United States, for example, about 13 percent of electric generating capacity is switchable (EIA 2020). Substitution between coal and natural gas is more complicated, because it requires refitting or construction of new plants. Retrofitting, however, has become increasingly common, especially in the United States. Nuclear and renewable energy are also substitutes for electricity generation.

Crude oil

The global oil market has experienced many price booms and busts. It has also been subject to supply management and price-fixing, most notably by Standard Oil from 1879 to 1910, the Interstate Oil Compact Commission (IOCC) and Seven Sisters between 1935 and the 1970s, OPEC since 1960, and OPEC+ since 2017 (figure 1.2; McNally 2017).

In the years following the breakup of the Standard Oil monopoly in 1910, the U.S. oil market experienced episodes of price booms and busts. After unsuccessful attempts to coordinate voluntary output reductions in the face of an oil glut, a group of U.S. states accounting for 80 percent of U.S. production combined to form the IOCC in 1935. The IOCC set enforceable quotas and could order reductions in production to keep prices stable. Because Texas was the largest producer, and effectively acted as a swing producer, the Texas Railroad Commission came to have a major role in setting prices.

Global oil production was dominated by a group of the seven largest oil companies (five of which were U.S. companies), later nicknamed the "Seven Sisters." These companies obtained concessions in key oil-producing countries, primarily in the Middle East,

FIGURE 1.2 Crude oil: Historical developments

Crude oil prices were low and stable between 1930 and 1970, in large part because of the federal government-administered IOCC in the United States, and the Seven Sisters international cartel. Prices have undergone sharp cycles since the rise of OPEC. Periods of high prices have periodically led to the emergence of new producers, often via new discoveries or new technologies, such as in the Middle East after the Second World War, and in Alaska, Mexico, and the North Sea in the 1970s.

A. Long-run crude oil prices

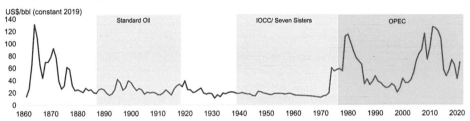

B. Global oil production, 1900-75

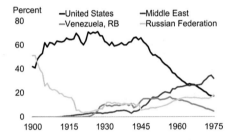

C. Global oil production, 1970-2019

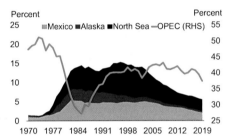

Sources: BP Statistical Review of World Energy 2021; International Energy Agency; World Bank.
Note: IOCC = Interstate Oil Compact Commission; OPEC = Organization of Petroleum Exporting Countries.
A. Oil price refers to the U.S. average between 1861 and 1944, Arabian Light between 1945 and 1983, and Dated Brent between 1984 and 2021. Arabian Light and Dated Brent refer to global oil price benchmarks. Real price series deflated using U.S. Consumer Price Index.
B. Middle East includes Iran, Islamic Rep.; Iraq; Kuwait; Qatar; and Saudi Arabia.
C. North Sea includes Norway and the United Kingdom. RHS = right-hand side.

giving them wide-ranging control of production in exchange for royalty payments. As a result, the Seven Sisters controlled the majority of global production in the mid-1900s, despite substantial oil discoveries during this period. They chose to benchmark oil prices relative to the U.S. price, therefore translating U.S. oil price stability to global oil price stability (McNally 2017). The group did not use its monopoly to push aggressively for higher prices because it wanted to avoid government intervention. This informal arrangement lasted for more than three decades but began to break down in the 1960s, in part because the United States had run out of excess capacity and was increasingly dependent on crude oil imports, but also because the oil-producing countries in the Middle East sought more control over their production and prices (Baumeister and Kilian 2016; Stern and Imsirovic 2020).

OPEC, formed in 1960, accounted for about half of world output by 1970. After raising prices several times in the early 1970s, OPEC generated a global oil price shock by quadrupling the price in 1973-74. A second price shock occurred in 1979-80 when the Iranian revolution and war between Iraq and Islamic Republic of Iran resulted in a significant loss of global oil production and a sharp increase in prices.

Although oil producers benefited from increased oil revenue, the high prices reduced oil demand and encouraged the development of non-OPEC oil production. Between 1979 and 1983, global oil demand fell by 10 percent, or 6 mb/d, with demand in AEs declining by 18 percent. Oil-importing countries mandated increases in fuel efficiency standards and encouraged the use of substitutes, for example, by prohibiting the construction of oil-powered electricity power stations.[2] At the same time, high oil prices resulted in a sharp increase in non-OPEC supply, particularly from high-cost sources (Gately 1986). Output from Alaska, the Gulf of Mexico, and the North Sea rose from 2.2 percent of global production in 1975 to 14.0 percent in 1985, with market share taken at the expense of OPEC.

Because of these developments, oil prices declined every year between 1980 and 1985. To offset the sustained declines in prices, OPEC set production quotas for the first time in March 1982. Quotas were successively lowered, and Saudi Arabia accepted the role of a swing producer, absorbing the brunt of production cuts. However, noncompliance by other OPEC members was widespread, and by mid-1985 Saudi Arabia's oil production had fallen by more than three-quarters (Hamilton 2010). In 1985, Saudi Arabia changed its strategy and announced that it would cease its role as swing supplier and increase production, causing oil prices to collapse. In addition to raising Saudi Arabia's market share, the price war was meant to invoke production discipline among all OPEC members. OPEC again set quotas in 1987, along with a price target. However, apart from a spike at the onset of the Gulf War in 1990, prices continued to slide, reaching a low of US$10.00 per barrel of crude oil (bbl) in 1999.

The 1970s oil crisis and nationalization of company assets helped trigger the broader development of the oil market, including the emergence of market pricing mechanisms. The New York Mercantile Exchange introduced the WTI (West Texas Intermediate) oil futures contract in 1983, and the Brent contract was launched shortly thereafter. Today, there are three main oil price benchmarks—Brent, WTI, and Dubai—as well as many regional price benchmarks.[3] Oil futures are widely traded on futures exchanges, with WTI the most active. Of all commodity markets, oil futures have the longest horizon, although liquidity declines rapidly as the contract term lengthens.

---

[2] Oil demand was also depressed by a steep rise in interest rates caused by the Federal Reserve's policy of reducing inflation, and by a global economic recession.

[3] Brent refers to crude oil produced in the North Sea. It is used to price two-thirds of the world's trade in crude oil, including that produced in Africa, Europe, and some parts of the Middle East (ICE 2021). WTI is the U.S. benchmark, and Dubai is generally used to price crude oil exports from the Persian Gulf to Asia. Differences between types of crude oil are primarily based on their sulfur content and their density, which determine if they are "sweet" or "sour" and "light" or "heavy" (EIA 2012). Brent and WTI are light, sweet crude oils, whereas Dubai is at the opposite end of the scale as a heavy, sour oil. In general, crude oil grades that are lighter and sweeter are more valuable than heavy, sour oils, because it is easier to produce gasoline and diesel from them.

The 2000s saw a surge in oil prices, mainly reflecting larger-than-expected demand among EMDEs (figure 1.3; World Bank 2018). Oil consumption in China rose by nearly 70 percent during 2000-08, and in India by 40 percent. In contrast, oil demand among AEs was broadly unchanged over this period. In addition to increases in demand, only modest increases in supply from OPEC contributed to rising prices (Baumeister and Peersman 2013; Kilian 2009; Kilian and Murphy 2014). At the peak in 2008, oil prices reached well over $100/bbl. The boom ended abruptly during the global financial crisis, but oil prices recovered rapidly thanks to robust growth in China and production cuts among OPEC countries.

Between January 2011 and mid-2014, oil prices plateaued at just over $100/bbl. In contrast, most other commodity prices gradually declined over this period because of weak global demand and rising supplies. Through 2013, the impact of soft global demand on oil prices was offset by geopolitical factors on the supply side. These factors included a collapse in exports from Libya due to internal conflict, as well as reduced exports from the Islamic Republic of Iran following the imposition of sanctions by the United States and the European Union (Baumeister and Kilian 2016).

Oil prices began to drop in mid-2014 and continued to decline until a trough of $40/bbl was reached at the start of 2016—a decline of more than 70 percent from the highs earlier in the decade. Several factors were at play. High and stable prices before 2014 facilitated the development of other forms of crude oil, most notably U.S. shale oil, as well as Canadian tar sand production and biofuels. U.S. crude oil production increased by 55 percent between 2011 and 2014, and its share of global oil production rose from 7.6 percent to 11.2 percent. In addition, oil supply disruptions arising from geopolitical events—including conflict in Libya, the impact of sanctions on the Islamic Republic of Iran, and fears of supply outages in Iraq—had less impact on production than expected, and oil demand, although continuing to grow, consistently came out below market expectations (Baffes et al. 2015).

The drop in prices was exacerbated by a change in OPEC strategy. At its meeting in November 2014, OPEC opted to maintain a production level of 30 mb/d instead of anticipated production cuts (OPEC 2014). This decision signaled that OPEC would no longer act as the swing oil producer and would let prices be set by the marginal producer, U.S. shale. Shale oil projects differ from conventional drilling projects in that they have a shorter life cycle and relatively low capital costs, and production tends to respond more rapidly to price changes (Kilian 2020).

The sharp fall in prices was expected to have a substantial negative impact on U.S. shale production. However, the U.S. shale industry adapted to lower prices and sharply reduced production costs via efficiency gains and innovation. As a result, U.S. production declined only modestly in 2016 before recovering rapidly as prices rebounded. In 2018, U.S. crude oil production rose by a record 1.5 mb/d. With this increase, the United States overtook the Russian Federation and Saudi Arabia to become the world's largest oil producer, accounting for nearly 15 percent of global production (EIA 2018).

FIGURE 1.3 Crude oil: Developments since 2000

After surging through the 2000s, oil prices averaged over $100/bbl between 2011 and 2014 before collapsing. The price surge was driven by a sharp increase in demand among EMDEs, while demand among advanced economies has declined. U.S. oil production has risen sharply as a result of the shale oil revolution. Amid surging global output, OPEC has attempted to manage oil markets by reducing its own production, and expanding its influence with the OPEC+ grouping. The COVID-19 pandemic presented a unique shock to oil markets, triggering a fall in oil demand more than twice as large as any previous decline.

A. Brent crude oil prices

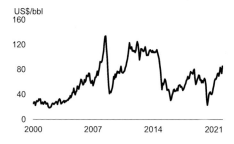

B. Oil demand

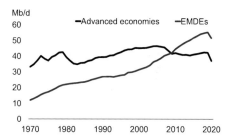

C. Oil consumption in EMDEs

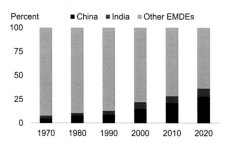

D. Crude oil production, three largest producers

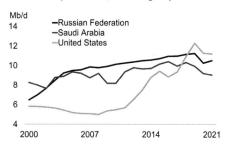

E. OPEC+ production management

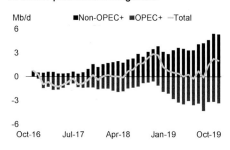

F. Oil demand declines since 1965

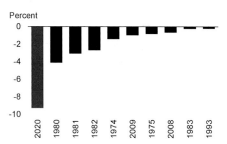

Sources: BP Statistical Review of World Energy 2021; International Energy Agency; World Bank.
Note: bbl = barrel of crude oil; EMDE = emerging market and developing economies; mb/d = million barrels per day; OPEC = Organization of Petroleum Exporting Countries.
E. Figure shows change in production relative to October 2016. Last observation is December 2019. OPEC+ includes OPEC members and 10 non-OPEC countries that collectively agree to production quotas.
F. Figure shows the top-10 declines in annual oil demand.

As in the previous period, the increase in the U.S. share of oil production came at the expense of OPEC. In response to the rapid increase in U.S. production and relatively low prices, in December 2016 OPEC reached an agreement with 10 non-OPEC countries to cut oil production by a collective 1.2 mb/d.[4] The group became known as OPEC+ and continues to collectively set production targets. Between 2017 and 2019, OPEC+ had some success in maintaining prices, although it came at the expense of market share and may have served to benefit the U.S. shale industry.

In 2020, the COVID-19 pandemic had a large impact on oil markets (Kabundi and Ohnsorge 2020). The one-month decline in oil prices in April 2020 was the largest on record, with the WTI price briefly turning negative (World Bank 2020). Oil consumption fell sharply because of government restrictions to stem the spread of the pandemic, with demand declining by almost 10 percent in 2020, more than twice as large as any previous decline (World Bank 2020). Amid plummeting prices, OPEC and its partners agreed in April 2020 to cut production by a record 9.7 mb/d.[5] Prices rose during the remainder of the year and accelerated in 2021 as the global economy recovered. While production rose, some producers struggled to increase output, hindered by various factors, including shortages of labor, transportation bottlenecks, and bad weather (World Bank 2021).

Oil markets were once again disrupted by the war in Ukraine. In response to the invasion, several countries, including Canada, the United Kingdom, and the United States announced they would ban or phase out imports of oil from Russia. The International Energy Agency estimated about 3 mb/d of Russia's production was disrupted as a result. The longer-term implications of the war in Ukraine are examined in box 1.1.

Coal

Coal has been used extensively as a fuel throughout history and was instrumental in the industrial revolution. Thermal (or steam) coal, which accounts for more than 80 percent of global coal consumption, is chiefly used for electricity generation. The remainder is coking or metallurgical coal and is used to smelt iron ore for steel production. China is the largest consumer of coal, accounting for more than half of the world's consumption. China also accounts for half of global production, followed by India (10 percent), Indonesia (7 percent), and Australia and the United States (about 6 percent each).

Before the 1960s, international trade of coal was limited, mostly land-based, and regional, reflecting the high cost of transportation—even today, transportation costs can make up half of total costs of coal supply (Paulus 2012). Former West Germany, for

---

[4] The 10 non-OPEC countries are Azerbaijan, Bahrain, Brunei, Kazakhstan, Malaysia, Mexico, Oman, Russia, Sudan, and South Sudan.

[5] The group had previously failed to reach an agreement at its meeting in March 2020, which triggered the end of the existing cuts. Saudi Arabia announced it would increase oil production by more than 2 mb/d, to 12 mb/d, exacerbating the fall in prices.

example, exported coal to other countries in Western Europe while Poland and the Soviet Union supplied Eastern European countries. There was also some land-based trade between Canada and the United States. The only seaborne coal trade was from the United States (the world's largest producer at that time) to Japan and Western Europe.

An international market for coal began forming after the oil price shocks of the 1970s, which made coal competitive with crude oil for power generation despite higher transportation costs. The increasing use of coal for electricity generation was facilitated by the International Energy Agency's decision to ban its member countries from building new oil-fired electricity plants (IEA 1979). As a result, global coal consumption rose more than one-fifth between 1970 and 1980, leading to large increases in coal prices (figure 1.4). In addition, several countries—including Australia, Canada, and South Africa—developed their coal reserves and became coal exporters. The result was a doubling of the quantity of coal traded between 1970 and 1990 (Wårell 2005).

Coal prices began to decline in the 1980s and plateaued in the 1990s despite continued growth in coal consumption. The decline was driven by supply-side factors, including the emergence of additional coal exporters in the 1980s, including China, Colombia, and Indonesia, as well as technological developments, particularly in the United States, where the cost of producing coal fell sharply (Ellerman 1995). Between 1985 and 1995, the labor productivity of coal miners in the United States doubled, from 2.7 tons per employee per hour to 5.4 tons (EIA 2021). The 1980s saw the first international coal price benchmark, which was the outcome of negotiations between a leading Australian coal supplier, BHP Billiton, and Japanese power and steel companies.[6]

The coal market changed significantly from 2000 onward as rapid growth in EMDEs, notably China, led to a surge in demand (Baffes, Kabundi, and Nagle 2022; World Bank 2018). Global coal consumption rose by almost 50 percent during 2000-08, with China accounting for more than two-thirds of the increase. Although China rapidly increased domestic production of coal, the increase was insufficient to meet the rise in domestic demand. As a result, the country became a significant importer of coal, driving up global prices (which peaked in mid-2008). The global financial crisis caused prices to fall sharply as the global economy contracted, but prices bounced back rapidly as the economy recovered, with China once again driving the increase in demand.

Demand for coal peaked in 2014 and has slightly declined since, as China's growth has slowed and shifted away from manufacturing and investment toward consumption and services (World Bank 2019a). Coal demand has been further affected by the U.S. shale revolution, which led to plentiful supplies of low-cost natural gas, enabling gas-to-coal switching in electricity generation (EIA 2020). Concerns about climate change and pressures to reduce carbon emissions alongside a fall in the cost of solar- and wind-

---

[6] Today there are three widely used international coal price benchmarks: (1) free on board (fob) spot price at Richards Bay, representing thermal coal exports from South Africa, (2) fob spot at Newcastle, representing thermal coal exports from Australia, and (3) fob spot at Bolivar, representing thermal coal exports from Colombia, although numerous other prices are also used. Coal is also traded on several futures exchanges.

FIGURE 1.4 **Coal**

After a period of stability during the 1970s-2000s, coal prices surged in the 2000s, driven by rising demand from China and other EMDEs. Although the United States has the world's largest coal reserves, its share of coal production has fallen, while China, India, and Indonesia have seen increases. Coal consumption in advanced economies has been flat or declining since 2010 because of a decline in coal use in electricity generation. Coal-fired power plants are being retired in Europe and the United States, but China and India have installed additional capacity.

A. Global coal consumption

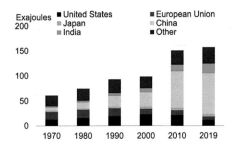

B. Monthly coal prices

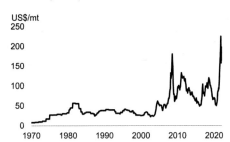

C. Shares of global coal production

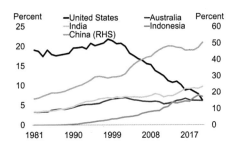

D. Global coal reserves

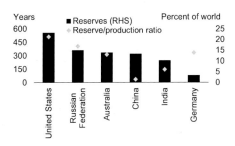

E. Use of coal in electricity generation

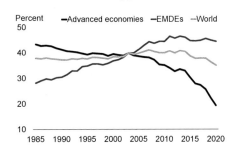

F. New coal capacity installation

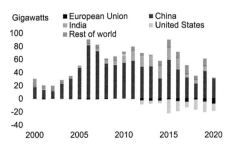

Sources: BP Statistical Review of World Energy 2021; Energy Information Administration; Global Energy Monitor; International Energy Agency; World Bank.
Note: EMDE = emerging market and developing economy; RHS = right-hand side.
B. Australian coal prices.
D. Reserve/production ratio refers to a country's known reserves relative to its production. Data for 2020.
F. Chart shows the net change in global coal-powered electricity generation capacity (additions of new capacity less retirement of existing capacity). A negative value indicates more coal generation capacity is being retired than is being added.

powered electricity have further suppressed demand, especially in AEs, resulting in a fall in coal-powered electricity. Reflecting these developments, coal-fired electricity capacity has declined in Europe and the United States in recent years, even as it has increased in China and India. However, coal still accounts for 30 percent of primary energy consumption and generates 40 percent of the world's electricity.

In 2020, the COVID-19 pandemic and the associated global recession caused a drop in demand for coal, and its price fell by nearly 30 percent between January and August. However, prices soared through 2021 and reached a new all-time high toward the end of 2021, as demand for imported coal rebounded in response to the economic recovery. Coal prices were further boosted by shortfalls in other sources of energy, including lower hydroelectric output, due to heat waves and droughts in North and South America as well as China (World Bank 2021). Amid worries about energy shortfalls, China's policy makers announced several initiatives to increase production; as a result, China's coal production reached a new all-time high by end-2021. In 2022, the war in Ukraine also disrupted coal markets, with several countries banning imports of Russian coal, leading to significant trade diversion (World Bank 2022).

Natural gas

Historically, natural gas markets have tended to be regional in terms of production, consumption, and pricing. In North America, natural gas has typically been transported through pipelines between Canada, the United States, and Mexico. Similarly, in Europe, most natural gas has, until recently, been transported by pipeline from major producers, such as Norway and Russia, to consuming countries across the continent.[7] In Asia, by contrast, a larger proportion of natural gas has been transported as liquefied natural gas (LNG), with Japan and the Republic of Korea the two largest consumers.

Pricing structures vary significantly by market. For gas transported by pipeline, prices can be set by open market mechanisms similar to those used in oil markets, or they may be set by direct negotiations between buyers and sellers. Prices are regulated in some markets. In contrast, LNG contracts are typically longer term, and indexed to the cost of feed gas, the floating price in the destination market, or indexed to oil or other commodities (Chandra 2020). In the European Union and the United States, gas supply and demand conditions help set prices at hubs, such as TTF (Title Transfer Facility) in the Netherlands and Henry Hub in the United States (IEA 2013).[8] In Asia and Central and Southern Europe, natural gas prices are typically indexed to oil prices (and occasionally to other energy prices, such as coal).

Over the past two decades, the natural gas market has changed substantially. On the production side, the shale boom in the United States has helped lift U.S. natural gas

---

[7] Natural gas is very capital-intensive, with substantial up-front costs in building pipelines, storage, and liquefaction and regasification facilities.

[8] The European Union gas market has undergone significant liberalization following the adoption of the Third Energy Package in 2009. This initiative contained several reforms to achieve a fully open market (European Commission 2009).

BOX 1.1 Comparing the effects of the war in Ukraine on commodity markets with the effects of earlier shocks

The Russian Federation's invasion of Ukraine has been a major shock to commodity markets and is causing significant disruptions to the production and trade of commodities. Earlier large commodity price shocks triggered policy and market responses that led to increased sources of supply and, for oil, substitution away from oil and greater consumption efficiency. Over time, the spike in prices following the war in Ukraine will likely once again spur more efficient energy consumption and a faster transition away from fossil fuels, particularly if supported by appropriate policy responses.

Introduction

The Russian Federation's invasion of Ukraine caused major shocks to commodity markets. It led to significant disruptions to the production and trade of commodities for which Russia and Ukraine are key exporters, especially energy and food. The shocks exacerbated existing COVID-19-related stresses in commodity markets, which had arisen as a result of rebounding global demand and constrained supplies. Together, the changes in nominal prices resulting from the post-COVID-19 rebound and the war in Ukraine led to the largest increase in energy prices since the 1973 oil price spike (figure B1.1.1; World Bank 2022). For food and fertilizers, the increase was the third largest (after 1974 and 2008).

The invasion affected commodity markets in the short term through two main channels: (1) the impact of blockades and the destruction of productive capacity, and (2) the impact on trade and production following sanctions. Ukrainian wheat production and trade were severely disrupted, which especially affected countries that rely heavily on Ukraine for wheat imports. In addition, many countries including Canada, European Union (EU) countries, and the United States, chose to ban or phase out imports of Russian energy, which led to a costly diversion of trade in energy, as countries sought out alternative suppliers to Russia.

Beyond their short-term effects, shocks such as the war in Ukraine have longer-term consequences. They can trigger shifts in government policies and changes in the behavior of consumers and producers, leading to lasting changes in patterns of consumption and production. This box draws lessons from major shocks to commodity markets over the past 50 years. These shocks include the 1970s oil and food price spikes and the broad-based rise in commodity prices during the 2000s. These price shocks induced policy and market responses that led to new supply sources, consumption efficiencies, and substitution among commodities.

This box addresses the following questions: What were the main policy and market responses during earlier commodity shocks? And how does the war in Ukraine compare with past episodes?

BOX 1.1 Comparing the effects of the war in Ukraine on commodity
markets with the effects of earlier shocks *(continued)*

FIGURE B1.1.1 Market responses to price shocks

Commodity prices (in nominal terms) rose sharply following the start of the war in Ukraine, particularly for commodities for which the Russian Federation and Ukraine are key exporters. Price increases from April 2020 to April 2022 were the largest for any equivalent two-year period since 1973 for energy and 2008 for fertilizers and food.

A. Energy price changes

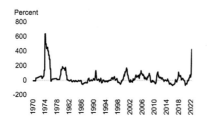

B. Fertilizer price changes

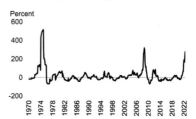

C. Food price changes

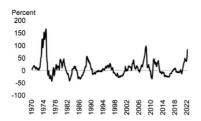

D. Real energy prices during price spikes

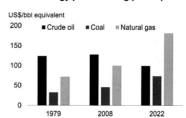

Sources: Bloomberg; World Bank.
A.-C. All prices in nominal U.S. dollar terms. Charts show the percent change in monthly price indexes over a two-year period. The last observation is based on April 2022 data. Because of data limitations, the energy price change before 1979 is proxied by the price of oil.
D. Chart shows the annual price of coal, Brent crude oil, and European natural gas, deflated using U.S. Consumer Price Index. Data for 2022 reflect forecasts from World Bank (2022). bbl = barrel of crude oil.

Policy responses during previous shocks

Energy

The global oil market has experienced three major price increases during the past 50 years. The first occurred in 1973 when several Gulf members of the Organization of the Petroleum Exporting Countries imposed an oil embargo on exports to the United States and its allies following the Yom Kippur War. The second occurred in 1979 as a result of the Iranian revolution and was intensified by the Iran-Iraq war leading to a tripling in oil prices within a year. The third

BOX 1.1 Comparing the effects of the war in Ukraine on commodity markets with the effects of earlier shocks *(continued)*

took place during the 2000s in a more gradual fashion as a result of strong demand in emerging market and developing economies (EMDEs), especially in China and India, with a spike in prices in 2008 and again in 2011-14 (Baffes et al. 2018).

The oil price spikes of the 1970s triggered a number of policy responses, which, alongside market forces, became the catalyst for demand reduction, substitution by other fuels, and the development of new sources of energy. After the first oil price shock, several members of the Organisation for Economic Co-operation and Development set up the International Energy Agency in 1974 to safeguard oil supplies under a binding oil emergency sharing system, and to promote common policy making and data collection and analysis. Key policy decisions included the requirement to create national oil reserves equal to 60 days of imports (later expanded to 90 days) and a ban on building new oil-fired electricity plants, which included a directive to switch to coal (enacted in 1977; Scott 1994). Additional policies were adopted after the second oil price shock, with member countries agreeing to reduce oil demand by 5 percent.

Policies varied at the country level. In the United States, price controls on oil (which had first been imposed in 1971, before the oil price shocks) contributed to shortages of oil products and were followed by the implementation of fuel allocation programs. These policies were generally deemed to have impeded the normal functioning of markets and led to significant distortions (McNally 2017). The country subsequently implemented numerous policy measures to address the underlying demand and supply imbalance with the Energy Policy and Conservation Act of 1975. On the demand side, measures included energy conservation programs as well as regulations such as the prohibition of the use of crude oil in electricity generation, and improved fuel efficiency standards for new automobiles and consumer appliances. The average fuel efficiency of U.S. autos rose from 13 miles per gallon in 1973 to 20 miles per gallon by 1990 (figure B1.1.2). On the supply side, measures included price incentives and production requirements to increase the supply of fossil fuels, including loan guarantees for new coal mines. The act also mandated the creation of the Strategic Petroleum Reserve and measures to improve data, which led to the formation of the Energy Information Administration. In addition, in 1979, the United States announced it would eliminate price controls for oil (which it did in January 1981), allowing market forces to address imbalances in supply and demand (Ilkenberry 1988).

In Japan, policies focused on measures to reduce energy use, develop alternative sources of energy to oil (notably nuclear power), and stabilize the supply of oil to Japan, for example through joint ventures with other countries (Shibata 1982).

BOX 1.1 Comparing the effects of the war in Ukraine on commodity markets with the effects of earlier shocks *(continued)*

FIGURE B1.1.2 Effects of price shocks on production and consumption

Rising oil prices led to increased production from alternative sources of oil such as Alaska and the North Sea in the 1970s-80s. The food price spikes of the 1970s encouraged the emergence of South American countries as major food exporters. The share of nonoil energy sources rose sharply after the 1979 oil price spike, notably nuclear and coal in advanced economies, but increases were smaller during the 2008 oil price spike. Higher prices also saw policies implemented to improve energy efficiency, including for vehicles in the United States.

A. Oil production

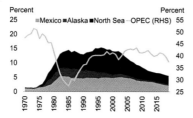

B. Maize and soybean production

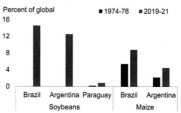

C. Changes in shares of energy demand

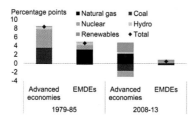

D. Fuel efficiency

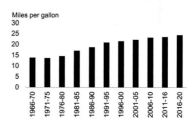

Sources: BP Statistical Review of World Energy 2021; Energy Information Administration; U.S. Department of Agriculture database, December 2021 update; World Bank. OPEC = Organization of the Petroleum Exporting Countries; RHS = right-hand side.
A. North Sea refers to production from Norway and the United Kingdom.
C. Chart shows the change in energy consumption in advanced economies and emerging market and developing economies (EMDEs) in the five years after the oil price shocks of 1979 and 2008. The total change reflects the equivalent decrease in oil consumption.
D. Figure shows the fuel efficiency of U.S. vehicles in miles driven per gallon of gasoline consumed.

The Japanese government also phased out energy-intensive industries such as aluminum and petrochemicals. European countries implemented some similar domestic policies (Ilkenberry 1988).

Steadily increasing oil prices in the 2000s again led to policies to address concerns about energy shortfalls. In the United States, the Energy Policy Act of 2005 and the Energy Independence and Security Act of 2007 included numerous provisions

BOX 1.1 Comparing the effects of the war in Ukraine on commodity markets with the effects of earlier shocks *(continued)*

to reduce demand and boost production (EPA 2007). They included improving fuel efficiency in vehicles, tax breaks for the purchase of hybrid vehicles, and tax breaks and incentives for investing in energy-efficient buildings, both for commercial use and housing. On the supply side, the act mandated a sharp increase in the use of biofuels, established renewable fuel standards, provided energy-related tax incentives for fossil fuels and renewable energy sources, and provided loan guarantees. Other countries adopted similar policies. For example, the EU introduced the Renewable Energy Directive in 2009, which mandated that 20 percent of all energy usage in the EU, including at least 10 percent of all road transportation fuels, be produced from renewable sources by 2020, alongside measures to increase energy efficiency (European Parliament 2009). These directives were further expanded by the European Green Deal of 2019. Biofuel policies were also introduced in some EMDEs, including Brazil and India.

Food

Food commodity markets have experienced two major price increases over the past half century, both during similar time periods to the oil price shocks. The first occurred during the 1972-74 oil crisis, and the second took place during the 2000s as part of the broader commodity price boom. As in the case of oil, food prices spiked in 2008 and again in 2011.

The 1970s food price spike was beneficial for food-exporting countries. In the United States, the government was able to reduce expensive support programs that it had previously implemented. Among commodity importers such as Japan, the price boom of the 1970s (as well as an embargo on soybean exports by the United States) reinforced the desire for self-sufficiency in food commodities. Japan promoted international cooperation to stabilize agricultural commodity prices and guarantee reliable supplies for importers (Honma and Hayami 1988). Other East Asian countries, including the Republic of Korea, increased protection of domestic agriculture and expanded the scope of state trading agencies.

During the 2008 price increase, governments in several EMDEs were confronted with difficult policy choices. Allowing domestic prices to adjust to world food price changes would have led to higher food price inflation, thereby causing a decline in real incomes of poor households that were net food buyers (Laborde, Lakatos, and Martin 2019). Instead, many countries attempted to reduce the transmission of international food price shocks to domestic markets. During the 2007-08 food price spike, close to three-quarters of EMDEs undertook policy actions to insulate their economies from the sharp increase in international food prices, especially for rice (World Bank 2019b). Similar policy actions were undertaken before and during the spike of 2010-11 (Chapoto and Jayne 2009;

BOX 1.1 Comparing the effects of the war in Ukraine on commodity markets with the effects of earlier shocks *(continued)*

Ivanic and Martin 2014). Several studies have shown that the use of such trade policy interventions compounded the volatility of world prices and also increased poverty (Laborde, Lakatos, and Martin 2019).

Market responses during previous shocks

Market mechanisms respond to price shocks and associated policies through three main channels: demand reduction, substitution, and supply response. This section discusses how these channels apply to energy and food commodities. Although substitution and supply responses are applicable across most commodities, the demand reduction channel is less applicable for food.

Energy

Demand reduction. Between 1979 and 1983, global oil demand fell by 11 percent, or 6 million barrels per day (mb/d), with demand in advanced economies shrinking by almost 20 percent. While the drop in oil demand was partly a result of the global recession in 1982, energy efficiency and substitution policies implemented by oil-importing countries caused a permanent reduction in underlying demand growth. Changes in consumer preferences in response to higher prices also played a role. For example, in the United States, preferences shifted away from domestically produced and less fuel-efficient vehicles in favor of more efficient Japanese-made cars—the share of Japanese cars in U.S. auto purchases rose from 9 percent in 1976 to 21 percent in 1980 (Cole 1981).

In the 2000s, high oil prices and policy changes once again induced efficiency improvements in the use of oil, but less switching to other fuels occurred because much less crude oil was being used in electricity generation. After peaking in 2005, oil consumption in advanced economies steadily declined such that by 2014 it had fallen 14 percent from its peak. Once again, consumer preferences played a role. For example, in the United States, there was a shift toward fuel-efficient hybrid cars (supported by government policies) away from sport utility vehicles. Indeed, in 2008, sales of sport utility vehicles began to plunge, and by mid-2008 they were down more than 25 percent from the same period a year earlier (Hamilton 2009).

Substitution. In the five years after the 1979 oil price shock, the share of crude oil in the energy mix in advanced economies fell by more than 7 percent. This shift was chiefly due to the prohibition of the construction of oil-powered electricity power stations—which were replaced by nuclear- and coal-powered stations. The shift to nuclear power, which had started in the late 1960s, was particularly pronounced in France and Japan, where its share in total energy consumption reached 23 and 8 percent, respectively, by 1984. Among EMDEs, the share of oil fell by 4 percent and was largely replaced by natural gas.

BOX 1.1 Comparing the effects of the war in Ukraine on commodity markets with the effects of earlier shocks *(continued)*

In the years following the 2008 oil price rise, the share of natural gas and renewables in the energy mix rose, reflecting the U.S. shale boom for natural gas, and mandates and technological improvements for renewables. However, because oil was no longer used widely in electricity generation, the decline in its share was of marginal significance. Moreover, substituting other energy commodities for oil in its main uses—transportation and petrochemicals—is much harder. As a result of mandates, the share of biofuels—ethanol and biodiesel—rose from about 0.15 percent of total oil consumption in 2005 to 1.70 percent in 2020, a large overall increase although still a very small share of overall oil consumption.

New sources of production. High oil prices in the 1970s induced investment in oil production facilities outside of the Organization for the Petroleum Exporting Countries, including Prudhoe Bay in Alaska, the North Sea offshore fields of the United Kingdom and Norway, the Cantarell offshore field of Mexico, and oil sands in Canada. High and stable prices in the 2000s also facilitated the development of alternative sources of crude oil. The most notable of these was the development of U.S. shale oil deposits, output from which rose from 5 mb/d in 2008 to 9 mb/d in 2014. In addition, Canadian oil sand production and Brazilian deep-water production rose rapidly.

Food

Substitution. In contrast to energy commodities, most of the substitution in food commodities takes place on the input side because different crops can be grown with much the same inputs of land, labor, machinery, and fertilizers. This flexibility allows shifts in crop patterns from one season to another, in turn preventing sustained price gaps among commodities. For example, the price spikes of the 1970s and 2000s were mostly focused in one commodity and subsequently spread to the prices of other crops. Indeed, despite the large increase in maize and edible oil demand for biofuels and animal feed over the past two decades, the prices of these commodities moved in tandem with other grains and oilseeds.[a]

Substitution on the consumption side does occur, but only for some agricultural commodities. For example, edible oils (including palm, soybean, and rapeseed oil) can be substituted for each other, which explains the high degree of comovement in edible oil prices. Substitutability also takes place in animal feed, especially between maize and soybean meal. Other food commodities, however,

---

a. For example, global demand for maize doubled during 2000-20, compared to the 26-28 percent increase in global demand for rice and wheat (in line with worlds population growth of 27 percent over this period).

BOX 1.1 Comparing the effects of the war in Ukraine on commodity markets with the effects of earlier shocks *(continued)*

are less substitutable because consumption patterns depend on cultural factors (for example, Asia is mostly a rice-consuming region while whereas the Americas and Europe are mostly wheat-consuming regions).

New sources of supply. The food price increases in the 1970s induced a supply response from some South American countries, including Argentina and Brazil. Today, these two countries account for 17 and 50 percent of global soybean production, respectively, whereas they produced virtually no soybeans in the 1970s. Over the same period, their share of global maize production almost doubled to about 8 percent and 4 percent, respectively. High food commodity prices in 2008 and 2011, however, did not bring any major new producers into the global food markets. Indeed, some of the factors behind the spikes reversed— for example, high energy prices started to decline, and restrictive trade policies were eased—thus replenishing stocks of most grains and oilseeds.

Comparing shocks from the war in Ukraine with earlier shocks

The shock from the war in Ukraine has a number of similarities to, but also some differences from, earlier shocks. In all three shocks, high energy prices pushed up fertilizer prices and other input costs, thereby causing food commodity prices to spike. Export bans were also used in all three shocks. The 1970s shocks and the war in Ukraine were associated with geopolitical tensions, ongoing stresses in commodity markets, and inflationary pressures.

Energy

Prices. All energy prices saw significant increases through 2021 and the start of 2022, particularly natural gas and coal. In contrast, in the earlier episodes, oil prices rose much more sharply than those for coal and gas. In March 2022, the price of oil in real terms averaged 35 percent below its 2008 peak, whereas the price of European natural gas reached a historical high. With all energy prices elevated, there is less opportunity to substitute with cheaper fuel. In fact, because oil is one of the cheapest fuels, it was used somewhat to substitute for natural gas in electricity generation in 2021 and 2022 (World Bank 2021). In addition, high prices of some commodities (such as energy) pushed up the production cost of other commodities (such as fertilizers, foods, and metals). Although renewables— mainly solar and wind power—offer an alternative source of energy, their cost also rose in 2022 as a result of sharply higher prices for the metals used in their construction, including aluminum and nickel.

Intensity. The amount of oil required to produce a unit of economic output (the "oil intensity of GDP") has fallen considerably since the 1970s. Similarly, consumer spending on energy as a share of total spending has also fallen,

BOX 1.1 Comparing the effects of the war in Ukraine on commodity markets with the effects of earlier shocks *(continued)*

especially in advanced economies (although it increased significantly in 2022). As a result, consumers may respond less to energy price changes, at least in the short term, than in the 1970s. Industry, by contrast, may be more vulnerable to price changes. There is some evidence that price elasticity of demand in energy-intensive industries may be higher than that of consumers. For example, in Europe high natural gas and electricity prices led to lower production of fertilizer and aluminum in 2021.

Policies. Policy responses to high energy prices following the war in Ukraine often focused on reducing fuel taxes or introducing subsidies—a marked reversal of a broader trend of declining subsidies over previous years. These policies were also in contrast to policy announcements to combat climate change (such as during the 26th session of the Conference of the Parties, COP 26, in 2021), which included promises to phase out fossil fuel subsidies. Although tax breaks and subsidies can somewhat alleviate the immediate impact of price spikes, they do not provide large benefits to vulnerable groups, and by increasing energy demand they tend to prolong the imbalance of demand and supply.

Energy supply disruptions following the war in Ukraine also complicated the energy transition, with several countries announcing plans to increase production of fossil fuels. China, for example, announced it would increase its coal production by 300 million tons (an amount equal to its imports), an increase of nearly 8 percent from its production during 2021. The EU also announced plans to increase imports of liquefied natural gas to reduce its reliance on Russian natural gas. Although increasing the supply of fossil fuels helps alleviate energy shortages, it makes achieving climate change goals more challenging. Although some countries announced intentions to boost energy production from renewable sources or to revive or extend nuclear power plants, such projects take time to materialize.

As in the earlier shocks, the war on Ukraine has prompted several countries to unveil plans to reduce energy demand. For example, the United States announced a faster increase in fuel efficiency requirements for car manufacturers, requiring fuel efficiency to increase to 49 miles per gallon by 2026, an increase of about one-quarter relative to 2021. The EU announced plans to encourage the installation of heat pumps, which are a more energy-efficient method of heating homes.

Food

A key similarity between the shock from the Ukraine war and the earlier food price shocks is the role of high energy (and fertilizer) prices in driving food price increases. However, the extent and breadth of price increases differed markedly across the three spikes. Whereas the 1970s food price increases were among the

BOX 1.1 Comparing the effects of the war in Ukraine on commodity markets with the effects of earlier shocks *(continued)*

largest of the past 100 years, the more recent increases have been much smaller in magnitude, reflecting, in part, the long-term downward path of agricultural prices (Baffes and Kabundi 2021). Whereas the 1970s price boom was broad-based, the boom in 2008-09 was led by rice, and that in 2022 was led by wheat, followed by edible oils.

Substitution has also played an important role and explains differences in price changes following the Ukraine war. Whereas prices of agricultural commodities of which Ukraine is a major exporter rose, increases were smaller for sunflower oil compared with wheat. That is because sunflower oil can be substituted by soybean and palm oil (the prices of all edible oils have risen since the war began, reflecting this substitutability). The larger price spike for wheat reflects the fact that it is less easily substituted by other commodities. Substitution of wheat will instead come from land reallocation, which takes place from one season to the next.

On the policy front, export bans and other trade restrictions were less common during the 2022 price spike compared to the previous events. However, the food price rises accelerated domestic food price inflation and increased food insecurity in many low-income countries, where it had already deteriorated during the pandemic.

Conclusions and policy implications

The war in Ukraine has dealt a major shock to commodity markets. In the past, policy responses were key to providing a long-term solution to shocks. The comparison with earlier shocks highlights how some policies have been highly effective and beneficial, whereas others have provided short-term fixes but at the expense of market distortions or new problems. Increased efficiency standards for automobiles, incentives for more efficient home appliances, and renewable energy mandates (except biofuels) have all generated long-term benefits. Similarly, the creation of institutions to improve market transparency, coordinate policy responses, improve data quality, and facilitate policy dialogue, have also been beneficial. These include the International Energy Agency (set up by the Organisation for Economic Co-operation and Development after the first oil price shock) and the Agricultural Marketing Information System (set up by the G20 in response to the 2007-08 price spike).

Some policies that provided short-term respite to higher prices exacerbated problems in the medium term or led to new problems. For example, price controls in the United States after the first oil price shock in 1973 distorted markets and may have increased oil demand. The promotion of coal use for electricity generation in the late 1970s reduced reliance on oil; however, it created environmental problems, including air pollution and the acceleration of climate

BOX 1.1 Comparing the effects of the war in Ukraine on commodity markets with the effects of earlier shocks *(continued)*

change. Similarly, the introduction of biofuels provided an alternative to crude oil and may have increased the share of renewable energy, but its overall effectiveness has been questioned because biofuel production requires large amounts of energy and fertilizers and leads to upward pressure on food prices. Export bans on food commodities during the 2007-08 and 2010-11 price increases, while temporarily softening the impact of food price inflation on poorer households, also induced high volatility in world prices and reciprocal policy responses by other countries.

The current shock, however, has three key features that could make addressing the energy shortfall more difficult. First, there is less room to substitute away from the most affected energy commodities—gas and coal—because price increases have been broad-based across all fuels. In addition, higher prices of some commodities such as energy have also increased the production costs of other commodities. Second, the energy intensity of GDP is much lower compared to the 1970s, so consumers may be less sensitive to relative price changes, at least in the short term. It may also be more difficult for countries to reduce energy use (that is, less low-hanging fruit is available because efficiency has already improved significantly in many areas such as lighting). Third, although many governments have implemented fuel subsidies or tax cuts, fewer have implemented policies to tackle the underlying supply and demand imbalance, thus risking prolonging the crisis.

production by more than 5 percent per year (on average) since 2010. The United States is now the largest producer of natural gas in the world (figure 1.5). This development came as a surprise to markets. From 2000 to 2007, U.S. production was flat, as existing fields matured. The United States was preparing to become a natural gas importer, with major investments in LNG terminals to accommodate LNG imports. These terminals have since been retrofitted to allow exports instead (EIA 2014). Gas production has risen rapidly elsewhere, especially in Qatar, Australia, and China. The United States became the world's largest exporter in late 2021, superseding Qatar and Australia.

Demand for natural gas has grown rapidly, particularly among EMDEs, where growth has averaged nearly 4 percent per year since 2000. Consumption also rose in AEs, in notable contrast to oil and coal, which have seen declines in AE demand over this period. The rise in demand for natural gas is due in part to its superior properties as a fuel—far less polluting than coal, with half the carbon dioxide emissions and fewer particulate emissions (IFC 2019). Coal-to-gas switching in power plants has become increasingly common, particularly in the United States and Europe (IEA 2019).

Historically, imports of LNG were concentrated in a few countries in Asia—Japan accounted for half of all LNG imports in 2000. Increasing availability of supply has

FIGURE 1.5 Natural gas

Natural gas markets have undergone significant changes over the past two decades, including a sharp increase in production in the United States and elsewhere, rapid growth in consumption among EMDEs, and a shift in trade toward liquefied natural gas. These trends have caused varying divergences in natural gas prices across countries.

A. Share of natural gas production in top-five producers

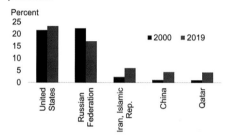

B. Natural gas demand

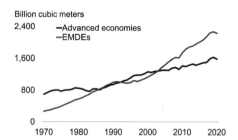

C. Natural gas trade, by type

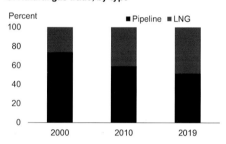

D. LNG imports

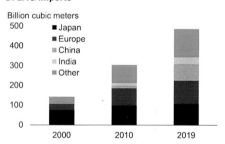

E. Destination of LNG exports for select countries

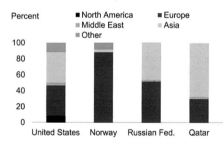

F. Natural gas prices

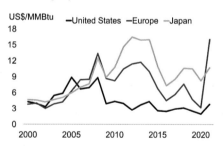

Sources: BP Statistical Review of World Energy 2021; World Bank.
Note: EMDE = emerging market and developing economy; LNG = liquefied natural gas; MMBtu = metric million British thermal units.

encouraged a considerable broadening of trade, however. China and numerous countries in Europe now import much more LNG compared to two decades ago. LNG now accounts for roughly half of natural gas trade, up from one-quarter in 2000.

With increased numbers of suppliers and importers, and increased volumes of trade, the market structures for LNG have evolved. Pricing has become more responsive to changes in market conditions and the global market has become more unified. Although the LNG market has traditionally relied on long-term contracts, short-term and spot-priced trades now account for more than one-third of all LNG trade. Exports from the United States account for much of this shift (IEA 2021a). That shift also helped increase the share of natural gas that is not indexed to other commodities, notably oil. Furthermore, LNG can be exported to a much wider range of countries than gas exported by pipeline (although it still requires infrastructure in the form of LNG terminals). As a result, cargos can be exported (or reexported) to countries where prices are highest, which can contribute to a reduction in price differentials between regions.

In 2010, large and persistent differentials opened up between the three main price benchmarks—United States, Europe, and Japan. Unlike the United States, natural gas prices in Europe and Japan were formally linked to oil prices. When oil prices surged in 2010-14, prices rose sharply in the European Union and even more so in Japan. At the same time, natural gas prices fell in the United States (to levels last seen in the 1990s) because of a sharp rise in natural gas production. Although European and Japanese prices eventually declined in 2015 alongside the fall in oil prices, differentials between the three benchmarks persisted. More recently, however, as LNG trade has expanded, the differentials between the prices have decreased. LNG from the United States is now transported to Asia or Europe, depending on where prices are highest (although the transportation costs to Asia are higher than those to Europe).

The global economic fallout from the COVID-19 pandemic had large repercussions on natural gas markets. The recession in 2020 triggered a sharp fall in demand, and surplus gas in the United States resulted in a large increase in LNG exports, especially to Europe. This increase pushed European prices to an all-time low, and to parity with U.S. prices. However, the following year saw a reversal when demand for energy rebounded rapidly as the global economy recovered. A shortfall in coal in China, as well as reduced output of renewable energy more broadly, led to a sharp increase in natural gas prices in China and elsewhere. The price of European natural gas rose more than 400 percent over the course of 2021, because Europe was in direct competition with the rest of the world for LNG.

Natural gas markets were also severely disrupted by the invasion of Ukraine. The European Union pledged to reduce its exports of natural gas from Russia by two-thirds by the end of 2022. Because almost 70 percent of Russia's natural gas exports went by pipeline to Europe, and with few alternative means of transporting natural gas, there was less scope for diversion to other countries and a larger share of Russia's production was disrupted.

Nuclear energy

Commercial use of nuclear energy began in the mid-1950s and grew rapidly from the 1960s, with installed capacity increasing by about 20 percent per year between 1965 and 1988. The oil price shocks of the 1970s provided a particular impetus for installation in several countries. For example, during 1970-84, nuclear capacity in France rose from 6 terawatt-hours to 191 terawatt-hours, such that nuclear energy accounted for about three-quarters of the country's total electricity production by 1985 (a share that has been fairly constant since then). The share of nuclear energy in total global energy consumption peaked at just under 7 percent in 2001, and its share of electricity generation was about twice as large (figure 1.6). Currently, the United States is the world's largest producer of nuclear energy, accounting for about 30 percent of global generation.

The use of nuclear energy has been subject to opposition and restrictions, however, limiting its use (Gamson and Modigliani 1989). Opposition has focused on the potential dangers associated with nuclear energy, including the disposal of radioactive waste, nuclear accidents, and the risk of nuclear proliferation and terrorism. For example, nuclear installations declined sharply after the Chernobyl disaster in 1986. More recently, following the Fukushima nuclear accident in 2011, Japan temporarily shut down its nuclear power plants (although it has since restarted some of them). Germany decided to gradually phase out its use of nuclear power following the Fukushima accident, a process due to be finalized in 2022. This decision has resulted in contradictory policy objectives. As a decreasing share of electricity in Germany has been generated through nuclear sources, coal and natural gas have mostly filled the gap, despite the policy priority of reducing the use of fossil fuels in electricity production— and with major health and social costs (Jarvis, Deschenes, and Jha 2019).

Over the past decade, global nuclear energy production has risen because of growth in EMDEs, notably China. China's nuclear generation capacity grew by 17 percent per year, on average, between 2010 and 2019. In contrast, nuclear generation in AEs has declined because of closures in several countries, including Germany and Japan. More recently, nuclear energy has been receiving renewed attention given the role it could play in aiding the energy transition as a reliable source of zero-carbon electricity (Birol and Malpass 2021). The International Energy Agency's net-zero emissions scenario envisions a 60 percent increase in nuclear energy over the next 30 years (IEA 2021b).

Renewable energy

Renewable sources of energy can be split into two main types—hydroelectricity and other renewables (such as solar, wind, geothermal, wave, tidal, and biomass). In contrast to fossil fuels, almost all energy from renewables is, at present, used to generate electricity. At present, renewables still account for a small share of global energy consumption: 11 percent in 2020, of which hydroelectricity accounted for more than half. However, installed capacity has been growing rapidly over the past decade, particularly of nonhydroelectricity renewables. In general, the share of zero-carbon fuels in total energy consumption is larger in AEs than in EMDEs, except for hydroelectricity (figure 1.6). This section focuses on hydroelectricity, solar, and wind.

Hydroelectricity

Hydropower is considered a more reliable base load source of electricity than solar and wind, because it is less intermittent and output can be varied to help with load balancing

FIGURE 1.6 Nuclear and renewables

Collectively, low-carbon sources of energy (nuclear, hydroelectric, and other renewables) in 2020 accounted for about 16 percent of global energy consumption. Although renewable energy and nuclear energy account for a larger share of total energy in advanced economies, consumption is growing much faster in EMDEs, particularly for renewables. Wind energy currently accounts for the majority of nonhydroelectric renewable energy, and solar is the fastest-growing source.

A. Share of nuclear energy in total primary energy consumption

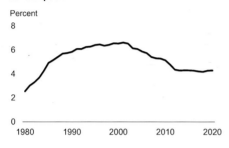

B. Share of nuclear in electricity generation

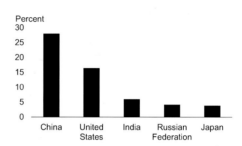

C. Share of renewable energy in total primary energy consumption

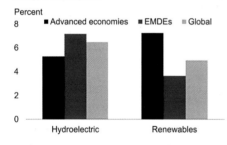

D. Growth rate of renewable energy consumption

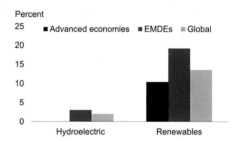

E. Share of other renewable energy in total primary energy consumption

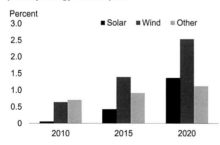

F. Growth rate of other renewable energy

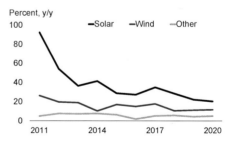

Sources: BP Statistical Review of World Energy 2021; World Bank.
Note: Renewables include solar, wind, geothermal, biomass, and other non-hydro renewables. EMDE = emerging market and developing economy.
B.C. Data for 2019.
D. Chart shows average annual growth rates over the period 2009-19.
E.F. "Other" includes geothermal, biomass, and other nonhydroelectric renewables. y/y = year over year.

by redirecting water flow through dams.[9] However, because hydropower depends on plentiful water supplies, production faces increasing threats from climate change, in particular the heightened risk of droughts.[10] In 2021, for example, hydropower in Brazil, China, and the United States was sharply reduced by drought, leading to increased demand for fossil fuels (World Bank 2021).

Hydroelectricity has been used as a source of electricity since the late 1800s. Capacity grew sharply throughout the 1900s, with its share of global energy rising from 1 percent of total energy in 1920 to 6 percent in the 1990s. Initial installations were primarily in AEs, but more recently new capacity has been concentrated in EMDEs. The largest producer of hydroelectricity is China, accounting for 31 percent of global production in 2020. In some countries, notably Brazil and Norway, hydropower is the primary source of electricity, accounting for more than 80 percent of total electricity.

Other renewables: Solar and wind

The commercial use of wind and solar power to generate electricity began in the 1970s following the oil price shocks, although adoption was initially relatively slow. By 2010, wind power accounted for just 0.6 percent of global energy consumption and solar power less than 0.1 percent. Over the past decade, however, their installation has accelerated, with solar capacity growing by almost 40 percent per year since 2010 and wind power increasing by about 16 percent per year. Growth has been particularly rapid in EMDEs, with China currently accounting for the largest share of global renewables generation (more than one-quarter of total renewable generation capacity).

The increase in global renewable installation has been driven by a combination of improved technology and manufacturing processes, as well as government policies, which have collectively reduced the cost of solar generation by 90 percent since 2010 (IRENA 2020). Solar and wind power are now the lowest-cost sources of new electricity in most parts of the world. The ongoing energy transition is expected to lead to a large increase in the share of electricity generated by renewables, although this increase will require improvements in energy storage or backup generating capacity, because solar and wind power are more intermittent and seasonal than hydropower.

Metals

Overview

Metals have been used since prehistoric times to cast tools, weapons, and other objects. Copper was the first to find widespread use. In the Bronze Age (roughly 3000 BCE to 1200 BCE), copper was mixed with tin to form bronze, which produced stronger

---

[9] Hydropower can also be used to store energy in the form of "pumped" hydro. When there is excess electricity, water can be pumped from the bottom of a reservoir to the top, and when there is a need for electricity (including to meet large surges in demand) the dam can be used to generate electricity. Pumped hydro is one option to help address issues of storage associated with the use of other renewables.

[10] Hydroelectric dams also present the risk of dam failure, which can have very severe consequences.

implements. Other metals, such as gold, silver, mercury, and lead, were used in this period, as trade routes developed. The advent of the Iron Age (from 1200 BCE to 600 BCE) brought stronger iron-made weapons and tools, which included agricultural implements such as scythes and plows, boat rudders, and numerous other products.[11]

There was little fundamental change to iron and steel production technology until the second industrial revolution in the late 1800s and early 1900s. New technologies to mass-produce steel led to the displacement of cast iron; steel was lighter, stronger, and more cost-effective. Steel applications expanded and included railroads, bridges, buildings, factories, machinery, weapons, ships, and automobiles. Advances in mechanization—water pumps, drilling, loading, and hauling ores—also helped expand mining. For base metals, the use of copper expanded greatly from the late 1800s because of its use in electrical materials. Another major development was the mass production of aluminum by electrolysis.[12] Aluminum's strong and lightweight traits extended to many uses in transportation, construction, packaging, and electrical and consumer goods. Aluminum demand grew rapidly, overtaking copper by volume in the 1960s, and today the volume of aluminum consumed is about two-and-a-half times that of copper.

Metal prices broadly declined during the 1900s because of advances in technology, efficiency improvements in processing and mineral extraction, and the discovery and development of large, low-cost mines (figure 1.7). Metal markets have experienced several boom-and-bust price cycles, with three longer-term cycles (Radetzki 2006). Strong post-WWII demand for the reconstruction of Western Europe and Japan and economic expansion in North America drove prices higher during the 1950s and early 1960s. A second cycle began in the 1970s, partly due to cost pressures following energy price shocks and the era of stagflation. A third cycle began in the 2000s, with the industrialization of China spurring enormous demand for metals—at a faster rate than previous industrial expansions—leading to higher prices. In all cases, prices eventually contracted because of recession or financial crises, or because high prices themselves generated additional supply. Apart from demand growth, a key reason for metal price cycles is the long lead times for discovery, exploration, and development. The average time from discovery to production for copper mines, for example, is 17 years (Khan et al. 2016). Consequently, at times of accelerated demand, a significant supply lag can occur and cause prices to rise. In contrast, softening demand is often met with lagged supply, causing prices to fall.

Since 2000, prices have rebounded largely because of surging import demand in China, which now produces and consumes over half the major base metals, iron ore, and steel, up from a tenth two decades earlier. Yet metal prices have not moved in a uniform

---

[11] The early adoption of copper (along with gold, silver, mercury, and lead) compared to iron ore reflected the lower melting temperatures of the former. Iron tools and weapons were also brittle. However, it was later discovered that heating wrought iron in a bed of charcoal, then quickly quenching in water or oil, would turn the outer layers into steel.

[12] According to the U.S. Geological Survey, global iron reserves are 230.0 billion metric tons, bauxite reserves are estimated at 55.0 billion to 75.0 billion metric tons, and copper reserves are 3.5 billion metric tons.

FIGURE 1.7 Drivers of metal prices since 1900

Metal prices have generally declined over the past 120 years, with decades-long boom-and-bust cycles (super cycles) around the trend. Spurts of industrialization of major economies, and a sluggish supply response, underlay such super cycles. Efforts by producer groups and governments to control prices through output restrictions, export bans, and stock accumulations have had limited success.

A. Real metal price index

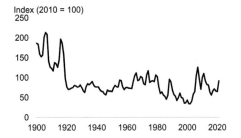

B. Copper demand share

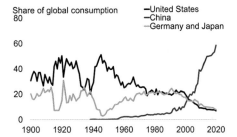

C. Global mine production and GDP growth

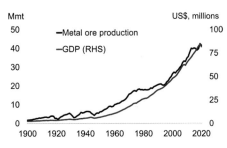

D. United States base metal stocks

E. Dry bulk freight rates

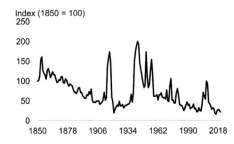

F. Real metal prices in different currencies

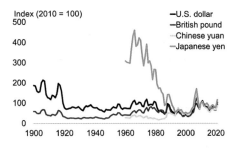

Sources: British Geological Survey; Federal Reserve Bank of Minneapolis; Jacks and Stuermer 2021; Maddison Historical Statistics, https://www.rug.nl/ggdc/historicaldevelopment/maddison/; Mitchell 1988; Schmitz 1979; U.S. Bureau of Labor Statistics; U.S. Geological Survey; World Bank; World Bureau of Metal Statistics.

A. Index is a weighted average of the prices of aluminum, copper, lead, nickel, tin, zinc, and iron ore. Weights used are from World Bank Commodity Markets (Pink Sheet) database. Prices are deflated using U.S. Consumer Price Index. Last observation is 2021.

B. Data for China available from 1938. Last observation is 2020.

C. Mine production of copper, lead, nickel, tin, and zinc. Growth rates are five-year moving averages. Last observation is 2020. Mmt = million metric tons; RHS = right-hand side.

D. Base metals are aluminum, copper, lead, nickel, tin, and zinc. Stocks held by industry, government, and commodity exchange warehouses. Last observation is 2017.

F. Last observation is 2020.

fashion. A striking example is the price differential between copper and aluminum. In 2001, copper and aluminum were trading at similar price levels. Whereas the real price of copper rose nearly fourfold during the past two decades, the real price of aluminum changed little, as China continued to build capacity in excess of domestic needs.

Over time, technological advances in production, such as ore leaching, solvent extraction, electrowinning, and productivity improvements, led to significant reductions in production costs for all metals, and to the opening of new sources of reserves. In addition, improved transportation technology has reduced freight rates. The application of steam power enabled the movement of goods on land by rail and across oceans by steamships in the latter half of the 1800s. At the same time, bulk carriers allowed economic transport of low-value products such as bauxite, coal, and iron ore (Lundgren 1996). Dry bulk freight rates declined almost 80 percent in real terms from 1850 to 2020, contributing to declining metal prices for importers.

Metal and mineral markets have been subjected to policy interventions at both international and country levels (Radetzki and Wårell 2016). At an international level, various efforts by producer groups and governments have sought to influence prices. Producer cartels operated in the aluminum, copper, lead, nickel, steel, and zinc industries during the first half of the 1900s, and an international commodity agreement operated in the tin market until its collapse in 1985.[13] The latter used buffer stocks to adjust imbalances in global supply and demand in an attempt to prevent excessive fluctuations in prices and export earnings. Motives for public intervention at the country level included support of industry during the Great Depression and restoring supply lines during WWII. During the 1960s and 1970s, a move toward state control of foreign-owned metal assets occurred in Africa and Latin America, similar to a trend toward state controls in the oil sector in these regions and the Middle East.

Looking ahead, demand for some metals may soften as global growth slows and China continues to rebalance its economy away from investment toward domestic consumption (chapter 2). Moreover, the global shift toward net-zero carbon emissions is likely to spur unprecedented demand for critical metals (for example, aluminum, copper, cobalt, lithium, and nickel) in low-carbon technologies. Prices for these metals could remain elevated for a prolonged period, depending on the speed and direction of the energy transition, the volume of mining capital investment, environmental constraints on these industries, and policy measures and incentives.

Iron ore

Iron ore is the key raw material used to make steel, which is mostly used in construction, infrastructure, and transportation, but also in machinery and consumer goods. Iron ore

---

[13] The high degree of metal production concentration has led to concerns about market manipulation and collusion. Metal production is typically concentrated in a few countries, and multinational or state-owned corporations have large market shares in the production and refining of some metals. For instance, three countries in Southeast Asia—Indonesia, Malaysia, and Thailand—together accounted for more than half of global tin mine production in the 1970s.

deposits are abundant, yet mining operations are concentrated in a few countries (Australia, Brazil, China, India, and Russia account for more than 80 percent of global output) by virtue of transportation infrastructure and low energy costs. China is a large producer of iron ore, but domestic production is insufficient to meet the considerable demand of the steel industry (China produces 57 percent of the world's steel). In addition, China's iron ore is low-grade and expensive to process, and its mines are being depleted. For steelmakers located in its coastal regions, the cost of domestic ore can be higher than the price of imports. Iron ore exports are dominated by Australia and Brazil, and China is by far the world's largest iron ore consumer, accounting for more than 70 percent of global demand in 2020.

Prices of iron ore historically have been set by producers or determined following negotiations between major mines and steel companies. After WWII, reference prices in Europe were set by Swedish producers and European steelmakers, with Brazil's main producer Vale (also known as CVRD for Companhia Vale do Rio Doce) taking over the producer role in the mid-1970s. In Asia, the rising importance of Japan's steel industry resulted in an Asia price benchmark arising from negotiations between Japanese steelmakers and iron ore producers.[14] In 2005, with the rising importance of China in the iron ore market, this negotiated price system began to shift toward a more market-based reference price, and by 2010 negotiated prices ended. The main price benchmark became a spot delivered price at Chinese ports.

Since 2005, iron ore prices have been subjected to three large price cycles. The first peak was reached in 2008 and quickly slumped during the financial crisis, in line with the boom/bust of other commodities. A second boom in 2011-14 was driven by a strong rebound in demand (also in conjunction with a recovery in other commodity prices), ended by a slowdown in China imports and expanding ore supply. Prices increased moderately in 2015 following the collapse of Vale's tailings dam in Brazil. A third spike occurred in 2021 when the extraordinary demand for goods in the wake of COVID-19 (partly due to fiscal stimulus) resulted in strong global steel demand.

Copper

Copper is one of the oldest metals, along with gold and silver, and was historically used to mold utensils, jewelry, and weaponry. The discovery of smelting expanded the use of copper and allowed it to be alloyed with tin to yield a stronger product, bronze. The rise of iron and steel limited copper's expansion, making them the first formidable competitors to copper (Radetzki 2009). In the late 1700s, the primary use of copper was to sheath the bottom of boats, but copper was later displaced by other alloys. In the late 1800s, copper use expanded because of its ability to conduct electricity and heat. The main uses of copper today are for construction, electric power infrastructure, industrial machinery, transportation, and various consumer goods. Copper faces competition from plastics, fiber optics, and aluminum, as well as from efficiency improvements, particularly when prices are high.

---

[14] Before 2005, iron ore prices changed infrequently, at most once a year, even during periods of inflation.

FIGURE 1.8 **Real metal prices**

Metal prices have always been volatile, with several boom-and-bust cycles, particularly for copper, lead, and zinc. Aluminum prices have seen a long-run declining trend. Tin prices increased until the start of the 1980s, with the decline in prices intensifying after the collapse of the International Tin Agreement in 1985. Iron ore and gold prices have increased substantially in the past few years.

A. Copper prices

B. Aluminum prices

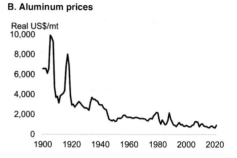

C. Tin and nickel prices

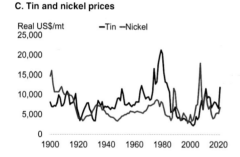

D. Lead and zinc prices

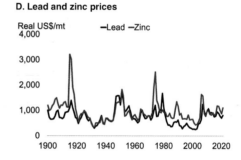

E. Iron ore prices

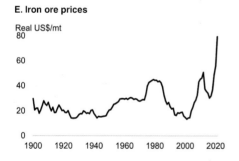

F. Gold prices

Sources: Federal Reserve Bank of Minneapolis; Mitchell 1988; U.S. Bureau of Labor Statistics; World Bank.
Note: mt = metric ton; troy oz = troy ounce (traditional unit of gold weight).
A.-F. Prices are deflated using U.S. Consumer Price Index (100 = 1982-84). Last observation is 2021.

Real copper prices declined during the 1900s amid high volatility, with prices bottoming in 2001. The booms in copper prices coincided with major periods of industrialization that drove global demand for many metals (figure 1.8). Prices rose during most of the 2000s because of strong import growth in demand from China and lagging supply. Three price spikes have occurred since 2005: the financial crisis in 2008, the subsequent economic recovery in 2011, and the rebound from the pandemic in

2021. Looking ahead, although demand growth may mature and slow in some sectors, copper stands to benefit from the energy transition in wind turbines, solar panels, grid connections, electric vehicles, and battery charging infrastructure.

There have been numerous attempts to manage the market and influence prices. In 1887-89, the Secrétan Syndicate led by the French fabricator Pierre Secrétan convinced bankers and investors to corner the market and lift prices on the London Metal Exchange (Slade 2020). It brought forth more supply than the syndicate could purchase, and the scheme collapsed. In 1899, the Amalgamated Copper Company was formed to consolidate the industry, resulting in a controlling stake in the Anaconda Copper Mining Company in Montana. The trust curtailed production and exports to Europe, causing prices to soar and stimulating higher production by other producers. When Amalgamated released copper stocks in 1901, prices fell sharply (Herfindahl 1959). Several subsequent attempts at price manipulation have led to short-term price swings (Mueller and Gorin 1985). The first copper cartel, managed by the Copper Export Association, was formed in 1918 to liquidate large inventories accumulated during World War I, and was disbanded in 1924 after achieving its aim (Walters 1944). A second cartel, Copper Exporters Inc., was formed in 1926 to restrict output, but its power declined after the Great Depression. A third attempt to manage the copper market, the International Copper Cartel, did not have a major influence on prices, although it may have smoothed them somewhat (Guzmán 2018).

During the first half of the 1900s, copper production was dominated by a few U.S. multinational companies, notably Anaconda, Kennecott, and Phelps Dodge. Copper production grew slowly until WWII, but then expanded rapidly during the postwar industrial expansion. Nationalization of assets in the 1970s, notably in Chile and Peru, altered the structure of local industries, although the adverse experience in Peru led to privatization in the 1990s (Lagos 2018). Subsequent improvements to the business climate and property rights in Africa and Latin America were an underlying factor encouraging the establishment of new mines (IMF 2015). Many new high-grade copper mines in Chile, such as Escondida, commenced production in the early 1990s. As a result, Chile accounted for about 35 percent of global copper supply in the 2000s. New greenfield copper mines in the Democratic Republic of Congo, Peru, and Zambia began production after 2010, reducing Chile's share to 27 percent by 2020. The growth in global mine supplies slowed after 2016 following a period of low prices. Growth was also negatively affected by COVID-19-related disruptions.

Aluminum

Widespread use of aluminum is a relatively new development. When production began in the late 1800s, aluminum was used only in luxury items. However, significant improvements in the smelting process greatly reduced the cost of production.[15] Because

---

[15] The Hall-Héroult process, developed in 1886, allowed large-scale commercial production, and the Bayer Process, developed in 1889, enabled bauxite to be refined to produce alumina (aluminum oxide), which is then refined to aluminum metal at a much lower cost.

of its light weight, strength, conductivity, and corrosion resistance properties, aluminum is now used in a wide range of industries, including construction, transportation, electrical, packaging, machinery, and consumer goods. It has taken market share from other metals, notably copper and tin. As with other metals, aluminum faces competition from other materials, namely carbon fiber, plastics, glass, and alloys.

Aluminum prices have declined significantly in real terms over the past 120 years. Unlike price spikes in the 2000s for other metals, aluminum prices have remained relatively flat—mostly in response to expansion of smelting capacity by China. However, steps by China to reduce emissions and energy consumption have led to a tightening in the aluminum market and thus higher prices in 2021 (box 1.2 places China's industrialization and commodity demand in a historical context). The industry has also benefited from recycled aluminum, which has risen to one-third of global aluminum production and is much less energy-intensive than primary production.

As with other metals, aluminum prices have been affected by numerous policy interventions, at both domestic and international levels. The industry was marked by a continuous series of cartels until WWII (Bertilorenzi 2013). At the turn of the twentieth century, five companies dominated the market—U.S. Alcoa, British Aluminum, Swiss AIAG, and two French companies. Three cartels were formed between 1901 and 1923 to set prices and allocate quotas; each ended because of competition from new entrants, recession, or war. In 1926, the European companies signed an agreement, but Alcoa stayed out because it was under antitrust scrutiny. The company spun off its non-U.S. holdings to its Canadian affiliate Aluminum Limited (later Alcan), and in 1931 Aluminum Limited joined the European companies to form a Swiss holding company, the Aluminum Alliance Company (Storli 2014). The aim was to allocate output during the Depression, which required the company to purchase excess stocks. Although the most successful aluminum cartel, it ended in 1939 with the start of WWII.

Although official prewar cartels stopped after 1945, cartel-like behavior continued and an agreed price list was set (Bertilorenzi 2016). Antitrust action was taken against Alcoa after WWII, but by the 1950s new entrants to the market dissuaded the government from breaking up the company. The European Commission also accused the industry of criminal cartel behavior in the 1970s. The era of cartelization ended in 1978, however, with the start of an aluminum futures contract on the London Metal Exchange.

Since 1978, global production has increased fivefold in response to strong industrial demand and new applications (figure 1.9). China has accounted for 70 percent of the gain, partly owing to abundant coal-powered energy in the western and northwestern regions. Outside China, given the energy-intensive nature of aluminum smelting, there has been a shift to concentrate production in countries with low-cost electricity, such as Canada, India, Norway, Russia, and the United Arab Emirates. There have been significant changes in sources for the raw material bauxite and intermediate product alumina. Previously, bauxite and alumina production were concentrated in a few advanced economies, even though those economies were poorly endowed with bauxite reserves. The geographic location of alumina production has now shifted toward

FIGURE 1.9 **Production of metals since 1900**

Global metal production has shifted from advanced economies to EMDEs. In the early 1900s, production was dominated by a few industrialized countries such as Australia, Canada, and the United States. Today, Asia, Africa, and Latin America account for most of the world's metal supplies.

A. Copper mine production

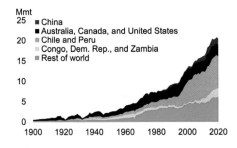

B. Primary aluminum production

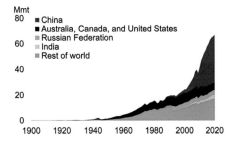

C. Tin mine production

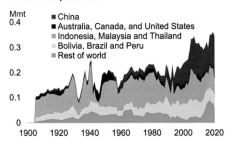

D. Lead mine production

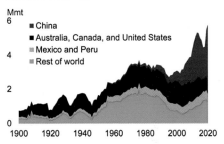

E. Nickel mine production

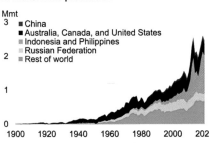

F. Iron ore production

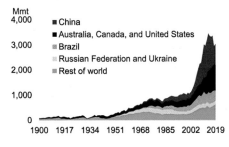

Sources: British Geological Survey; Schmitz 1979; U.S. Geological Survey; World Bank; World Bureau of Metal Statistics; WorldSteel.
Note: EMDE = emerging market and developing economy; Mmt = million metric tons.
A.-E. Last observation is 2020.
F. Last observation is 2019.

countries with access to abundant sources of bauxite (Nappi 2013). China is the largest alumina producer and imports more than two-thirds of its bauxite.

Looking ahead, aluminum is a critical raw material in the global energy transition, given its use in battery packaging, hydrogen fuel cells, and solar photovoltaics. However, because of its energy-intensive nature, the industry is also a significant source of greenhouse gas emissions. The ongoing strategy to site smelters near low-cost hydropower has the added benefit of constraining emissions.

Other base metals

Tin

The use of tin dates to antiquity when it was mixed with copper to produce bronze, tools, and weapons. Tin plating for cans began in Britain in the early 1800s and by the mid-1900s over half of tin use was for plating in cans for beverages and food. However, tin was gradually displaced by aluminum and other materials, including plastic, recyclable glass, and more recently paper. Today over half of tin supplies are used in solder for electronics. Other applications include industrial chemicals, tin plating, and lead-acid batteries. Tin's use in small electronic components (mainly in electric vehicles, solar panels, and battery storage) makes it critical to the low-carbon economy.

Unlike prices of other base metals, tin prices rose in real terms throughout most of the twentieth century. Prices increased sharply after WWII, driven mainly by rising demand from postwar reconstruction in Japan and Korea. Prices were also supported by policies, including the accumulation of inventories by the U.S. government in response to post-WWII supply concerns. Real prices peaked in 1979 but declined sharply in 1985 following the collapse of the Sixth Tin Agreement (see the following discussion and box 1.4 later in the chapter). Tin prices boomed during the early 2000s in response to strong demand from China. Following a period of relative stability, prices surged again during COVID-19 in response to strong demand for electronics and household appliances containing tin solder.

During most of the twentieth century, four countries—Bolivia, Indonesia, Malaysia, and Thailand—dominated global tin supplies. Today, China is the largest producer with almost half of the world's tin mine production (up from 5 percent in the 1980s), followed by Indonesia and Peru. Historical production trends for tin have been much more volatile than other metals because of interventions to manage supply and prices.

Policy intervention in the tin market began in the early twentieth century, starting with the formation of the Bandoeng Pool in 1921, which attempted to stabilize prices through inventory management. The pool was dissolved in 1924 when its stocks were exhausted (Baldwin 1983; Thoburn 1994). In 1956, 24 consuming and producing countries began a series of agreements aimed at stabilizing prices through buffer stock management. Each agreement was modified to account for membership and policy changes (Chandrasekhar 1989). However, tensions mounted between producer and consumer interests, with price targets shifting from a mutually agreed narrow band to one that favored producers. When global tin consumption fell in the early 1980s because of recession and substitution by aluminum, stocks began accumulating (Mallory 1990). The withdrawal of the United States (a member of only the Fifth Tin Agreement) and Bolivia, along with mounting financial difficulties, led to the agreement's insolvency in October 1985 and the suspension of buffer stock activity. Tin prices plunged and financial burdens were absorbed by bank lenders, London Metal Exchange traders, and tin miners (Prest 1986).

Lead and zinc

Lead has been used since ancient times and was widely used in the Roman Empire, especially for water pipes.[16] Its corrosion-resistant properties and malleability, along with its low boiling point and easy extraction from ores, made it a popular metal for ammunition, ships, underwater cables, and roofing. Lead was later used as an additive in various chemical applications, including paint and glass, and later as an additive to increase the octane rating of gasoline. The chemical uses, however, have been reduced or eliminated because of the metal's high toxicity and negative environmental impact. Today's primary use of lead is in lead-acid batteries, which account for four-fifths of global consumption.

Lead is often mined as a by-product of other metals—mainly zinc, but also copper and silver. Lead mine production grew during the post-WWII reconstruction. Most lead was produced in the Americas, followed by Europe and the Soviet Union. Production fell sharply after the collapse of the Soviet Union and reduced demand because of health and environmental issues. Today, China is the world's dominant lead producer, accounting for more than half of global output. Mine supply accounts for only one-third of global consumption because of the high rate of recycling from the battery sector—lead can be recycled indefinitely without any decrease in quality.

Although lead prices followed a downward path during the 1900s, they have been subjected to volatility in response to policies, environmental regulations, technological change, and, on some occasions, market manipulation.[17] For example, prices declined during the Great Depression, but they rose sharply after WWII following stockpiling policies by the United States in 1951. In the 1960s, prices were relatively stable, partly because of the lead and zinc mining stabilization program in the United States (Smith 1999). Prices increased in the 1970s amid strong demand from centrally planned economies but fell sharply in the early 1980s with the global recession. They remained low in the years that followed because of the gradual phaseout of lead use in gasoline, paints, solders, and water systems. Prices, however, rebounded after 2000 amid surging demand for batteries (both for vehicles and backup storage of electricity) and supply restrictions stemming from environmental constraints associated with mining and processing. Given that lead ore is a by-product of zinc production, the eventual phaseout of lead in batteries would affect the economics of zinc mining.

Zinc is the third most used nonferrous metal, after aluminum and copper. Its traditional use (since antiquity) has been as an alloy with copper to form brass. More recently it has

---

[16] Lead has been in use since at least 6500 BCE in ancient Egypt. Lead was commonly used as roofing material in Europe during the Middle Ages, for instance, as well as in ammunition.

[17] For example, in 1909 the Metallgesellschaft, a German company that controlled most of global output, withheld lead from the market to push prices up (Gibson-Jarvie 1983).

BOX 1.2 Industrialization of China and commodity demand in historical context

The structure of global industrial commodity demand has changed fundamentally over the past quarter century. Advanced economies' share of energy and metals consumption has declined markedly. Meanwhile, China has emerged as the world's largest consumer, accounting for more than half of global demand for coal, metals, and iron ore. Although China's industrialization draws many parallels with earlier industrializations, such as those of the United Kingdom and the United States, the speed of its ascent has been without precedent.

Introduction

Global metals consumption more than doubled during 1995-2020, with China accounting for 90 percent of the increase. Global energy demand rose 50 percent, with China contributing nearly 60 percent of the increase, mainly in the consumption of coal (chapter 2). The unprecedented commodity demand surge has coincided with strong and sustained growth in emerging market and developing economies (EMDEs). During 1995-2020, economic growth in EMDEs was 5.5 percent per year, and in China it was 8.8 percent, increasing its per capita income from $540 to $10,550.[a]

To better understand the structural shifts and their likely impact on future commodity demand, this box places the post-2000 industrial commodity demand boom into historical perspective by comparing it with three earlier surges in commodity demand: the industrial revolution in the United Kingdom from the late 1700s to the second half of the 1800s, the industrialization in the United States after the Civil War, and the reconstruction and expansion in Europe and Japan after World War II (WWII). Specifically, this box examines the following questions:[b]

- How has the structure of global industrial commodity demand changed over the past 25 years?

- How does China's structural shift in industrial commodity demand compare to major industrialization episodes since the nineteenth century?

Recent changes in the composition of industrial commodity demand

Over the past 25 years, the geographic location of global industrial commodity demand has undergone a fundamental change. In 1995, advanced economies

---

a. Data from World Bank, World Development Indicators Database (https://datatopics.worldbank.org/world-development-indicators/).

b. These demand surges have been studied in the context of price super cycles—that is, price cycles that are primarily demand driven and that may last several decades from peak to peak (Cuddington and Jerrett 2008; Erten and Ocampo 2013; Heap 2005; Jacks 2013; Stuermer 2018). In contrast, the typical business cycle has a duration of just a few years (see chapter 3).

BOX 1.2 Industrialization of China and commodity demand in historical context *(continued)*

accounted for one-half of global energy and nearly three-quarters of global metals consumption. By 2020, their share of energy consumption had declined to 34 percent, and their metals share to less than 25 percent.

Over the same period, demand from China increased enormously, underpinned by a rapid expansion of resource-intensive investment and manufacturing exports. Consumption of primary energy and especially metals is strongly correlated with industrial production (chapter 2). During 1995-2000, China's share of energy consumption more than doubled while its share of metals consumption increased sixfold, from 9 percent to 57 percent.

The acceleration of China's industrial commodity demand has been much stronger than other fast-growing, large EMDEs. For instance, although India's share of consumption of oil and coal doubled, in line with the increase in its share of global gross domestic product (GDP), its share of metals consumption increased only marginally. Other EMDEs collectively saw little change in their share of global commodity demand.

Coal contributed nearly 85 percent of the increase in China's energy consumption. Today, China consumes more than half of the world's coal, up from 30 percent in 1995 (figure B1.2.1). The country's dependence on coal reflects, in part, its large coal reserves (chapter 4). Although China's share of global oil consumption more than doubled over the same period, at 17 percent it is in line with the country's share of global GDP.

The increase in China's metal consumption has been even more remarkable. Its share of global copper consumption increased from 7 percent to 58 percent during 1995-2020. Consumption of other metals shows similar trends. The sharp rise in coal and iron ore demand has been driven, in large part, by the growth in Chinese steel production. Both coal and iron ore are key inputs in steel production. Coal is heavily used in the production of aluminum—about 90 percent of the electricity used in Chinese aluminum production is generated from coal.

Commodity consumption relative to GDP—often termed intensity of consumption—reveals some important trends. China's coal intensity follows a downward trend, like the rest of the world, in part reflecting a shift away from fossil fuel use. Its copper intensity, however, which was declining until the late 1990s, reversed its trajectory. This rise is in sharp contrast to the steady downward trajectory in the rest of the world. Similarly, its iron ore intensity picked up after 2000, although it began to fall in 2014. These diverging trends in intensity attest to the importance of country-specific developments at work in China, notably the focus on investment for construction, infrastructure, and manufacturing for domestic use and export, which are much more metals intensive than other consumption and services.

BOX 1.2 Industrialization of China and commodity demand in historical context *(continued)*

FIGURE B1.2.1 Changes in the composition and intensity of industrial commodity demand

Over the past 25 years, China's share of global energy consumption more than doubled, while its share of global metals consumption rose more than sixfold. The pace of China's commodity demand growth was much stronger than in India and other fast-growing, large emerging markets. Today, China accounts for more than half of the world's consumption of coal, metals, and iron ore. China's energy intensity has continued to decline, in line with the rest of the world; however, its metal intensity, which fell until the late 1990s, has since trended upward.

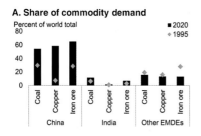

A. Share of commodity demand

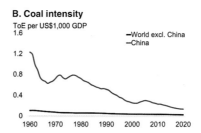

B. Coal intensity

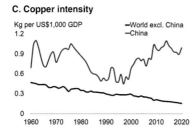

C. Copper intensity

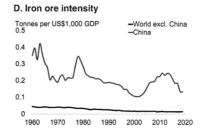

D. Iron ore intensity

Sources: BP Statistical Review of World Energy 2021; British Geological Survey; International Historical Statistics; U.S. Geological Survey; World Bank; World Bureau of Metal Statistics; World Steel Association.
Note: Intensity of a commodity is defined as the ratio of material used per unit of output. EMDE = emerging market and developing economies; kg = kilogram; ToE = tonnes of oil equivalent.
A. Share of country or country group in world total. Latest data for iron ore is 2019.
B.-D. GDP in constant 2015 U.S. dollars.

Industrial commodity demand since the nineteenth century

To place China's structural shift of industrial commodity demand in a broader and longer-term context, this section compares its recent industrial ascent with three historical episodes of industrialization.

- *Industrial revolution in the United Kingdom,* which began in the late 1700s and continued throughout the 1800s. Coal fueled the industrial revolution through its use in factories, railway locomotives, and steamships. An efficient fuel, it was essential for turning iron ore into the iron, and later steel, that

BOX 1.2 Industrialization of China and commodity demand in historical context *(continued)*

was used to build ships and railways (Clark and Jacks 2007). The advent of electricity in the late 1800s heralded a vast increase in copper demand for electrical wiring. The smelters in Swansea, Wales, processed much of the world's copper ore because of Britain's superiority in smelting technology (Evans and Saunders 2015; Radetzki 2009).

- *Industrialization in the United States*, which began in the mid-1800s and accelerated in the 1870s, after the Civil War. Innovations in mining and smelting techniques developed in the United States resulted in a dramatic expansion of the global copper market. The first half of the 1900s featured electrification and mass production of steel, automobiles, telecommunications, chemicals, and mechanized agriculture.

- *Post-WWII reconstruction of Europe and Japan.* The postwar reconstruction in Europe was assisted by financing through the U.S. Marshall Plan (Eichengreen and Uzan 1992). The recipient countries underwent similar rapid growth in construction, infrastructure, and manufacturing as experienced earlier by the United Kingdom and the United States.

The remarkable trends in commodity consumption brought about by these industrializations are clearly evident in figure B1.2.2, which shows country shares of global demand dating back to the 1800s for coal, iron ore, and copper.

Copper. During the industrialization cycles described above, the share of global copper demand peaked in the United Kingdom at 60 percent (the late 1870s), the United States at 58 percent (1945), and the combined shares of Western Europe and Japan at 40 percent (early 1990s). Although it took many decades to reach the peaks in the United Kingdom and the United States, the expansion in Europe/Japan was shorter. In contrast, China's share of global copper demand rose at unprecedented speed, from less than 10 percent in the 1990s to 58 percent in 2020. This share is broadly similar to the peak shares in the United Kingdom and the United States, suggesting that China may also be near its peak. Its consumption, however, shows no sign of plateauing.

Coal. The United Kingdom's share of global coal demand exceeded 60 percent in 1850 and has since steadily declined toward zero. The U.S. share peaked at 50 percent in 1918, whereas the combined shares of Western Europe and Japan hovered around 20 percent until 1970. Both have since declined, but coal remains a sizeable component of electricity generation in both areas. In contrast, China's share of global coal demand surpassed 50 percent in 2013, up from 20 percent in 1986. Its coal consumption has broadly plateaued in recent years, and the country intends to start phasing out coal beginning in 2026.

BOX 1.2 Industrialization of China and commodity demand in historical context *(continued)*

FIGURE B1.2.2 Commodity demand during major industrialization periods

Four major periods of industrialization have driven commodity demand growth since the beginning of the 1800s: the industrial revolution in the United Kingdom beginning in the late 1700s, industrialization in the United States after the Civil War, expansion of Western Europe and Japan after World War II, and the industrial rise of China since the 1990s. China's strong and sustained commodity demand growth is consistent with the experiences of earlier industrializing countries, but its remarkable pace is unprecedented.

A. Copper demand

B. Coal demand

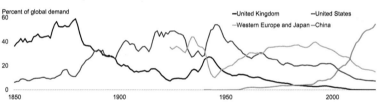

C. Iron ore demand

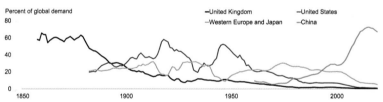

Sources: Abstract of British Historical Statistics; BP Statistical Review of World Energy 2021; British Geological Survey; Bureau of Mines Minerals Yearbook; Historical Statistics of the United States; International Historical Statistics; Lemon 1838; Mineral Statistics of the British Empire and Foreign Countries; Statistical Summary of the Minerals Industry; Schmitz 1979; Smil 2017; Stuermer 2017; The Copper Handbook; U.K. Department for Business, Energy & Industrial Strategy; U.S. Energy Information Administration; U.S. Geological Survey; World Bank; World Bureau of Metal Statistics; World Steel Association.

A.-C. Share of country or country group in world total. Share of global consumption plotted as three-year moving average to improve readability. Where consumption is not available, apparent consumption (production + imports - exports) is used. When data are missing, especially in the earlier years, linear interpolation is applied.

A. Data from 1850 to 2020.

B. Data from 1850 to 2020.

C. Data from 1857 to 2019. China's iron ore consumption based on gross weight.

BOX 1.2 Industrialization of China and commodity demand in historical context *(continued)*

Iron ore. The declines in advanced countries' shares of iron ore are similar to those for coal. However, the huge increase in China's demand for the metal is even more striking than that of coal. Its share of global iron ore demand reached 73 percent in 2013, up from 20 percent in 1991. The rate of increase and the current market share of China's consumption have no historical equivalent.

In terms of intensity of use, China's per capita consumption of copper and coal is now comparable to that of the advanced economies when they had similar per capita incomes (figure B1.2.3). Despite China's extensive use of coal, its peak per capita coal consumption is much lower than that of the United Kingdom and the United States, partly reflecting the broader range of fuels available today. For example, in 1860, nearly all primary energy consumption in the United Kingdom came from coal; similarly, in the United States, 80 percent of energy consumption in 1910 was from coal.

Iron ore, however, presents a vastly different picture. China's per capita consumption has reached levels far beyond those seen in earlier industrialization episodes, driven almost entirely by the growth in steel production for domestic and export markets. The primary domestic sources of demand for steel are construction, infrastructure, and manufacturing. A large part of the increase in construction and infrastructure has been driven by the large growth in China's urban population, from 20 percent in 1980 to more than 60 percent in 2020. [c] Rising incomes and new housing have in turn led to increased demand for steel-using durable goods such as automobiles, machinery, and home appliances.

Conclusion

Global commodity demand has shifted significantly over the past 25 years from advanced economies toward EMDEs. The shift has been concentrated in China, which today accounts for more than half of the global demand for coal, metals, and iron ore. Many features of China's industrialization and commodity demand growth are broadly in line with the experiences of the United Kingdom and the United States in the 1800s and early 1900s, as well as in post-WWII Europe and Japan. However, the speed at which China's consumption of commodities, especially iron ore, has increased is unprecedented, and reflects China's rapid industrialization and export-led economy. In addition, a massive shift of population into urban areas has driven large-scale infrastructure projects and soaring residential investment, amplifying the demand for steel and iron ore.

---

c. In contrast, it took the United States 80 years (1860-1940) to achieve a similar degree of urbanization (Boustan, Bunten, and Hearey 2013).

BOX 1.2 Industrialization of China and commodity demand in historical context *(continued)*

FIGURE B1.2.3 Consumption of industrial commodities per capita and income per capita

The growth in China's per capita consumption of copper and coal has been similar to the run-up in other industrializing nations. However, the pace and scale of China's per capita consumption of iron ore—a key raw material in steel production—is unprecedented, reflecting China's rapid economic development, industrialization, and urbanization. The primary sources of demand for steel in China are residential property construction, public infrastructure, and manufacturing.

A. Copper in China, the United Kingdom, and the United States

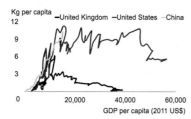

B. Copper in Germany and Japan

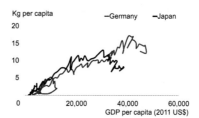

C. Coal in China, the United Kingdom, and the United States

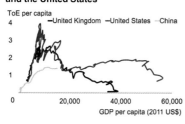

D. Coal in Germany and Japan

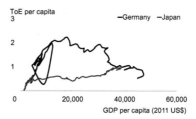

E. Iron ore in China, the United Kingdom, and the United States

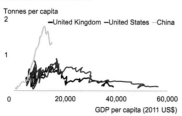

F. Iron ore in Germany and Japan

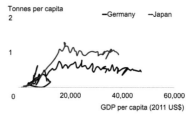

Sources: Maddison Project Database 2020; World Bank; and sources for figure B1.2.2.
A-C. GDP per capita in constant 2011 U.S. dollars. Lines show the evolution of income and commodity consumption per capita. When consumption is not available, apparent consumption (production + imports - exports) is used. When data are missing, especially in the earlier years, linear interpolation is applied.
A.B. Data from 1820 (A) and 1850 (B) to 2020.
C.D. Data from 1820 (C) and 1872 (D) to 2020. ToE = tonnes of oil equivalent.
E.F. Data from 1855 to 2019. China's iron ore consumption based on gross weight.

been used as an anticorrosion material to galvanize steel. Zinc is also used as an alloy in the manufacturing of electrical components, and to produce zinc oxide, which is used for rubber manufacture and skin ointment. As with other metals, China accounts for half of global consumption owing to its vast steel production. Zinc is mined in many countries, and, like other metals, production has shifted from AEs to EMDEs. The expansion has been most notable in China in the 2000s. The country currently produces more than one-third of global mine output, with Australia and Peru the next largest producers (chapter 4).

The price dynamics of zinc are broadly similar to those of lead, although price peaks have been sharper. Early cartel behavior influenced prices, and there have been several attempts at cartel action since (Stuermer 2018). For example, some European producers in the 1960s attempted to form a cartel but ultimately failed to stabilize prices (Tolcin 2012).

Nickel

Nickel has been known since ancient times, but it was not available for use until technological improvements during the industrial revolution made its separation from other minerals possible. The first commercial nickel smelting facility was developed in Norway in 1848. Nickel's resistance to corrosion makes it an important alloy, especially in stainless steel, which accounts for about 70 percent of nickel demand. Nickel is also used as an alloy for nickel steels, nickel cast iron, brass, and bronze. Other uses include rechargeable batteries and lithium-ion batteries, used in electric and hybrid vehicles.

Real nickel prices experienced a broad decline during the 1900s. Post-WWII demand helped lift prices through the 1970s, but the recession of the early 1980s and the emergence of lower-cost suppliers drove prices lower. Following the breakup of the Soviet Union, large volumes of nickel were released into the global market. Combined with weak demand during the East Asian financial crisis, this flood pushed prices to historical lows in 1998. The demand boom in China (which today accounts for more than half of the world's nickel demand), alongside recent growth in use in batteries, reversed the downward price trend.

Nickel is found in two types of ores: sulfide ores, which are typically found in underground rock formations, especially in Canada and Russia (figure 1.10), and laterite ores, found near the surface of humid, tropical areas—such as Indonesia, New Caledonia, and the Philippines. Sulfide was originally preferred because of its higher purity and less complex production process, but technological improvements in laterite ore (the majority of global reserves) made it profitable in the 1970s and it is used extensively today.

Historically, New Caledonia has been a key nickel supplier, but Canada emerged as the dominant producer in the 1960s. Canadian International Nickel Company enjoyed a near monopoly outside the former Soviet Union, setting global prices and thereby

FIGURE 1.10 Consumption of metals since 1900

In 1900, Europe and the United States consumed almost all of the world's metal output. Today, China alone accounts for 50 to 60 percent of global consumption.

A. Refined copper consumption

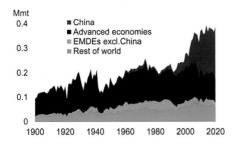

B. Primary aluminum consumption

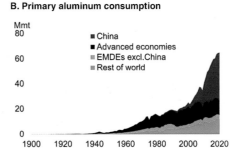

C. Refined tin consumption

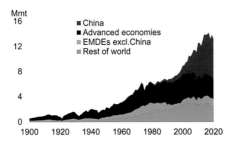

D. Refined lead consumption

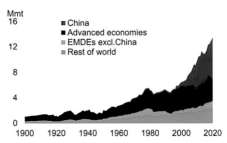

E. Refined zinc consumption

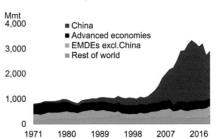

F. Iron ore consumption

Sources: British Geological Survey; Schmitz 1979; Stuermer 2017; U.S. Geological Survey; World Bank; World Bureau of Metal Statistics; WorldSteel.
Note: EMDE = emerging market and developing economy; EMDEs excluding China = Brazil, India, and the Russian Federation; Mmt = million metric tons.
A.-E. Last observation is 2020.
F. Last observation is 2017.

extracting considerable resource rents (Kooroshy and Preston 2014). However, the emergence and subsequent profitability of laterite ore weakened the oligopoly structure of the industry (Erhlich 2018). Furthermore, the introduction of a futures contract in 1979 by the London Metal Exchange gave a further impetus to competitive pricing (Kuck 1999).

Trade flows and prices of nickel have been affected by trade policies as well, especially policies in Indonesia, currently the world's largest producer. In 2014, Indonesia introduced an export ban on unprocessed ores in order to increase its share of the value added to its mineral resources (UNCTAD 2017). Following a sharp fall in exports, Indonesia relaxed the ban in 2017 but reintroduced it in 2020.

From an energy transition perspective, nickel is deemed a "winning" commodity because of the ongoing electrification of transport and growing demand for large-scale battery storage capacity for wind- and solar-generated electricity. However, further advancements in battery technology will determine which type of commodity will be in high demand, and ultimately which will gain a dominant position in global production.

Precious metals

Gold has been used by humans since ancient civilizations, first for jewelry and later as a store of wealth and medium of exchange. Jewelry and transactions remained the most important uses of gold well into the 1900s. Britain was the first to adopt a gold standard for its currency in 1821 and had been on a de facto gold standard since 1717 (George 2012). The price of gold has been intricately linked with the gold standard, in use during 1871-1914, during the interwar period, and during the Bretton Woods (1944-71) period. This link kept the price of gold stable for 200 years until the U.S. Gold Reserve Act of 1935 raised the price from $20.67 per troy ounce to $35.00 per troy ounce (Cooper 1982). During the Bretton Woods period, the U.S. dollar was the principal reserve currency, with the price of gold set at $35.00 per troy ounce (Meltzer 1991).

Delinking gold from the U.S. dollar in 1971 set the stage for the flexible exchange rate regimes adopted by many countries. Real gold prices peaked in 1980 on safe haven buying and hedging against inflation. Prices stayed relatively low in the 1980s and 1990s in part because of sales by European central banks, which preferred to hold their foreign reserves in the form of interest-bearing assets in major currencies. Prices started to rise in 2001 in response to terrorist attacks and a long period of low mine production (George 2012). During the past two decades, gold prices have responded to real interest rates and, to a lesser degree, inflation and geopolitical concerns (Barsky et al. 2021).

Gold production was long dominated by South Africa, but that country's share in global gold production has steadily declined. In 2020, South Africa accounted for just 3 percent of global mine production, compared to change to 62 percent in 1970. Production has risen, notably in Australia, Canada, China, Russia, and the United States. Recycled gold makes up about 30 percent of supply. A large proportion of gold demand comes from China and India, mostly associated with jewelry fabrication. Central bank buying in these and other EMDEs has added to physical demand. Gold exchange-traded funds have increased in popularity as investment vehicles, providing an easier and less costly way to own gold. Gold's use in industry is primarily in electronics because of its high electrical conductivity and resistance to tarnishing.

Other precious metals include silver and platinum-group metals. Silver prices are more aligned to economic cycles because more than half of silver's demand comes from industrial applications, such as in electronics, solar panels, batteries, and photographic equipment. Silver stands to benefit from the energy transition given some of these applications and multiple components in electric vehicles.

Platinum and palladium prices are heavily influenced by vehicle demand, because both metals are used in emissions-reducing catalytic converters in car exhaust systems. Mexico and Peru are the top producers of silver, whereas production of platinum and palladium is dominated by South Africa and Russia. Both metals are expected to benefit in the energy transition, mainly through use in fuel cells, and most aspects of the envisioned hydrogen economy.

Agriculture supply and demand

Introduction

Agricultural commodities have been traded for centuries, beginning with high-value products such as spices and coffee. As the cost of transportation declined and communications improved at the start of the 1900s, trade became profitable for bulky commodities, such as grains, in turn allowing countries to make produce and trade agricultural commodities according to their comparative advantage. Tropical commodities, including cocoa, coffee, and tea, were exported from Africa and Asia, while grains and other temperate commodities were exported from Argentina, Russia, and the United States. Raw materials were exported from key producing countries to countries with large industries using those materials, such as the export of cotton produced in the United States to the textile industry in the United Kingdom. Specialization provided incentives for the adoption of new technologies and production practices to increase output and exports.

Technological improvements have been a key driver of agricultural production and trade. Early in the 1900s, the introduction of hybrid varieties changed the path of yields for most agricultural commodities. Before the 1930s, one hectare (ha) of land produced 1.6 metric tons (mt) of maize in the United States, with virtually no change from year to year. Today it produces more than 10 mt. Similar developments have taken place for many other commodities and, after the 1960s, in many other countries. Other improvements, such as transportation (including containerization), bulk storage, cold storage, and packaging, have enabled most consumers to consume almost every agricultural commodity throughout the year. More recent productivity improvements, including biotechnology, precision farming, real-time information from satellites and weather stations, and controlled-release fertilizers, are expected to further boost productivity as they are adopted more widely. Productivity improvements along the supply chain, lower transportation costs, and better information technology have exerted a downward impact on most agricultural commodity prices over time (figure 1.11).

FIGURE 1.11 **Real agricultural commodity prices since 1900**

Most agricultural commodity prices have followed a long-term downward path in real terms. Prices have also been volatile, especially during the first three decades of the 1900s. Volatility patterns differ among commodities, with the exception of grains (in part due to land substitutability). The price spike during the oil crises of the 1970s was similar to that of other commodities.

A. Maize, wheat, and rice

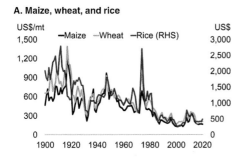

B. Sugar and palm oil

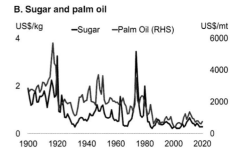

C. Cocoa, coffee, and tea

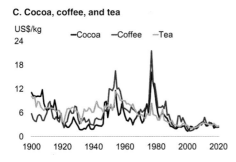

D. Cotton and natural rubber

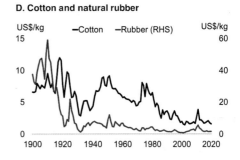

Source: World Bank.
Note: Prices deflated by Consumer Price Index. kg = kilogram; mt = metric ton; RHS = right-hand side.

Technological change

Improvements in technology during the 1900s and early 2000s have boosted the production and trade of agricultural commodities, essentially satisfying the basic caloric needs of the growing world population. Technology has fundamentally altered how agricultural commodities are produced, transported, stored, and consumed. Information and communication technology has encouraged the ongoing development of markets and the creation of sophisticated hedging facilities (box 1.3).

Production. The first major productivity improvement in agriculture was the development of hybrid maize in the United States, often called the biggest agricultural miracle of the twentieth century (Crow 1998). Hybrid seeds, formed by crossing four interbred lines, became commercially available during the 1920s and were widely adopted in the major maize growing areas of the United States by 1940. For example, in the U.S. state of Iowa, a key maize producing state, hybrid seeds accounted for nearly 97 percent of the area allocated to maize by 1941, with yields reaching 3.20 mt/ha, up from 1.95 mt/ha a decade earlier. Mechanization, improved production practices, fertilizer, and chemical use, and continued improvements in the genetic material resulted in further productivity gains. In 2016-21, maize yields in the United States exceeded 10 mt/ha, an eightfold increase since the introduction of hybrid varieties (figure 1.12). Similar productivity improvements have occurred for most other agricultural commodities on a continuous basis.

Productivity improvements in grains attained in AEs during the 1940s and 1950s were replicated in EMDEs during the Green Revolution. The high-yielding varieties of rice and wheat now used in EMDEs were developed at the International Maize and Wheat Center in Mexico and the International Rice Research Institute in the Philippines, and adapted to EMDE agroecological and climatic conditions.[18] The outcome included improved hybrid seeds, increased effectiveness of fertilizers and chemicals, and expanded irrigation and mechanization. The wheat yield increases achieved by the United States in the 1940s were achieved in India by the mid-1960s. Similarly, rice yields in China, India, and Vietnam quadrupled between 1960 and 2020, while wheat yields in Argentina doubled.

The location of production shifted as these changes occurred. Brazil became a major soybean producer and exporter during the second half of the 1900s, accounting for more than one-third of global production in 2020, from near zero in 1950 (figure 1.13). Indonesia and Malaysia became leaders in palm oil production. Vietnam now accounts for nearly one-fifth of global coffee supply, from zero in 1980. Cotton production shifted from the United States to China and India (figure 1.14).

A further increase in productivity began in the mid-1990s with the introduction of genetically modified crops in the United States.[19] Such crops can reduce costs because they reduce chemical applications. Biotechnology had a much larger positive impact on yields in EMDEs than in AEs because chemical applications in EMDEs were already relatively low, and thus suboptimal for conventional seed varieties (Baffes 2012; Qaim and Zilberman 2003). Not all countries, however, have adopted biotechnology. Among advanced economies, Australia, Canada, and the United States have used biotechnology extensively, whereas the European Union has left it up to the member states to decide. Among EMDEs, Argentina, Brazil, Paraguay, and South Africa are adopters.

Transportation and marketing. In the first half of the 1900s, the combined effects of mature railroad networks, oil-fueled ships, and the motor vehicle reduced transportation costs, increased trade, and brought greater integration in commodity markets. The pace of change accelerated after 1945. Investments in the shipping industry enabled the

---

[18] Both the center and the institute are members of the Consultative Group for International Agricultural Research, an umbrella organization that unites 14 international agricultural research institutes and provides evidence, innovation, and new tools to "harness the economic, environmental, and nutritional power of agriculture" (from the organization's "How We Work" page at https://www.cgiar.org/how-we-work/).

[19] A genetically modified crop is "a plant used for agricultural purposes into which one or several genes coding for desirable traits have been inserted through the process of genetic engineering. These genes may stem not only from the same or other plant species, but also from organisms totally unrelated to the recipient crop" (Qaim 2009, 665).

FIGURE 1.12 **Yield trends in AEs and EMDEs for selected food commodities**

Innovations during the 1930s set the stage for productivity improvements for most food commodities. During 1930-2020, each hectare of land in the U.S. produced, on average, 108 kg more maize and 23 kg more wheat each year. After the Green Revolution got under way in the 1960s, EMDEs achieved similar productivity gains. More recent technological improvements, including biotechnology, precision farming, smart fertilizers, and extensive use of satellite and weather station data, have sustained productivity gains in both advanced economies and EMDEs.

A. Maize, United States, 1885-2020

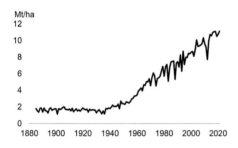

B. Wheat, United States, 1885-2020

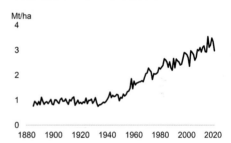

C. Maize, selected countries, 1960-2021

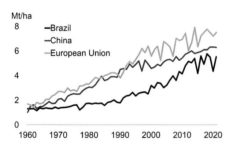

D. Wheat, selected countries, 1960-2021

E. Rice, selected countries, 1960-2021

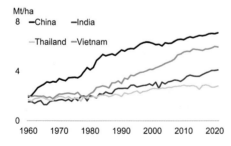

F. Soybeans, selected countries, 1964-2021

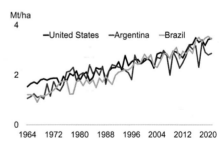

Sources: U.S. Department of Agriculture 2019; U.S. Department of Agriculture database, December 2021 update; World Bank.
Note: Data until 2021. EMDE = emerging market and developing economy; mt/ha = metric tons per hectare.

FIGURE 1.13 **Production and consumption shares: Food commodities**

The past six decades have seen significant shifts in the production and consumption of food commodities. China has emerged as a key producer and consumer of maize (to feed the rapidly expanding number of livestock). The European Union and the Russian Federation play an important role in global wheat markets. China and India dominate global production and consumption of rice, and Thailand is a large exporter. Argentina and Brazil have become key players in the soybean market.

A. Global production of rice and wheat

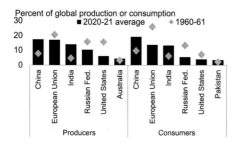

B. Global production of maize and soybean

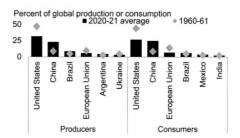

C. Wheat

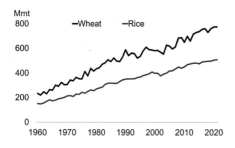

D. Maize

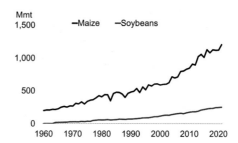

E. Rice

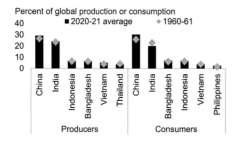

F. Soybean

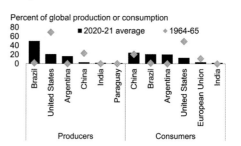

Sources: U.S. Department of Agriculture database, December 2021 update; World Bank.
A.B. Data until 2021. Mmt = million metric tons.

FIGURE 1.14 Production and consumption shares: Export commodities

Production of export commodities has been dominated by EMDEs. Côte d'Ivoire and Ghana dominate the cocoa market. Cotton production and consumption has shifted to China and India at the expense of the United States. China and India dominate global tea production and consumption, but Kenya is the biggest exporter. Thailand has emerged as the main global supplier of natural rubber, and China is the main buyer.

A. Global production of cocoa and tea

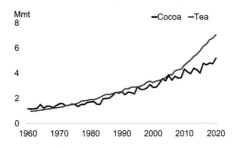

B. Global production of cotton and natural rubber

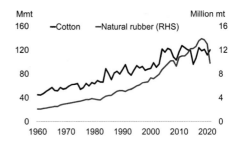

C. Cocoa

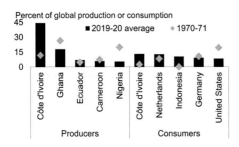

D. Cotton

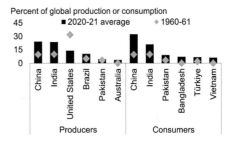

E. Tea

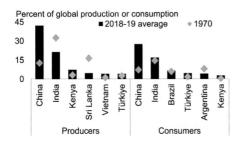

F. Natural rubber

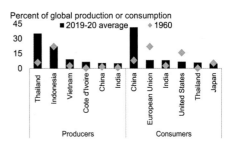

Sources: Food and Agriculture Organization of the United Nations; Grilli, Agostini, and Hooft-Welvaars 1980; International Cocoa Organization; International Coffee Organization; International Rubber Study Group; U.S. Department of Agriculture database, December 2021 update; World Bank.
Note: Mmt = million metric tons; RHS = right-hand side.
A. Data until 2020.
B. Data until 2021.

BOX 1.3 The development of price benchmarking in commodity markets

Global commodity price benchmarks set a guideline for prices at which transactions in commodities take place. They are essential to the futures contracts used in organized exchanges. Benchmark pricing based on competitive commodity markets flourished from the late 1800s for commodities such as cotton and grains. However, further progress in the mid-1900s was hindered by protectionist trade policies and a proliferation of supply management schemes. The development of competitive markets and associated price benchmarks reemerged following rounds of trade liberalization in the 1950s and 1960s. The collapse of the Bretton Woods fixed exchange rate system gave impetus to futures markets for currencies, and to associated innovations in hedging techniques that have influenced organized markets generally. Today, the main commodity markets have mature global price benchmarking mechanisms, which assist in the efficient allocation of resources and the reduction of market risks for producers and consumers alike.

Introduction

A benchmark price is the price of a standard unit of a good (or financial asset) with a reputation for consistent quality and wide availability in its market. It sets a baseline for the pricing of other goods in the same category, which may have somewhat different qualities and characteristics. A product in the group with inferior qualities will trade at a discount to the benchmark, whereas one with superior qualities will trade at a premium. Benchmark prices for commodities are calculated and published daily from the trading on organized futures exchanges (for example, the Brent crude futures on the Chicago Mercantile Exchange). Traders do not deal in physical commodities but in precisely defined contracts for which a standardized quality and delivery date are essential. Because only the price is negotiable, the benchmarks from futures exchanges provide a transparent and accurate guide for the pricing of the physical products that are actually delivered. As an integral part of the market mechanism, they help increase economic efficiency, and reduce risks, to the benefit of producers and consumers alike.

Global commodity price benchmarks, principally formed at commodity exchanges, encapsulate worldwide supply and demand conditions. For this reason, they influence the prices at which most transactions in primary commodities take place. Global price benchmarks were first formed in the mid-1800s when the speed of information transmission was decoupled from the speed at which commodities were transported. That, in turn, enabled market participants to incorporate information on demand and supply conditions that went beyond the geographic coverage of the transaction in question.

Price benchmarks for cotton and some grains were fully developed by the end of the 1800s. Benchmarks for industrial commodities emerged rather later. For

BOX 1.3 The development of price benchmarking in commodity markets *(continued)*

some commodities, such as iron ore, the formation of mechanisms for international price benchmarks is still a work in process, and, in some cases, such as fertilizers and rare earth metals, the process is either at an early stage or has not yet begun. For natural gas, the high cost of transocean transportation means that existing benchmarks apply only to regional markets—there have been wide differences between prices on futures exchanges in the United States and Europe.

Against this background, this box answers the following questions:

- How has price benchmarking evolved in commodity markets?

- What are the recent trends and impediments in price benchmarking?

The evolution of competitive pricing in commodity markets

The London Tea Auction began operation in 1679 and was the world's most important tea pricing center until it closed in 1998 (Pettigrew and Richardson 2013). Amsterdam also saw the emergence of commodity trading in the 1600s, and the use of a primitive futures contract (Goss and Yamey 1978; Stringham 2003). Price benchmarking as it is known today began during the mid-1800s on two parallel tracks. First, the global cotton market emerged from regional trading hubs in Alexandria (Egypt), Liverpool, New York, and New Orleans. Second, Chicago became the trade hub for grains produced in the midwestern United States. In both cases, price benchmarks began to emerge—a regional benchmark in grains and a global benchmark in cotton.

Japan has been credited with the birth of futures trading, starting with trading at the Dōjima rice market in Osaka in 1730 (Markham 1987; Schaede 1989). Key characteristics of the Dōjima market, presaging the characteristics of modern futures trading, were the central clearing of contracts, contract standardization, mark-to-market accounting rules, and the concept of settlement price.

The origins of the global cotton market go back to cotton trading in Liverpool in the mid-1700s (Dumbell 1923). Liverpool was the port of entry to the textile industry in northern England for cotton from Egypt, India, and North America. The Liverpool Cotton Exchange originated early versions of futures contracts in the 1840s, making it the first global cotton pricing center. Cotton futures contracts were traded in Alexandria as early as 1849, although the Alexandria Cotton Exchange was not formally established until 1861 (Baffes 2005).

Developments in transportation and information technology in the mid-1800s—first the steamship and later the telegraph—were instrumental in accelerating and broadening the informational content of commodity prices. With the

BOX 1.3 The development of price benchmarking in commodity markets *(continued)*

introduction of steamships in the 1820s and their expanded use in the next two decades, the time taken to cross the Atlantic was reduced from two months to two weeks (Armstrong 1859). Early mail steamships were faster than cargo ships, allowing information about cotton supply conditions in the United States, the principal cotton supplier to England at the time, along with cotton samples, to arrive much earlier than the cotton itself. Using the early arrival of information on U.S. supply conditions, merchants in Liverpool were able to trade "to arrive" or "intransit" contracts more than one month before the physical arrival of the product. These contracts formed the basis for forward and futures contracts (Dumbell 1923). However, the defining moment that turned the cotton market into a global market was the installation of the first successful transatlantic cable in 1865. Information on market conditions in the United States could now be transmitted instantaneously to Europe and vice versa. [a] By the end of the 1880s, five cotton futures exchanges were connected by cable (Alexandria, Le Havre, Liverpool, New Orleans, and New York), giving birth to the world's first global competitive pricing mechanism (Baffes and Kaltsas 2004).

In North America, the Chicago Board of Trade (CBOT) was founded in 1848 to facilitate cash transactions in grains. Forward ("to arrive") contracts began to be traded shortly thereafter (Williams 1986). [b] Grain traders in Kansas followed suit by establishing the Kansas City Board of Trade. In 1859, the Illinois legislature granted CBOT self-regulatory authority, thereby enabling CBOT to facilitate the standardization of contracts. Shortly thereafter, formal trading rules were instituted regarding delivery procedures. In 1868, rules were adopted against certain manipulative activities, such as cornering the market, that is, buying a good in a large enough quantity to be able to later push the price artificially high. [c] Together, the adoption of trading rules and rules defining manipulation marked the beginning of grain (wheat, corn, and oats) futures trading in CBOT. The global cotton market in conjunction with the grain market in Chicago (and New York) set the stage for the golden era of competitive commodity pricing.

---

a. The effects of the steamship and the transatlantic cable on cotton pricing are summarized by Dumbel (1923, 259):

> So long as cotton and news travelled across the sea at the same pace there could be no volume of dealings except in cotton on the spot. But as soon as the mail steamer, carrying letters and samples, outstripped the sailing ship with its cargo of cotton, that cargo could be bought and sold while still at sea. The gradual extinction of the sailing ship would have eliminated the time interval which made that practice possible, but in the meantime the telegraph came to magnify and perpetuate the difference between the transmission of news and the shipment of cotton.

b. According to Williams (1982, 312): "Although the western ports did not get a telegraph until 1848, Buffalo and New York were connected in late 1846. Perhaps then, the flurry of trading in 1847 accompanied the introduction of the telegraph."

c. From the Commodity Futures Trading Commission's "History of the CFTC" web page (https://www.cftc.gov/About/HistoryoftheCFTC/history_precftc.html).

BOX 1.3 The development of price benchmarking in commodity markets (continued)

Further advances in competitive price benchmarking were hindered by policy developments in the interwar period and after World War II. During the Great Depression, many countries adopted protectionist trade policies, beginning with the passage of the U.S. Tariff Act of 1930 (the Smoot-Hawley Tariff). Exchange rate movements that were deemed excessive encouraged further protectionist measures (Irwin 2012).

After World War II, recognition of the harmful effects of protectionist policies underlaid a more open approach to international trade policy, enshrined in the General Agreement on Tariffs and Trade (1947). As the recovery from the war gained momentum in the 1950s and 1960s, governments effected large reductions in tariffs on a vast range of goods in several rounds of international negotiations. However, the high tariffs and other trade restrictions in agriculture were largely left untouched. [d] And nontariff interventions, including subsidies, discriminatory domestic taxes, and trade-distorting regulations on investment, continued to obstruct competitive commodity pricing in various other areas. Price benchmarks for many commodities were also influenced by international supply management schemes (see box 1.4). The Uruguay Round achieved some easing of nontariff protectionist measures, but even so substantial barriers to trade in agriculture have remained (Baffes and de Gorter 2005; Tyers and Anderson 1992).

These interventions weakened global benchmarking mechanisms in agricultural commodities and halted progress toward the competitive pricing of industrial commodities. Many attempts to establish futures contracts on organized exchanges failed. Traders were reluctant to take positions because prices were either too stable to generate hedging interest or susceptible to abrupt changes resulting from political decisions they could not predict. [e]

Post-Bretton Woods developments in price benchmarking

A number of post-World War II developments facilitated the development of price benchmarking as we know it today. First, following the collapse of the Bretton Woods fixed exchange rate system, and the subsequent adoption of flexible exchange rates for major currencies, the Chicago Mercantile Exchange launched currency futures contracts (Clifton 1985). Second, agricultural policies

---

d. Before the Uruguay round, there were seven General Agreement on Tariffs and Trade rounds: Geneva (1947), Annecy (1949), Torquay (1950-51), Geneva (1955-56), Dillon (1961-62), Kennedy (1963-67), and Tokyo (1973-79).

e. The absence of competitive pricing, along with the public ownership of resources, created rent-seeking conditions (Krueger 1964). Carlton (1984) and Hieronymus (1977) cited commercial interests as a key reason for the frequent failure of commodity futures contracts after World War II.

BOX 1.3 The development of price benchmarking in commodity markets *(continued)*

in high-income countries gradually became more market-oriented, initially with the replacement of stockholding mechanisms by price supports, and later by the introduction of direct support to farmers in place of price supports and government-organized supply management (Gardner 1987). Pivotal policy shifts in this respect were the 1985 U.S. Farm Bill and the 1992 Common Agricultural Policy reform in the European Union (Baffes and Meerman 1998). Third, the transition from central planning in Central and Eastern Europe and Central Asia, and later in China, expanded the geographical scope of international markets. Developing economies followed suit, with the dismantling of parastatals in charge of marketing and trading of commodities (Akiyama et al. 2003). Fourth, rapid advances in computer technology and in options pricing algorithms led to the increasing use of derivative instruments and sophisticated hedging strategies in futures markets, and to a large rise in trading volumes.

Today, most major commodity markets have benchmarking mechanisms in place. Yet the transition to global benchmark pricing has not been the same across all commodity markets. Crude oil benchmarks, for example, emerged relatively quickly after the 1970s crises. The New York Mercantile Exchange introduced the West Texas Intermediate oil futures contract in 1983, which became the price benchmark for the midcontinent United States. Shortly thereafter, the Brent contract developed into an alternative world price barometer. Numerous other futures oil contracts have been launched since then (Yang and Zhou 2020).

Futures markets for some commodities, however, have developed more slowly, as highlighted by the following examples.

- *Coal.* The first international coal price benchmark was the outcome of negotiations between a key Australian supplier and a group of Japanese power and steel companies. This pricing system was replaced by a Reference Price System in the late 1990s. Spot markets emerged in the early 2000s, providing an alternative means of benchmark pricing. Today there are three widely used international coal price benchmarks—in Australia, Colombia, and South Africa. Coal futures are also traded on several exchanges, and began with New York Mercantile Exchange (now owned and operated by Chicago Mercantile Exchange Group) in 2001, followed by the Intercontinental Exchange in Europe, and more recent exchanges including Amsterdam and Australia. Yet coal futures are not as liquid as other commodities, and studies have concluded that the international coal market continues to be weakly integrated (Liu and Geman 2017; Zaklan et al. 2012).

- *Natural gas.* In contrast to most other commodity markets, natural gas does not have a global price benchmark. Because of the costs of transportation,

BOX 1.3 **The development of price benchmarking in commodity markets** *(continued)*

especially across oceans, there are several segmented markets whose prices can move quite independently of each other. Markets connected by pipeline have a much higher degree of integration, but can still show local differences (for example, between Alberta in Canada and Texas in the United States). The U.S. natural gas market has a mature pricing mechanism, including a futures contract that was launched in the early 1980s. Prices of European natural gas and liquefied natural gas (LNG) have been traditionally benchmarked to crude oil. This practice has been changing, however, through the so-called spotification of the LNG market (Colombo, Harrak, and Sartori 2016). [f]

- *Iron ore.* As recently as 2005, international iron ore prices were set through negotiations between Vale, Brazil's largest iron ore-producing company, and European steel manufacturers. During the 1980s and 1990s, Brazil was the world's top iron ore producer and Europe was one of the largest consumers, along with the United States and Japan (Vale 2012). The rapid expansion of China's steel consumption radically altered this nexus. The pricing of the iron ore market changed in 2005 from negotiated to spot pricing (Astier 2015).

Over the past 25 years, the strong economic expansion of EMDEs in Asia, especially China, has led to a corresponding rise of commodity trading activity in that region. Benchmark commodity prices in centers such as Dalian, Shanghai, and Singapore offer increasingly viable alternatives to those from established locations in Chicago, London, and New York (Tamvakis 2018).

Conclusion

Price benchmarking is instrumental in allocating resources efficiently among producers and consumers. The associated development of future markets and hedging instruments allows both sides to reduce exposures to risks. Organized price benchmarking goes back to the London Tea Auction (1679) and the Dōjima rice market in Osaka (1730). Defining moments for regional and global benchmarks came in the 1800s. The introduction of the mail steamship, and a few decades later the transatlantic cable, accelerated the transmission of information well ahead of the physical movements of commodities. By the late 1800s, the cotton futures exchanges on both sides of the Atlantic had effectively coalesced into a well-integrated global market. Markets for other commodities were to follow a similar path into the 1900s.

---

f. LNG could act as "insurance" against geopolitically driven embargoes or, as Nakano (2016) put it, "democratization of LNG."

BOX 1.3 The development of price benchmarking in commodity markets (continued)

However, trade protectionism during the Great Depression, and economic disruptions from World War II, slowed the spread of this development. Global trade liberalization in the 1950s and 1960s allowed organized markets to progress once again. Price benchmarking as it exists today got under way after the collapse of the Bretton Woods fixed exchange rate system and the subsequent evolution of futures markets. Advances in computer technology led to the increasing use of sophisticated instruments and trading techniques, which depend on benchmark prices, and a large expansion of trading volumes.

Today, many important commodities are traded in organized futures exchanges. For some commodities, such as fertilizers and rare earth metals, global price benchmarking is still in the early stages of development. For others, geography will always pose barriers to global integration. For example, price benchmarking for natural gas is still segregated—and based on regional demand and supply conditions—because of the high cost of transocean transportation.

capacity of cargo ships to double in the three decades following 1950 (Levinson 2016). Increasing demand for bulk transportation spurred other technological improvements, including dry bulk, supertankers, and container ships, which allowed greater economies of scale (Jacks and Stuermer 2021).[20] The decline in transportation costs contributed to increased commodity trade and lower commodity prices as countries were able to exploit their comparative advantage. Ocean freight rates for bulk cargo, such as coal and grains, halved in real terms during the past 50 years.[21]

The ratio of transportation costs to grain prices has remained relatively constant during the past 70 years as the cost of ocean transport and grain prices have declined at similar rates. More efficient port handling facilities have contributed to the decline in shipping costs, as has the weakening of shipping cartels and increased competition, advances in propulsion technology, and electronic navigation (Sjostrom 2004; World Bank 2000). Shipping of nongrain agricultural products, including meat and fresh produce, has benefited greatly from the growing use of refrigerated storage and intermodal containers (which may be carried on ships, airplanes, trains, and trucks). As a result, countries with temperate climates have been able to import tropical and off-season produce year-round and on a large scale. Innovations in processing, packaging, and retailing continue to expand the food choices open to consumers.

---

[20] Closures of the Suez Canal in 1956-57 and 1967-75 accelerated these innovations.

[21] This decline has not been smooth. There have been several spikes in ocean freight rates, including during WWII in the 1940s, the Korean War in the 1950s, the oil crises in the 1970s, and the commodity price boom in the 2000s.

Evolution of food consumption

An important aspect of overall demand for food is that income elasticity declines as incomes rise beyond subsistence levels (chapter 2). Global per capita consumption over time has risen more slowly than per capita real income during the past 60 years, indicating an income elasticity of less than unity. Declining income elasticities have been more noticeable for basic foods. Total consumption of wheat and rice, for example, has grown at a rate similar to the population growth rate, implying a per capita income elasticity close to zero (figure 1.15; chapter 2). However, per capita consumption of other items, including protein-rich seeds and meats, beverages, and oils, has continued to increase as per capita incomes have risen.

Between 1965 and 2020, global edible oil consumption increased nearly 20-fold (Kearney 2010). Per capita consumption in EMDEs increased by a factor of 13, and in AEs by a factor of 4. Three trends explain these increases. First, as per capita income grows, people tend to consume more food in packaged form and to use restaurants and fast food more frequently—forms of food that are typically more oil-intensive. Second, for health reasons, consumers also reduce consumption of animal fats for cooking (in favor of edible oils) as incomes rise. Third, edible oils are used to produce biofuels.

The rapid growth in consumption of meats, dairy, and packaged foods was made possible by advances in transportation, refrigerated storage, and packing technology. Associated with these developments was the expansion of supermarkets, which made access to these products more convenient. Whereas supermarkets have been common in advanced economies, their presence grew briskly in Asia and Latin America only toward the end of the 1900s. Supermarkets have also made inroads in Africa during the past 20 years (figure 1.15). In a review of 66 studies covering 48 African countries, Colen et al. (2018) report average income elasticities of less than 0.4 for cereals, close to 0.8 for meats, and more than 1.2 for beverages. As income grows, especially in low-income countries, consumption of animal products and packaged foods is expected to continue to grow relatively strongly, in turn increasing the demand for animal feed, such as maize and soybean meal, and for cooking oil.[22]

Biofuels are a newer source of demand for agricultural products. Currently, Brazil, the European Union, and the United States account for nearly two-thirds of global biofuel production. The crops most commonly used to produce biofuels are sugarcane and maize (for ethanol) and edible oils (for biodiesel). Several countries have announced their intention to increase biofuel production as part of efforts to meet climate change targets. China, for example, is expected to more than double its ethanol production over the next five years. Other countries, including India, Indonesia, and Malaysia, have set ambitious targets. According to some estimates, biofuel production could increase as much as 50 percent by the end of the 2020s.

---

[22] As shown in figure 1.15C, it takes about 25 kg of feed to produce 1 kg of beef. The corresponding feed requirements for pork and chicken meat are 6.4 kg and 3.3 kg of feed, respectively.

FIGURE 1.15 Demand for agricultural commodities

During the past six decades, rice and wheat consumption have grown in line with population growth. Consumption of edible oils and (less so) maize has grown much faster, oils because of their use in packaged foods and maize because of biofuel demand. Among export commodities, consumption of natural rubber has grown the most because it responds to industrial activity; demand for other commodities grew more in line with population. Looking ahead, animal products (especially some meats that require considerable amounts of feed) will continue to be key sources of demand growth. Biofuels could also play an important role, if the announced policy mandates (in response to the energy transition) materialize.

A. Output, population, and commodity consumption growth, food commodities

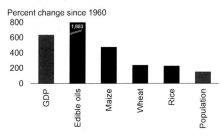

B. Output, population, and commodity consumption growth, export commodities

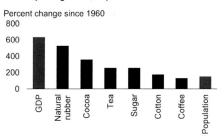

C. Feed conversion ratios for animal products

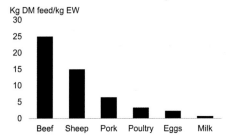

D. Production of biofuels

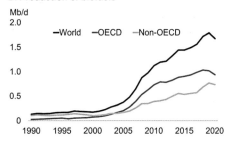

E. Supermarket food retail sales in Sub-Saharan Africa

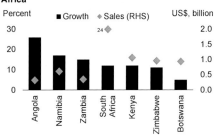

F. Consumption of edible oils

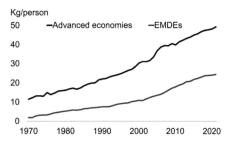

Sources: Alexander et al. 2016; BP Statistical Review of World Energy 2021; Grilli, Agostini, and Hooft-Welvaars 1980; International Cocoa Organization; Reardon et al. 2021; U.S. Department of Agriculture database, December 2021 update; World Bank.
A. "Edible oils" includes coconut, olive, palm, palm kernel, rapeseed, soybean, and sunflower seed oil. The base year corresponds to the 1964-65 average.
C. The "Sheep" category also includes goat and some other meats. Feed conversion ratios were adjusted to express feeding requirements per unit of EW and also to account for the need to raise sire and dam animals (Smil 2002). kg DM feed/kg EW = kilograms of dry matter feed per kilogram of edible weight.
D. Biofuel volumes have been adjusted for energy content. Mb/d = million barrels per day; OECD = Organisation for Economic Co-operation and Development.
E. RHS = right-hand side.
F. "Edible oils" includes coconut, olive, palm, palm kernel, rapeseed, soybean, and sunflower seed oil. EMDE = emerging market and developing economy.

Agricultural policies

Agricultural commodity markets have been influenced by government policies since the early twentieth century. These policies continue to affect markets today, albeit in a less distortionary manner. Policies have different objectives and effects—some encourage higher production through price supports and trade measures, whereas others seek to nationalize production and trade. The latter objective leads to stagnation and often the collapse of commodity sectors. International policies (including schemes that managed supplies at an international level and various trade agreements) have also played a key role, especially during the twentieth century (box 1.4 discusses the rise and collapse of international supply management schemes).

Policy intervention in agricultural commodity markets in AEs began in the United States shortly after World War I when the loss of export markets in Europe caused prices to fall. Policy interventions began in Western European countries shortly after the formation of what is now the European Union. Specifically, the creation of the Common Agricultural Policy in the early 1960s aimed to keep farm incomes comparable to those of nonfarm workers. At the time, Europe was a major importer of most agricultural commodities, but high and stable prices under the Common Agricultural Policy encouraged higher production and turned the European Union into a commodity exporter. Similarly, Japan's agricultural policies were aimed at maintaining self-sufficiency and to keep farm incomes comparable to those of nonfarm sectors. EMDEs introduced high taxes on crop exports to promote food self-sufficiency and keep food prices low (a practice aligned with EMDE efforts to promote industrialization). Last, centrally planned economies aimed at self-sufficiency through public ownership of most aspects of production and trade.

United States

The loss of European markets after the end of World War I, together with depressed agriculture prices, resulted in pressure for government intervention. After initial attempts at price support failed, the Federal Farm Board was established in 1929 with the aim of stabilizing agricultural commodity prices through government-financed inventory building. The effort failed, however, because of inadequate financing and the overwhelming impact of the Great Depression. In 1930, the U.S. Congress passed the Smoot-Hawley Act, which raised tariffs sharply (Irwin 1998). These trade barriers against the backdrop of the depression led to a spiraling of trade restrictions around the world.

Widespread distress among agricultural communities during the Great Depression had a lasting impact on policies. With the aim of raising domestic prices, the United States initiated a wide array of measures to pay farmers for cutting their output, to finance the purchase and storage of crops, and to subsidize exports of products deemed to be hurt by foreign government intervention. The Agricultural Adjustment Act of 1933 introduced

BOX 1.4 The rise and collapse of international supply management

Numerous efforts to manage commodity supplies at an international level throughout the 1900s had initial success but ultimately ended in failure. Their main objective was usually a profitable and stable level of prices, to be achieved via limits and quotas on production. Attempts to reduce supplies following World War I included export quotas and planting restrictions for coffee, and export quotas for copper. Attempts to control the market through stockpiling included government purchases of wool and buffer stocks of tin. Falling prices during the Great Depression spurred numerous schemes, which included tea, natural rubber, sugar, coffee, and copper. Buyers as well as producers were involved in attempts to revive supply management schemes during the shortages and inflations after World War II, and in the 1970s. Initially, some of the schemes achieved their stated objectives. However, attempts to set up longer-term supply arrangements laid the foundation for their eventual failure. The high prices that such arrangements may have created induced investment and innovation, brought new suppliers to the market, and caused consumers to substitute alternative products. The Organization of the Petroleum Exporting Countries may have been an exception in its longevity, but it has not succeeded in reducing the volatility of oil prices.

Introduction

Internationally coordinated supply management schemes have been applied to numerous commodity markets since the early 1900s. This box analyzes such arrangements with respect to industrial commodities and perennial agriculture. [a] Sometimes these arrangements were managed by producer cartels, and other times they were negotiated among countries importing or exporting commodities. Objectives of these attempts included an orderly transition from periods of high stress (for example, collapse of demand, or high levels of inventories), a general reduction of price volatility, and, in the case of cartels, price increases. Some of these arrangements fulfilled their objectives for a substantial period, but others failed outright. In several instances, the period of success laid the foundation for a later failure, because it facilitated the emergence of new entrants to the market or induced the development of substitute products.

The box adds to the literature in two ways. First, it considers a full cohort of commodity agreements, thereby providing a greater breadth of historical evidence. Existing studies have analyzed either a single commodity such as oil

---

a. Perennial agriculture refers to tree-based products such as natural rubber, coffee, and tea. Unlike annual agriculture, production capacity cannot be switched from one use to another from year to year in response to changing market conditions. Domestic policies toward the management of agriculture in general are discussed in the main text of chapter 2. Although these policies may have international ramifications, governments generally enact them independently. Trade agreements often impose constraints on the supply-management measures that a government might adopt, but these agreements differ from the coordinated steps negotiated under an international supply management system.

**BOX 1.4 The rise and collapse of international supply management
(*continued*)**

(Kaufmann et al. 2004; McNally 2017), coffee (Akiyama and Varangis 1990), tin
(Chandrasekhar 1989), and natural rubber (Verico 2013), or a group of nonoil
commodities (Davis 1946; Gilbert 2011; Roberts 1951). Second, it considers the
policy implications of the experiences with such schemes. Whereas most studies
have warned of the difficulties associated with international supply management,
this box takes a more nuanced approach and considers circumstances in which
globally coordinated action may be appropriate. This approach has particular
relevance in the context of the post-2000 boom-and-bust price cycle, the
COVID-19 pandemic, and the ongoing energy transition. To shed light on the
issues facing commodity markets today, this box draws on historical experiences
to examine the following questions:

- What short- and long-run objectives have governed coordinated efforts to
  manage commodity supplies?

- What impact have those efforts had on commodity markets?

Short- and long-term objectives of supply management mechanisms

Supply management arrangements have had both short- and long-term
objectives. A common short-term objective has been to restore orderly markets
after a crisis. A common long-term objective has been to maintain stable prices at
a profitable level for producers.

The short-term objective has been paramount in the policy response to large
destabilizing events, such as the Great Depression or the aftermath of war.
Transition to an orderly market involves a reduction in price volatility and a
restoration of viable conditions for both producers and consumers. Because the
objective is essentially short-run, and limited in ambition, actions aiming at an
orderly postcrisis transition have often been successful. They may involve no
more than the temporary use of buffer stocks to increase or reduce supply on the
market. For example, the 1921-23 coordinated liquidation of tin inventories,
which had accumulated during World War I, is considered a success. In response
to the sharp fall in oil demand at the onset of the recession caused by the
COVID-19 pandemic, the Organization of the Petroleum Exporting Countries
(OPEC) responded with large cuts in production, which were matched by some
nonmember producers (Indonesia and Norway).

Schemes with long-term objectives for the management of commodity markets
have rarely survived in an operative form. They confront an economic dilemma
that has usually led to their demise: any initial success in controlling output and
raising prices encourages new entrants, and thus an expansion of supply. It also
stimulates substitution by consumers into alternative products, reducing demand.

BOX 1.4 The rise and collapse of international supply management (*continued*)

Over time, these reactions in the market wear down the attempt at supply management. Their ultimate failure is evident empirically in the volatility and long-term downtrends of a range of real commodity prices subject to supply management (figure B1.4.1.).

Attempts to lift and stabilize prices through supply management nevertheless occurred throughout the 1900s (see table B1.4.1 later in this box for a comprehensive list of nonoil supply management schemes). An early attempt at international supply management followed the 1902 International Coffee Conference in New York (Hutchinson 1909; Wickizer 1943). Brazil agreed to reduce coffee supplies, with other Latin American producers joining the effort shortly after (Hutchinson 1909; Krasner 1973; Wickizer 1943). To reduce disruptions to international trade after World War I, agreements were reached for the orderly liquidation of tin and wool inventories accumulated during the war (Baranyai 1959; Blau 1946; Briggs 1947; Tsokhas 1993). Lifting prices was the objective for private cartels in copper (Walters 1944) and silver (Bratter 1938; Friedman 1992).

During and after the Great Depression, numerous agreements sought to address chronic surpluses and deflationary pressures—despite the fact that the cause was the collapse in aggregate demand, not overproduction. Agreements covered the entire commodity spectrum, including agricultural raw materials, timber, food commodities, beverages, metals, and precious metals (table B1.4.1; Davis 1946; Glesinger 1945). Examples are the agreements covering tea (Roberts 1951), sugar (Fakhri 2011; Hagelberg and Hannah 1994), and beef (Tsou and Black 1944). Some one-off interventions, such as those for wool, beef, and timber, had limited but well-defined objectives, and were deemed successful. [b]

Supply management schemes put in place after World War II were inspired by the United Nations Conference on Food and Agriculture (1943) and the Havana Charter (1948). These schemes—targeting coffee, cocoa, natural rubber, tin, and sugar—had more ambitious goals and broader international membership, including both exporting and importing countries (Baranyai 1959; Swerling 1968). Their principal objective was price stabilization through export restrictions and inventory management (Gilbert 1996). These attempts at supply management broke down before long. [c]

---

b. The silver cartel, however, did not succeed.

c. The mid-1970s was a period of inflation and high relative prices for commodities. Some governments attempted to limit further price increases through independent direct action. For example, the United States imposed price controls and drew down strategic stocks of metals (Cooper and Lawrence 1975). These measures had little success against the inflation and were soon abandoned.

BOX 1.4 The rise and collapse of international supply management (*continued*)

FIGURE B1.4.1 Prices of commodities subjected to supply management schemes after World War II

Five of the six commodities subjected to supply management after World War II were also subjected to supply management before the war, the exception being cocoa. Since then, the International Wheat Agreement ceased market operations in 1971, whereas agreements for coffee, sugar, and tin lasted until the late 1980s. The last cocoa agreement lasted until 1993, and the natural rubber agreement (the last nonoil agreement) collapsed after the 1997-98 Asian financial crisis.

A. Wheat

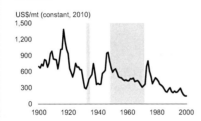

B. Tin

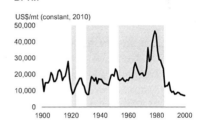

C. Natural rubber

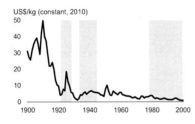

D. Sugar

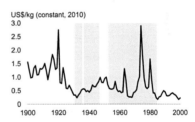

E. Coffee

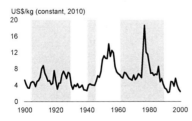

F. Cocoa

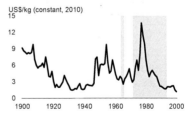

Source: World Bank.
Note: The series has been deflated by the U.S. Consumer Price Index. The shaded areas denote periods of supply management. kg = kilogram; mt = metric ton.

BOX 1.4 **The rise and collapse of international supply management** (*continued*)

The most durable international arrangement for supply management has been OPEC. It has attempted to set production quotas for its members and thereby stabilize the price of oil at a high level. Adherence to the quotas by members has, however, been mixed. And the periods of high prices that OPEC has achieved have encouraged new sources of supply—such as North Sea oil and shale oil. Moreover, changes in strategy by leading members have caused occasional extreme volatility in oil prices.

Impact of supply management schemes

There is strong empirical evidence that international agreements have had an impact on commodity prices. However, measuring their exact impact is challenging because other things are continually shifting. For example, although the Tin Agreement in itself may have put upward pressure on tin prices, concurrent technological advances were making aluminum a superior substitute. The rest of this section summarizes the literature on the subject, discusses some summary statistics, and gives some model-based results looking at all commodities.

Brazil's first coffee supply restriction in 1905 successfully raised and stabilized prices, and was renewed twice (Krasner 1973). Similarly, the 1921 agreement to limit the sale of tin inventories accumulated during World War I succeeded in stabilizing prices (Baldwin 1983). Numerous studies have concluded that most post–World War II agreements had a substantial impact on prices. See, for example, Akiyama and Varangis (1990) for coffee, Chandrasekhar (1989) for tin, and Verico (2013) for natural rubber.

Figure B1.4.2 reports price changes after the collapse of an agreement for six nonoil commodities. The change is gauged by the three-year average of the inflation-adjusted price after the collapse minus the three-year average before it. In four cases (sugar, Arabica coffee, Robusta coffee, and tin), prices dropped by about 50 percent after the collapse of the agreement. However, prices increased substantially after the cocoa and wheat agreements expired, but did not change for natural rubber. These declines in prices suggest that the agreements, as long as they were in effect, helped lift prices. It is also important to note that the increase in the price of wheat coincided with the 1970s commodities price boom.

To further examine the relationship between commodity agreements and prices, we present summary results adopted from the price decomposition model reported in chapter 3. The model, which looks at the behavior of 27 inflation-adjusted commodity prices from January 1970 to December 2019, decomposes real prices into cycles (up to 20 years) and trends. One can then examine the

BOX 1.4 The rise and collapse of international supply management (*continued*)

degree of nonlinearity of the trends. The analysis finds that trends differ across most commodities. Six commodities subjected to agreements within the sample period—cocoa, Arabica coffee, Robusta coffee, crude oil, natural rubber, and tin—exhibit a much higher degree of nonlinearity than the rest of the commodities. Indeed, the root mean square error—a measure of how much the long-term trends deviate from a linear trend—of the six commodities subjected to intervention is almost 11, compared to 4 for the remaining commodities. Subject to the caveats discussed earlier, this finding could suggest that interventions in commodity markets may be associated with deviations of real prices from their long-run trends.

Although higher and more stable prices benefited participating countries in the short term, they often unleashed forces that led to their own eventual collapse. First, higher prices reduce consumption by encouraging more efficient usage and a switch to alternative products. For example, the more than 10-fold increase in oil prices in the 1970s induced conservation and efficiency gains, as well as substitution by other fuels, which led to a four-year, 10 percent decline in global consumption. World oil demand growth never fully recovered from the price shocks, because improved efficiency reduced the energy intensity of world output. In addition, as noted earlier, high tin prices maintained by the Tin Agreement accelerated the use of aluminum and other products in the canning industry.

Second, commodity agreements frequently suffered from low compliance. Although constrained production by some members led to higher prices, it increased the rewards for cheating. Poor compliance was the main reason why oil agreements before the World War II collapsed. (OPEC has often suffered from poor compliance with quotas.) The most successful agreements were those that had a legal mandate to enforce production restrictions.

Third, higher prices attract the entry of new producers that operate outside the agreement—"free riders" benefiting from the output constraints on members of the agreement. High coffee prices, along with a lack of access to the global coffee market, prompted Eastern European countries and the Soviet Union (which were not members of the coffee agreement) to seek new coffee supplies. They provided technical and financial assistance to Vietnam to develop its coffee industry outside the coffee agreement. High tin prices brought new tin suppliers, such as Brazil, into the market. For oil, high prices have repeatedly stimulated the development of new high-cost supplies—offshore oil in Brazil and the North Sea, and nonconventional sources like U.S. shale.

Thus, the passage of time brings to bear market forces that eventually overwhelm supply management schemes. In some cases, organizations originally established

BOX 1.4 The rise and collapse of international supply management (*continued*)

to intervene in commodity markets have modified their objective to providing information, via market monitoring and the provision of statistics, thus improving market transparency through information-sharing, analysis, and consultation on market and policy developments. Such organizations serve a useful purpose by providing a public good.[d] Looking forward, ongoing efforts to substitute environmentally friendly energy sources for fossil fuels could benefit from the sharing of technical information among producers and consumers (see energy transition discussion in box 1.1).

Conclusion

Over the past century, coordinated supply management efforts have been implemented in numerous commodity markets and with various stated motives. For some, the objective was to facilitate an orderly transition in response to a large destabilizing event, such as the Great Depression or the aftermath of war. For example, OPEC's production cuts in response to the sharp fall in oil demand in 2020 had limited and essentially short-run objectives. These actions aiming at an orderly postcrisis transition have often been successful.

However, the original primary objective of most internationally negotiated supply management schemes has been more ambitious: to increase and stabilize prices over a longer term through agreed controls on production and exports or inventory management. Some of these schemes have been successful for a while, but they have often become victims of their own early success. High and stable prices have encouraged new producers to enter the market and consumers to reduce consumption. High oil prices, for example, encourage the expansion of non-OPEC supplies, the adoption of energy efficiency measures, and substitution of products. Moreover, enforcing quotas on members becomes more difficult as the benefits of adherence become more elusive. For these reasons, the passage of time tends to wear out supply management schemes.

From a policy perspective, the historical experience of supply management mechanisms with longer-run goals is not encouraging. Although they appear to be an attractive tool to mitigate the adverse effects of the boom-and-bust cycles of commodity prices, these mechanisms distort markets by keeping prices stable or elevated, which in turn has frequently led to the eventual collapse of the mechanisms. At their worst, these mechanisms can exacerbate commodity price cycles and can harm producers of a given commodity by encouraging consumers

---

d. These "new" organizations include the International Cocoa Organization, the International Coffee Organization, and the International Grains Council.

BOX 1.4 The rise and collapse of international supply management (*continued*)

FIGURE B1.4.2 Impact of collapse of supply management schemes on commodity prices

The collapse of supply management schemes has most often led to declining prices. Prices of commodities subjected to supply management are characterized by a high degree of nonlinearity.

A. Change in prices after agreements collapse

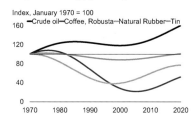

B. Real commodity price decomposition

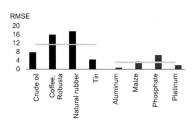

C. Long-term trend of commodity prices subjected to supply management

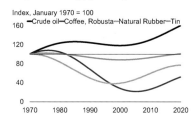

D. Long-term trend of commodity prices not subjected to supply management

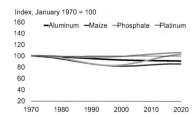

Source: World Bank.
A. The change is based on the three-year nominal average before and after the year of the collapse of the agreement. The year of collapse is noted in the parenthesis and is excluded from the comparison.
B. RMSE = root mean square error, which is a proxy for nonlinearity. Yellow line denotes group averages.

to switch to alternatives, which may lead to a permanent reduction in demand for the commodity.

Some international organizations that originated with the intention to manage supply have shifted focus to become providers of market information as a public good. Looking forward, ongoing efforts to substitute environmentally friendly energy sources for fossil fuels could benefit from the sharing of information among producers and consumers on technical research.

BOX 1.4 The rise and collapse of international supply management (*continued*)

TABLE B1.4.1 Nonoil commodity management schemes

	Mechanism (membership), duration	Nature
Before World War II		
Coffee	Export quotas and planting restrictions (State of São Paolo), 1905-29	**Valorization schemes** raised and stabilized prices and were profitable to the participating banks.
Wool	Government purchases (1 importer and 3 exporters), 1916-20	**Imperial Wool and Sheepskin Contract Scheme** maintained price stability and was terminated in 1920, as scheduled.
Copper	Export quotas (4 exporters), 1918-24	**Copper Export Association** succeeded in an orderly liquidation of copper inventories and was disbanded in 1924.
Tin	Buffer stocks (2 exporters), 1921-25	**Bandoeng Pool** was successful in liquidating inventories and led to the establishment of the International Tin Committee.
Tea	Production quotas (3 exporters), 1929-33	**Tea Restriction Scheme** raised prices of lower quality tea, but consumer preferences changed toward higher-priced teas.
Rubber	Export quotas and production restrictions (2 exporters), 1922-28	**Stevenson Plan** raised prices but led to output expansion by other exporters.
Copper	Export quotas (European and U.S. mining companies), 1926-32	**Copper Exporters, Inc.** raised prices, but a strike by buyers and imposition of a U.S. import tax led to its dissolution in 1932.
Coffee	Prohibition of plantings and coffee destruction (Brazil), 1930-37	**Coffee Control Scheme** was a costly scheme; eventually the government allowed free competition.
Tin	Buffer stocks and export quotas (5 exporters), 1931-46	**International Tin Control Scheme** failed to stabilize prices because of rapid changes in demand during and after WWII.
Sugar	Export and production quotas (associations in 7 exporters), 1931-35	**The Chadbourne Agreement** failed to stabilize prices and collapsed a year before its termination date.
Silver	Government purchases (5 exporters and 3 importers), 1933-37	**London Silver Agreement** did not increase prices as expected but benefited some exporting countries and companies.

BOX 1.4 The rise and collapse of international supply management (*continued*)

TABLE B1.4.1 Nonoil commodity management schemes *(continued)*

	Mechanism (membership), duration	Nature
Before World War II		
Wheat	Export and import quotas (9 exporters 12 importers), 1933-34	**International Wheat Agreement** failed to stabilize prices and broke down after one year of operation.
Tea	Export quotas and planting restrictions (3 exporters), 1933-47	**Tea Regulation Scheme** stabilized prices initially but the agreement collapsed following increased demand after WWII.
Rubber	Export quotas and planting restrictions (5 exporters), 1934-44	**International Rubber Regulation Agreement**, despite being extended for a second 5-year period, was not successful in reducing price volatility.
Copper	Production quotas (mining companies from 7 exporting countries), 1935-39	**International Copper Cartel** stabilized prices but was terminated with the outbreak of WWII.
Timber	Export quotas (9 exporters), 1935-39	**European Timber Exporters Convention** raised prices, but the scheme collapsed in 1939 following the outbreak of WWII.
Beef	Export and import quotas (6 exporters), 1937-40	**Beef Agreement** operated successfully but was suspended with the outbreak of WWII.
Sugar	Export quotas and other restrictions (21 exporters and importers), 1937-46	**Regulation of Production and Marketing of Sugar** failed to address high-cost production among exporters.
Wool	Government purchases (1 importer and 3 exporters), 1940-46	**Imperial Wool Purchase Scheme** successfully coordinated allocation of wool and managed high wool inventories after WWII.
Coffee	Export quotas and import quotas (14 exporters and the United States), 1941-45	**Inter-American Coffee Agreement** raised prices but brought new producers, especially from Africa.
After World War II		
Wheat	Export and import quotas (5 exporters and 36 importers), 1949-71	**International Wheat Agreement** failed to stabilize prices and collapsed shortly before the 1970s commodity price boom.
Sugar	Export and import quotas (26 exporters and 18 importers), 1953-84	**International Sugar Agreement** did not achieve price stability despite being renewed three times (it was not implemented in between renewals).

BOX 1.4 **The rise and collapse of international supply management** (*continued*)

TABLE B1.4.1 **Nonoil commodity management schemes** (*continued*)

	Mechanism (membership), duration	Nature
After World War II		
Tin	Buffer stocks and export quotas (7 exporters and 18 importers), 1954-85	**International Tin Agreement** raised and stabilized prices, but new entrants and substitution by aluminum led to its insolvency.
Coffee	Export quotas (42 exporters and 7 importers), 1962-89	**International Coffee Agreement** raised prices, but disagreements among members resulted in the termination of the agreement.
Cocoa	Export quotas (6 exporters), 1964-65	**International Cocoa Agreement** lasted only one year because of a bumper crop.
Cocoa	Buffer stocks and export quotas (9 exporters and 35 importers), 1972-93	**International Cocoa Agreement** had limited impact on prices despite being extended four times.
Rubber	Buffer stocks (13 exporters and 49 importers), 1979-99	**International Natural Rubber Agreement** did not stabilize prices and collapsed during the East Asian financial crisis.

Source: World Bank summary of various sources.
Note: The schemes appear in chronological order. WWII = World War II.

various policy instruments, in effect rendering the government buyer of last resort.[23] Price stabilization was to be achieved by loan and storage programs that removed supplies from the market while a system of nonrecourse loans was initiated. Under the program, a producer could receive a government loan on their crop at the price support level and repay the loan by delivering the crop to the government. Because it was often impossible to export commodities at the support price, a system of export subsidies had to be instituted. The system was buttressed by a high tariff and by import quotas. All of these practices in effect isolated the United States from world markets.

Although strong commodity demand after WWII brought booming commodity markets, efforts to institute a more flexible agricultural support mechanism in the late 1940s failed. In the mid-1950s, demand slowed, stocks rose sharply, and program costs began to escalate, despite large-scale land retirement programs and increased food aid to

---

[23] Although the Supreme Court declared the act unconstitutional, subsequent modifications kept most of its key elements intact.

developing countries. A different support system, with deficiency payments when prices fell below a threshold level, was instituted in 1973.

In a sudden turnaround in world market conditions, surplus stocks soon disappeared as the Soviet Union became a large-scale grain importer. World grain production experienced a shortfall, and input costs increased sharply with the oil price spike. Concerns about commodity surpluses and low prices were replaced by near panic over high prices and short supplies, which led to price controls for some meat products and a soybean export ban in 1974. High commodity prices during the late 1970s and early 1980s, along with strong exports, meant that little support from the U.S. government was required. However, the price collapse of the mid-1980s meant that the cost of the price support program spiraled again.

Policy revisions in 1985 and 1990 were aimed largely at controlling program costs. The boom in grain prices in the mid-1990s, which obviated the need for price deficiency payments, presented the opportunity for a thorough redesign of U.S. agricultural policy. The 1996 Freedom to Farm Act gave farmers fixed support payments, independent of current farm prices and production (Baffes and de Gorter 2005).

Over the past two decades, U.S. agricultural policies have shifted to reflect environmental and conservation concerns. These policies included a more flexible approach featuring countercyclical payments, subsidized insurance, and conservation programs (Glauber and Smith 2021). In a further shift, in 2019 the United States introduced cash compensation for farmers hurt by the escalation of tariffs in a trade dispute with China.

Western Europe

Before WWII, each Western European country had different agricultural structures and policies. France was a relatively low-cost producer with surplus capacity. The United Kingdom pursued a liberal trade policy with heavy dependence on imports. Germany's agriculture was heavily protected, with large, productive agricultural estates in the east, and small, less-efficient farms in the west. The Netherlands had an efficient, export-oriented sector. During WWII and the years that followed, European countries experienced food shortages due to disruptions in production, distribution, and trade.

In recognition of the need for secure supplies of food for its population, and of the difficulties facing European farmers, a founding principle of the European Economic Community (EEC) in 1957 was the establishment of a Common Agricultural Policy (CAP). It had multiple mandated objectives: to increase productivity through technological progress and the best use of resources, to ensure a fair standard of living for rural communities, to stabilize markets, to secure the availability of supplies, and to enforce fair prices. CAP began operating in the early 1960s, using common internal prices, tariffs, and financing as instruments to achieve the objectives. Measures included import levies to maintain price targets, export subsidies to gain global market share, and storage programs to keep excess supplies off the market.

When CAP was formulated, most member states were net importers of agricultural commodities. At first, CAP brought price stability in the internal market and posed no threat to external competitors. However, high and stable prices incentivized farmers to increase production, and within a decade the EEC went from being a major food importer to an exporter of grains, meats, sugar, and other food commodities.

Moreover, to maintain parity between farm incomes and rising urban incomes, the EEC had to repeatedly raise internal agricultural support prices (and thus widen the gaps between domestic and world prices). Doing so imposed increasingly heavy costs on members for commodity purchases, storage, and export subsidies. To sustain CAP objectives, the EEC looked to international commodity agreements to achieve higher and more stable world prices. This became the EEC's main negotiating objective in the Tokyo Round of General Agreement on Tariffs and Trade negotiations.

Declining world commodity prices during the 1980s, however, intensified the difficulties with CAP. Stocks rose at unsustainably high rates, costs skyrocketed—in the 1980s CAP accounted for about 60 percent of total EEC spending—and farm incomes still lagged those of nonfarm sectors. Reforms to CAP since then reduced the fiscal burden on the European Union (established in 1992) to 35 percent of the budget in 2020. Markets opened up, support prices were phased out, and European Union storage spending was capped. The reforms marked a policy reorientation—from price support per se toward supporting incomes of farmers directly, improving food quality, and encouraging environmental sustainability. For example, the European Union has measures to retire farmland in favor of afforestation. Policy reforms in Western Europe combined with reforms in the United States and other AEs have resulted in a decline in overall agricultural support to Organisation for Economic Co-operation and Development countries by more than one-third during the past two decades (figure 1.16).

Japan and East Asia

Before WWII, Japan depended on imports from China, Korea, and elsewhere in the region to supplement domestic food production. Following WWII, the main government objectives were a high degree of self-sufficiency in rice and maintaining farmer incomes. Key aspects of the policies included support of an extensive system of cooperatives for small farmers and the establishment of state trading agencies for imports. Marketing of basic commodities—including rice, wheat, beef, and dairy products, but excluding other commodities such as soybeans and coarse grains—was another feature. Domestic prices were protected by import quotas.

The commodity price boom of the 1970s along with the soybean export embargo by the United States reinforced the desire for self-sufficiency in food commodities and fueled Japan's interest in international agreements to stabilize agricultural commodity prices and to guarantee reliable supplies of imports. Other East Asian countries, including the Republic of Korea, also adopted policies that placed a heavy emphasis on high domestic protection and extensive use of state trading agencies.

FIGURE 1.16 Developments since 2000

Despite high food commodity prices during 2020-22, world food markets are much better supplied than in the early 2000s, according to the aggregate stocks-to-use ratio, a measure of demand relative to supply. Input costs, however, have risen, posing important risks if such increases become permanent. On the technology front, biotech commodities have been used by both advanced economies and EMDEs, with considerable productivity gains for the latter. Most of global cotton, maize, and soybean production comes from biotech varieties. Domestic support to agriculture by OECD countries has declined during the past two decades. On the demand side, food marketed through formal channels, such as supermarkets, has increased in most regions, including Sub-Saharan Africa. However, challenges regarding undernourishment remain, especially following COVID-19.

A. Biotechnology use in selected EMDEs in 2018

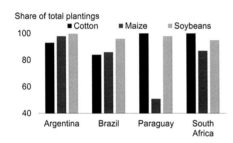

B. Biotechnology use in selected advanced economies in 2018

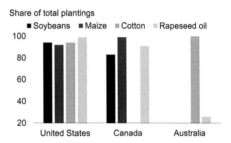

C. Agricultural support in OECD countries

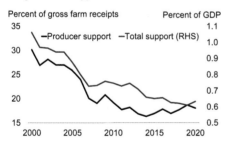

D. Undernourishment

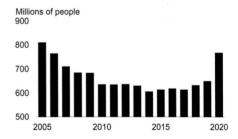

Sources: Brookes and Barfoot 2020; Food and Agriculture Organization of the United Nations; Organisation for Economic Co-operation and Development; U.S. Department of Agriculture database, December 2021 update; World Bank (Commodity price database).
Note: EMDE = emerging market and developing economies; OECD = Organisation for Economic Co-operation and Development; RHS = right-hand side.
D. Data from FAO 2021. Data for 2020 are estimates.

Centrally planned economies

The Soviet Union nationalized agricultural production, marketing, and internal distribution in the 1930s. After WWII, it imposed a similar system on most Eastern European countries (with the exception of Poland, where small farmers retained control of their land). The two objectives of the centrally planned system were self-sufficiency and low costs of food for urban consumers. In sectors that could not achieve self-sufficiency, trade was undertaken with other centrally planned economies, with crude oil often used in the barter exchange.

These policies were not successful. Inefficient production and marketing systems could not produce adequate supplies to meet consumer demand at artificially low prices. Consumption was rationed because of severe shortages, ultimately forcing the Soviet Union and several Eastern European countries to import grains and meats in the early 1970s.

Large and erratic Soviet imports had a destabilizing effect on international commodity markets during the 1970s and 1980s. In 1975, the United States signed an agreement with the Soviet Union under which the latter agreed to import at least 6 million metric tons of grains annually. The Soviet Union also agreed not to exceed a maximum amount, although domestic U.S. policies prevented any upper limit from being enforced. In the early 1980s, in response to the Soviet invasion of Afghanistan, the United States imposed an embargo on grain exports to the Soviet Union, triggering a collapse of grain prices in the global market.

Although the Soviet Union was producing large amounts of wheat before 1990, it was an inefficient producer. It relied on imports in the 1980s for grains to feed its livestock sector, which was growing rapidly under the incentive of heavy subsidies.[24] The breakup of the Soviet Union in 1991, and the transition to market economies, led to a major liberalization of agriculture, the removal of livestock subsidies, and substantial improvements in productivity. Russia, along with Kazakhstan and Ukraine, became a key player in the global grain market.

Other centrally planned economies, notably China, began importing grains in the 1970s to offset domestic shortfalls. In the late 1970s, China began liberalizing its domestic commodity markets, albeit in a gradual manner. Initial reforms included the right to trade surplus production (Huang and Rozelle 2006). More reforms followed record production growth in the mid-1980s, including a reduction of production quotas (implying that farmers could sell more in open markets). New reforms were launched in the early 2000s, including the removal of all marketing restrictions and the elimination of government intervention in grain prices (Huang, Rozelle, and Chang 2004).

Agriculture policies of other EMDEs

Government intervention in agriculture in EMDEs has had multiple objectives. They include support for rural incomes, protection of domestic output (or self-sufficiency), maintenance of secure supplies, low prices of basic foods, and conservation of the environment. Managing the trade-offs between these objectives is a difficult task, fraught with political and social pitfalls. For reasons of economic efficiency, economists often advocate the replacement of distortionary subsidies and price controls with direct income supplements to farmers and low-income households. However, attempts to enact such proposals generally meet overwhelming opposition from interested parties (through regular political channels and through street demonstrations). Another

---

[24] During 1970-90, meat production in the Soviet Union increased by two-thirds, and by the end of this period its per capita meat consumption was on par with that of AEs (Liefert 2002).

challenge is that governments often do not have the administrative capacity to deliver individualized support payments to targeted households in countries where a large proportion of the population works in the informal sector (Ohnsorge, Okawa, and Yu 2021). In these circumstances, government welfare payments may not be a feasible alternative to subsidized price-controlled food, such as bread or flour provided to poor people from a government outlet.

Some EMDEs had adopted policies aimed at shifting resources from raw materials and agriculture to processing and manufacturing. This industrialization-focused approach was based on the observation that rising incomes tend to boost demand for manufactured goods and services while having noticeably less impact on demand for primary products. That, in turn, would have a negative impact on primary commodity prices relative to manufacturing goods (Kindleberger 1943; Prebisch 1950; Singer 1950; see also chapter 2). This view dominated the development agenda of the 1950s and 1960s and set the stage for the widespread industrialization policies pursued by low-income countries in the following decades. Import substitution, whereby domestic manufacturing is heavily protected from foreign competition, was a favored approach for promoting industrialization. At the same time, government parastatals assumed sole authority to manage all aspects of domestic commodity markets, including marketing, trade, provision of inputs, and exports—at considerable cost to these economies. Many EMDEs assumed large external debts to finance industrialization projects.

Numerous authors warned against such interventions from the outset. Johnson (1947) argued that the agricultural sector should not be subjected to interventions. Friedman (1954) disputed the benefits of managing income variability for agricultural producers. Johnston and Mellor (1961) criticized the pro-urban policies followed by many developing countries in pursuit of the industrialization agenda.

In the end, poor results undermined the arguments for industrialization and import-substitution policies, largely because programs were poorly conceived and managed. Government interventions in Africa have been found to amount to expropriation from agricultural producers for the benefit of urban populations (Bates 1981). More fundamentally, the strategic decisions of government planners were undone by the realities of world markets. Lal (1985) criticized the rigid approach to planning (where governments actively dictate economic decision-making) and advocated for more reliance on the price mechanism for allocating resources. The industrialization programs were ill-prepared to adapt to changes in technology and patterns of demand—or to the policy changes of foreign governments. Many authors highlighted the growing distortions associated with interventions in commodity markets (for example, Krueger, Schiff, and Valdès 1992; World Bank 1986). Through the commodities price boom of the 1970s, rising revenues and heavy borrowing kept programs afloat, but the bust of the early 1980s and the following EMDE debt crisis fully exposed their deficiencies.

On a practical level, international organizations pushed for market-oriented reforms as a condition of financial assistance. The World Bank introduced Structural Adjustment Loans in the early 1980s to assist EMDEs with debt issues caused by poor fiscal management. The associated conditions included reduced intervention by the state along with a reduction of subsidies and trade barriers. Some authors, however, have questioned the effectiveness of the adjustment programs (for example, Harrigan and Mosley 2007). Reappraisal of conditionality in World Bank and International Monetary Fund lending in the 2000s has led to less prescriptive programs, with more focus on results and the specific circumstances facing borrowing countries (Koeberle et al. 2005).

Conclusion

The chapter has reviewed developments in three commodity sectors—energy, metals, and agriculture—over the past century. It has looked at demand patterns, the impact of technology on supply, and the evolution of policy.

On the demand side, consumption of energy and metals has expanded more rapidly than world population and per capita income in recent decades. For agricultural commodities, demand has expanded at about the same pace, especially that of basic foodstuffs. Over the past half century, the location of demand growth for all commodities has shifted from AEs toward EMDEs, with a large shift in the consumption of primary products to China. Similarly, production of some commodities, especially refined metals, has also shifted to EMDEs. Technological improvements have taken place in all sectors, at varying rates, and with different effects both for consumption and production. The shale revolution, for example, upended oil and natural gas market dynamics in the 2010s. Among metals, innovation has led to widespread substitution (notably aluminum for other metals) and to the discovery and development of new reserves. In addition, the technology behind the energy transition will increasingly drive demand for metals. Spectacular increases in agricultural productivity followed the development of hybrid grains in the 1930s and the Green Revolution of the 1960s-70s. Advances in technology have also encouraged consumption via the creation of new products and thus new uses of commodities.

Commodity prices have always been volatile. Over the past half century, oil prices have seen large fluctuations following shifts in strategy by OPEC and the emergence of new sources of oil. Metals prices have seen prolonged cycles caused mainly by macroeconomic developments in the main consuming markets. Agricultural prices on the world market have followed a downward path in real terms, mostly because of the large increases in agricultural productivity. Volatility around the downtrend has been caused by geopolitical factors (such as intermittent grain purchases by the Soviet Union in the 1970s) and variations in harvests.

Policies at the national level have had multiple objectives, for example, stabilizing prices, protecting domestic industries, ensuring secure supplies, and raising rural incomes. Policy tools have included border policies (such as export subsidies, export or import bans, and tariffs) and internal policies (such as subsidies, taxes, and other types of support). Policies at the international level, such as international commodity agreements, have generally been directed toward stabilizing world markets and prices. They have included agreements to limit output, such as production quotas. In practice, however, policies have had distortionary and, in the long run, destabilizing effects on commodity markets. For example, in the oil market, the changing strategies of OPEC have caused steep jumps and drops in prices. And the long-run outcome of agricultural support programs, despite their intention, has generally been excess supplies and stockpiling, and heightened downward pressure on prices.

References

Akiyama, T., J. Baffes, D. F. Larson, and P. Varangis. 2003. "Commodity Market Reform in Africa: Some Recent Experience." *Economic Systems* 27 (1): 83-115.

Akiyama, T., and P. Varangis. 1990. "The Impact of the International Coffee Agreement on Producing Countries." *World Bank Economic Review* 4 (2): 157-73.

Alexander, P., C. Brown, A. Arneth, J. Finnigan, and M. D. A. Rounsevell. 2016. "Human Appropriation of Land for Food: The Role of Diet." *Global Environmental Change* 41 (November): 88-98.

Armstrong, R. 1859. *High-Speed Steam Navigation*. London: E. & N. F. Spon.

Astier, J. 2015. "Evolution of Iron Ore Prices." *Mineral Economics* 28: 3-9.

Baffes, J. 2005. "History of Cotton Trade: From History to the Twentieth Century." In *Cotton Trading Manual*, edited by the Secretariat of the International Cotton Advisory Committee. Cambridge, U.K.: Woodhead Publishing Limited.

Baffes, J. 2012. "How Africa Missed the Cotton Revolution." In *African Agricultural Reforms: The Role of Consensus and Institutions*, edited by M.A. Aksoy, 125-50. Washington, DC: World Bank.

Baffes, J., and H. de Gorter. 2005. "Experience with Decoupling Agricultural Support." In *Global Agricultural Trade and Developing Countries*, edited by M. A. Aksoy and J. C. Beghin, 75-90. Washington, DC: World Bank.

Baffes, J., and A. Kabundi. 2021. "Commodity Price Shocks: Order Within Chaos?" Policy Research Working Paper 9792, World Bank, Washington, DC.

Baffes, J., A. Kabundi, and P. Nagle. 2022. "The Role of Income and Substitution in Commodity Demand." *Oxford Economic Papers* 74 (2): 498-522.

Baffes, J., A. Kabundi, P. Nagle, and F. Ohnsorge. 2018. "The Role of Major Emerging Markets in Global Commodity Demand." Policy Research Working Paper 8495, World Bank, Washington, DC.

Baffes, J., and I. Kaltsas. 2004. "Cotton Futures Exchanges: Their Past, Their Present, and Their Future." *Quarterly Journal of International Agriculture* 43 (2): 153-76.

Baffes, J., A. Kose, F. Ohnsorge, and M. Stocker. 2015. "The Great Plunge in Oil Prices: Causes, Consequences, and Policy Responses." Policy Research Note 15/01, World Bank, Washington, DC.

Baffes, J., and J. Meerman. 1998. "From Prices to Incomes: Agricultural Subsidization without Protection?" *World Bank Research Observer* 13 (2): 191-211.

Baldwin, W. 1983. *The World Tin Market: Political Pricing and Economic Competition.* Durham, NC: Duke University Press.

Baranyai, L. 1959. "History of Commodity Agreements." Report No. EC-74b, World Bank, Washington, DC.

Barsky, R., C. Epstein, A. Lafont-Meuller, and Y. Yoo. 2021. "What Drives Gold Prices." *Chicago Fed Letter* 464, November 2021. https://www.chicagofed.org/publications/chicago-fed-letter/2021/464.

Bates, R. 1981. *Markets and States in Tropical Africa: The Political Basis of Agricultural Policies.* Berkeley, CA: University of California Press.

Baumeister, C., and L. Kilian. 2016. "Forty Years of Oil Price Fluctuations: Why the Price of Oil May Still Surprise Us." *Journal of Economic Perspectives* 30 (1): 139-60.

Baumeister, C., and G. Peersman. 2013. "The Role of Time-Varying Price Elasticities in Accounting for Volatility Changes in the Crude Oil Market." *Journal of Applied Econometrics* 28 (7): 1087-109.

Bertilorenzi, M. 2013. "From Patents to Stock Buffering Schemes: The Historical Evolution of the International Aluminum Cartels (1886-1945)." *Revue économique* 64 (6): 1145-69.

Bertilorenzi, M. 2016. *The International Aluminum Cartel 1886-1973.* Routledge: New York.

Birol, F., and D. Malpass. 2021. "It's Critical to Tackle Coal Emissions." *Voices* (blog), October 8, 2021. https://blogs.worldbank.org/voices/its-critical-tackle-coal-emissions.

Blau, G. 1946. "Wool in the World Economy." *Journal of the Royal Statistical Society* 109 (3): 179-242.

Boustan, L. P., D. Bunten, and O. Hearey. 2013. "Urbanization in the United States, 1800-2000." NBER Working Paper 19041, National Bureau of Economic Research, Cambridge, MA.

Bratter, H. M. 1938. "The Silver Episode: I." *Journal of Political Economy* 46 (5): 601-52.

Briggs, A. 1947. "The Framework of the Wool Control." *Oxford Economic Papers* 8 (November): 18-45.

Brookes, G., and P. Barfoot. 2020. *GM Crops: Global Socio-Economic and Environmental Impacts 1996-2020.* Dorchester, U.K.: PG Economics Ltd.

Carlton, D. W. 1984. "Futures Markets: Their Purpose, Their History, Their Growth, Their Successes and Failures." *Journal of Futures Markets* 4 (3): 237-71.

Chandra, V. 2020. "How Is Natural Gas Priced?" *Geo ExPro* 17 (6): 42-45.

Chandrasekhar, S. 1989. "Cartel in a Can: The Financial Collapse of the International Tin Council." *Northwestern Journal of International Law and Business* 10 (2): 308-32.

Chapoto, A., and T. S. Jayne. 2009. "Effects of Maize Marketing and Trade Policy on Price Unpredictability in Zambia." Food Security Collaborative Working Papers 54499, Michigan State University.

Clark, G., and D. Jacks. 2007. "Coal and the Industrial Revolution, 1700-1869." *European Review of Economic History* 11 (1): 39-72.

Clifton, E. V. 1985. "The Currency Futures Market and Interbank Foreign Exchange Trading." *Journal of Futures Markets* 5 (3): 375-85.

Cole, R. 1981. *The Japanese Automotive Industry. Model and Challenge for the Future?* Ann Arbor, MI: University of Michigan Center for Japanese Studies.

Colen, L., P. C. Melo, Y. Abdul-Salam, D. Roberts, S. Mary, and S. Gomez Y Paloma. 2018. "Income Elasticities for Food, Calories and Nutrients Across Africa: A Meta-Analysis." *Food Policy* 77 (May): 116-32.

Colombo, S., M. El Harrak, and N. Sartori. 2016. *The Future of Natural Gas: Markets and Geopolitics.* The Netherlands: Istituto Affari Internazionali, OCP Policy Center, and Lenthe Publishers/European Energy Review.

Cooper, R. and R. Lawrence. 1975. "The 1972-75 Commodity Boom." *Brookings Papers on Economic Activity* 6 (3): 671-724.

Cooper, R. N. 1982. "The Gold Standard: Historical Facts and Figures and Future Prospects." *Brookings Papers on Economic Activity* 1982 (1): 1-56.

Crow, J. F. 1998. "90 Years Ago: The Beginning of Hybrid Maize." *Genetics* 148 (1): 923-28.

Cuddington, J., and D. Jerrett. 2008. "Super Cycles in Real Metal Prices? *IMF Staff Papers* 55 (4): 541-65.

Davis, J. S. 1946. "Experience under Intergovernmental Commodity Agreements." *Journal of Political Economy* 54 (3): 193-220.

Dumbell, S. 1923. "Early Liverpool Cotton Imports and the Organization of the Cotton Markets in the Eighteenth Century." *Economic Journal* 33 (131): 363-73.

EIA (U.S. Energy Information Administration). 2012. "Crude Oils Have Different Quality Characteristics." *Today in Energy*, July 16, 2012. https://www.eia.gov/todayinenergy/detail.php?id=7110.

EIA (U.S. Energy Information Administration). 2014. "Global Natural Gas Markets Overview: A Report Prepared by Leidos, Inc., Under Contract to EIA." EIA Working Paper, U.S. Energy Information Administration, Washington, DC.

EIA (U.S. Energy Information Administration). 2018. "The United States Is Now the Largest Global Crude Oil Producer." *Today in Energy*, September 12, 2018. https://www.eia.gov/todayinenergy/detail.php?id=37053.

EIA (U.S. Energy Information Administration). 2020. "More Than 100 Coal-Fired Plants Have Been Replaced or Converted to Natural Gas since 2010." *Today in Energy*, August 5, 2020. https://www.eia.gov/todayinenergy/detail.php?id=44636.

EIA (U.S. Energy Information Administration). 2021. *Annual Coal Report 2020*. Washington, DC: U.S. Energy Information Administration.

Eichengreen, B., and M. Uzan. 1992. "The Marshall Plan: Economic Effects and Implications for Eastern Europe and USSR." *Economic Policy* 7 (14): 13-75.

Ellerman, A. 1995. "The World Price of Coal." *Energy Policy* 23 (6): 499-506.

EPA (U.S. Environmental Protection Agency). 2007. "Summary of the Energy Independence and Security Act; Public Law 110-140." U.S. Environmental Protection Agency, Washington, DC. https://www.epa.gov/laws-regulations/summary-energy-independence-and-security-act.

Erhlich, L. G. 2018. "What Drives Nickel Prices—A Structural VAR Approach." Research Paper 186, Hamburg Institute of International Economics.

Erten, B., and J. A. Ocampo. 2013. "Super Cycles of Commodity Prices since the Mid-nineteenth Century." *World Development* 44 (C): 14-30.

Evans, C., and O. Saunders. 2015. "A World of Copper: Globalizing the Industrial Revolution, 1830-70." *Journal of Global History* 10 (1): 3-26.

European Commission. 2009. "Directive 2009/73/EC of the European Parliament and of the Council of 13 July 2009 Concerning Common Rules for the Internal Market in Natural Gas and Repealing Directive 2003/55/EC." European Commission, Brussels.

European Parliament. 2009. "Directive 2009/28/EC of the European Parliament and of the Council of 23 April 2009, on the Promotion of the Use of Energy from Renewable Sources." European Commission, Brussels. https://eur-lex.europa.eu/legal-content/EN/TXT/?uri=CELEX%3A02009L0028-20151005.

Fakhri, M. 2011. "The 1937 International Sugar Agreement: Neo-Classical Cuba and Economic Aspects of the League of Nations." *Leiden Journal of International Law* 24 (4): 899-922.

FAO (Food and Agriculture Organization of the United Nations). 2021. *The State of Food Security and Nutrition in the World: Transforming Food Systems for Food Security. Improved Nutrition, and Affordable Healthy Diets for All*. Rome: FAO.

Friedman, M. 1954. "The Reduction of Fluctuations in the Incomes of Primary Producers: A Critical Comment." *Economic Journal* 64 (256): 698-703.

Friedman, M. 1992. "Franklin D. Roosevelt, Silver, and China." *Journal of Political Economy* 100 (1): 62-83.

Gamson, W. A., and A. Modigliani. 1989. "Media Discourse and Public Opinion on Nuclear Power: A Constructionist Approach." *American Journal of Sociology* 95 (1): 1-37.

Gardner, B. 1987. "Causes of Commodity Farm Programs." *Journal of Political Economy* 95 (2): 290-310.

Gately, D. 1986. "Lessons from the 1986 Oil Price Collapse." *Brookings Papers on Economic Activity* 2 (1986): 237-84.

George, M. W. 2012. *Metals Prices in the United States until 2010.* Reston, VA: U.S. Geological Survey.

Gibson-Jarvie, R. 1983. *The London Metal Exchange: A Commodity Market.* Cambridge, U.K.: Woodhead-Faulkner.

Gilbert, C. L. 1996. "International Commodity Agreements: An Obituary." *World Development* 24 (1): 1-19.

Gilbert, C. L. 2011. "International Agreements for Commodity Price Stabilization: An Assessment." OECD Food, Agriculture and Fisheries Paper 53, Organisation for Economic Co-operation and Development, Paris.

Glauber, J., and V. Smith. 2021. "Trends in Agricultural Policy since 2000 and Implications for the Next Twenty Years." *EuroChoices* 20 (2): 58-63.

Glesinger, E. 1945. "Forest Products and the World Economy." *American Economic Review, Papers and Proceedings* 35 (2): 120-29.

Goss, B. A., and B. S. Yamey. 1978. *The Economics of Futures Trading: Readings Selected, Edited and Introduced.* London: Macmillan Press.

Grilli, E. R., B. B. Agostini, and M. J. Hooft-Welvaars. 1980. *The World Rubber Economy: Structure, Changes, and Prospects.* Baltimore, MD: John Hopkins University Press.

Guzmán, J. I. 2018. "The International Copper Cartel, 1935–1939: The Good Cartel?" *Miner Econ* 31 (1): 113-25.

Hagelberg, G. B., and A. C. Hannah. 1994. "The Quest for Order: A Review of International Sugar Agreement." *Food Policy* 19 (1): 17-29.

Hamilton, J. 2009. "Causes and Consequences of the Oil Shock of 2007-08." NBER Working Paper 15002, National Bureau of Economic Research, Cambridge, MA.

Hamilton, J. 2010. "Historical Oil Shocks." In *Routledge Handbook of Major Events in Economic History*, edited by R. E. Parker and R. Whaples. New York: Routledge Taylor and Francis Group.

Harrigan, J., and P. Mosley. 2007. "Evaluating the Impact of World Bank Structural Adjustment Lending: 1980-87." *Journal of Development Studies* 27 (3): 63-94.

Heap, A. 2005. "China—The Engine of a Commodities Super Cycle." Citigroup Global Markets.

Herfindahl, O. 1959. *Copper Costs and Prices: 1870-1957.* Baltimore, MD: John Hopkins University Press.

Hieronymus, T. A. 1977. *Economics of Futures Trading for Commercial and Personal Profit.* New York: Commodity Research Bureau.

Honma, M., and Y. Hayami. 1988. "In Search of Agricultural Policy Reform in Japan." *European Review of Agricultural Economics* 15 (4): 367-95.

Huang, J., and S. Rozelle. 2006. "The Emergence of Agricultural Commodity Markets in China." *China Economic Review* 17 (2006): 266-80.

Huang, J., S. Rozelle, and M. Chang. 2004. "The Nature of Distortions to Agricultural Incentives in China and Implications of WTO Accession." *World Bank Economic Review* 18 (1): 59-84.

Hutchinson, L. 1909. "Coffee 'Valorization' in Brazil." *Quarterly Journal of Economics* 23 (3): 528-35.

ICE (Intercontinental Exchange). 2021. *Global Crude Benchmarks: Brent Sets the Standard.* Atlanta, GA: Intercontinental Exchange.

IEA (International Energy Agency). 1979. "Principles for IEA Action on Coal: Decision on Procedures for Review of IEA Countries' Coal Policies." Press release, International Energy Agency, Paris.

IEA (International Energy Agency). 2013. "Developing a Natural Gas Trading Hub in Asia." IEA Country Report, International Energy Agency, Paris.

IEA (International Energy Agency). 2019. "The Role of Gas in Today's Energy Transitions." *World Energy Outlook* special report, International Energy Agency, Paris.

IEA (International Energy Agency). 2021a. "Gas Market Report: Q1 2021." International Energy Agency, Paris.

IEA (International Energy Agency). 2021b. *Net Zero by 2050. A Roadmap for the Global Energy Sector.* Paris: International Energy Agency.

IFC (International Finance Corporation). 2019. "Natural Gas and the Clean Energy Transition." EM Compass Note 65, International Finance Corporation, Washington, DC.

Ilkenberry, G. 1988. *Reasons of State: Oil Politics and the Capacities of American Government.* Ithaca, NY: Cornell University Press.

IMF (International Monetary Fund). 2015. *World Economic Outlook: Adjusting to Lower Commodity Prices.* October. Washington, DC: International Monetary Fund.

IRENA (International Renewable Energy Agency). 2020. *Renewable Power Generation Costs in 2019.* Abu Dhabi: International Renewable Energy Agency.

Irwin, D. 1998. "The Smoot-Hawley Tariff: A Quantitative Assessment." *Review of Economics and Statistics* 80 (2): 326-32.

Irwin, D. A. 2012. *Trade Policy Disaster: Lessons from the 1930s.* Cambridge, MA: MIT Press.

Ivanic, M., and W. Martin. 2008. "Implications of Higher Global Food Prices for Poverty in Low-Income Countries." Policy Research Working Paper 4594, World Bank, Washington, DC.

Ivanic, M., and W. Martin. 2014. "Implications of Domestic Price Insulation for Global Food Price Behavior." *Journal of International Money and Finance* 42 (1): 272-88.

Jacks, D. 2013. "From Boom to Bust: A Typology of Real Commodity Prices in the Long Run." NBER Working Paper 18874, National Bureau of Economic Research, Cambridge, MA.

Jacks, D. S., and M. Stuermer. 2021. "Dry Bulk Shipping and the Evolution of Maritime Transport Costs, 1850-2020." *Australian Economic History Review* 61 (2): 204-27.

Jarvis, S., O. Deschenes, and A. Jha. 2019. "The Private and External Costs of Germany's Nuclear Phase-Out." NBER Working Paper 26598, National Bureau of Economic Research, Cambridge, MA.

Johnson, D. G. 1947. *Forward Prices for Agriculture.* Chicago: University of Chicago Press.

Johnston, B., and J. Mellor 1961. "The Role of Agriculture in Economic Development." *American Economic Review* 51 (4): 566-93.

Kabundi, A., and F. Ohnsorge. 2020. "Implications of Cheap Oil for Emerging Markets." Policy Research Working Paper 9403, World Bank, Washington, DC.

Kaufmann, R. K., S. Dees, P. Karadeloglou, and M. Sanchez. 2004. "Does OPEC Matter? An Econometric Analysis of Oil Prices." *Energy Journal* 25 (4): 67-90.

Kearney, J. 2010. "Food Consumption Trends and Drivers." *Philosophical Transactions of the Royal Society B* 365: 2793-807.

Khan, T., T. Nguyen, F. Ohnsorge, and R. Schodde. 2016. "From Commodity Discovery to Production." Policy Research Working Paper 7823, World Bank, Washington, DC.

Kilian, L. 2009. "Not All Oil Price Shocks Are Alike: Disentangling Demand and Supply Shocks in the Crude Oil Market." *American Economic Review* 99 (3): 1053-69.

Kilian, L. 2020. "Understanding the Estimation of Oil Demand and Oil Supply Elasticities." CESifo Working Paper 8567, Center for Economic Studies, Munich.

Kilian, L., and D. Murphy. 2014. "The Role of Inventories and Speculative Trading in the Global Market for Crude Oil." *Journal of Applied Econometrics* 29 (3): 454-78.

Kindleberger, C. P. 1943. "Planning for Foreign Investment." *American Economic Review* 33 (1): 347-54.

Koeberle, S., H. Bedoya, P. Silarszky, and G. Verheyen, eds. 2005. *Conditionality Revisited: Concepts, Experiences, and Lessons.* Washington, DC: World Bank.

Kooroshy, J, and F. Preston. 2014. "Cartels and Competition in Mineral Markets: Challenges for Global Governance." Chatham House, London.

Krasner, S. D. 1973. "Manipulating International Coffee Markets: Brazilian Coffee Policy 1906 to 1962." *Public Policy* 21 (4): 493-523.

Krueger, A. O. 1964. "The Political Economy of the Rent Seeking Society." *American Economic Review* 64 (3): 291-303.

Krueger, A. O., M. Schiff, and A. Valdès. 1992. *The Political Economy of Agricultural Pricing Policy*. Baltimore, MD: Johns Hopkins University Press.

Kuck, P. 1999. *Metals Prices in the United States through 1998*. Reston, VA: U.S. Geological Survey.

Laborde, D., C. Lakatos, and W. Martin. 2019. "Poverty Impact of Food Price Shocks and Policies." In *Inflation in Emerging and Developing Economies—Evolution, Drivers, and Policies*, edited by Jongrim Ha, M. Ayhan Kose, and Franziska Ohnsorge, 371-401. Washington, DC: World Bank Group.

Lagos, G. 2018. "Mining Nationalization and Privatization in Peru and in Chile." *Miner Econ* 31: 127-39.

Lal, D. 1985. *The Poverty of Development Economics*. Cambridge, MA: Harvard University Press.

Lemon, C. 1838. "The Statistics of the Copper Mines of Cornwall." *Journal of the Statistical Society of London* 1 (2): 65-84.

Levinson, M. 2016. *The Box: How the Shipping Container Made the World Smaller and the World Economy Bigger, Second Edition*. Princeton, NJ: Princeton University Press.

Liefert, W. M. 2002. "Comparative (Dis?)Advantage in Russian Agriculture." *American Journal of Agricultural Economics* 84 (3): 762-67.

Liu, B., and H. Geman. 2017. "World Coal Markets: Still Weakly Integrated and Moving East." *Journal of Commodity Markets* 5 (March): 63-76.

Lundgren, N. 1996. "Bulk Trade and Maritime Transport Costs: The Evolution of Global Markets." *Resources Policy* 22 (1-2): 5-32.

Mallory, I. A. 1990. "Conduct Unbecoming: The Collapse of the International Tin Agreement." *American University International Law Review* 5 (3): 835-92.

Markham, J. W. 1987. *The History of Commodity Futures Trading and Its Regulation*. New York: Praeger Publishers.

McNally, R. 2017. *Crude Volatility: The History and the Future of Boom-Bust Oil Prices*. New York: Columbia University Press.

Meltzer, A. H. 1991. "U.S. Policy in the Bretton Woods Era." *Federal Reserve Bank of St. Louis Review* 73 (3): 53-83.

Mitchell, B. 1988. *British Historical Statistics.* New York: Cambridge University Press.

Mueller, M., and D. Gorin. 1985. "Informative Trends in Natural Resource Commodity Prices: A Comment on Slade." *Journal of Environmental Economics and Management* 12 (1): 89-95.

Nakano, J. 2016. "The Evolution of Japan's LNG Strategies and Their Geopolitical Implications." In *The Future of Natural Gas: Markets and Geopolitics,* edited by Silvia Colombo, Mohamed El Harrak, and Nicolò Sartori. Houboerweg, the Netherlands: Lenthe/ European Energy Review.

Nappi, C. 2013. *The Global Aluminium Industry: 40 Years from 1972.* London: International Aluminium Institute.

Ohnsorge, F., Y. Okawa, and S. Yu. 2021. "Lagging Behind: Informality and Development." In *The Long Shadow of Informality: Challenges and Policies,* edited by F. Ohnsorge and S. Yu, 125-202. Washington, DC: World Bank.

OPEC (Organization of the Petroleum Exporting Countries). 2014. "OPEC Monthly Oil Market Report." Organization of the Petroleum Exporting Countries, Vienna.

Paulus, M. 2012. "The Economics of International Coal Markets." PhD dissertation, University of Cologne. http://inis.iaea.org/search/search.aspx?orig_q=RN:46021454.

Pettigrew, J. and B. Richardson. 2013. *A Social History of Tea: Tea's Influence on Commerce, Culture Community.* Danville, KY: Benjamin Press.

Prebisch, R. 1950. *The Economic Development of Latin America and Its Principal Problems.* New York: United Nations.

Prest, M. 1986. "The Collapse of the International Tin Agreement." *IDS Bulletin* 17 (4): 1-8.

Qaim, M. 2009. "The Economics of Genetically Modified Crops." *Annual Reviews of Resource Economics* 1: 665-93.

Qaim, M., and D. Zilberman. 2003. "Yields Effects of Genetically Modified Crops in Developing Countries." *Science* 299 (5608): 900-2.

Radetzki, M. 2006. "The Anatomy of Three Commodity Booms." *Resources Policy* 31(1): 56-64.

Radetzki, M. 2009. "Seven Thousand Years in the Service of Humanity—The History of Copper, the Red Metal." *Resources Policy* 34 (December): 176-84.

Radetzki, M., and L. Wårell. 2016. *A Handbook of Primary Commodities in the Global Economy.* Cambridge, U.K.: Cambridge University Press.

Reardon, T., D. Tschirley, L. S. O. Liverpool-Tasie, T. Awokuse, J. Fanzo, B. Minten, R. Vos, et al. 2021. "The Processed Food Revolution in African Food Systems and the Double Burden of Malnutrition." *Global Food Security* 28 (March): 100466.

Roberts, T. J. 1951. "A Study of International Commodity Agreements." Master's thesis, University of British Columbia, Canada.

Schaede, U. 1989. "Forwards and Futures in Tokugawa-Period Japan: A New Perspective on the Dōjima Rice Market." *Journal of Banking and Finance* 13 (September): 487-513.

Schmitz, C. 1979. *World Non-Ferrous Metal Production and Prices 1700-1976.* London: Frank Cass.

Scott, R. 1994. *The History of the International Energy Agency. Volume Two. Major Policies and Actions.* Paris: International Energy Agency.

Shibata, H. 1982. "The Energy Crises and Japanese Response." *Resources and Energy* 5 (2): 129-54.

Singer, H. W. 1950. "The Distribution of Gains between Investing and Borrowing Countries." *American Economic Review* 40 (2): 473-85.

Sjostrom, W. 2004. "Ocean Shipping Cartels: A Survey." *Review of Network Economics* 3 (2): 107-34.

Slade, M. E. 2020. "Vertical Restraints Imposed by Buyers: The Secrétan Copper Cartel, 1887–1889." *Antitrust Law Journal* 83 (1): 75-97.

Smil, V. 2002. "Worldwide Transformation of Diets, Burdens of Meat Production and Opportunities for Novel Food Proteins." *Enzyme and Microbial Technology* 30 (3): 305-11.

Smil, V. 2017. *Energy and Civilization. A History.* Cambridge: MIT Press.

Smith, G. 1999. "Lead." In *Metal Prices in the United States through 1998,* edited by P. A. Plunkert and T. S. Jones. Reston, VA: U.S. Geological Survey.

Stern, J., and A. Imsirovic. 2020. "A Comparative History of Oil and Gas Markets and Prices: Is 2020 Just an Extreme Cyclical Event or an Acceleration of the Energy Transition?" Energy Insight 68, Oxford Institute for Energy Studies.

Storli, E. 2014. "Cartel Theory and Cartel Practice: The Case of the International Aluminum Cartels, 1901-1940." *Business History Review* 88 (3): 445-67.

Stringham, E. 2003. "The Extralegal Development of Securities Trading in Seventeenth-Century Amsterdam." *Quarterly Review of Economics and Finance* 43 (2): 321-44.

Stuermer, M. 2017. "Industrialization and the Demand for Mineral Commodities." *Journal of International Money and Finance* 76 (September): 16-27.

Stuermer, M. 2018. "150 Years of Boom and Bust: What Drives Mineral Commodity Prices?" *Macroeconomic Dynamics* 22 (3): 702-17.

Swerling, B. C. 1968. "Commodity Agreements." In *International Encyclopedia of the Social Sciences,* edited by D. L. Sills. New York: Macmillan Co. and Free Press.

Tamvakis, M. 2018. "From Chicago to Shanghai and Dalian: Apprehending the Future of Chinese Commodity Derivative Markets." In *The Financialization of Commodity Markets: A Short-Lived Phenomenon*, edited by Y. Jegourel. Ramat, Morocco: OCP Policy Center.

Thoburn, J. 1994. *Tin in the World Economy*. Edinburgh, U.K.: Edinburgh University Press.

Tolcin, A. C. 2012. *Metals Prices in the United States through 2010. Zinc.* Reston, VA: U.S. Geological Survey.

Tsokhas, K. 1993. "British Economic Warfare in the Far East and the Australian Wool Industry." *Agricultural History Review* 41 (1): 44-59.

Tsou, S. S., and J. D. Black. 1944. "International Commodity Arrangements." *Quarterly Journal of Economics* 58 (4): 521-52.

Tyers, R., and K. Anderson. 1992. *Disarray in World Food Markets: A Quantitative Assessment.* Cambridge, U.K.: Cambridge University Press.

UNCTAD (United Nations Conference on Trade and Development). 2017. "Using Trade Policy to Drive Value Addition: Lessons from Indonesia's Ban on Nickel Exports." United Nations, Geneva.

USDA (United States Department of Agriculture). 2019. *Crop Production Historical Track Records.* April. Washington, DC: USDA.

Vale. 2012. *Vale: Our History.* Rio de Janeiro: Vale. http://www.vale.com/en/aboutvale/book -our-history/pages/default.aspx.

Verico, K. 2013. "Economic Cooperation in Natural Rubber: The Impacts on Natural Rubber's World Supply and Indonesia's Economy." *Asian Journal of Agriculture and Development* 10 (2): 1-19.

Walters, A. 1944. "The International Copper Cartel." *Southern Economic Journal* 11 (2): 133-56.

Wårell, L. 2005. "Defining Geographic Coal Markets Using Price Data and Shipments Data." *Energy Policy* 33 (17): 2216-30.

Wickizer, V.D. 1943. *The World Coffee Economy with Special Reference to Control Schemes.* Palo Alto, CA: Stanford University Press.

Williams, J. C. 1982. "The Origin of Futures Markets." *Agricultural History* 56 (1): 306-16.

Williams, J. 1986. *The Economic Function of Futures Markets.* Cambridge MA: Harvard University Press.

World Bank 1986. *The World Development Report: Trade and Pricing Policies in World Agriculture.* New York: Oxford University Press.

World Bank. 2000. *Global Commodity Markets. A Comprehensive Review and Price Forecast.* Washington, DC: World Bank.

World Bank. 2018. *Global Economic Prospects: The Turning of the Tide?* June. Washington, DC: World Bank.

World Bank. 2019a. *Commodity Markets Outlook: The Role of Substitution in Commodity Demand.* October. Washington, DC: World Bank.

World Bank. 2019b. *Commodity Markets Outlook: Food Price Shocks: Channels and Implications.* April. Washington, DC: World Bank.

World Bank. 2020. *Commodity Markets Outlook: Implications of COVID-19 for Commodities.* April. Washington, DC: World Bank.

World Bank. 2021. *Commodity Markets Outlook: Urbanization and Commodity Demand.* October. Washington, DC: World Bank.

World Bank. 2022. *Commodity Markets Outlook: The Impact of the War in Ukraine on Global Commodity Markets.* April. Washington, DC: World Bank.

Yang, J., and Y. Zhou. 2020. "Return and Volatility Transmission between China's and International Crude Oil Futures Markets: A First Look." *Journal of Futures Markets* 40 (6): 860-84.

Zaklan, A., A. Cullmann, A. Neumann, and von Hirschhausen, C. 2012. "The Globalization of Steam Coal Markets and the Role of Logistics: An Empirical Analysis." *Energy Economics* 34 (1): 105-16.

CHAPTER 2
Commodity Demand: Drivers, Outlook, and Implications

John Baffes and Peter Nagle

Commodity consumption has surged over the past half century. Metal commodities led the way, their consumption rising fourfold between 1970 and 2019, followed by a threefold increase in consumption of energy and agricultural commodities. Key drivers of this growth have been income and population growth, with demand for metals the most responsive to rising income. Technological innovations have heavily influenced the commodity intensity of output by boosting efficiency in the consumption and production of commodities. Government policies, through taxes, subsidies, and regulation, have also had strong effects. These factors, along with changes in relative prices reflecting the relative scarcity of resources, affect the composition of demand as well as the total. Over the decades ahead, the energy transition is expected to be a primary driver of substitution among commodity groups. The switch to low-carbon sources of energy is anticipated to reduce consumption of hydrocarbons but increase consumption of the metals used to produce clean energy, such as copper.

Introduction

Global consumption of natural resource-based commodities has seen a substantial increase over the past half century, but at significantly varying speeds across the major commodity groups. Consumption of base metals rose more than fourfold from 23 million metric tons in 1970 to 107 million metric tons in 2019—a growth similar to that of global gross domestic product, or GDP (figure 2.1). Consumption of energy materials nearly tripled over the same period, from just over 200 exajoules to 580 exajoules, as did consumption of food commodities. Aluminum experienced the fastest growth of the base metals, rising more than sixfold because of its increasing use as a substitute for other metals, particularly in the transportation industry (Chen and Graedel 2012). Among energy commodities, natural gas consumption rose fourfold, thanks to its clean-burning properties relative to crude oil and coal. Among food commodities, the sharpest increases were for inputs to processed consumer products, animal feed, and biofuels, with consumption of edible oils rising eightfold and corn fourfold. Consumption of other grains doubled, broadly in line with the increase in world population over the past 50 years.

The speed of these increases has varied over time. After rapid growth in the 1960s and 1970s, commodity demand slowed sharply in the 1980s-90s, before picking up again in the 2000s. The post-2000 demand surge was driven by strong growth in emerging market and developing economies (EMDEs), most notably China. China's exceptionally rapid economic growth, focused on commodity-intensive manufacturing and investment, raised the country's share of world metal consumption to 50 percent in 2019, up from 10 percent two decades earlier (figure 2.2; World Bank 2018a, 2018b).

FIGURE 2.1 **Changes in commodity demand**

Commodity demand has surged over the past 50 years. Demand for metals has grown particularly rapidly with more than a fourfold increase, similar to GDP growth. Energy and agricultural demand tripled, slightly faster than the increase in global population. Among individual commodities, natural gas has seen the fastest growth of the energy commodities, aluminum has seen the fastest growth among metals, and soybeans have seen the fastest growth among agricultural commodities.

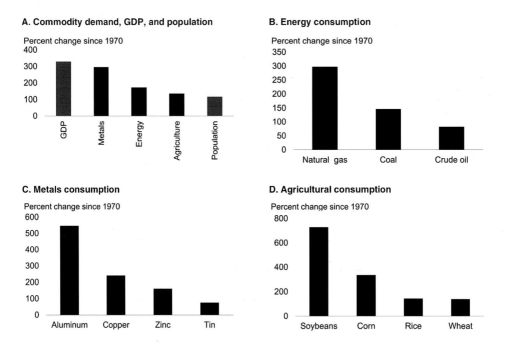

A. Commodity demand, GDP, and population

B. Energy consumption

C. Metals consumption

D. Agricultural consumption

Sources: BP Statistical Review of World Energy 2021; U.S. Department of Agriculture; World Bureau of Metals Statistics; World Bank.
Note: Panels show change in commodity demand, GDP, and population between 1970 and 2020.

Although commodity consumption also rose strongly in other EMDEs, their share of global consumption remained relatively constant.

Understanding the causes of variations in the long-term growth in commodity demand is of critical importance for the economic prospects of EMDE commodity exporters. Knowing how key drivers—such as population growth, income growth, technology, or policies—shape long-term trends is a first step in making projections of future commodity demand growth. For commodity exporters, this crucial input aids in projecting future fiscal and export revenue. For commodity importers, it can inform estimates of future resource needs, which in turn can help safeguard energy and food security. Long-term dependence on resource-based sectors can leave a country vulnerable to external shocks to the terms of trade. The scale and nature of resource extraction also have strong environmental implications.

The current outlook for commodity demand has an unusually large and unpredictable component. Transformative change is on the horizon because of the energy transition.

FIGURE 2.2 **Changing shares of consumption of industrial commodities**

Between 1997 and 2017, China's share of global GDP tripled, while its share of population shrank 10 percent. At the same time, its share of oil consumption doubled, and its share of metals consumption rose fivefold to about 50 percent. In contrast, although India's share of global GDP doubled, its share of consumption of all major industrial commodities increased more slowly. The increase in China's share of global commodity consumption came about primarily because consumption fell in advanced economies, with a particularly steep fall in their share of metal consumption.

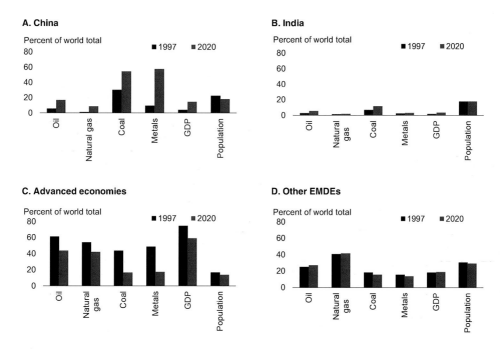

Sources: BP Statistical Review of World Energy 2021; U.S. Department of Agriculture; World Bank; World Bureau of Metals Statistics.
A.-D. Sample of countries included in this figure collectively accounted for 97 percent of global GDP and 83 percent of global population in 2017. Because of data limitations fewer countries are available for metals demand.
C. Advanced economies contains 29 countries for all categories except metals, which contains 27 countries.
D. Panel shows data for 33 EMDEs for all categories except metals, for which it shows data for 29 EMDEs. EMDE = emerging market and developing economy.

Clean energy technology and related industrial innovation are advancing at a rapid rate, including cost reductions in generating electricity from renewable resources, battery storage, and electric vehicles. Policies strongly encouraged these changes, with governments and international institutions announcing measures to mitigate the impact of climate change as well as other environmental issues related to the consumption and production of commodities.

Against this backdrop of accelerated innovation, and the likelihood of fundamental changes in commodity use, this chapter addresses the following questions:

- What have been the historical determinants of commodity demand?

- How does commodity demand evolve quantitatively as economies develop?

• What are the prospects for global commodity demand, and what are the implications for policy makers?

Contribution to the literature. This chapter presents estimates of income elasticities of demand for the energy, metals, and food commodity groups. It builds on the research in Baffes, Kabundi, and Nagle (2022), which estimates income elasticities of demand for the individual commodities within each of these sectors. The results reported in this chapter control for the presence of long-term substitutions between commodity groups, in both production and consumption. The use of a common framework facilitates a comparison of income elasticities across commodity groups. Previous studies have typically focused more narrowly on a single commodity group, with much of the literature focusing on energy.

The chapter uses a methodology that enables the estimation of income-varying elasticities of demand, in contrast to most previous studies that for a given commodity provide estimates of linear income elasticities, uniform across all levels of per capita income. Calculating nonlinear elasticities of demand enables an analysis of how commodity demand changes at different stages of economic development.

Main findings. This chapter has three main findings. First, population and income growth are the two primary drivers of aggregate commodity demand in the long run. Whereas income is a key driver of growth for metals and energy, it is less important for food commodities, which tend to be driven chiefly by population growth. Other factors, including relative prices, technology, substitutions from one commodity group to another, and government policies, are also important drivers of demand growth. These factors can lead to changes in the intensity of commodity demand for a given level of per capita income, as well as changes in the relative importance of individual commodities.

Second, per capita income elasticities of demand vary significantly between commodity groups. Base metals have the highest income elasticity of demand, followed by energy. The lowest income elasticity is for food. Growth in metals consumption over the past 50 years has closely tracked growth in income (reflecting growth in both population and GDP per capita), whereas growth in food consumption has more closely followed population growth, particularly for grains. In addition, income elasticities vary with per capita income levels. At low levels of income, elasticities of demand for commodities are high (in some cases well above unity). As per capita income levels rise, the marginal income elasticities fall. At high levels, the marginal elasticities may go to zero, or even negative, reflecting shifts in consumption patterns toward goods with high-value-added content, and toward services, as per capita incomes rise. This decline was larger for metals and energy than for agriculture; however, because the starting elasticity for metal was high, it remains the most income elastic component of commodity demand.

Third, overall commodity demand is likely to continue to increase in the years ahead, but at a slower rate than over the past two decades. This slower pace is due to slower anticipated population and income growth, as well economic changes, such as China's shift toward a more service- and consumer-based economy. Demand for individual commodities could see transformative substitutions because of innovations and policy-driven initiatives to mitigate climate change. The energy transition is likely to feature a wave of disruptive change that will cause large, permanent changes in the demand for commodities. A shift to low-carbon sources of energy is expected to raise demand for metals used for clean energy (such as copper), and much reduce the consumption of fossil fuels.

The rest of this chapter is structured as follows. The next section presents a historical description of trends in the key drivers of commodity demand—population, income levels, and commodity intensity (that is, changes in the efficiency of commodity consumption and production due to innovation). The third section presents empirical estimates of income elasticities of demand for the three sectors: metals, energy, and food, and considers the prospects for future commodity demand growth, based on expected income and population trends. The final section offers some policy implications. Boxes investigate the relationship between urbanization and commodity demand, and some notable historical examples of commodity substitution.

Classifying the determinants of commodity demand

Population and income growth, and technological progress, have been fundamental drivers of demand for commodities. Innovations in production have often caused large-scale substitutions from one commodity to another. They have also led to changes in the commodity intensity of output—that is, commodity consumption per unit of GDP.

Commodity demand, C_t, can be expressed as the following identity:

$$C_t = (pop_t) * \left(\frac{Y_t}{pop_t} \right) * \left(\frac{C_t}{Y_t} \right), \tag{2.1}$$

where pop_t and Y_t denote population and income at time t. The three factors included in the parentheses—population, per capita income, and commodity intensity—are inter-related. For example, as countries get wealthier, demand tends to shift from goods that are intensive in commodities toward products with a higher component of value added, notably services. With economic development, GDP per capita increases, and output becomes less commodity intensive over time. The three subsections that follow describe historical trends in the way each of these factors has affected commodity demand.

Population

Demographics have been a key driver of commodity demand over the past 50 years. Commodity consumption at the global level is directly linked to the size of the global population. Basic material needs, such as food, clothing, shelter, and heat, are an important part of this link, as are other material wants. Agricultural commodities provide food, clothing, and other raw materials; metals and minerals are essential components of shelter; and energy commodities fuel transportation, heating, and lighting. In addition to material needs, people have material wants for goods and services for which resource-based commodities are essential inputs (for example, beverage crops such as coffee, precious metals for jewelry, and energy use in leisure activities such as flying). If each additional person has a similar consumption pattern to the existing population, an increase in population leads to a proportional in commodity demand, as per the identity in equation (2.1).

Over the past 50 years, the global population has more than doubled, from 3.7 billion people in 1970 to 7.8 billion people in 2020. The rate of population growth in percentage terms has gradually slowed, from almost 2 percent per year in the 1970s to just over 1 percent in the 2010s (the increase in the absolute number of population has remained stable, at almost 80 million people per year).

However, demand for commodities has not grown at the same rate as population. One reason is that per capita commodity demand varies significantly between countries. For example, whereas per capita energy consumption at the global level averaged 75 gigajoules in 2019, it averaged 173 gigajoules in advanced economies (AEs) and only 55 gigajoules in EMDEs. For metals, differences between AEs and EMDEs were less striking, largely because of China's high per capita metal consumption. Across individual countries, differences are more stark. For example, per capita energy and metal consumption in 2019 were approximately 10 times higher in the United States than in India (figure 2.3). Differences in agricultural consumption are less marked, with U.S. consumption roughly two-and-a-half times higher than in India.

An associated reason for the change in global per capita consumption in commodities over the past 50 years is the unevenness of population growth. Most of the increase in population has occurred in countries with per capita commodity consumption levels below the global average. Since 1970, EMDEs have accounted for 77 percent of growth, with 14 percent from low-income countries and less than 10 percent from AEs. As a result of rich countries' declining share of the global population, the increase in commodity demand due to population growth has been less than global demographics might imply.

This point can be illustrated with a simple, if counterfactual, numerical scenario. Suppose that per capita commodity consumption for each country remains at the 1970 level. Consumption in each country then grows at a rate equal to its specific population growth rate. Under this stylized scenario, although world population more than doubled between 1970 and 2019, global energy demand would have increased by just 55 percent, and metal demand by 44 percent. The increase in commodity consumption due to population growth is smaller than the actual increase in population growth because much of it happened in countries with below-average per capita commodity consumption. In contrast, the increase in food consumption under the scenario is 84 percent, far closer to population growth, because of the relatively small difference in per capita food consumption between AEs and EMDEs.

This numerical exercise assumes, counterfactually, that commodity demand per capita remains constant. In fact, it has increased significantly over the past 50 years in many countries. This change does not invalidate the relevance of the scenario as an illustration

FIGURE 2.3 **Population and commodity demand**

Global per capita consumption of commodities has risen over the past 50 years, driven by an increase among EMDEs. Among advanced economies, per capita commodity consumption has fallen slightly, although consumption levels are still much higher. Agricultural consumption has changed less, with smaller disparities in consumption between advanced economies and EMDEs. Although global population increased by about 80 million people per year in the past 50 years, growth is expected to slow over the next 50 and will be increasingly driven by low-income countries.

A. Energy consumption per capita

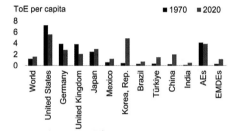

B. Metal consumption per capita

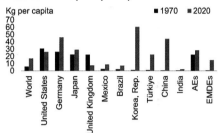

C. Agricultural consumption per capita

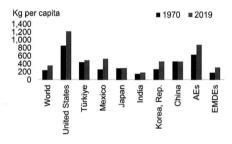

D. Global population growth forecasts, by income group

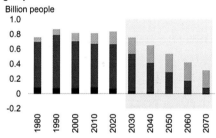

Sources: BP Statistical Review of World Energy 2021; World Bank; World Bureau of Metals Statistics.
Note: Energy includes oil, natural gas and coal. Metals include aluminum, copper, and zinc. AE = advanced economy; EMDE = emerging market and developing economy; kg = kilogram; ToE = tonnes of oil equivalent.

of the important effect of differences across countries on the growth of global demand. However, it does indicate that the two factors other than population in equation (2.1)— per capita income and the intensity of commodity demand—must also have had a sizable impact. These factors are investigated in the next two parts of this section.

Per capita income

The relationship between economic development and commodity demand is, on the surface, straightforward: as people's incomes rise, their material demands increase.[1] For example, in the case of transportation, as people get wealthier, they shift from

---

[1] Early studies on the relationship between income and commodity consumption such as the declining terms of trade hypothesis implicitly assumed that the relationship was stable over time and invariant across commodities and countries (Prebisch 1950; Singer 1950).

predominantly muscle-powered transportation such as walking, cycling, or animal transport, toward motorized forms of travel, such as cars and trains. In addition, they travel more for pleasure, notably by sea and air (Parikh and Shukla 1995). This shift leads to greater material consumption, including metals (for making vehicles), and energy commodities (especially crude oil in the past half century). Similarly, as incomes rise people use more space, including larger houses, which is associated with the use of more resources, including construction material and energy to heat, cool, and light the larger space, and to fuel transportation for commuting and shopping in less densely built locations (Brounen, Kok, and Quigley 2012; Liu et al. 2003).

The relationship between per capita income growth and commodity demand is non-linear.[2] The relationship has been estimated to follow an inverse U or an S shape, with demand for commodities initially growing rapidly at low levels of income, and then plateauing or even declining at higher income levels. Four factors account for this pattern: the evolution of an economy's production and consumption as it develops, differences in sectoral growth patterns across countries, urbanization, and improvements in technology and efficiency. The rest of this subsection explores these factors.

Per capita GDP at the global level rose from just under US$5,000 in 1970 to US$11,000 in 2019 (in constant-value, 2019 dollars). In EMDEs, per capita GDP quadrupled from US$1,200 to nearly US$5,000, an average annual growth rate of 3 percent. Per capita GDP growth was particularly rapid in China, where it increased from less than US$300 in 1970 to more than US$10,000 in 2020, an average annual growth rate of 7.7 percent. Because the majority of rapid economic growth occurred in countries with low levels of per capita income, that growth led to an overall increase in commodity demand of similar magnitude.

However, per capita consumption of most commodities shows a profile that first rises, as per capita income increases from a low level, and then plateaus, as income grows above a certain range (figure 2.4).[3] There is even some evidence of declining per capita consumption at higher levels of income for some commodities. The precise form of the

---

[2] The nonlinear nature of the commodity consumption-income relationship throughout the development process has led to a strand of literature that comes under various names: the material or environmental Kuznets curve, S-shaped curve, inverted U-shaped curve, dematerialization hypothesis, the intensity of material use hypothesis, and plateauing hypothesis (Bogmans et al. 2020; Clark 1940; Cleveland and Ruth 1998; Herman, Ardekani, and Ausubel 1990; Kuznets 1971; Radetzki et al. 2008; Tilton 1990).

[3] The empirical literature on the commodity consumption-income relationship is rich, with a split between studies focused on individual commodities and a smaller literature on group aggregates, primarily energy. At a primary commodity level, Fernandez (2018a, 2018b), Lahoni and Tilton (1993), and Stuermer (2017), among others, examined individual base metals; Jaunky (2012) looked at aluminum; Bailliu et al. (2019) and Guzmán, Nashiyama, and Tilton (2005) studied copper; and Crompton (2015) and Wårrel (2014) covered steel. Other studies looked at individual energy commodities, including oil (Gately and Huntington 2002; Hamilton 2009), natural gas (Erdogdu 2010; Krichene 2002), and coal (Chan and Lee 1997; Shealy and Dorian 2010). Demand for final products has also been studied extensively—see Kamerschen and Porter (2004) for electricity; Dahl (2012), Drollas (1984), and Gately and Streifel (1997) for gasoline and diesel. At the aggregate level, several studies look at the demand for energy (Bogmans et al. 2020; Burke and Csereklyei 2016; Csereklyei and Stern 2015; Dahl and Roman 2004; Jakob, Haller, and Marschinski 2012), and Baffes, Kabundi, and Nagle (2022) cover both individual and group aggregates for energy and metals.

FIGURE 2.4 Income and commodity demand

The relationship between income per capita and commodity consumption per capita shows signs of plateauing for most commodities as income rises. Whereas the relationship for energy is similar across countries, the relationship for metals diverges among countries. China stands out as having higher metals consumption per capita at lower levels of income than other countries, particularly in the case of aluminum. Agriculture shows less relationship with income, with signs that demand plateaus at low levels of income.

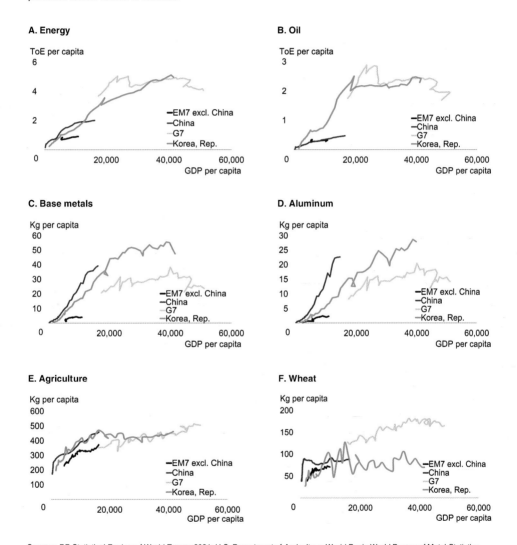

A. Energy

B. Oil

C. Base metals

D. Aluminum

E. Agriculture

F. Wheat

Sources: BP Statistical Review of World Energy 2021; U.S. Department of Agriculture; World Bank; World Bureau of Metal Statistics.
Note: GDP per capita in constant 2010 U.S. dollars. Lines show the evolution of income and commodity consumption per capita over the period 1965-2019. Each data point represents one country or group for one year. EM7 excl. China = Brazil, India, Indonesia, Mexico, the Russian Federation, and Türkiye; kg = kilogram; ToE = tonnes of oil equivalent.

relationship between commodity demand and income can vary substantially among countries. For example, China's per capita consumption of most metals is comparable to or higher than that of AEs, despite a much lower level of income.

The plateauing in commodity demand can be interpreted as a decrease in the commodity intensity of GDP. As economies get wealthier, the quantity of commodities used in the production of an additional unit of GDP decreases. Indeed, over the past 50 years, the commodity intensity of demand at the global level has, in general, decreased for most commodities, driven by the increasing importance of the service sector in the global economy and reduced infrastructure requirements and efficiency improvements (figure 2.5; Evans and Lewis 2005; Fernandez 2018a). However, there have been some notable differences: the intensity of energy and food in GDP has declined steadily over this period, whereas that of metal demand fell until about 2000, then began rising, before plateauing in recent years.

These patterns reflect major differences between countries. Although energy intensity has decreased at the global level, it has done so chiefly because of reductions among AEs. Energy intensities have risen for most EMDEs as they have industrialized. Two notable exceptions are China and Poland, which had among the highest energy intensities in the world in 1970.[4] For metals, the sharp reversal of the global downtrend in the intensity of demand in 1995 was driven entirely by China's industrialization. Excluding China, intensity declined at a similar rate to that of energy. For agriculture, intensity fell at the fastest rate of all commodity groups and fell in most countries, consistent with the low income elasticity of demand for agricultural products.

Commodity intensity of demand

At a given level of per capita GDP, four factors may influence an economy's commodity intensity of demand: the degree of industrialization, urbanization, technology, and government policies at the country level and the international level. This subsection examines each factor.

Industrialization

Historically, as economies develop, their consumption patterns change. For economies already at high income levels, incremental growth in income typically leads to increased consumption of services, rather than goods, and services are much less commodity intensive. In addition, as economies mature, they increasingly fulfill their infrastructure needs, reducing their need for construction materials (Radetzki et al. 2008; Stuermer 2017; Tilton 1990). A similar pattern occurs in terms of production: as economies move

---

[4] Countries that industrialized under central planning tend to exhibit high energy intensity because of inefficient resource allocation (Dienes, Dobozi, and Radetzki 1994; Ruhl et al. 2012; Urge-Vorsatz, Miladinovab, and Paizs 2006). Following the collapse of the Soviet Union, and coinciding with rapid per capita income growth, the energy intensity of demand in these countries fell steadily, although it remains elevated. China has a similar profile, with its energy intensity (measured as energy use relative to GDP) extremely high in the 1980s and steadily declining subsequently as its per capita incomes rose.

FIGURE 2.5 Intensity of commodity demand

Over the past 50 years the intensity of commodity demand—the amount of commodities consumed per unit of GDP—generally declined for energy and agriculture, but declined and then rose for metals. The global aggregates are driven by diverging trends at the country level, with intensities of demand typically falling in advanced economies and rising for EMDEs. An exception is agriculture, where the sharpest changes were for EMDEs.

A. Energy intensity of demand

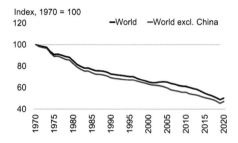

B. Energy intensity of demand, select countries

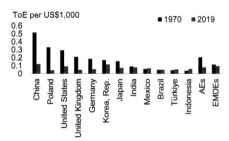

C. Metal intensity of demand

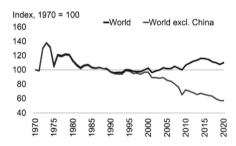

D. Metal intensity of demand, select countries

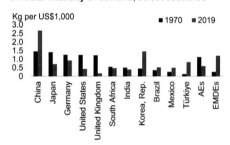

E. Agricultural intensity of demand

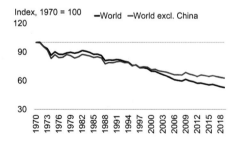

F. Agricultural intensity of demand, select countries

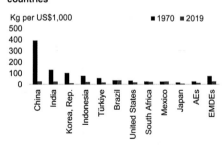

Sources: BP Statistical Review of World Energy 2021; U.S. Department of Agriculture; World Bank; World Bureau of Metals Statistics.
Note: Intensity of demand is calculated as the amount of energy, metal, or agricultural commodities used per unit of GDP. Energy includes crude oil, natural gas and coal. Metals includes aluminum, copper, lead, nickel, tin, and zinc. AE = advanced economy; EMDE = emerging market and developing economy; kg = kilogram; ToE = tonnes of oil equivalent.

from predominantly agricultural economies toward manufacturing, their commodity demand rapidly increases because manufacturing is more resource-intensive than agriculture, particularly for metals. At a later stage of development, economic growth tends to be increasingly accounted for by the service sector.

These trends are evident in the global data. For example, the share of the service sector in world GDP rose from about 50 percent in 1970 to 64 percent in 2019. Natural endowments can make a difference to the commodity composition of GDP. For example, Australia, Canada, and Chile are resource-rich countries with relatively large extractive industries. In contrast, the large East Asian economies have based their industrial development on manufacturing sectors.

Urbanization

The degree of urbanization has been linked to commodity demand growth (Jacks and Stuermer 2018; Yu 2011). The share of the global population living in urban areas has risen rapidly over the past 50 years, alongside a major increase in commodity consumption. Urban areas have large resource needs, for their construction and maintenance, for materials for their factories, and for everyday needs of their households. However, the effect of migration from the countryside to a city on commodity demand depends on the relative efficiency of resource use in the two areas (World Bank 2010). Furthermore, economic growth is also a key driver of urbanization, such that the relationship between urbanization and commodity demand is complex. Research on this relationship is surveyed in box 2.1.

Technology

Technological innovation is a key determinant of commodity demand. Disruptive innovation is a change that renders existing products or industries obsolete. It may involve the introduction of an entirely new product (such as the mobile phone), new methods of production (such as robots), or new techniques for marketing (such as internet shopping). Technological developments can also introduce significant efficiency gains on both the consumption and the production side, which, in turn, can encourage large-scale commodity substitution (Baffes, Kabundi, and Nagle 2022; Tilton and Guzmán 2016). For example, improvements in global energy efficiency, such as increased thermal efficiency of fossil fuel power plants and improved fuel economy of internal combustion engines, have been estimated to have lowered global energy consumption by about 1.2 percent per year between 1971 and 2017 (Bogmans et al. 2020). Similarly, innovations in production processes can sharply reduce resource use and production costs in manufacturing processes (for example, 3D printing; Campbell et al. 2011).

Oil is an important case in point. The first commercial discoveries in the mid-1800s led to rapid advances in drilling technology and a steep drop in the relative price of oil. Along with the simultaneous invention of the internal combustion engine, these advances resulted in the gradual displacement of coal in transport (from steam engines to

BOX 2.1 Urbanization and commodity demand

The past 50 years have seen a rapid increase in urbanization rates in emerging market and developing economies, which is set to continue over the next 30 years. Urbanization can have a major impact on the composition of commodity demand given the size of cities and their concentration of people and economic activity. Empirical evidence shows that, even after controlling for income and population, an increase in the share of the population living in urban areas has generally been associated with higher energy consumption. High-density cities, however, have lower per capita energy consumption than less densely populated cities. Adoption of well-designed policies would allow increased urbanization to proceed along with a reduction in commodity use. Such policies would include policies to encourage public transit, greater population intensity, improved insulation of buildings, and investment in modern energy-saving equipment.

Introduction

Over the past 50 years the share of the world's population living in urban areas has risen from 37 percent to 56 percent, an increase of 3 billion people (figure B2.1.1; United Nations 2019; World Bank 2021a). The sharpest increase came from emerging market and developing economies (EMDEs), where the share of the urban population nearly doubled from 28 percent to 54 percent. The largest increase came from China, where the share of the urban population jumped from 17 percent to 61 percent between 1970 and 2020. Urbanization in advanced economies mainly took place earlier in the 1900s. Urban areas cover less than 3 percent of the world's land area, but account for roughly two-thirds of global energy consumption (UN Habitat 2020).

The shift from rural to urban areas is set to continue, with the share of the urban population at the global level expected to reach 68 percent by 2050, before plateauing thereafter (United Nations 2019). Most of this growth is expected to continue to occur in EMDEs and in low-income countries, especially in South Asia and in Sub-Saharan Africa.

The increase in the share of the urban population has occurred alongside a rising trend in per capita commodity demand. Although population and income growth are primary drivers of commodity demand, urbanization also has the potential to have a major impact, especially on the composition of demand, because city dwellers have different propensities to consume resources than rural dwellers (Baffes, Kabundi, and Nagle 2022).

Urbanization can affect commodity demand through several channels, but the impacts vary depending on the nature of urbanization (World Bank 2010, 2021b). Density of urban areas varies, ranging from high-density mega cities, to smaller cities, to low-density urban sprawls that result in dependency on

BOX 2.1 Urbanization and commodity demand *(continued)*

FIGURE B2.1.1 Urban population trends

Urban populations have risen rapidly in EMDEs and LICs since 1970. China saw the largest increase in its urban population, followed by India. Over the next 30 years, the largest increases in urbanization are expected to occur in Sub-Saharan Africa and South Asia.

A. Urban population share

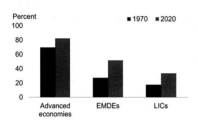

B. Change in urban population and urbanization rate, 1970-2020, select countries

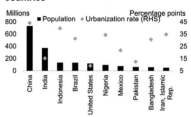

C. Urban population share forecasts

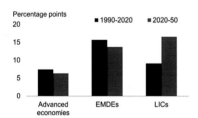

D. Urban population share forecasts, by region

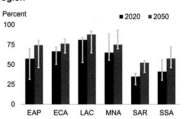

Sources: United Nations 2019; World Bank.
Note: Orange whiskers indicate minimum and maximum range. EAP = East Asia and Pacific; ECA = Europe and Central Asia; EMDE = emerging market and developing economy; LAC = Latin America and the Caribbean; LIC = low-income country; MNA = Middle East and North Africa; SAR = South Asia; SSA = Sub-Saharan Africa.
A.-D. Charts show data and forecasts for urbanization rates and urban populations from the United Nations (2019).
D. Bars show average urbanization rates within regions. Lines show interquartile range of the urbanization rates of individual countries within regions.

automobiles and prohibit walking (Benfield, Raimi, and Chen 1999; Brody 2013; Burchell et al. 1998). Evidence suggests that urbanization, by itself, has generally caused increased consumption of commodities. But this effect is not uniform. High population density in the cities of advanced economies is associated with reduced per capita consumption of energy. Given the sharp increase in the urban population expected over the next 30 years, it is critical to understand how urbanization can affect demand for different types of commodities, beyond the broader impact of population and income growth.

BOX 2.1 Urbanization and commodity demand *(continued)*

Against that backdrop, this box reviews the literature on the relationship between urbanization and commodity demand and asks the following questions:

- What is the nature of urbanization?

- What are the channels through which urbanization can affect commodity demand?

- What are the empirical effects of urbanization on commodity demand?

The nature of urbanization

Although the share of the population living in urban areas has risen globally, the density of urban areas varies significantly across and within countries and has changed over time.

Defining urban areas. Definitions of what constitutes an urban area differ greatly between countries, with officially designated minimum sizes ranging from 200 people in Denmark and Sweden, to 50,000 in Japan (figure B2.1.2; United Nations 2019). Furthermore, some countries use metrics such as population density instead of population size. In addition, definitions of what areas to include in urban regions vary substantially across countries.[a] For example, suburban areas may not be officially part of the city but may be considered for economic purposes part of the urban area. The size of defined urban areas varies considerably, from megacities containing 10 million or more people, to urban areas with fewer than 300,000 people. Although a majority of the world's population lives in an urban area, two-fifths live in urban areas of fewer than 300,000 people.

Density of urban areas. On average, the larger a city is, the denser it is. However, similar-sized cities can vary substantially (Dijkstra, Florczyk et al. 2020). Cities in Asia have much higher density than cities in the United States—among the 100 largest cities in the world, 9 of the 10 least densely populated are in the United States. Population densities of large cities in India are orders of magnitude greater than those U.S. cities. The types of density also vary. For example, the skyline of cities can be vastly different between countries. Richer cities tend to be more "pyramid shaped"—that is, with more taller buildings and skyscrapers, whereas

---

a. To facilitate the comparison of urban areas, the United Nations endorsed a new methodology to define cities, towns, and rural areas on the basis of total population and population density within population grids (Dijkstra, Florczyk et al. 2020; United Nations 2020). Under this definition, the share of the population living in urban areas increases substantially (in 2015, by 22 percentage points), in part because several large countries classify most towns as rural areas (Dijkstra, Hamilton et al. 2020).

BOX 2.1 Urbanization and commodity demand *(continued)*

FIGURE B2.1.2 Urban population share and population density

The population threshold for defining an urban area varies greatly across countries. On the basis of official definitions, about 60 percent of the world's population lives in urban areas. About 50 percent of the urban population lives in cities of fewer than 300,000 people. Population densities of the largest cities in EMDEs, especially in Asia, are an order of magnitude greater than of cities in the United States.

A. Population threshold for "urban area"

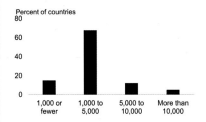

B. Global distribution of population, by city size

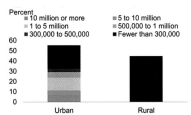

C. Population density of cities

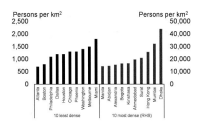

D. Population density and carbon emissions in selected cities

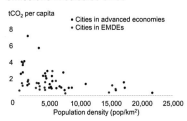

Sources: Our World in Data; UN Habitat 2020; World Bank.
Note: EMDE = emerging market and developing economy; km = kilometer; RHS = right-hand side; tCO$_2$ = metric tons of carbon dioxide emission.
A. Chart shows the variances in definitions among countries for the minimum number of inhabitants needed for a settlement to classify as an "urban area." Sample includes 100 countries. It does not include countries that do not rely on a population threshold and instead consider other metrics, including population density.
B. Chart shows the percent of the world's population living in urban and rural areas, with urban areas split by size of city.
C. Population density of world's 100 largest cities. Chart shows the 10 least dense and most dense cities. Data from 2014.
D. The y-axis shows metric tons of CO$_2$ emissions per capita from transportation; the x-axis shows population density of 40 major cities. Data are from 2016 to 2019.

low- and lower-middle-income cities tend to be "pancake-shaped" or flatter. In EMDEs, the combination of high population density and low-rise residences makes the cities prone to overcrowding and reduces quality of life (Lall et al. 2021).

Changes over time. Cities can grow outward, inward (infill of undeveloped spaces), or upward. In low-income and lower-middle-income countries, 90

BOX 2.1 Urbanization and commodity demand *(continued)*

percent of urban built-up area expansion occurred as horizontal or outward growth between 1990 and 2015, and only 10 percent as infill. In high-income countries, however, about 30 percent occurred as infill (Lall et al. 2021). Population densities have generally increased, however, as urban populations have grown faster than urban areas have expanded. Between 1990 and 2015, global population densities of cities rose by 8 percent, with larger cities experiencing the biggest increase in density (Dijkstra, Florczyk et al. 2020). In contrast, small cities (fewer than 250,000 people) experienced declines in population density.[b]

Channels: From urbanization to commodity demand

Urbanization affects commodity consumption through several channels. These channels include the impact of urbanization on transportation behavior, infrastructure needs, household characteristics, and consumer choice.

Transportation. Urbanization has the potential to either raise or lower energy demand from transportation. Studies finding that urbanization reduces energy demand from transportation typically focus on the fact that high-density neighborhoods facilitate journeys by foot or by bicycle, and effective mass transit systems provide alternatives to personal motorized vehicles (figure B2.1.3; Brownstone and Golob 2009; Kahn 2000; Liddle and Lung 2010; Newman 2006). In contrast, studies finding that an increase in the urban population increases transportation energy demand focus on factors that can result in increased journeys. In the absence of mass transit systems, rising urban populations can result in increased dependence on cars, because residences and workplaces are typically separated in cities (Glaeser and Kahn 2010; Jones 2004; Marshall 2007). Urban sprawl can exacerbate this issue and lead to increased auto use (Burchell et al. 1998; Hankey and Marshall 2010; VandeWeghe and Kennedy 2007).[c]

In EMDEs, the move from rural to urban areas may see a shift from mainly muscle-powered transportation (such as walking or biking) to motorized transportation (such as cars, motorcycles, and buses), leading to a net increase in energy consumption (Parikh and Shukla 1995). This increase occurs particularly when cities have not been well planned (Wahba 2019). In addition, the reliance of cities on commodities, such as food, produced outside their borders can result in increased energy use because these products need to be transported and stored;

---

b. In contrast, earlier studies found that population densities had decreased over time. Those studies had a higher estimate of the increase in urban areas because they used different methodologies (Angel et al. 2016; UN Habitat 2020).

c. Causation may also run in the opposite direction, whereby the development of the automobile facilitated lower-density cities.

BOX 2.1 Urbanization and commodity demand *(continued)*

FIGURE B2.1.3 Urban populations and transportation-related energy demand in the United States

Low levels of population density are associated with much higher energy consumption from transportation in the United States. Rural populations tend to drive more and walk less than their urban counterparts. Similarly, high rates of urban density facilitate the use of public transportation, with commuter rates much higher in large, dense cities. Household energy use is higher in detached houses than in apartments, and energy use is also higher in smaller households.

A. Population density and transportation-related energy consumption in the United States

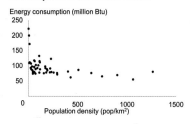

B. Miles driven per year

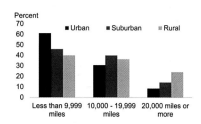

C. Frequency of walking for travel

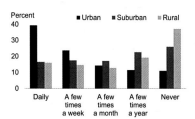

D. Share of workers commuting by public transport

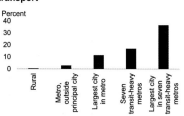

Sources: Federal Highway Administration, National Household Travel Survey 2017; World Bank.
Note: Btu = British thermal unit; km = kilometer.
A. Vertical axis presents data for total energy consumption per capita in the transport industry for 50 U.S. states, whereas population density is shown on the horizontal axis. Data for 2019.

this need does not arise for mostly self-sufficient rural areas (Parikh and Shukla 1995). [d]

Infrastructure requirements. Densely populated cities have vast infrastructure needs, including mass transit, electricity generation, and water and sewerage

---

d. Because urbanization facilitates economies of scale and specialization as part of the industrialization process, it may lead to the increased movement of raw materials and intermediate goods in the production process (Jones 1991, 2004).

BOX 2.1 Urbanization and commodity demand *(continued)*

services (Eberts and McMillen 1999). Economies of scale and network effects may, however, make the provision of the service more efficient (that is, on a per capita basis). At the same time, it is possible that urbanization and high-density living create new demands for infrastructure. For example, high-density urban populations have greater need than low-density rural areas for sewerage systems.

Household size and type of accommodation. An increase in the share of the urban population can lead to differences in household characteristics, with either positive or negative impacts on energy consumption. Apartments are much more common in cities than in rural areas because of higher land costs. Apartments have lower energy use than detached houses because apartments have fewer exterior walls, which reduces energy loss from heating and cooling (Brounen, Kok, and Quigley 2012; Satterthwaite 2011). However, differences in household composition may partly offset this advantage. Average household size tends to be smaller in urban areas, as young people move away from their family home and delay forming households (Cole and Neumayer 2004). Smaller households tend to have higher per capita energy consumption because they benefit less from economies of scale in energy consumption compared with larger households (Liu et al. 2003).

Changes in the composition of energy demand. Urbanization can also lead to changes in the types of fuel consumed within a country. As households move from rural to urban areas, they typically move from more basic forms of energy, such as biomass, toward more modern energy forms, such as electricity from centralized power stations fueled by coal or natural gas (Barnes, Krutilla, and Hyde 2005). This shift has the potential to reduce commodity demand because the provision of energy in the form of centrally generated electricity or natural gas is typically more efficient (Pachauri and Jiang 2009; Poumanyvong and Kaneko 2010). However, greater access to better-quality, cheaper energy such as electricity may lead to increased consumption of energy (Gillingham, Rapson, and Wagner 2016; IEA 2008).

The heat island effect. Urban areas give rise to the heat island effect, whereby structures such as roads and buildings absorb and reemit heat from the sun to a greater degree than natural landscapes (Imhoff et al. 2010). Urban areas, particularly cities with larger and denser populations, are hotter than nearby rural or natural areas, although the effect can vary between cities depending on the extent of green space within them. These variations can increase energy demand for cooling in hotter countries and during summer; however, it can reduce energy demand for heating in countries with cold winters.

Increased consumer choice. Consumers living in cities benefit from a larger choice of goods and services, which can lead to increased consumption by

BOX 2.1 Urbanization and commodity demand *(continued)*

increasing access to new products. Access to larger markets enables producers and retailers to specialize and supply a wider variety of goods and services. All else equal, a rise in consumption due to increased choice, beyond that caused by increased income, would result in an increase in commodity demand. For example, urban diets are typically more varied and include a greater share of meat and processed food, which require more energy and other commodities in their production (Hovhannisyan and Devadoss 2020; Regmi and Dyck 2001). However, because income is the primary driver of per capita commodity demand, and higher incomes generate more choices for the consumer, these studies leave open the size and direction of the impact of urbanization on commodity demand.

Effect of urbanization on commodity demand: Empirical estimates

This section is based on a survey of literature on how urbanization affects commodity demand (see table 2.2 in the main text of the chapter). The research can be broadly split into two fields: studies that investigated the effect of the share of the urban population and studies that delve deeper by considering urban density (differences between high- and low-density urban areas within a country). The majority of the studies on the share of urban populations used panel data sets with a wide range of economies. They focused mainly on aggregate energy consumption, although some looked at individual sources of demand for energy. This group included some single-country studies, with two for food consumption. In contrast, the studies examining urban density in individual countries covered only advanced economies (Canada, Japan, the Netherlands, and the United States), likely because of greater data availability. Their main focus was on sectoral demand for energy (for example, transportation or dwellings). All studies in the literature review controlled for per capita income.

Share of urban populations. Higher urban population shares were positively correlated with energy demand in almost all cross-country studies. One study found the relationship varied by income level, with a negative relationship for low-income countries, but a positive relationship for higher-income countries; this finding was attributed to efficiency gains arising from shifts to more modern fuels (Poumanyvong and Kaneko 2010). A study investigating metals consumption also found a positive impact of urbanization on demand (Baffes, Kabundi, and Nagle 2022). Three studies investigated food consumption and found little impact from urbanization after controlling for income (Hovhannisyan and Devadoss 2020; Pandey et al. 2020; Stage, Stage, and McGranahan 2010).

Urban density. Of the studies examining the impact of urban density, all found a negative relationship with energy demand. These studies considered a variety of energy uses, including for transportation, dwellings, transportation and dwellings

BOX 2.1 Urbanization and commodity demand *(continued)*

together, and consumption from the service sector.[e] Higher-density cities had lower energy demand than lower-density ones, at least in advanced economies. The extent to which these results apply to EMDEs is unclear. Many cities in low-income countries, particularly in Sub-Saharan Africa, struggle with high road congestion and commuting costs due to poor planning, inadequate transportation infrastructure, and limited public transit options, despite high population density (Hommann and Lall 2019).

Conclusions and policy implications

The share of the global population living in urban areas has risen rapidly over the past 50 years alongside a major increase in commodity consumption. Although income and population growth have been the primary drivers of commodity demand over time, urbanization per se has also had an effect. In general, an increase in the share of the urban population is associated with increased energy demand per capita. But the quantitative impact will depend on the nature of urbanization in particular countries. Compact, high-density cities have lower per capita energy consumption than low-density cities, particularly in advanced economies, because of greater resource efficiency in heating, shorter distances between home and work and recreation, and economies of scale in mass transit.

With urban populations expected to continue to increase, strategic urban planning that increases population density, and integrates transportation and land use, will become even more important in managing the impact of urbanization on commodity demand.[f] Key policy measures include the expansion of the capacity, affordability, and access of public mass transportation systems. Fiscal policies can also play a role; for example, fuel taxes have been shown to increase population density and preserve open space (Creutzig 2014; Creutzig et al. 2015). Many countries may be close to the upper limit of such taxes, however, because the tax burden falls on workers in certain urban sectors (such as truckers and taxi drivers).

In addition, well-devised incentives and regulations are required. Incentives for reduced energy consumption, including upgraded insulation in existing homes, provide a public good. Building codes can ensure that new homes meet high energy-efficiency standards. Regulations to reduce the use of private vehicles in

---

e. These studies considered various channels, including transportation (Brownstone and Golob 2009; Liddle 2004); dwellings (Brounen, Kok, and Quigley 2012; Lariviere and Lafrance 1999); transportation and dwellings together (Glaeser and Kahn 2010; Larson and Yezer 2015); and consumption from the service sector (Morikawa 2012).

f. The development of green and sustainable cities is a key component of the World Bank's Climate Change Action Plan and is in line with the United Nations' Sustainable Development Goal 11 to make cities and human settlements inclusive, safe, resilient, and sustainable (World Bank 2021c).

> **BOX 2.1 Urbanization and commodity demand (continued)**
>
> congested districts have proved effective. Zoning laws to encourage intensification through infill housing, and building up instead of out, can help reduce long commutes, increase use of public transit, and lower energy use and greenhouse gas emissions (Lall et al. 2021). Early planning and installation of transportation infrastructure is particularly crucial in rapidly growing cities because it can help guide and shape future urban growth (Hommann and Lall 2019).

gasoline and diesel). More recent innovations in oil production (in part due to a rise in oil prices after 1973), led to the exploitation of offshore oil, oil sands, and more recently shale oil. Innovations on the demand side have expanded the use of oil in new sectors, but efficiency improvements have also reduced oil use. For example, innovations in the petrochemicals industry have led to new products such as plastics and fertilizers, and the development of the jet airplane made long-distance travel and tourism available to a mass market. This development, in turn, increased demand for oil—jet fuel currently accounts for about 5 percent of global oil consumption. At the same time, innovations have sharply improved the efficiency of oil consumption, reducing the aggregate increase in demand for oil. The average fuel consumption of a new aircraft fell by 45 percent between 1968 and 2014, an average annual reduction of 1.3 percent (Kharina and Rutherford 2015).

Disruptive innovation has been common throughout history. It has been a major cause of transformation in the structure of commodity demand and a crucial factor for economic growth (Aghion, Antonin, and Bunel 2021).[5] The industrial revolution led to massive, permanent, demand shifts for several commodities. Inventions during the 1700s transformed the textile industry from its cottage structure (that is, home-based factories employing a few workers) to the world's largest industry. Innovations included John Kay's flying shuttle in 1733, James Hargreaves' spinning jenny in 1764, and James Watt's steam engine in 1769, which all led to cotton replacing wool and flax.

The steam engine revolutionized land and ocean transportation. Iron replaced timber for ship bodies, and coal-fired steam engines replaced cotton sails. The internal combustion engine revolutionized transportation (both ocean and land) in the first half of the twentieth century, replacing coal with gasoline and diesel. In the second half of that century, kerosene became the main fuel for air transport. In addition, innovations in chemistry saw synthetic rubber overtake the use of natural rubber in the production of tires (figure 2.6). Unlike the routine substitutions that occur in response to a change in

---

[5] The causation is not always unidirectional. Innovation may be induced by price changes. Discussions of substitutability go back to Hicks (1932), who argued that a change in the relative prices of the factors of production spurs innovation. Hicks' hypothesis, known as induced innovation hypothesis, has been tested extensively, including in Hayami and Ruttan 1970; Olmstead and Rhode 1993; Hanlon 2015; and Newell, Jaffe, and Stavins 1999.

FIGURE 2.6 Drivers of commodity demand: Technology, innovation, and policies

The invention of the steam engine led to the replacement of sailing ships by steamships, and of wooden frames along with cotton- and linen-based sail cloth (all agricultural commodities) by steel frames (made from iron ore) and steam engines (running on coal instead of wind energy). Innovations in chemistry led to synthetic rubber and polyester (made from crude oil) displacing natural rubber and cotton (agricultural commodities). Government policies can also sharply influence commodity consumption. For example, concerns about the health impact of asbestos in construction materials, and lead in paint and gasoline, led to their use being gradually phased out and eventually banned. Aided by improvements in battery technology, charging infrastructure, and government incentives, the share of hybrid and electric vehicles has enjoyed impressive demand growth.

A. Share of synthetic rubber in global rubber consumption

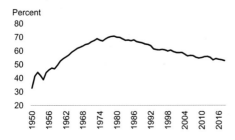

B. Asbestos use

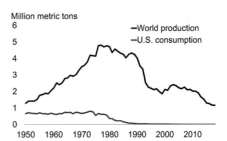

C. Consumption of lead in the United States

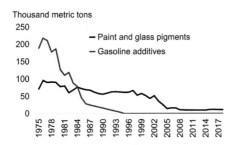

D. Sales of alternative vehicles in the United States

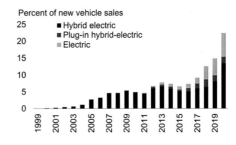

Sources: International Rubber Study Group; U.S. Department of Commerce; U.S. Geological Survey; World Bank.
A. Synthetic rubber is a substitute for natural rubber.

relative prices, substitutions from transformative technical change are usually nonreversible.

Two notable technology-driven transitions are currently under way. The first concerns communications and information storage. The inventions of the telegraph and subsequently the telephone led to increased use of copper wire in place of messengers. More recently, the development of the internet, mobile devices, wireless technology, and fiber optics has reduced the commodity intensity of much consumer and business activity. For example, video conferencing tools have reduced the need for personal and business travel. For more than five centuries (since the invention of the printing press in the mid-1400s) information was typically stored and transmitted on paper made from natural fiber. Following advancements in digital technology during the late 1900s, paper is being rapidly replaced by digital storage and reading devices, thus replacing natural fibers with rare earth metals and energy. The second notable development, which has far more important implications for commodity demand and has only just begun, is the energy transition away from fossil fuels. Box 2.2 summarizes aspects of historical and current structural changes.

Country-level policies

Changes in government policies have resulted in major changes in commodity demand. Governments routinely use subsidies and taxes to incentivize or discourage the consumption of commodities. For example, energy subsidies are prevalent in most countries (in terms of both production subsidies and consumption subsidies) and are often used to lower the cost of energy for consumers, which would typically lead to an increase in consumption. At the same time, to reduce pollution, governments often use fuel taxes to reduce driving and consumption of gasoline or diesel. More recently, several countries have introduced special taxes on single-use plastics to address rising concerns about plastic pollution in the oceans.

Governments have sometimes introduced outright bans on the production or use of dangerous or unhealthy commodities. For example, growing awareness of the adverse health effects of lead poisoning saw the United States gradually phase out the use of lead in gasoline, paint, and plumbing. This process began around 1970, and most other countries followed suit. More recently, China has implemented a range of regulations to improve air pollution in cities, including restrictions on metal smelting.

International policies

Throughout the twentieth century, numerous international commodity agreements have had a major impact on consumption patterns.[6] These agreements, often negotiated among both commodity-exporting and commodity-importing countries, were designed to mitigate the negative impacts of boom-and-bust cycles and reduce price volatility common to commodity prices. However, in practice, the agreements have distorted commodity markets by keeping prices high and stable, which encouraged consumers to reduce consumption, raise efficiency, or use substitute products (World Bank 2020). For example, the International Tin Agreement restricted the supply of tin and kept prices elevated for several years, but it resulted in the widespread substitution of aluminum for tin, especially in the beverage can industry. All efforts to manage non-energy commodity markets through international agreements have failed.

---

[6] Commodity agreements have covered the entire spectrum of commodity markets and have been researched in the literature, including for coffee (Akiyama and Varangis 1990), tin (Chandrasekhar 1989), natural rubber (Verico 2013), and groups of nonoil commodities over time (Davis 1946; Gilbert 2011; Roberts 1951).

BOX 2.2 Substitution among commodities: Reversible and permanent shifts

Substitution among commodities is a key feature of market behavior. Substitution of one good for another may follow changes in relative prices or incomes, with technology remaining basically the same. It often involves routine, reversible, shifts among similar commodities, for example, natural gas for oil, or plastic for paper packaging. However, the underlying cause of transformative substitutions since the industrial revolution has been the development and adoption of new technologies. Historical examples are the replacement of animal and wind power by steam, or the substitution of jet fuel for bunker oil in transcontinental travel. Technology and policies in response to climate change could drive a new transformation, to a lower-carbon economy. These forces will profoundly transform the structure of commodity consumption over the next few decades. The metals and other materials required to produce clean energy could see a strong rise in output, whereas the consumption of fossil fuels will start a permanent decline.

Introduction

Substitution between commodities is a routine but key feature of markets. For example, in many countries over the past 15 years natural gas has been supplanting coal for the generation of electricity. This substitution represents the normal functioning of the market mechanism, as an increased global supply of gas (especially due to rising U.S. shale gas production) caused a decline in its relative price that induced a matching increase in demand. In 2021, a surge in natural gas prices led to a reversal of this change, with countries switching to coal (and even crude oil) as fuel for electricity generation (World Bank 2021b).

Substitution among materials used as inputs in the production of final goods can take place at both short- and long-term horizons, as well as within and across commodity groups (Tilton and Guzmán 2016).[a] If a good or service can be provided more cheaply via the use of a different commodity, consumers will switch. In the long run, such substitution of inputs, in response to price changes or other incentives, can occur on a much larger scale as new capital equipment and production processes move to the least-cost options.

Substitution is very common as a response to changes in relative prices or relative scarcity among commodities belonging to the same group. In agriculture, soybean oil is a close substitute for palm oil for human consumption, and soybean meal

---

a. As Wellmer (2012, 11) noted:

> [W]e do not consume resources per se but their inherent functions or their physical and chemical properties. We do not need one tonne of copper: we need its electrical conductivity for transmitting power supply or transferring messages via electric pulses in telephone wires. This latter function can be ensured via fiber cables, directional antennae or mobile phone. So, we have substitution in the narrow sense (glass fiber vs. copper) and functional substitution to obtain the same function. Every technical solution has its own raw-material profile.

BOX 2.2 Substitution among commodities: Reversible and permanent shifts *(continued)*

FIGURE B2.2.1 Historical episodes of substitution

By 1890, steam accounted for more ship power than sail, and by 1920 that replacement was almost total. Following the introduction of aluminum beer cans in the mid-1960s, their share of shipments reached three-quarters by 1986 (they replaced refillable glass bottles and tin cans). In the early 1800s, wool and flax dominated fiber consumption. They were gradually replaced by cotton over the next 150 years. After World War II, synthetic fibers accounted for more than half of global fiber consumption. When prices of oil increased sevenfold after the oil crises of the 1970s, crude oil's share in electricity generation declined rapidly, replaced by natural gas and, to a lesser extent, coal. More recently, the share of renewable energy in electricity generation has risen rapidly, driven by a sharp decline in renewable energy costs.

A. Shipping capacity in the United Kingdom

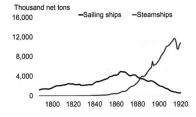

B. World fiber consumption, by type

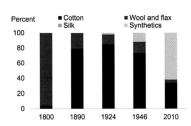

C. Global electricity generation, by fuel

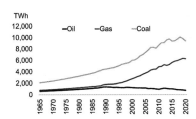

D. Share of aluminum cans in beverage containers

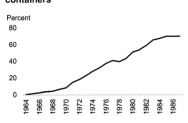

Sources: Original calculations; BP Statistical Review of World Energy 2021; World Bureau of Metal Statistics; World Bank.
A. Denotes ocean transportation capacity of ships registered in the United Kingdom.
C. TWh = terawatt hours

and maize are substitutes for animal feed. In energy, different fuels are direct substitutes, such as coal and natural gas in electricity generation; in metals, tinplate steel has been replaced by aluminum for beverage containers (figure B2.2.1). Examples of substitution across groups include transportation, in which ethanol (from maize or sugarcane) and biodiesel (from edible oils) can be substituted for gasoline (from crude oil), and the beverage container industry, in

BOX 2.2 Substitution among commodities: Reversible and permanent shifts *(continued)*

which plastic bottles (a by-product of crude oil) or paper (agriculture-based) can be substituted for aluminum cans (metal-based). Such substitutions can later be reversed just as easily if relative prices go back to their previous level.

Substitution can also be driven by policies. Domestic policies often change the relative prices of commodities. For example, many oil-producing countries subsidize oil, thus encouraging its consumption at the expense of other energy sources. Trade policies (such as tariffs) and industrial policies (such as protection of agriculture) can induce substitution. Regulations to protect the environment or to control dangerous substances also affect the composition of commodity demand. Changing consumer preferences can also lead to substitution. For example, following environmental concerns, consumers have sought to minimize the use of petrochemical-based materials (such as plastic) by replacing them with natural or biodegradable alternatives (such as paper).

Historically, more permanent major changes in the use of commodities have been caused by innovation. Technical advances, and their adaptation by entrepreneurs, have profoundly transformed existing economic structures. The resulting transformational commodity substitutions are not easily, and hardly ever, reversed. For example, the introduction of jet planes caused a switch from bunker oil to kerosene as the source of power for transcontinental travel. Moreover, transformational substitutions can cross commodity groups. The invention of the internal combustion engine eventually led to the substitution of metal and oil for horses and animal feed. There is no turning back from this kind of transformational change—also known as disruptive innovation or creative destruction (Aghion, Antonin, and Bunel 2021).

It can be challenging to distinguish episodes of transformative commodity substitution from routine substitution because forces like technological advances, resource discoveries, innovation, population growth, urbanization, and income growth are endlessly intertwined.[b] The distinction, however, can shed light on the economic history of commodity use. And it is especially relevant today in what is likely the beginning of an era of accelerated technical change and innovation under the impetus of climate change and government policies to mitigate its impact.

---

b. Theoretical discussions on commodity substitution and its relationship with innovation and prices go back to Hicks (1932, 124), who wrote that "a change in the relative prices of the factors of production is itself a spur to invention, and to invention of a particular kind—directed to economizing the use of a factor which has become relatively expensive." Hicks' view, later coined the induced innovation hypothesis, has been discussed extensively, including in Hanlon (2015); Hayami and Ruttan (1970); Newell, Jaffe, and Stavins (1999), and Olmstead and Rhode (1993). Substitutability among commodities has been cited as the antidote to resource scarcity (Goeller and Weinberg 1978; Pei and Tilton 1999).

BOX 2.2 Substitution among commodities: Reversible and permanent shifts *(continued)*

Against that background, this box examines the following questions:

- What have been the quantitative drivers of commodity substitution episodes over the past half century, and how have they affected commodity demand?

- What will be the role of commodity substitution in the energy transition that is only just under way?

The box confirms that new technologies and innovation have been the key forces behind long-term substitution, especially after the industrial revolution. On some occasions, however, policies too have played an important role. Each of the substitution episodes saw substantial changes in commodity demand, but with important differences. For some episodes substitution has been complete, with one commodity completely replaced by another; for others substitution is incomplete, with both commodities still used, albeit with a smaller share for the original commodity.

As efforts to transition away from fossil fuels accelerate (in the context of energy transition and pollution), substitution is expected to occur across commodity groups. Consumption of fossil fuels will likely decline while consumption of the metals associated with production of renewable energy and electric vehicle technology will rise. Demand for agricultural commodities may also increase, depending on whether policy announcements regarding the production of biofuels materialize.

How have past substitution episodes affected commodity demand?

Substitution among commodities on the demand side has played a key role in economic development at the macro level and has affected the entire spectrum of industries. To illustrate, this section examines the role of substitutability in three industries: transportation, packaging, and electricity generation.

Transportation

Substitution, driven by innovation, has been an ongoing process in the transportation industry since the industrial revolution, with profound implications for economic development. In the late 1700s, the recently invented steam engine was first adapted to the textile industry. Innovations over the next century led to its widespread adoption for land and ocean transportation. As animal traction was replaced by trains, animal feed gave way to coal as the source of power. Steel and iron replaced wood for the bodies of ships, and coal-powered steam engines replaced cotton and linen sail cloth. More generally, the industrial revolution brought a transition from agricultural commodities to mineral energy and to metals (Lundgren 1996).

BOX 2.2 Substitution among commodities: Reversible and permanent shifts *(continued)*

In the late nineteenth and early twentieth centuries, technological developments in the transportation industry induced further substitution among agricultural and energy commodities. The invention of the automobile saw three competing technologies in the late nineteenth century. The first cars were powered by steam and electricity and led to the partial replacement of animal traction, which meant that food commodities were largely supplanted by coal and coal-powered electricity. Next, the first-generation internal combustion engine vehicles that used biofuels replaced the early electric vehicles (Kovarik 2013). Later, vehicles powered by gasoline and diesel became the dominant form of ground transportation. Similar trends took place in ocean transportation, with steam engines replaced by internal combustion engines, again substituting diesel and bunker fuel for coal.

More recently, biofuels have again emerged as a substitute fuel for transport. Numerous countries legislated biofuel policies in the late 1900s, mostly in the form of mandates (de Gorter and Just 2009). Policies included the use of maize-based ethanol in the United States, edible oil-based biodiesel in the European Union, and sugarcane-based ethanol in Brazil. More recently several other countries (including China, Indonesia, and Thailand) have introduced biofuel policies and are expected to produce substantial amounts of biofuels—if or when policies are enacted. Biofuels currently account for about 4 percent of total land allocated to food crops, and less than 2 percent of global liquid energy consumption. Substitution in the transportation industry continues into the twenty-first century with internal combustion engine vehicles being replaced by electric vehicles (see the section on the energy transition, later in this box).

Packaging: Beverage and bottle industries

Until the 1960s, glass, steel, and tinplate were the main materials used to manufacture beverage containers (chiefly for soft drinks and beer). However, the emergence of aluminum in the 1960s, with its superior properties (being lightweight and easy to recycle, and featuring technological developments like the pull-up and crimp can) significantly changed the beer industry, and to a lesser extent the soft drink sector (Nappi 1990). The share of aluminum cans used in the U.S. beer industry reached 80 percent by 1986, with tinplate cans being completely replaced. In the soft drink industry, however, the share of aluminum cans was limited by the dramatic rise of plastic bottles following their introduction in the late 1970s.

Aluminum's expanded use at the expense of tin was also aided by the International Tin Agreement, which kept tin prices artificially high through the management of buffer stocks (see chapter 1). The agreement, first negotiated in 1954 with the objective of maintaining tin prices within a desired range through

BOX 2.2 Substitution among commodities: Reversible and permanent shifts (continued)

the management of buffer stocks, collapsed in 1985 following several years of insufficient funds to maintain stocks (Chandrasekhar 1989). Tin lost market share not only because of technological advances of its competitors but also by its own pricing decisions.

Innovation in beverage containers continues, particularly for soft drinks. Glass, plastics, and increasingly paper (for example, Tetrapak) dominate the bottle market, although aluminum remains the main material for the can industry. Substitution between these materials occurs when relative prices change. Environmental concerns, particularly regarding plastics, have also favored recyclable (aluminum, glass) and compostable (paper) containers. Thus, what initially began as substitution among metals turned into substitution between metals and energy (plastics) and, recently, between metals/energy and agriculture (paper).

Electricity generation

In the decade before 1972, global oil consumption grew at almost 8 percent a year in response to the rapid postwar expansion of transportation, industry, and electricity consumption (generated using crude oil). The use of oil in these industries was aided by artificially low prices (during 1945-72, oil prices averaged about US$16 per barrel of crude oil in 2017 constant terms because of price controls by the Seven Sisters oil cartel), making it comparatively cheaper than coal. The cartel's control gradually weakened as emerging market and developing economies increased their share of oil production.

The 1973 and 1979 energy crises, which resulted in a sevenfold increase in oil prices, set in motion powerful market forces and policies to reduce oil consumption and seek alternative supplies. Efficiency improvements, often mandated by government policies, led to reductions in the amount of oil used by the transportation sector, while coal, nuclear power, natural gas, and renewable sources (such as hydro and geothermal) displaced oil for electricity generation.

Both national and international policies encouraged the increasing use of coal in electricity generation. The International Energy Agency's 1979 Principles for IEA Action on Coal directive required member countries to promote the use of coal as an alternative to crude oil and minimize the use of crude oil in electricity generation, including by preventing new or replacement oil-fired capacity (IEA 1979, 1995). This directive was complemented by domestic policies, such as the U.S. Powerplant and Industrial Fuel Use Act of 1978, which mandated that no new baseload electric power plant could be constructed or operated without the capability to use coal or another nonoil or nongas alternate fuel as a primary energy source.

BOX 2.2 Substitution among commodities: Reversible and permanent shifts *(continued)*

What will be the role of commodity substitution in the ongoing efforts of energy transition?

Efforts to decarbonize the global economy will induce further substitution among commodities, with important implications for commodity demand. Substitution will occur across several fronts, including both the source of energy and its use.

Electricity generation: Substitution of fossil fuel commodities by metals

As discussed in box 2.3, the energy transition is expected to see renewable energy replacing fossil fuel energy in electricity generation, which entails a sharp increase in demand for the metals and minerals used to produce renewable energy. This substitution is being driven by both demand and supply factors (IPCC 2021). Demand has shifted in response to changes in consumer preferences (for example, growing interest in renewable energy and installation of solar panels) as well as policies (such as tax incentives for solar installation or purchase of electric vehicles, and the use of carbon pricing mechanisms). In terms of supply, technological developments have led to sharp reductions in the cost of renewable energy, increasing its relative competitiveness.

Transportation: Switch to electric vehicles, batteries, and biofuels

Transitioning toward a lower-carbon energy environment will radically transform the transportation industry. Over the next decade, land transportation will see large-scale replacement of gasoline- and diesel-powered vehicles by electric vehicles (EVs). Initially, EVs faced numerous headwinds, including high prices, long charging times, sparse charging stations, and limited driving range. However, aided by improvements in battery technology and charging infrastructure and by government incentives, EVs have recently enjoyed impressive demand growth. In 2018, the global electric car fleet, at 5 million units, was up 2 million from the previous year (IEA 2019a). In the United States, electric and hybrid vehicles in 2021 accounted for nearly 10 percent of total passenger vehicle purchases. China is currently the world's largest EV market, followed by Europe and the United States. Norway has the highest use of EVs, at 46 percent of recent vehicle sales. Growth of the EV market share is expected to accelerate, because numerous countries have set high targets for phasing out new gasoline and diesel-powered vehicles.

EVs will induce substitution of commodities because of their fuel requirements—which favor sources of energy that generate electricity (most likely renewables) over crude oil—as well as their physical design. An EV, for example, contains four times more copper (for the battery, motor, and wiring) than an internal-combustion engine vehicle. Large volumes of copper will also be needed for the

BOX 2.2 Substitution among commodities: Reversible and permanent shifts *(continued)*

EV charging infrastructure. For a standard battery pack with the most common battery chemistry, the main materials are aluminum, copper, cobalt, graphite/carbon, lithium, nickel, and manganese.

Electric technology is less suited to shipping and air transportation, but these sectors may find substitutes to petroleum-based fuels, such as hydrogen or biofuels. Hydrogen can be produced from water using either natural gas (although this process produces carbon emissions) or electrical energy. Biofuels currently account for about 2 percent of global liquid energy consumption. Biodiesel produced from agricultural products or waste products may also be used as a low- or zero-carbon alternative, because the feedstock comes from plants and trees that absorb carbon as they grow. The International Energy Agency estimates that a fourfold increase in biofuels production by 2050 would be needed to achieve a net-zero emissions objective (IEA 2021a). Several countries (including China, Indonesia, and Thailand) have recently introduced biofuel policies, which could potentially produce substantial amounts of biofuels if enacted. However, the policy-driven expansion of biofuels is a highly controversial and hotly debated topic in terms of its environmental benefits and its impact on food prices.

Conclusion

This box examined historical commodity substitution in three sectors (beverage packaging, electricity generation, and transportation) and analyzed how substitution may affect commodity demand due to the energy transition. Ocean transportation has undergone two complete substitution cycles (from sail ship to steam ship and from steam ship to bunker fuel and diesel). Both cycles were driven by technology and innovation, and substitution was complete, resulting in large changes in commodity demand. Substitution in retail packaging was also driven by technology and innovation, with a shift from tinplate steel to aluminum (and later to plastic bottles, and more recently to paper). Substitution in electricity generation reflects a combination of innovation (such as the introduction of nuclear power) and government policies. For all three sectors, substitution continues today because of advances in technology (such as the falling cost of solar energy), policies to limit greenhouse gases (such as carbon-emission pricing, biofuel mandates), and consumer preferences (such as for recyclable or compostable materials in packaging).

The ongoing energy transition will likely cause major substitution among commodities. Consumption of metals will likely increase considerably at the expense of fossil fuels (Boer, Pescatori, and Stuermer 2021). Depending on policies, the use of biofuels for transport may increase considerably, effectively substituting food commodities for fossil fuels.

The Organization of the Petroleum Exporting Countries (OPEC), is the only remaining example of a major international commodity agreement. OPEC was founded in the 1960s with members coming together to negotiate better prices for oil and ultimately to use their market power to influence oil prices. OPEC interventions in the oil market have occurred frequently over the past 20 years, albeit with mixed success (Baffes et al. 2015). Notable examples include OPEC's decision to abandon quotas in November 2014 and more recently to introduce massive cuts (in partnership with other countries) following the collapse in demand due to COVID-19 (World Bank 2020). Like other production agreements, OPEC's' historical attempts to manipulate prices have triggered other market forces—by keeping prices high they have encouraged consumers to reduce consumption by increasing efficiency, substituting other fuels for oil, and inducing innovation in the production of crude oil. However, the group continues to actively manage its production of crude oil.

Whereas earlier international agreements were motivated by economic objectives, more recent agreements reflect environmental and climate change concerns. For example, the Montreal agreement in 1987 began the gradual phase-out of the use of chlorofluorocarbons because of their detrimental impact on the ozone layer. An example of international action for health reasons is the outright ban on asbestos in 16 countries (2003), which followed the accumulation of scientific evidence on the carcinogen. More recently, countries have begun to phase out the use of high-sulfur fuels in shipping under the agreement known as IMO 2020 (World Bank 2019). Of note are efforts to combat climate change by reducing greenhouse gas emissions, including the signing of the Paris (2015) and Glasgow (2021) agreements (IPCC 2021). Potential policies to accelerate the energy transition include carbon taxes, subsidies for renewable energy and electric vehicles (including battery development), and mandates to use certain types of commodities such as biofuels—all of which will materially alter commodity consumption patterns.

Modeling commodity demand

Following a literature review, this section estimates income elasticities of demand for energy, metals, and agriculture at the group level.[7] This estimation enables a comparison across the three different commodity groups and a better understanding of the role played by identified drivers for each commodity.

Literature review on income elasticities

Estimates of long-run income elasticities of demand vary by commodity, between countries, and over time (table 2.2). For energy, most studies have found an income elasticity of demand of less than unity (Burke and Csereklyei 2016; Csereklyei and Stern 2015; Jakob, Haller, and Marschinski 2012). That elasticity implies per capita energy

---

[7] This section extends and builds on the work of Baffes, Kabundi, and Nagle (2022) by including agriculture and estimating income elasticities using GDP in purchasing power parity terms.

consumption grows more slowly than per capita real GDP, consistent with a declining energy intensity of demand. Several studies have also found that income elasticities of demand for energy decline as income rises (Dahl 2012; Fouquet 2014; Jakob, Haller, and Marschinski 2012). An exception is Burke and Csereklyei (2016), who find the long-run income elasticity of demand increases as per capita real GDP rises. This finding likely reflects a country sample that included a number of low-income countries whose long-run income elasticity of demand may initially be very low, as a result of their reliance on noncommercial fuels (that is, biomass). As income rises beyond a certain low level, an increasing switch to purchasing fuel would imply a rising income elasticity, up until the switch is complete. Elasticities in low-income countries may also be kept low by policies such as energy subsidies (Joyeux and Ripple 2011).

For metals, the elasticity of income depends on the availability of substitutes and the range of uses. Because of its wide applicability, demand for aluminum grows more than proportionately with rising manufacturing output (that is, with an above-unitary elasticity); demand for tin and lead, because of environmental concerns, grows less than proportionately (that is, with a below-unitary elasticity; Stuermer 2017). Fernandez (2018a) also finds a higher income elasticity of demand for aluminum (and nickel and zinc) than for lead.

Methodology and data

To estimate the relationship between income and commodity demand, a standard demand equation is used (Baffes, Kabundi, and Nagle 2022): [8]

$$c_t = \mu + \theta_1 y_t + \theta_2 y_t^2 + \theta_3 p_t + \varphi' X_t + \varepsilon_t \,, \tag{2.2}$$

where c_t denotes per capita commodity consumption at year t; y_t is real per capita income in purchasing power parity terms; p_t is the real price of the commodity; X_t is an $h \times 1$ vector of control variables, such as fixed effects and various country-specific characteristics; ε_t is the stochastic error term; μ, θ_1, θ_2, and θ_3 denote parameters; and φ' denotes a vector, all to be estimated.

This approach is common in the literature (Adeyemi and Hunt 2007; Burke and Csereklyei 2016; Crompton 2015; Stuermer 2017). The quadratic income term y_t^2, intended to capture the nonlinearities discussed earlier, allows the calculation of income elasticities that vary across income levels and is consistent with an inverse U-shape theory of commodity demand.[9] Changes in commodity intensity of demand are captured by

---

[8] The model is estimated by the pooled mean group estimation procedure, which assumes homogeneity across all long-run estimators but allows for differences across countries in the short term (Pesaran, Shin, and Smith 1999) —an appropriate assumption because demand tends to be more similar across countries over the long term than the short term. For more details on estimation see Baffes, Kabundi, and Nagle (2022). All variables are in logs.

[9] An alternative specification would include a cubic term, y_t^3, which would be consistent with an S-shape consumption path—low growth initially, high growth at medium income levels, and a return to low growth at high income levels. Bogmans et al. (2020) find evidence for an S-shaped curve in energy consumption. Because the sample in this chapter has relatively few low-income countries (because of data limitations), the inverse U-shape seems more appropriate.

the control variables in X_t. Industrialization and urbanization are proxied, respectively, by the investment share and the urbanization share. A time trend proxies for technology-driven efficiency gains. By using group aggregates instead of individual commodities, the approach also controls for within-commodity group substitution (such as coal to natural gas) when overall demand for energy remains unchanged. However, it does not control for between-group substitution (such as coal to renewable energy made from metals).

Relationship (2.2) can be used to derive income elasticities as follows:

$$\eta_t = \frac{\partial c_t}{\partial y_t} = \theta_1 + 2\theta_2 y_t \, , \tag{2.3}$$

where η_t denotes the long-run income elasticity for the given commodity. Because η_t varies with income, it enables an estimation of whether consumption of a commodity plateaus as income rises. A large and positive value for the coefficient on y_t indicates a high initial elasticity, whereas a large and negative value for the coefficient on y_t indicates a rapid decrease in the elasticity.

The model was estimated for energy consumption (weighted by calorific energy content), metals consumption (aggregated using physical weights; a robustness check weighting with nominal values was also conducted), and agricultural consumption (weighted by calorific values). The analysis used annual data from 1970 to 2019 for up to 77 countries and GDP per capita in purchasing power parity terms.

Results

Table 2.1 reports the results for the energy, metal, and agriculture group aggregates. The parameter estimates for both income variables and price variables have the expected signs—positive for y_t, negative for y_t^2, and negative for p_t, thus confirming that consumption of the aggregate commodity groups increases as income grows, but at a decelerating rate. The estimates are all significantly different from zero at the 1 percent level. The estimates of this parameter for the metals aggregate are greater than for energy, and much larger than for agriculture, implying that metal consumption exhibits a stronger response to income and price changes. In addition, the results from the error-correction component of the model show that metals adjust to long-run equilibrium faster than energy and much faster than agriculture. This finding is consistent with the higher variability of metal intensity compared to energy and agriculture as well as the cyclical nature of metals, which tend to move in tandem with industrial activity (Roberts 1996).

The estimated income elasticities of demand show a considerable drop as the level of per capita income rises (figure 2.7). A value of one indicates commodity demand grows at the same rate as income, larger than one it grows faster than income, and below one it grows more slowly. A negative value indicates declining commodity demand as income grows.

FIGURE 2.7 Income elasticity estimates

The income elasticity of metals was high at very low levels of income but declined rapidly, reaching unity at about US$12,000 per capita, and close to zero at the current level of U.S. income per capita. For energy, the initial elasticity was lower than for metals, but it declined more slowly and remained positive at the current level of U.S. income per capita. In contrast, agricultural elasticities were much lower than for energy and metals, indicating that population growth is the primary driver of agricultural consumption growth.

A. Aggregate income elasticity estimates

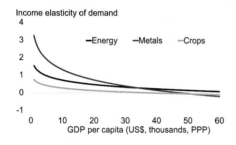

B. Energy income elasticity estimates for select economies

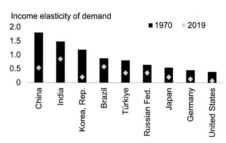

C. Metal income elasticity estimates for select economies

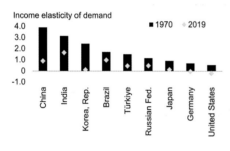

D. Agriculture income elasticity estimates for select economies

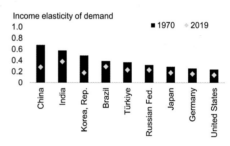

Sources: Original calculations; BP Statistical Review of World Energy 2021; U.S. Department of Agriculture; World Bank; World Bureau of Metal Statistics.
A. Lines show implied income elasticity of demand estimates derived from coefficients in table 2.1. PPP = purchasing power parity.
B.-D. Bars and diamonds indicate income elasticity of demand estimates at 1970 and 2019 per capita income levels. Russian Fed. = Russian Federation.

When calculated at the median level of per capita income in 2020, the income elasticity of demand for metals was 1.0, followed by energy at 0.6 and agriculture at 0.2. All commodities show a decrease in income elasticity as income rises, starting high and approaching zero or turning negative at higher levels of income. This result is consistent with the dematerialization hypothesis, which predicts a switch of consumption from commodity-intensive material goods to goods and services with a higher-value-added component. It can explain the plateauing of commodity demand shown in figure 2.4— as income rises, commodity demand grows at a decreasing rate.

The evidence shows a significant variation of income elasticities across commodities. Elasticities for metals and energy are well above unity at lower per capita incomes. As incomes rise, the elasticities decline, to below unity for both commodities at a per capita income of more than US$20,000. The elasticity for metals declined faster, equal to energy at a per capita income level of US$35,000 (in purchasing power parity terms), and turning negative at US$50,000. In contrast, energy had a positive income elasticity at all income levels. The estimate for the income elasticity of agriculture showed the least change for different levels of income. This estimate was less than unity even at the lowest income levels, which indicates that population is the primary driver of growth in agricultural commodities.

For each country, the implied path of income elasticities of demand over time can be derived. For most EMDEs, income elasticities started high and fell as economies industrialized and developed. In the case of China, its demand elasticity for metals fell from 4.0 in 1970 to 0.7 in 2019, while for energy it fell from 1.5 to 0.5. These elasticities imply that China's demand for commodities is now growing more slowly than its economy—in the case of energy, at half the rate. In other words, the commodity intensity of demand is declining. In advanced economies, elasticities were lower in 1970 and by 2019 had fallen to near zero for energy and slightly negative for metals and agriculture, indicating a modest decline in per capita consumption as incomes rose from an already high level.

Scenarios of commodity demand growth

Two factors suggest that overall demand for commodities will grow more slowly in the decades ahead than in the past three decades. First, population growth is slowing. The world's population is expected to reach 9.8 billion by 2050 from 7.6 billion in 2020, a 30 percent increase (United Nations projection; figure 2.8). The increase over the preceding 30 years was more than 40 percent. Moreover, almost all the expected growth will take place in EMDEs, especially in Sub-Saharan Africa, a region with the world's lowest per capita commodity demand.

Second, GDP growth is expected to slow. Consensus expectations for global growth 10 years ahead have repeatedly been revised down. The Organisation for Economic Co-operation and Development's long-term forecasts for GDP growth in EMDEs indicate a slowdown in growth from an average of 4.8 percent per year between 2011 and 2019 to an average of 3.7 percent per year between 2021 and 2030, largely due to slower growth in China. As China slows, it is expected to increasingly shift toward less commodity-intensive activities. For metals, however, the concentration of projected GDP growth in regions with relatively low incomes is a positive factor because of the high income elasticities of demand at lower income levels. Growth will instead shift toward economies that are currently much less commodity-intensive than China.

A key question is whether India (with a population similar in size to China's) or another group of EMDEs, such as those in Sub-Saharan Africa, could experience levels of commodity consumption growth commensurate with that of China. For India, this growth is unlikely, for two reasons. First, India is not expected to grow at the double-digit rates experienced by China through much of the 2000s. Second, India's economy

FIGURE 2.8 Future determinants of commodity demand

Global population is expected to continue to grow, driven increasingly by LICs, albeit at a slower pace than over the past half century. Similarly, global economic growth is expected to slow and be driven by EMDEs. Based on scenario estimates, demand for commodities in EMDEs is expected to slow, although metals demand growth will remain above that of energy and crops. When excluding China, however, EMDE demand for metals is expected to increase.

A. Cumulative population growth forecasts

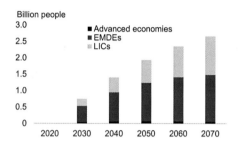

B. Long-term growth forecasts

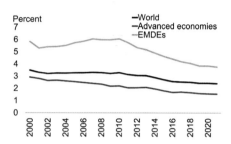

C. Scenario estimates of commodity demand growth in EMDEs

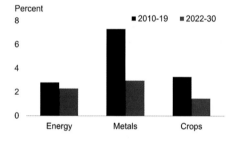

D. Scenario estimates of commodity demand growth in EMDEs excluding China

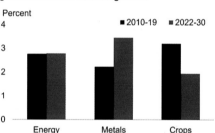

Sources: Consensus Economics; Organisation for Economic Co-operation and Development; United Nations; World Bank.
Note: EMDE = emerging market and developing economy; LIC = low-income country.
A. Chart shows cumulative increase in global population, by income levels, relative to 2020.
B. Chart shows 10-year-ahead consensus global growth forecasts.
C.D. Original estimates using United Nations population data, Organisation for Economic Co-operation and Development
 growth rates, and estimated income elasticities of demand.

is noticeably different, with the service sector playing a much larger role than it did in China at an equivalent stage of development. However, the current low levels of per capita commodity demand and expected population growth in other EMDEs and low-income countries represent a long-term future source of growth for commodity demand. As these economies develop and industrialize, their commodity demand will rise; given their very low levels of commodity consumption, these economies present a substantial amount of pent-up demand.

A scenario of future commodity demand growth to 2030 can be derived from a simulation experiment using the model described in equation 2.2. The main inputs for the projection are the estimated income elasticities of demand, population growth forecasts from the United Nations, and estimates for GDP growth from the

Organisation for Economic Co-operation and Development.[10] The scenario focuses on EMDEs, given that the majority of population growth and commodity demand growth is expected to occur in these economies. The scenario does not take into account structural changes in commodity demand, however, such as the energy transition. The likely impact of the energy transition on commodity demand is explored in box 2.3.

The simulation implies that growth in EMDE consumption of energy, metals, and crops slows over the next decade compared to 2010-19. The slowdown in metals is most pronounced, declining from an annual average of 7 percent to about 3 percent. However, this growth rate remains above that of energy and crops. The slowdown can be entirely attributed to China. If China is excluded, EMDE metal demand growth increases over the next decade as income elasticities of demand in the scenario stay above 1 in many EMDEs. For the other commodity groups, energy demand is expected to remain relatively constant, and crop consumption growth is estimated to halve.

The structural trends generated in the model simulation take explicit account only of income and population growth. Other factors, such as advances in global technology, shifts in consumer preferences, environmental concerns, and policies to encourage cleaner fuels, could trigger much more radical changes in the global use of some commodities. Of particular importance is the energy transition from fossil fuels toward low- or zero-carbon sources of energy. A technological transformation of this magnitude brings an unusually large and unpredictable component to long-run quantitative forecasts of the demand for commodities.

The direction of some changes, however, seems clear. The energy transition will lead to a reduction in the growth of demand for fossil fuels, particularly coal and crude oil, in favor of renewable energy sources (IEA 2021a). At some point, fossil fuel consumption will start to decline. In contrast, low-carbon energy systems are very intensive in their use of metals such as copper, nickel, cobalt, and lithium. Demand for these metals will likely grow rapidly because of the transition, although their production capacity may pose potential bottlenecks for the transition (Boer, Pescatori, and Stuermer 2021; World Bank 2017). Although the energy transition will likely have less direct effect on agricultural commodities, a sharp increase in demand for biofuels could reduce the availability of resources to grow other crops, putting upward pressure on food prices. This would be an unwelcome development, given that the poorest households spend a high proportion of their income on food, and that climate change also poses a threat to food harvests.

Conclusions and policy implications

The past half century has seen rapid growth in the consumption of most commodities. This growth is accounted for by population growth, income growth, and changes in the

---

[10] The Organisation for Economic Co-operation and Development data contain growth forecasts for 31 AEs and 17 EMDEs that collectively account for more than 90 percent of global GDP. For countries without growth forecasts, annual growth was held constant at their 2010-19 average.

BOX 2.3 **The energy transition: Causes and prospects**

The energy transition—the shift away from fossil fuels toward zero-carbon sources of energy—is already under way. Although the speed and magnitude of the transition are uncertain, it will have significant implications for commodity markets. Consumption of fossil fuels, especially coal and crude oil, is expected to decline. In contrast, demand for metals and minerals is likely to see a boost from the transition, because renewable energy infrastructure, such as wind turbines and solar, requires significant amounts of metal in its manufacturing. For agriculture, a surge in demand for biofuels could see increasing competition for these crops with traditional food crops, putting upward pressure on prices.

Introduction

The energy transition refers to the shift from an economy predominately driven by fossil fuels to one powered largely by zero-carbon energy sources. Such a shift is essential to sharply reduce greenhouse gas emissions to address global warming and achieve the objectives of the Paris Agreement. The transition is already under way; between 2000 and 2019, production of renewable energy increased by 300 percent, its share of total energy rose from 5 to 10 percent, and its share of electricity rose from 18 to 26 percent (figure B2.3.1). Despite this increase, the share of fossil fuels in total energy has remained relatively flat at the global level because of a fall in nuclear generation. Significant challenges remain, and further progress will be needed to avoid the worst outcomes of climate change.

Despite varying expectations for the speed of the transition, there is greater consensus that the energy transition will trigger a substantial change in the demand for commodities, leading to reduced demand for fossil fuels, particularly coal, and increased demand for the metals and minerals required for renewable energy infrastructure. Against that backdrop, this box examines the following questions:

- What is driving the energy transition?

- What are the challenges facing the transition?

- How fast is the transition expected to occur?

- How will it change patterns of demand for commodities?

What is driving the energy transition?

Government policies and consumer preferences. Policies are a potent tool in driving the energy transition. Almost all countries have signed on to the Paris Accord, and more than 100 countries have either set or are considering net-zero targets, although timelines differ (IEA 2021b; van Soest, den Elzen, and van Vuuren 2021). Subsidies for renewable energy sources and associated technologies such as electric vehicles can encourage investment in these sources of energy. To

BOX 2.3 The energy transition: Causes and prospects *(continued)*

FIGURE B2.3.1 The energy transition and its drivers

Since 2000, the share of renewable energy has increased sharply, with rapid growth in solar and wind power. The energy transition is being assisted by government policies to reduce CO_2 emissions, and by a sharp fall in renewable energy costs, both for electricity generation and storage.

A. Share of renewables in global supply

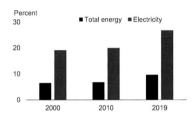

B. Share of solar and wind power in global energy

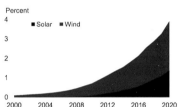

C. Number of national net zero pledges and share of global CO_2 emissions covered

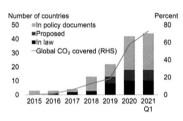

D. Renewable generation and electricity storage costs

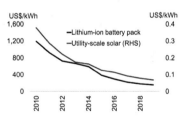

Sources: BP Statistical Review of World Energy 2021; International Energy Agency; International Renewable Energy Agency; Our World in Data; World Bank.
Note: CO_2 = carbon dioxide; RHS = right-hand side.
A. Renewables include hydroelectric, solar, wind, geothermal, biomass, and other renewable sources.
D. Installed cost of utility-scale photovoltaic solar power, measured as U.S. dollars per kilowatt-hour (US$/kWh) of generation. Consumer cost for lithium-ion cells, measured as dollars per kilowatt hour of storage.

reduce the use of fossil fuels, many countries have enacted carbon taxes or carbon pricing (OECD 2021). Many private sector companies, including fossil fuel producers, have announced zero-target ambitions, often in response to pressure from investors. The energy transition has also been influenced by the growth of green investment, a component of the ESG (environmental, social, and corporate governance) investor movement. The Institute for International Finance estimates that ESG debt issuance grew to US$2 trillion in 2021Q1 (IIF 2021).

Declining cost of renewables. Improving technology and better manufacturing processes have resulted in a sharp decline in the cost of renewable energy. The price of utility-scale solar energy fell by 80 percent between 2010 and 2019, and

BOX 2.3 **The energy transition: Causes and prospects** *(continued)*

the price of onshore wind power declined by nearly 40 percent (IRENA 2020).[a] As a result, solar and wind energy are now the lowest-cost sources of new electricity in many parts of the world, including China, India, and the United States (IEA 2020). Installed capacity is expected to grow rapidly over the next five years, and costs are expected to continue to decline with technological improvements, increasing solar and wind energy's competitiveness against traditional fossil fuels even more.[b] Decreasing costs of energy storage, including the development of new storage technologies, will be critical in facilitating a growing share of renewables in energy production. The ongoing development of low-cost lithium-ion batteries has been driven by the needs of the rapidly growing electric vehicle industry. In 2020, global electric vehicle sales rose nearly 20 percent, whereas sales of traditional cars declined. As storage costs continue to decrease and battery ranges improve, electric vehicle sales are expected to accelerate.

What are the challenges to achieving the transition to net-zero carbon emissions?

As the world economy has grown over the past 30 years, the carbon intensity of gross domestic product has declined, but total emissions have nonetheless kept rising. Achieving a transition to zero poses several challenges.

Insufficient investment. If investment in fossil fuel production falls faster than investment in renewable production increases, it could result in a shortfall of energy. Investment in oil and gas production is currently at a level broadly in line with the International Energy Agency scenario for a net-zero transition (figure B2.3.2; IEA 2021c). Investment in low-carbon technology, however, is currently only about one-third of what is required. The surge in energy prices in 2021 is a reminder of how rapidly fossil fuel prices increase when demand outstrips supply. Unexpectedly high energy prices, or interruptions to supply, could weaken political support for the energy transition.

Reserves and stranded assets. Although renewables are increasingly the lowest-cost source of new energy, significant reserves of fossil fuels remain and are concentrated in emerging market and developing economies (EMDEs). With energy demand expected to continue to increase in EMDEs, particularly among low-income countries where access to energy has been limited, countries may

---

a. Utility-scale solar farms are large installations of solar panels. They vary in size from a few acres to more than 20 square kilometers. The costs of residential rooftop solar panels are higher because of their small size. Nevertheless, residential costs fell in the past decade by an estimated 47 to 80 percent, depending on the market.

b. The cost of solar panels and wind turbines increased in 2021 because of the broader rise in commodity prices, including the metals and minerals used in their construction (for example, aluminum, silicon).

BOX 2.3 The energy transition: Causes and prospects *(continued)*

FIGURE B2.3.2 **Challenges to the energy transition**

The energy transition faces several challenges. Current levels of investment in clean energy are insufficient to offset the decline in oil and gas investment. Significant reserves of fossil fuels, particularly among EMDEs, encourage accelerated investment to sidestep the risk of stranded assets. Renewable energy also faces the issue of intermittency and seasonality. Other uses of energy will prove harder to decarbonize than road travel and electricity generation, and achieving a net-zero target in these industries will require significant technological developments, including in biofuels and the use of hydrogen.

A. Investment needs

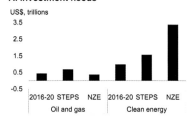

B. Fossil fuel reserves

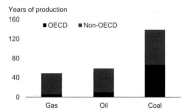

C. Renewable generation, EU28

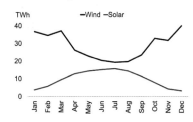

D. Share of global carbon emissions, by sector

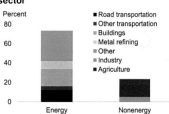

E. Biofuel production under IEA's NZE scenario

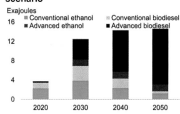

F. Use of hydrogen fuels by sector under IEA's NZE scenario

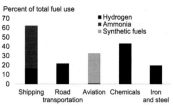

Sources: BP Statistical Review of World Energy 2021; Eurostat; International Energy Agency; Our World in Data; World Bank.

Note: STEPS and NZE refer to the International Energy Agency's stated policies and net-zero emissions scenarios, taken from IEA (2021b).

C. Chart shows monthly solar and wind energy production averaged over 2015-20. EU28 = all European Union countries; TWh = terrawatt hours.

D. "Energy" refers to carbon emissions from the consumption of energy by sectors of the economy. "Other" includes all other carbon emissions from energy consumption by nonspecified sectors of the economy (such as industry, agriculture). "Nonenergy" refers to carbon emissions from other sources, such as industrial emissions from the manufacture of chemicals, and agricultural emissions from livestock and rice production.

E.F. Charts show scenario estimates for production of biofuels and hydrogen-based fuels, taken from the Net Zero scenario in IEA (2021b).

BOX 2.3 The energy transition: Causes and prospects *(continued)*

choose to continue using fossil fuels, particularly if they have significant domestic reserves. Policy measures, such as border carbon taxes, can be introduced to address this environmental impact, but equity considerations must also be taken into account. Stranded assets—resources tied to fossil fuels and no longer able to generate an economic return because of carbon pricing—present another set of challenges. For example, regulators have been focusing on the risks that such assets present to financial stability.

Energy storage. A notable problem with renewable energy is the issue of intermittency. Electricity generation can fluctuate with weather, the time of day, and the season. For example, solar panels produce more energy when it is sunny, during the day, and during summer. At present, renewable electricity generation requires either storage or backup production for when renewable production drops. As renewable energy becomes increasingly widespread, this problem will become more acute, as seen in areas that have substantial solar capacity, such as California. Natural gas provides one method of backup generation of electricity and was used during 2021 when drought and low wind speed reduced renewable production in many countries (World Bank 2021b). However, natural gas still produces CO_2 emissions, and as such low-carbon sources of backup power will be needed. Improved large-scale methods of storing electricity could help with the problem of interrupted supply. Measures to improve load-balancing, or adjusting electricity demand to synchronize with supply, will also be critical. For example, whereas solar production peaks in summer and is lowest in winter, wind production tends to be higher in winter and lower in summer. Integration of power markets across regions and countries, including transmission lines, can help balance generation from renewables.

Energy subsidies. Subsidies for traditional sources of energy remain high, despite progress in reducing them in recent years. In response to soaring energy prices in 2021, many governments in both advanced economies and EMDEs reintroduced subsidies or used price caps to prevent the higher cost of natural gas and coal from being passed onto consumers. To the extent that subsidies make fossil fuels cheaper, they will delay the energy transition.

Carbon-intensive industries and novel technologies. Despite the existence of the technology to move to zero-carbon electricity and road transportation, about one-third of emissions comes from sectors that do not have an economically feasible alternative to fossil fuels. These sectors include ocean shipping, air transportation, metal refining, and agriculture. Replacing crude oil-based fuels in shipping and air transportation with battery power is not currently an option because of the length of journeys and the size of the vehicles. Many industrial processes, including the refining of metals, notably steel, are carbon-intensive—the smelting of iron ore into steel uses coking coal and currently accounts for about 7 percent of global emissions. A potential solution could be biofuels for some forms of

BOX 2.3 The energy transition: Causes and prospects *(continued)*

transport, or hydrogen, which could be used as both a fuel for transport and a replacement for fossil fuels, such as coal, in the smelting of steel (IEA 2019b; IRENA 2020). However, further technological development is required before these solutions become viable.

Agricultural emissions. Greenhouse emissions from agriculture present a challenge. Agriculture tends to be very capital and energy intensive in advanced economies, whereas in EMDEs it is typically more labor intensive. Agriculture also produces nonenergy greenhouse gas emissions, including the production of methane from livestock, especially cows, and from rice paddy fields. The euro area stands out for its energy intensity, driven by a few countries, notably Belgium and the Netherlands, which farm very intensively on small areas of land and use energy for heating and lighting. In contrast, southern countries have much lower energy intensities because they rely more on the sun.

How fast is the energy transition expected to occur?

Although the transition is under way, the timing is uncertain and depends on the approach taken by governments, and on the pace of technological change. Both industry and international organizations have developed several scenarios (BP 2020; EIA 2021; IEA 2021c; Royal Dutch Shell 2021). Figure B2.3.3 shows two scenarios by the International Energy Agency.[c] The first is the stated policies scenario (the "business-as-usual" approach), which incorporates current government policies but no additional progress. The second is the net-zero emissions scenario, which assumes significant policy changes by governments as well as substantial technological development in renewable generation, storage, and carbon capture, and results in an energy transition fast enough to limit warming to 1.5 degrees.

Under the stated policies scenario, the use of coal is anticipated to have already peaked and is expected to gradually decline over the next 30 years, whereas demand for oil sees a slight increase, driven by demand from EMDEs, before plateauing and declining after 2035, but broadly unchanged from current levels by 2050. Natural gas consumption continues to rise, given its cleaner properties and use as a backup fuel for renewables. Demand for renewable and biofuels rises rapidly, approximately doubling over the next 30 years, and nuclear sees a small rise.

The net-zero scenario is similar in terms of the direction and order of trajectory but differs in terms of speed and magnitude. Use of coal falls substantially by

---

c. These scenarios are broadly similar to those of BP and Shell. Differences chiefly pertain to the speed of the transition, which depends on policy choices and technological developments.

BOX 2.3 The energy transition: Causes and prospects *(continued)*

FIGURE B2.3.3 Speed and implications of the energy transition

The energy transition will result in significant changes in energy demand. Coal and crude oil will be the first to decline and see the sharpest falls, whereas natural gas may continue to increase. Renewables and biofuels will see the fastest growth, and nuclear will see modest gains. Demand for metals will likely increase sharply because renewable technologies are very metals intensive.

A. Energy demand growth by 2050 under different scenarios

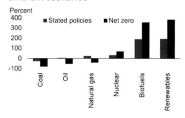

B. Copper use in electricity generation

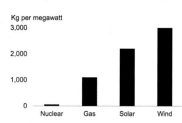

Sources: Copper Alliance; International Energy Agency; World Bank 2017; World Bank.

A. Chart shows the change in energy demand for different fuels relative to their 2019 level under different scenarios from IEA (2021b).

B. Chart shows the amount in kilograms (kg) of copper required to generate one megawatt of electricity using different generation methods.

about 80 percent by 2050, and oil declines by 50 percent. A significant proportion of oil will continue to be used in the petrochemical industry (currently about one-third of total consumption), which limits the reduction in use by 2050. Natural gas plateaus for the next decade before falling rapidly. For renewables, growth is expected to surge, rising more than fourfold over the next 30 years, with growth in solar power expected to be roughly double that of wind power. Similarly, biofuels are expected to rise fivefold by 2050. Nuclear is also expected to grow, albeit less rapidly, with a 70 percent increase.

Regardless of the scenario or forecaster, some commonalities hold. Coal is unlikely to see further increases and could start to see a rapid decline. Oil demand has broadly plateaued and will start to decline, albeit more slowly than coal, whereas natural gas is expected to see robust demand, at least in the next decade. Renewables and biofuels are set to see the fastest growth of any fuel, but the outlook for nuclear is less certain.

How will the energy transition affect demand for commodities?

Outlook for energy. Consumption of fossil fuels, especially coal, is expected to decline because of the increasing competitiveness of renewables. Increased take-up of electric vehicles will reduce oil demand. Further out, demand for fossil fuels will remain for industrial uses, such as petrochemicals and fertilizer production.

BOX 2.3 The energy transition: Causes and prospects *(continued)*

The impact of the energy transition on the production of fossil fuels, and consequently on prices, is more uncertain. The production of fossil fuels (especially natural gas and crude oil) requires significant investment in exploration and drilling simply to maintain current levels of production. Natural gas and oil wells can have high decline rates, particularly in the case of shale oil. Even if demand for these fuels falls, substantial new investment will still be needed. As a result of ESG investing and shareholder activism, there has been a shift away from investment in new oil production by the oil majors. State-owned companies, however, have been under less pressure to diversify. Therefore, future production is likely to increasingly be accounted for by the Organization of the Petroleum Exporting Countries and its partners. The remaining producers will likely be those with the lowest cost of production, whereas higher-cost producers will be the first to curtail production.

Outlook for metals. In contrast to fossil fuels, demand for certain metals and minerals is likely to benefit from a shift to a zero-carbon future. Low-carbon-emission technology is typically more metals intensive than fossil fuel energy. The key metals needed for a low-carbon future are aluminum (including alumina and bauxite), chromium, cobalt, copper, iron ore and steel, lithium, manganese, molybdenum, nickel, platinum group metals, rare earth metals (which include cadmium, indium, and neodymium), silver, titanium, and zinc (World Bank 2017). At present, solar-generated electricity requires twice as much copper as natural gas does, and wind requires three times as much (World Bank 2017). The same is true for electric vehicles. A traditional internal combustion engine car uses about 20 kilograms of copper, but electric vehicles require more than four times as much (ICA 2017). The wiring of the electric vehicle charging infrastructure will also imply a boost in demand for both aluminum and copper.

Outlook for agriculture. For agricultural commodities, the main impact of the energy transition is likely to be through increased demand for biofuels. Projected scenarios anticipate a sharp increase in biofuel consumption wherever electricity is not a feasible energy substitute for crude oil. The main crops for biofuels are corn/maize (United States), sugarcane (Brazil), and vegetable oils such as canola and palm (European Union). Biofuels currently account for about 4 percent of total land allocated to food crops. However, rapid-transition scenarios anticipate a fourfold increase in production, which would represent a massive diversion of land from food crops. In addition, biofuels' net environmental benefits are limited by the energy required to produce and process the crops (Searchinger et al. 2008). To mitigate this pressure, a significant further increase in agricultural yields, or the development of advanced biofuels made from crop waste or algae, would be required. Climate change could also affect agricultural production. For example, temperature and precipitation changes affect crop yields and could render large areas unsuitable for cropping (Schmidhuber and Tubiello 2007).

commodity intensity of output. Technological change, per capita income, and government policies have had important effects on commodity intensity.

Since 1970, global population has doubled, with growth concentrated mainly in EMDEs and low-income countries. Per capita income at the global level has more than doubled, and it has quadrupled among EMDEs. Thus, although global per capita consumption of commodities has leveled off over the past 20 years, consumption relative to GDP has declined. The decline in the commodity intensity of global output has been focused in energy and agricultural commodities. For metals, a similar downward trend in intensity was evident until about 2000, when the rapid industrialization of China brought a turnaround.

Econometric estimates of the income elasticities of demand for commodities indicate a causal pattern underlying these trends. The estimated elasticity, at median per capita income, is greater for metals than for energy, and lower for food than either. Demand for food has been almost entirely driven by population growth. Estimated income elasticities for all three commodity groups decline as incomes rise, providing support for the hypothesis that economic development involves a shift from material-intensive goods toward products with a higher-value-added component, notably services.

EMDE demand for metals, and to a lesser extent for energy, is expected to continue to grow over the next few decades, because many countries are still in a development phase associated with high income elasticities of demand. However, it is unlikely that EMDE commodity demand growth will repeat the growth rates experienced during the past two decades, because income growth and industrialization policies in other countries are unlikely to replicate those of China. Further, whereas demand for energy will continue to grow, demand for fossil fuels is expected to decline; energy will instead be provided by zero-carbon sources, such as renewables or nuclear energy.

The evolution of the drivers of commodity demand, together with likely changes resulting from the energy transition, will have significant implications in the years ahead. Aggregate commodity demand is expected to slow, reflecting the slowdown in income and population growth, and China's shift toward services. However, the outlook for different commodities varies substantially. Growth in demand for metals is likely to be higher than for other commodities because of metals' high income elasticity of demand, as well as the energy transition. Energy demand should continue to grow, albeit at a slower rate. With the shift away from fossil fuels, however, demand for hydrocarbons will grow more slowly or decline, compared to the past 50 years. Demand growth for agricultural crops is likely to moderate in line with the slowdown in population growth. The slowing will likely be concentrated in basic foods such as grains; demand for the more income-elastic foods, such as meat and dairy, may see faster growth.

The emerging energy transition implies transformative substitutions among commodities, and underlays the robust growth projected for metal consumption. The switch to clean electric power implies a permanent increase in the demand for copper, nickel, cobalt, and lithium, and an eventual drop in the use of fossil fuels. With respect to agriculture, a slowdown in growth in demand for basic foods could be offset by an acceleration in the use of biofuels, the production of which is currently concentrated in a handful of countries, notably Brazil, the European Union countries, and the United States.

The expected growth in demand for most commodities is likely to be met over time by commensurate increases in productive capacity, as technology advancements induce innovation and increase possibilities for substitution (Schwerhoff and Stuermer 2019). However, the supply of minerals needed for renewable energy might encounter bottlenecks, especially in view of the long development period before new facilities come onstream. A key policy question in this regard is whether resources will be produced and consumed in an environmentally sustainable manner, given the substantial externalities. Local externalities may be relatively easy to address, because the approvals process typically concerns a single policy maker (such as a national or state government), although it can nevertheless be controversial, politically difficult, and time-consuming. Global externalities, with respect to climate change, plastic waste, water pollution, and other environmental challenges, extend beyond country jurisdictions. Action or inaction by one country affects other countries, for better or for worse. An effective program for environmentally sustainable production growth necessarily includes international measures to promote the beneficial spillovers of environmental protection.

TABLE 2.1 Parameter estimates

	Energy	Metals	Food
y_t	3.99***	9.08***	1.28***
	(0.44)	(0.42)	(0.17)
y_t^2	-0.18***	-0.42***	-0.05***
	(0.02)	(0.02)	(0.01)
p_t^{ENERGY}	0.22***	–	–
	(0.02)		
p_t^{METALS}	–	0.24***	–
		(0.04)	
p_t^{FOOD}	–	–	-0.07***
			(0.01)
ρ	-0.08***	-0.18***	-0.27***
	(0.01)	(0.02)	(0.02)
Key statistics			
No. observations	3,195	2,123	3,799
No. countries	62	42	77
Log-likelihood	5,442	1,778	4,227

Source: World Bank.
Note: The dependent variable is the logarithm of the specific commodity consumption. Asymptotic standard errors in parentheses.
— = not available. Significance level: * = 10 percent, ** = 5 percent, *** = 1 percent.

TABLE 2.2 Literature review of income elasticities

Author (year)	Data/sample	Methodology	Results
Baffes, Kabundi, and Nagle (2022)	Three energy and six base metals, 63 countries, annual, 1965-2018	ARDL	At world median per capita income levels, 0.9 for metals and 0.7 for energy; elasticities decline as income rises.
Bogmans et al. (2020)	Energy, 127 countries, annual, 1850-2017	OLS	Supports Kuznets curve: elasticity increases at low-income levels, peaks at middle-income levels at around unity, and declines toward zero at high-income levels.
Bailliu et al. (2019)	Copper, 25 countries, annual, 1970-2015	PSTR	Elasticity of copper intensity to the investment share is fairly constant at about 0.5.
Fernandez (2018a)	Steel and 6 base metals, world and 8 regions, annual, 1980-2015	OLS and SUR	Long-run income elasticities: 1.3 (nickel), 1.1 (aluminum and tin), 1.0 (steel), 0.9 (zinc), 0.7 (copper), and 0.5 (lead). By region: steel elasticities were all unity or higher; for base metals varied widely across regions.
Huntington, Barrios, and Arora (2017)	Energy, price, and income elasticity estimates of demand from 38 papers	Literature review	On average, 0.5 for oil and 0.9 for natural gas.
Stuermer (2017)	Five base metals, 12 and 3 EMDEs, annual, 1840-2010	ARDL	Estimates (based on manufacturing output growth): 1.5 (aluminum), 0.9 (copper), 0.7 (zinc), 0.6 (tin), and 0.4 (lead).
Burke and Csereklyei (2016)	Energy, 132 countries, annual data, 1960-2010, energy	Panel OLS	Aggregate income elasticity is 0.7 for energy; it rises as income increases.
Crompton (2015)	Steel, 26 OECD countries, annual, 1970-2012	Fixed effects panel model	Inverse-U relationship between steel consumption and GDP per capita. Estimates range from zero to 4.1 and are negatively related to the country's GDP.
Csereklyei and Stern (2015)	Energy, 93 countries, annual data, 1971-2010	OLS	On average 0.6 to 0.8; as income rises, the rate of growth of energy use per capita declines.
Fouquet (2014)	Energy, United Kingdom, annual data, 1700-2000	VECM	As income rises, long-run income elasticity for transport energy peaks at 3.0 before declining to 0.3.
Valin et al. (2014)	Agricultural commodities, 10 economic models	Literature review (models)	Median income elasticities for rice and wheat estimated to be close to 0.1. First and third quartile range of estimates range from 0 to 0.2.
Wårrel (2014)	Steel, 61 countries, annual, 1970-2011	OLS, panel time series	Intensity of use holds for countries with real per capita GDP (2011 terms) between US$6,000 and US$30,000. The turning point occurs at US$19,000. A reverse relationship is found among high-income countries.

TABLE 2.2 Literature review of income elasticities (*continued*)

Author (year)	Data/sample	Methodology	Results
Dahl (2012)	Energy, 240 gasoline studies (70 countries) and 60 diesel studies (55 countries)	Literature review	As per capita income increases, elasticity for gasoline falls from 1.26 to 0.66.
Jakob, Haller and Marschinski (2012)	Energy, 30 EMDEs and 21 AEs, annual, 1971-2005	Difference-in-differences, panel data	Estimated at 0.63 for EMDEs and 0.18 for AEs.
Joyeux and Ripple (2011)	Energy, 30 OECD and 26 non-OECD countries, annual data, 1973-2007, energy	ECM estimator	It is 1.1 for OECD countries and 0.9 for and for non-OECD countries.
Guzman, Nashiyama, and Tilton (2005)	Copper, Japan, annual, 1960-2000	Various forms of time trend models	Intensity of copper use in Japan increased until GDP per capita reached US$18,285 (in 1969) and has declined since then.
Gately and Huntington (2002)	Energy and oil, 96 countries, OECD and non-OECD, annual, 1971-1997	Pooled demand equation, Koyck-lag model	Oil: 0.5 in OECD, 1.0 in non-OECD oil exporters, and 0.5 in other non-OECD.
Krichene (2002)	Crude oil and natural gas, World, annual, 1918-99	2SLS and ECM	Estimated at 0.6 for the full sample, it declines from 1918-73 to 1973-99.
Tcha and Takashina (2002)	Steel and 6 base metals, 1960-93 (world) and 1973-93 (7 regions)	Divisia moments	Estimates range 0.6 (lead) to 1.3 (nickel).
Gately and Streifel (1997)	Eight oil products, 37 developing countries, annual, 1971-93	OLS	Estimated at 1.0 for most countries, and much higher for some oil exporters (for example, 5.6 for Venezuela, RB, and 5.2 for Nigeria).

Source: World Bank.
Note: 2SLS = two-stage least squares; AE = advanced economy; ARDL = autoregressive distributed lag; ECM = error correction model; EMDE = emerging market and developing economy; OECD = Organisation for Economic Co-operation and Development; OLS = ordinary least squares; PSTR = panel smooth transition regression; SUR = seemingly unrelated regressions; VECM = vector error correction model.

TABLE 2.3 Literature review of urbanization and commodity demand

Author (year)	Data	Main topic	Main findings
Baffes, Kabundi, and Nagle (2022)	Panel of 63 advanced economies and EMDEs, 1965-2017	Aggregate energy and metal consumption	Urbanization has a positive effect on energy and metal consumption (positive on coal and natural gas consumption but negative effect on oil).
Dasgupta, Lall, and Wheeler (2021)	1,236 cities in 138 countries, 2014-2020	CO_2 emissions	Urban areas with higher population density have higher CO_2 emissions at very low levels of per capita income, but lower CO_2 emissions at higher income levels (above US$1,000 per capita).
Hovhannisyan and Devadoss (2020)	Panel data on consumer food expenditure in China, 2005-12	Food consumption	Urbanization has reduced demand for grains, vegetables, and fats and oils while increasing demand for meats, fruit, and eggs.
Pandey et al. (2020)	Consumer expenditure survey data covering 124 food commodities at the household, district, and state level in India	Food consumption	Although urbanization leads to varied diets, most of the change in food consumption patterns between urban and rural areas is due to income, not urbanization.
Larson and Yezer (2015)	Theoretical model calibrated with empirical estimates of model parameters with calibration target of 10 U.S. cities	Energy use from transport and dwellings	A doubling in urban population leads to a 2.6 percent reduction in energy use from transportation and dwelling use.
Salim and Shafiei (2014)	Panel of 29 OECD countries, 1980-2011	Aggregate energy use (renewable and nonrenewable)	Urbanization has a positive effect on nonrenewable energy use (due to changing consumer needs and increased transport demand) but little effect on renewable energy use.
Sadorsky (2013)	Unbalanced panel of 76 developing countries, 1980-2010	Energy intensity	Urbanization has an insignificant effect on energy use in most versions of the model; income is a statistically significant negative driver of energy intensity.
Brounen, Kok, and Quigley (2012)	Sample of 300,000 households in the Netherlands, 2008-09	Energy use from dwellings	Apartments and row homes had significantly lower energy consumption than detached and semidetached homes. An additional person per household reduced per capita natural gas and electricity consumption by 26 percent and 18 percent, respectively.
Morikawa (2012)	Microdata covering up to 66,000 service sector firms in Japan, 2007-08	Energy use by service sector	The efficiency of energy consumption in service companies is higher in densely populated cities. Energy efficiency increases by 12 percent when density doubles.
Poumanyvong, Kaneko, and Dhakal (2012)	Panel data set of 92 countries (low- medium- and high-income), 1975-2005	Energy use from transport	Urbanization leads to more energy use in transportation for all income groups, especially high-income countries.

TABLE 2.3 Literature review of urbanization and commodity demand (*continued*)

Author (year)	Data	Main topic	Main findings
Glaeser and Kahn (2010)	Single-year survey and census data for U.S. metropolitan areas	GHG emissions from energy use	Higher-density cities have lower emissions than low-density cities. Emissions from driving and electricity are lower, but emissions from public transportation and heating are higher.
Poumanyvong and Kaneko (2010)	Panel data set of 92 countries (low, middle, and high income) 1975-2005	Aggregate energy consumption	Urbanization results in lower energy use in low-income countries (perhaps due to switching from inefficient to efficient fuels). Urbanization leads to increased energy use in middle- and high-income countries.
Brownstone and Golob (2009)	Single-year survey data for California, United States	Energy use from transport	Lower-density households travel more and consume more fuel because of increased travel time and self-selection of less efficient cars.
Liu (2009)	China, 1978-2008	Aggregate energy consumption	Urbanization has a positive effect on energy consumption—much smaller than that of income and decreasing over time.
Mishra, Smyth, and Sharma (2009)	Nine Pacific island countries, 1980-2005	Aggregate energy consumption	In aggregate, a 1.0 percent increase in the rate of urbanization generates a 2.4 percent increase in energy consumption. However, the effect was positive in only four of the nine countries (negative in one, and insignificant in the other).
York (2007)	Panel of 14 EU countries, 1960-2000	Aggregate energy consumption	Urbanization leads to more energy consumption.
Liddle (2004)	Panel data, 23 OECD countries, 1960-2000	Energy consumption by transportation	Highly urbanized and more densely populated countries have lower personal transportation consumption.
Lariviere and Lafrance (1999)	Single-year data on electricity consumption, 45 cities in Canada	Electricity consumption	High-density cities use slightly less electricity than lower-density ones.
Parikh and Shukla (1995)	Panel data set of 72 countries, 1965-87	Aggregate energy consumption	A 1.00 percent rise in urbanization leads to a 0.28 percent rise in energy use, driven by transportation and attributed to greater intraurban commuting and congestion.

Source: World Bank 2021b.
Note: EMDE = emerging market and developing economy; EU = European Union; GHG = greenhouse gas; OECD = Organisation for Economic Co-operation and Development.

References

Adeyemi, I. O., and L. C. Hunt. 2007. "Modelling OECD Industrial Energy Demand: Asymmetric Price Responses and Energy-Saving Technical Change." *Energy Economics* 29 (4): 693-709.

Aghion, P., C. Antonin, and S. Bunel. 2021. *The Power of Creative Destruction: Economic Upheaval and the Wealth of Nations.* Cambridge, MA: Harvard University Press.

Akiyama, T., and P. Varangis. 1990. "The Impact of the International Coffee Agreement on Producing Countries." *World Bank Economic Review* 4 (2): 157-73.

Angel, S., A. M. Blei, J. Parent, P. Lamson-Hall, N. G. Sánchez, D. L. Civco, R. Q. Lei, and K. Thom. 2016. *Atlas of Urban Expansion—2016 Edition.* New York: NYU Urban Expansion Program at New York University, UN-Habitat, and the Lincoln Institute of Land Policy.

Baffes, J., A. Kabundi, and P. Nagle. 2022. "The Role of Income and Substitution in Commodity Demand." *Oxford Economic Papers* 74 (2): 498-522.

Baffes, J., M. A. Kose, F. Ohnsorge, and M. Stocker. 2015. "The Great Plunge in Oil Prices: Causes, Consequences, and Policy Responses." Policy Research Note 1, World Bank, Washington, DC.

Bailliu, J., D. Bilgin, K. Mo, K. Niquidet, and B. Sawatzky. 2019. "Global Commodity Markets and Rebalancing in China: The Case of Copper." Staff Discussion Paper 03, Bank of Canada, Ottawa.

Barnes, D., K. Krutilla, and W. Hyde. 2005. *The Urban Household Energy Transition.* Milton Park, U.K.: Routledge.

Benfield, F., M. Raimi, and D. Chen. 1999. *Once There Were Green Fields: How Urban Sprawl Is Undermining America's Environment, Economy and Social Fabric.* New York: Natural Resources Defense Council.

Boer, P., A. Pescatori, and M. Stuermer. 2021. "Energy Transition Metals" IMF Working Paper 243, International Monetary Fund, Washington, DC.

Bogmans, C., L. Kiyasseh, A. Matsumoto, and A. Pescatori. 2020. "Energy, Efficiency Gains and Economic Development: When Will Global Energy Demand Saturate?" IMF Working Paper 253, International Monetary Fund, Washington, DC.

BP (British Petroleum). 2020. "Energy Outlook 2020 Edition." https://www.bp.com/content/dam/bp/business-sites/en/global/corporate/pdfs/energy-economics/energy-outlook/bp-energy-outlook-2020.pdf.

Brody, S. 2013. "The Characteristics, Causes, and Consequences of Sprawling Development Patterns in the United States." *Nature Education Knowledge* 4 (5): 2.

Brounen, D., N. Kok, and J. Quigley. 2012. "Residential Energy Use and Conservation: Economics and Demographics." *European Economic Review* 56 (5): 931-45.

Brownstone, D., and T. Golob. 2009. "The Impact of Residential Density on Vehicle Usage and Energy Consumption." *Journal of Urban Economics* 65 (1): 91-98.

Burchell, R., N. Shad, D. Listokin, and H. Phillips. 1998. *The Costs of Sprawl Revisited.* Report 39. Transit Cooperative Research Program, Transportation Research Board. Washington, DC: National Academy Press.

Burke, P., and Z. Csereklyei. 2016. "Understanding the Energy-GDP Elasticity: A Sectoral Approach." *Energy Economics* 58 (8): 199-210.

Campbell T., C. Williams, O. Ivanova, and B. Garrett. 2011. "Could 3D Printing Change the World? Technologies, Potential, and Implications of Additive Manufacturing." Strategic Foresight Initiative, Atlantic Council, Washington, DC.

Chan, H. L., and S. K. Lee. 1997. "Modelling and Forecasting the Demand for Coal in China." *Energy Economics* 19 (3): 271-87.

Chandrasekhar, S. 1989. "Cartel in a Can: The Financial Collapse of the International Tin Council." *Northwestern Journal of International Law and Business* 10 (2): 308-32.

Chen, W., and T. E. Graedel. 2012. "Anthropogenic Cycles of the Elements: A Critical Review." *Environmental Science & Technology 46* (16): 8574-86.

Clark, C. 1940. *The Conditions of Economic Progress.* London: Macmillan.

Cleveland, C. J., and M. Ruth. 1998. "Indicators of Dematerialization and the Materials Intensity of Use." *Journal of Industrial Ecology* 2 (3): 15-50.

Cole, M., and E. Neumayer. 2004. "Examining the Impact of Demographic Factors on Air Pollution." *Population and Environment* 26: 5-21.

Creutzig, F. 2014. "How Fuel Prices Determine Public Transportation Infrastructure, Modal Shares and Urban Form." *Urban Climate* 10 (December): 63-76.

Creutzig, F., G. Baiocchi, R. Bierkandt, P. P. Pichler, and K. C. Seto. 2015. "A Global Typology of Urban Energy Use and Potentials for an Urbanization Mitigation Wedge." *Proceedings of the National Academy of Sciences* 112 (20): 6283-88.

Crompton, P. 2015. "Explaining Variation in Steel Consumption in the OECD." *Resources Policy* 45 (September): 239-46.

Csereklyei, Z., and D. Stern. 2015. "Global Energy Use: Decoupling or Convergence?" *Energy Economics* 51 (September): 633-41.

Dahl, C. 2012. "Measuring Global Gasoline and Diesel Price and Income Elasticities." *Energy Policy* 41 (C): 2-13.

Dahl, C. A., and C. Roman. 2004. "Energy Demand Elasticities Fact or Fiction? A Survey Update." Paper presented at the 24th Annual North American Conference of the United States and International Association for Energy Economics (USAEE/IAEE), "Energy, Environment and Economics in a New Era," Washington, DC, July 7-10.

Dasgupta, S., S. Lall, and D. Wheeler. 2021. "Urban CO_2 Emissions: A Global Analysis with new Satellite Data." Policy Research Working Paper 9845, World Bank, Washington, DC.

Davis, J. S. 1946. "Experience under Intergovernmental Commodity Agreements, 1902-45." *Journal of Political Economy* 54 (3): 193-220.

de Gorter, H., and D. R. Just. 2009. "The Economics of a Blend Mandate for Biofuels." *American Journal of Agricultural Economics* 91 (3): 738-50.

Dienes, L., I. Dobozi, and M. Radetzki. 1994. *Energy and Economic Reform in the Former Soviet Union*. London: Palgrave Macmillan.

Dijkstra, L., A. Florczyk, S. Freire, T. Kemper, M. Melchiorri, M. Pesaresi, and M. Schiavina. 2020. "Applying the Degree of Urbanisation to the Globe: A New Harmonised Definition Reveals a Different Picture of Global Urbanisation." *Journal of Urban Economics* 125 (2).

Dijkstra, L., E. Hamilton, S. Lall, and S. Wahba. 2020. "How Do We Define Cities, Towns, and Rural Areas?" *Sustainable Cities* (blog), World Bank, March 10, 2020. https://blogs.worldbank.org/sustainablecities/how-do-we-define-cities-towns-and-rural-areas.

Drollas, L. P. 1984. "The Demand for Gasoline: Further Evidence." *Energy Economics* 6 (1): 71-82.

Eberts, R., and D. McMillen. 1999. "Agglomeration Economies and Urban Public Infrastructure." In *Handbook of Regional and Urban Economics*, Vol. 3, Applied Urban Economics, edited by P. Cheshire, and E. S. Mills, 1455-195. Amsterdam: ScienceDirect.

EIA (U.S. Energy Information Administration). 2021. *Annual Coal Report 2020*. Washington, DC: United States Energy Information Administration.

Erdogdu, E. 2010. "Natural Gas Demand in Turkey." *Applied Energy* 87: 211-19.

Evans M., and A. C. Lewis. 2005. "Dynamics Metal Demand Model." *Resources Policy* 30: 55-69.

Fernandez, V. 2018a. "Price and Income Elasticity of Demand for Mineral Commodities." *Resources Policy* 59: 160-83.

Fernandez, V. 2018b. "Mineral Commodity Consumption and Intensity of Use Re-assessed." *International Review of Financial Analysis* 59 (10): 10-16.

Fouquet, R. 2014. "Long-Run Demand for Energy Services: Income and Price Elasticities over Two Hundred Years." *Review of Environmental Economics and Policy* 8 (2): 186-207.

Gately, D, and H. G. Huntington. 2002. "The Asymmetric Effects of Changes in Price and Income on Energy and Oil Demand." *Energy Journal* 23 (1): 19-55.

Gately, D., and S. Streifel. 1997. "The Demand for Oil Products in Developing Countries." Discussion Paper 359, World Bank, Washington, DC.

Gilbert, C. L. 2011. "International Agreements for Commodity Price Stabilization: An Assessment." OECD Food, Agriculture and Fisheries Papers No. 53, OECD Publishing, Paris.

Gillingham, K., D. Rapson, and G. Wagner. 2016. "The Rebound Effect and Energy Efficiency Policy." *Review of Environmental Economics and Policy* 10 (1): 68-88.

Glaeser, E., and Kahn, E. 2010. "The Greenness of Cities: Carbon Dioxide Emissions and Urban Development." *Journal of Urban Economics* 67 (3): 404-18.

Goeller, H. E., and A. M. Weinberg. 1978. "The Age of Substitutability." *American Economic Review* 68 (6): 1-11.

Guzmán, J. I., T. Nashiyama, and J. E. Tilton. 2005. "Trends in the Intensity of Copper Use in Japan since 1960." *Resources Policy* 30 (March): 21-27.

Hamilton, J. 2009. "Understanding Crude Oil Prices." *Energy Journal* 30 (2): 179-206.

Hankey, S., and J. Marshall. 2010. "Impacts of Urban Form on Future US Passenger-Vehicle Greenhouse Gas Emissions." *Energy Policy* 38 (9): 4880-87.

Hanlon, W. W. 2015. "Necessity Is the Mother of Invention: Input Supplies and Directed Technical Change." *Econometrica* 83 (1): 67-100.

Hayami, Y., and V. W. Ruttan. 1970. "Prices and Technical Change in Agricultural Development: The United States and Japan, 1880-1960." *Journal of Political Economy* 78 (5): 1115-41.

Herman, R., S. A. Ardekani, and J. H. Ausubel. 1990. "Dematerialization." *Technological Forecasting and Social Change* 38 (4): 333-47.

Hicks, J. R. 1932. *The Theory of Wages.* New York: Macmillan.

Hommann, K., and S. Lall. 2019. *Which Way to Livable and Productive Cities? A Road Map for Sub-Saharan Africa.* International Development in Focus Series. Washington, DC: World Bank.

Hovhannisyan, V., and S. Devadoss. 2020. "Effects of Urbanization on Food Demand in China." *Empirical Economics* 58 (2): 699-721.

Huntington, H., J. Barrios, and V. Arora. 2017. "Review of Key International Demand Elasticities for Major Industrializing Economies." U.S. Energy Information Administration Working Paper, Washington, DC.

ICA (International Copper Alliance). 2017. "The Electric Vehicle Market and Copper Demand." International Copper Alliance, New York.

IEA (International Energy Agency). 1979. "Principles for IEA Action on Coal: Decision on Procedures for Review of IEA Countries' Coal Policies." Press release, Paris, International Energy Agency.

IEA (International Energy Agency). 1995. *The History of the International Energy Agency. 1974-1994.* Paris: International Energy Agency.

IEA (International Energy Agency). 2008. *World Energy Outlook 2008*. Paris: International Energy Agency.

IEA (International Energy Agency). 2019a. *Global EV Outlook 2019*. Paris: International Energy Agency.

IEA (International Energy Agency). 2019b. "The Role of Gas in Today's Energy Transitions." *World Energy Outlook* special report, International Energy Agency, Paris.

IEA (International Energy Agency). 2020. *World Energy Outlook 2020*. Paris: International Energy Agency.

IEA (International Energy Agency). 2021a. *World Energy Balances 2021*. Paris: International Energy Agency.

IEA (International Energy Agency). 2021b. *World Energy Outlook 2021*. Paris: International Energy Agency.

IEA (International Energy Agency). 2021c. *Net Zero by 2050. A Roadmap for the Global Energy Sector*. Paris: International Energy Agency.

IIF (Institute of International Finance). 2021. *Sustainable Debt Monitor: Race to Net Zero Drives ESG Flows*. Washington, DC: Institute of International Finance.

Imhoff, M., P. Zhang, R. Wolfe, and L. Bounoua. 2010. "Remote Sensing of the Urban Heat Island Effect across Biomes in the Continental USA." *Remote Sensing of Environment* 114 (3): 504-13.

IPCC (Intergovernmental Panel on Climate Change). 2021. *Climate Change 2021: The Physical Science Basis. Contribution of Working Group I to the Sixth Assessment Report of the Intergovernmental Panel on Climate Change*. Cambridge, U.K.: Cambridge University Press.

IRENA (International Renewable Energy Agency). 2020. *Renewable Power Generation Costs in 2019*. Abu Dhabi: International Renewable Energy Agency.

Jacks, D. S., and M. Stuermer. 2018. "What Drives Commodity Price Booms and Busts?" *Energy Economics* 85 (1): 104035.

Jakob, M., M. Haller, and R. Marschinski. 2012. "Will History Repeat Itself? Economic Convergence and Convergence in Energy Use Patterns." *Energy Economics* 34 (1): 95-104.

Jaunky, V. C. 2012. "Is There a Material Kuznets Curve for Aluminium? Evidence from Rich Countries?" *Resources Policy* 37 (3): 296-307.

Jones, D. 1991. "How Urbanization Affects Energy-Use in Developing Countries." *Energy Policy* 19 (7): 621-30.

Jones, D. 2004. "Urbanization and Energy." *Encyclopedia of Energy* 6: 329-35.

Joyeux, R., and R. D. Ripple. 2011. "Energy Consumption and Real Income: A Panel Cointegration Multi-country Study." *Energy Journal* 32 (2): 107-41.

Kahn, M. 2000. "The Environmental Impact of Suburbanization." *Journal of Policy Analysis and Management* 19 (4): 569-86.

Kamerschen, D. R., and D. V. Porter. 2004. "The Demand for Residential, Industrial and Total Electricity, 1973-1998." *Energy Economics* 26 (1): 87-100.

Kharina, A., and D. Rutherford. 2015. "Fuel Efficiency Trends for New Commercial Jet Aircraft: 1960 to 2014." White Paper series, International Council on Clean Transportation, Washington, DC.

Kovarik, C. 2013. "Biofuels in History." In *Biofuel Crops: Production, Physiology and Genetics*, edited by B. P. Singh. Wallingford, U.K.: Centre for Agriculture and Bioscience International.

Krichene, N. 2002. "World Crude Oil and Natural Gas: A Demand and Supply Model." *Energy Economics* 24 (6): 557-76.

Kuznets, S. 1971. *Economic Growth of Nations: Total Output and Production Structure.* Cambridge, MA: Harvard University Press.

Lahoni, P. R., and J. E. Tilton. 1993. "A Cross-Section Analysis of Metal Intensity of Use in the Less-Developed Countries." *Resources Policy* 19 (3): 145-54.

Lall, S. V., M. Lebrand, H. Park, D. Sturm, and A. J. Venables. 2021. *Pancakes to Pyramids: City Form to Promote Sustainable Growth.* Washington, DC: World Bank.

Lariviere, I., and G. Lafrance. 1999. "Modelling the Electricity Consumption of Cities: Effect of Urban Density." *Energy Economics* 21 (1): 53-66.

Larson, W., and A. Yezer. 2015. "The Energy Implications of City Size and Density." *Journal of Urban Economics* 90 (November): 35-49.

Liddle, B. 2004. "Demographic Dynamics and Per Capita Environmental Impact: Using Panel Regressions and Household Decompositions to Examine Population and Transport." *Population and Environment* 26 (1): 23-39.

Liddle, B., and S. Lung. 2010. "Age-Structure, Urbanization, and Climate Change in Developed Countries: Revisiting STIRPAT for Disaggregated Population and Consumption-Related Environmental Impacts." *Population and Environment* 31 (5): 317-43.

Liu, J., G. Daily, P. Ehrlich, and G. Luck. 2003. "Effects of Household Dynamics on Resource Consumption and Biodiversity." *Nature* 421 (6922): 530-33.

Liu, Y. 2009. "Exploring the Relationship between Urbanization and Energy Consumption in China Using ARDL and FDM." *Energy* 34 (11): 1846-54.

Lundgren, N.-G. 1996. "Bulk Trade and Maritime Transport Costs: The Evolution of Global Markets." *Resources Policy* 22 (1): 5-32.

Marshall, J. 2007. "Urban Land Area and Population Growth: A New Scaling Relationship for Metropolitan Expansion." *Urban Studies* 44 (10): 1889-904.

Mishra, V., R. Smyth, and S. Sharma. 2009. "The Energy-GDP Nexus: Evidence from a Panel of Pacific Island Countries." *Resource and Energy Economics* 31 (3): 210-20.

Morikawa, M. 2012. "Population Density and Energy Efficiency in Energy Consumption: An Empirical Analysis of Service Establishments." *Energy Economics* 34 (5): 1617-22.

Nappi, C. 1990. "The Food and Beverage Container Industries: Change and Diversity." In *World Metal Demand: Trends and Prospects*, edited by J. E. Tilton, 38. New York: Resources for the Future Press.

Newell, R. G., A. B. Jaffe, and R. N. Stavins. 1999. "The Induced Innovation Hypothesis and Energy Saving Technical Change." *Quarterly Journal of Economics* 114 (3): 941-74.

Newman, P. 2006. "The Environmental Impact of Cities." *Environmental Urbanization* 18 (2): 275-95.

OECD (Organisation for Economic Co-operation and Development). 2021. "Carbon Pricing in Times of COVID-19: What Has Changed in G20 Economies—OECD." Organisation for Economic Co-operation and Development, Paris.

Olmstead, A. L., and P. Rhode. 1993. "Induced Innovation in American Agriculture: A Reconsideration." *Journal of Political Economy* 101 (1): 100-18.

Pachauri, S., and L. Jiang. 2009. "The Household Energy Transition in India and China." *Energy Policy* 36 (11): 4022-35.

Pandey, B., M. Reba, P. Joshi, and K. Seto. 2020. "Urbanization and Food Consumption in India." *Scientific Reports* 10: 17241.

Parikh, J., and V. Shukla. 1995. "Urbanization, Energy Use and Greenhouse Effects in Economic Development: Results from a Cross-National Study of Developing Countries." *Global Environmental Change* 5 (2): 87-103.

Pei, F., and J. Tilton. 1999. "Consumer Preferences, Technological Change, and the Short-Run Income Elasticity of Metal Demand." *Resources Policy* 25 (2): 87-109.

Pesaran, M. H., Y. Shin, and R. Smith. 1999. "Pooled Mean Group Estimation of Dynamic Heterogeneous Panels." *Journal of the American Statistical Association* 294 (446): 621-34.

Poumanyvong, P., and S. Kaneko. 2010. "Does Urbanization Lead to Less Energy Use and Lower CO_2 Emissions? A Cross Country Analysis." *Ecological Economics* 70 (2): 434-44.

Poumanyvong, P., S. Kaneko, and S. Dhakal. 2012. "Impacts of Urbanization on National Transport and Road Energy Use: Evidence from Low-, Middle- and High-Income Countries." *Energy Policy* 46 (July): 268-77.

Prebisch R. 1950. *The Economic Development of Latin America and Its Principal Problems.* New York: United Nations.

Radetzki, M., R. Eggert, G. Lagos, M. Lima, and J. E. Tilton. 2008. "The Boom in Mineral Markets: How Long Might It Last?" *Resources Policy* 33 (3): 125-28.

Regmi, A., and J. Dyck. 2001. "Effects of Urbanization on Global Food Demand." Changing Structure of Global Food Consumption and Trade / WRS-01-1, Economic Research Service, U.S. Department of Agriculture, Washington, DC.

Roberts, M. C. 1996. "Metals Use and the World Economy." *Resources Policy* 22 (3): 183-96.

Roberts, T. J. 1951. "A Study of International Commodity Agreements." Master's thesis, University of British Columbia, Canada.

Royal Dutch Shell. 2021. "The Energy Transformation Scenarios." Shell International B.V., London.

Ruhl, C., P. Appleby, J. Fennema, A. Naumov, and M. Schaffer. 2012. "Economic Development and the Demand for Energy: A Historical Perspective on the Next 20 Years." *Energy Policy* 50 (November): 109-16.

Sadorsky, P. 2013. "Do Urbanization and Industrialization Affect Energy Intensity in Developing Countries?" *Energy Economics,* 37 (May): 52-59.

Salim, R., and S. Shafiei. 2014. "Non-renewable and Renewable Energy Consumption and CO_2 Emissions in OECD Countries: A Comparative Analysis." *Energy Policy* 66 (C): 547-56.

Satterthwaite, D. 2011. "How Urban Societies Can Adapt to Resource Shortage and Climate Change." *Philosophical Transactions: Mathematical, Physical and Engineering Sciences* 369 (1942): 1762-83.

Schmidhuber, J., and F. N. Tubiello. 2007. "Global Food Security and Climate Change." *Proceedings of the National Academy of Science* 104 (50): 19703-08.

Schwerhoff, G., and M. Stuermer. 2019. "Non-Renewable Resources, Extraction Technology and Endogenous Growth." Working Paper 1506, Federal Reserve Bank of Dallas.

Searchinger, T., R. Heimlich, R. A. Houghton, F. Dong, A. Elobeid, J. Fabiosa, S. Tokgoz, D. Hayes, and T.-H. Yu. 2008. "Use of U.S. Croplands for Biofuels Increases Greenhouse Gases through Emissions from Land-Use Changes." *Science* 319 (5867): 1238-40.

Shealy, M., and J. P. Dorian. 2010. "Growing Chinese Coal Use: Dramatic Resource and Environmental Implications." *Energy Policy* 38 (5): 2116-22.

Singer, H. W. 1950. "The Distribution of Gains between Investing and Borrowing Countries." *American Economic Review* 40 (2): 473-85.

Stage, J., J. Stage, and G. McGranahan. 2010. "Is Urbanization Contributing to Higher Food Prices?" *Environment and Urbanization* 22 (1): 199-215.

Stuermer, M. 2017. "Industrialization and the Demand for Mineral Commodities." *Journal of International Money and Finance* 76 (September): 16-27.

Tcha, M., and G. Takashina. 2002. "Is World Metal Consumption in Disarray?" *Resources Policy* 28 (1-2): 61-74.

Tilton, J. 1990. *World Metal Demand: Trends and Prospects.* Washington, DC: Resources for the Future Press.

Tilton, J., and J. I. Guzmán. 2016. *Mineral Economics and Policy.* New York: RFF Press.

UN Habitat. 2020. *World Cities Report 2020: The Value of Sustainable Urbanization.* Nairobi, Kenya: United Nations Human Settlements Programme.

United Nations. 2019. *World Urbanization Prospects: The 2018 Edition.* New York: United Nations.

United Nations. 2020. "Statistical Commission: Report on the Fifty-First Session (3-6 March 2020)." Economic and Social Council, Official Records, 2020, Supplement No. 4. United Nations, New York. https://unstats.un.org/unsd/statcom/51st-session/documents/Report-2020-Draft-EE.pdf.

Urge-Vorsatz, D., G. Miladinovab, and L. Paizs. 2006. "Energy in Transition: From the Iron Curtain to the European Union." *Energy Policy* 34 (15): 2279-97.

Valin, H., R. Sands, D. van der Mensbrugghe, G. Nelson, H. Ahammad, E. Blanc, B. Bodirsky, et al. 2014. "The Future of Food Demand: Understanding Differences in Global Economic Models." *Agricultural Economics* 45 (1): 51-67.

van Soest, H. L., M. G. J. den Elzen, and D. P. van Vuuren. 2021. "Net-Zero Emission Targets for Major Emitting Countries Consistent with the Paris Agreement." *Nature Communications* 12 (1): 2140.

VandeWeghe, J., and C. Kennedy. 2007. "A Spatial Analysis of Residential Greenhouse Gas Emissions in the Toronto Census Metropolitan Area." *Journal of Industrial Ecology* 11 (2): 133-44.

Verico, K. 2013. "Economic Cooperation in Natural Rubber: The Impacts on Natural Rubber's World Supply and Indonesia's Economy." *Asian Journal of Agriculture and Development* 10 (2): 199419.

Wahba, S. 2019. "Smarter Cities for an Inclusive, Resilient Future." *Sustainable Cities* (blog), December 3, 2019. https://blogs.worldbank.org/sustainablecities/smarter-cities-inclusive-resilient-future.

Wårrel, L. 2014. "Trends and Developments in Long-Term Steel Demand: The Intensity-of-Use Hypothesis Revisited." *Resources Policy* 39 (March): 134-43.

Wellmer, F.-W. 2012. "Sustainable Development and Mineral Resources." In *Géosciences No. 15: Ressources minerals; Contribution des au sommet de la Terre 2021.* https://www.brgm.fr/en/news/journal/geosciences-no-15-mineral-resources.

World Bank. 2010. "Cities and Climate Change: An Urgent Agenda." Urban Development series, Knowledge Paper 10, World Bank, Washington, DC.

World Bank. 2017. *The Growing Role of Minerals and Metals for a Low Carbon Future.* Washington, DC: World Bank.

World Bank. 2018a. *Commodity Markets Outlook: The Changing of the Guard—Shifts in Commodity Demand.* October. Washington, DC: World Bank.

World Bank. 2018b. *Global Economic Prospects: The Turning of the Tide?* June. Washington, DC: World Bank.

World Bank. 2019. *Commodity Markets Outlook: Food Price Shocks: Channels and Implications.* April. Washington, DC: World Bank.

World Bank. 2020. *Commodity Markets Outlook: Implications of COVID-19 for Commodities.* April. Washington, DC: World Bank.

World Bank. 2021a. *Demographic Trends and Urbanization.* Washington, DC: World Bank.

World Bank 2021b. *Commodity Markets Outlook: Urbanization and Commodity Demand.* October. Washington, DC: World Bank.

World Bank. 2021c. *World Bank Group Climate Change Action Plan 2021-2025: Supporting Green, Resilient, and Inclusive Development.* World Bank, Washington, DC.

York, R. 2007. "Demographic Trends and Energy Consumption in European Union Nations, 1960-2025." *Social Science Research* 36 (3): 855-72.

Yu, Y. 2011. "Identifying the Linkages between Major Mining Commodity Prices and China's Economic Growth—Implications for Latin America." IMF Working Paper 86, International Monetary Fund, Washington, DC.

CHAPTER 3

The Nature and Drivers of Commodity Price Cycles

Alain Kabundi, Garima Vasishtha, and Hamza Zahid

Price cycles occur regularly in commodity markets, bringing with them major macroeconomic implications for both exporters and importers of commodities. The impact of these cycles, however, depends significantly on whether they are transitory or permanent. This chapter investigates the features and drivers of commodity price cycles. Across commodities, transitory and permanent components are found to be equally important in explaining price cycles. At the group level, however, they have marked differences. The permanent component dominates agricultural prices, whereas the transitory component is more important for industrial commodity prices. Energy and metal prices generally move in line with global economic activity, and this tendency has strengthened in recent decades. Given the heterogeneity in the magnitude, duration, and drivers of price cycles, appropriate policy responses will depend on the specific terms of trade faced by each country and their export and import commodity mix.

Introduction

The recent commodity price upswing has once again brought to the fore the vulnerability of emerging market and developing economies (EMDEs) to large fluctuations in commodity prices. Such price fluctuations are common across commodity groups (figure 3.1). Macroeconomic performance in commodity exporters has historically varied closely in line with commodity price cycles, especially in EMDEs that rely on a rather narrow set of commodities.

For policy makers, formulating the appropriate policy response depends on whether commodity price changes are expected to be permanent or temporary. To the extent that commodity price movements are temporary, they can be looked through, or smoothed by fiscal and monetary policies. For longer-lasting price shifts, however, structural changes may be needed. Understanding what is behind commodity price cycles is also critical for policy makers in both exporters and importers of commodities. For example, the likely impact of commodity price movements and the appropriate policy response depend heavily on whether movements were driven by global factors or commodity-specific factors, as well as whether they are predominantly demand or supply driven.

Shocks to commodity markets can have both permanent and transitory effects. Shocks with a transitory impact can originate from recessions, such as the 1997-98 Asian financial crisis and the 2007-09 global financial crisis (both of which affected a wide range of commodities); trade tensions (such as in 2018-19 and of special relevance to metals and soybeans); and the bans on grain exports during 2007 and 2011 (World Bank 2018). They can also arise from adverse weather conditions, most common to agriculture, such as El Niño and La Niña episodes or drought-related production shortfalls (such as for coffee in 1975 and 1985, and grains in 1995). Transitory shocks

FIGURE 3.1 Real commodity price indexes

Price shocks and price cycles occur regularly in commodity markets. Movements in global commodity prices have often been associated with global business cycles as well as developments specific to commodity markets.

A. Energy and metals

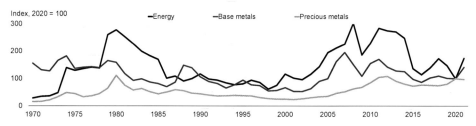

B. Agriculture and fertilizers

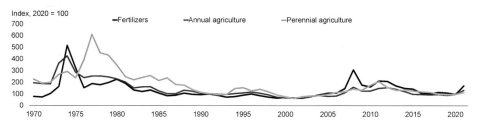

Source: World Bank.
Note: Indexes have been deflated by the U.S. Consumer Price Index. Last observation is 2021.

can also result from accidents (for example, the 2019 Vale accident in Brazil, which disrupted iron ore supplies); conflicts (for example, the first Gulf War, when oil production in Kuwait and Iraq was halted); and terrorist attacks (for example, the attack on Saudi oil facilities in 2019, which halted oil exports temporarily; see World Bank 2019).

Shocks with a permanent impact can arise from technological changes. For example, the emergence of shale technology in the natural gas and oil industries rendered the United States a net energy exporter in 2019 for the first time since 1952 (EIA 2020). The biotechnology shock of the 1990s increased crop productivity by more than 20 percent (Klümper and Qaim 2014). Policy shocks can also have long-lasting impacts on commodity prices. Examples include government efforts to encourage biofuel production, which caused global land use to shift from food to biofuel production (Rulli et al. 2016); interventions in agricultural markets by most Organisation for Economic Co-operation and Development countries, which have been shown to exert long-term downward pressures on food prices (Aksoy and Beghin 2004); and decisions by the Organization of the Petroleum Exporting Countries (OPEC) to manage oil supplies (Kaufmann et al. 2004).

Shocks, especially those related to energy markets, often trigger additional shocks. For example, the COVID-19 oil demand shock, which caused an estimated 10 percent decline in oil consumption during 2020, triggered a policy-driven supply shock of similar magnitude by OPEC+ (composed of OPEC and 11 non-OPEC members) when it cut oil production by 9.7 million barrels per day in April 2020. The oil price increases of the mid-2000s (driven by EMDE demand, OPEC supply cuts, and geopolitical concerns) rendered shale technology profitable, pushed up the costs of food production, and triggered biofuel policies. Following the oil price collapse of 2014, food production costs declined, but production of shale (through innovation and cost reduction) and biofuels (diverted from food commodities) appears to have a permanent character.

Against that backdrop, this chapter investigates the behavior of commodity price cycles, their duration, and their main drivers. Specifically, it answers the following questions:

- How large are the transitory and permanent components of commodity price cycles?

- What have been the main drivers of common cycles in commodity prices?

This chapter adds to the literature in two important ways. First, whereas the existing literature analyzes price movements in the context of either super cycles or cyclical-versus-trend behavior, the analysis in this chapter focuses on business and medium-term cycles, in line with the macroeconomic literature. Specifically, it separates the transitory component into two parts: (1) the traditional 2-to-8-year cycle, which is associated with economic activity; and (2) the medium-term cycle with a duration of 8 to 20 years. The first has been studied extensively in the macroeconomic literature and, in the case of commodities, for metals markets; the second has only recently begun to receive significant attention in the literature.[1]

Second, using a cutting-edge econometric approach, this chapter examines both global and commodity-specific cycles for a large number of commodities as well as the underlying drivers of those cycles. In contrast, earlier literature either focuses on a small set of commodities (examining commodity demand and supply rather than aggregate demand and supply) or simply documents the existence of comovement without identifying the underlying drivers. This chapter also provides an in-depth analysis of price cycles in key commodities since 1970 and compares the rebound in commodity prices after the COVID-19-induced global recession in 2020 with the price recoveries following past recessions and slowdowns.

Main findings. This chapter offers three main findings.

First, the permanent component accounts for 47 percent of commodity price variability, on average, across all commodities. The transitory component accounts for the remainder: the medium-term and business cycle components account for 32 percent and 17 percent, respectively, whereas short-term fluctuations account for only 4 percent of

---

[1] For short-term cycles, see Davutyan and Roberts (1994); Labys, Lesourd, and Badillo (1998); and Roberts (2009). For medium-term cycles, see Marañon and Kumral (2019); McGregor, Spinola, and Verspagen (2018); and Ojeda-Joya, Jaulin-Mendez, and Bustos-Pelaez (2019).

commodity price variability. These shares, however, mask heterogeneity. The permanent component dominates for agricultural commodity prices while the transitory component is more relevant for industrial commodities. This finding is consistent with studies that find business- and investment-driven cycles more important for industrial commodities (Marañon and Kumral 2019; Roberts 2009).

Second, the analysis identifies three medium-term cycles: the first (from the early 1970s to the mid-1980s) and the third (from the early 2000s to 2020 onward) exhibit similar duration and involve all commodities, whereas the smaller second cycle (spanning the 1990s) applies mostly to metals and (less so) agricultural commodities. The permanent component differs across commodities as well, with an upward trend for most industrial commodities and downward trend for agricultural commodities. Commodities subjected to policy interventions exhibit persistent price deviations from their respective linear trends. Nonlinearities in the permanent component, which coincide with the two post-World War II super cycles, are dominant in prices of commodities where investment is irreversible, such as energy, metals, and tree crops, but not in prices of annual agricultural crops where there is more flexibility on investment allocation and input use.[2]

Third, the chapter finds that, when considering cyclical and shorter-run movements, global macroeconomic shocks have been the main source of commodity price volatility over the past 25 years—particularly for metals. Global demand shocks have accounted for 50 percent of the variance of global commodity prices, and global supply shocks for 20 percent. In contrast, during 1970-96, supply shocks specific to particular commodity markets—such as the 1970s and 1980s oil price shocks—were the main source of variability in global commodity prices. These results suggest that the role played by developments specific to commodity markets in driving commodity price volatility may have diminished over time.

The chapter proceeds as follows. The first section examines the key features of commodity price cycles, including decomposing cycles into their transitory and permanent components. The second section looks at the main drivers of commodity price cycles. Box 3.1 provides an analysis of previous commodity price cycles for six major commodities: crude oil, coal, aluminum, copper, maize, and coffee. Box 3.2 estimates the comovement between commodity prices and compares the COVID-19-driven fall and recovery in commodity prices with previous recessions.

Explaining commodity price variability: Transitory versus permanent components

Data and methodology

To decompose commodity price movements into transitory and permanent components, a novel frequency domain approach is used that has thus far mostly been

---

[2] Annual agricultural commodities, often termed crop commodities, are produced on an annual basis; as such, land (and other factors of production) can change each crop year, depending on demand and supply conditions. These commodities include cotton, maize, rice, soybeans, and wheat.

BOX 3.1 Evolution of commodity cycles

Since 1970, slumps in the prices of industrial commodities have been associated mainly with declines in global economic growth, geopolitical events affecting supply, and the emergence of new producers. In contrast, slumps in the prices of agricultural commodities have been associated mostly with commodity-specific supply and policy shocks and less so with aggregate demand shocks. This box summarizes how various shocks affected the prices of two energy commodities (oil and coal), two base metals (aluminum and copper), and two agricultural commodities (coffee and maize).

Introduction

To illustrate commodity price cycles, six major commodities are examined in detail—coal, crude oil, aluminum, copper, coffee, and maize. These commodities are the most traded in their respective commodity groups. Price booms and slumps are identified for each commodity using standard techniques to date business cycles (World Bank 2022).[a] A boom for each commodity is defined as a trough-to-peak rise in commodity prices and a slump as a peak-to-trough decline. Price troughs and their causes are the focus of this box.

Coal

Coal prices have gone through eight troughs since 1970. The troughs can mainly be attributed to global recessions and slowdowns, policy-driven changes in China's growth model, and the emergence of new producers.

Global recessions. The global financial crisis of 2007-09 and the resulting global recession led to a sharp fall in coal prices. Prices bounced back rapidly in 2010-11 as the global economy recovered, with China driving the increase in demand. In 2020, the COVID-19 pandemic and the associated global recession caused a drop in demand for coal, with its price falling by nearly 30 percent between January and August. Although demand subsequently rebounded in 2021 alongside the economic recovery, production recovered more slowly, with weather events, including flooding in China and Indonesia, causing disruptions (World Bank 2021).

Policy-driven changes in China's growth model. The coal market changed significantly in the 2000s as rapid economic growth in China led to a surge in demand for coal, both for power generation and for metallurgical uses. To meet the surging demand, China rapidly increased its domestic production as well as its imports of coal. These developments slowed and went into reverse in the 2010s, as China's growth moderated and government policy shifted from a focus on

---

a. Specifically, the procedure applied is a widely used algorithm for dating business cycles, and largely follows Cashin, McDermott, and Scott (2002) and Harding and Pagan (2002).

BOX 3.1 Evolution of commodity cycles (continued)

investment and manufacturing toward less energy-intensive consumption and services. This shift contributed to a steady decline in prices from 2011 to 2015, with prices reaching a trough by end-2015.

Emergence of new producers. After increasing steadily through the 1970s, real coal prices declined through much of the 1980s and 1990s. The fall in prices through the 1980s in part reflected the emergence of additional coal producers, particularly China and Indonesia. By the 1990s, China had overtaken the United States as the world's largest coal producer and, by 2020, accounted for about 50 percent of global coal production.

Crude oil

Oil prices (represented by the unweighted average of Brent, Dubai, and West Texas Intermediate prices, in real terms) have experienced 11 troughs since 1970 (figure B3.1.1). The troughs were associated primarily with global recessions and with production agreements and decisions by the Organization of the Petroleum Exporting Countries (OPEC).

Global recessions. Four of the identified troughs (1975, 1998, 2001, 2020) in oil prices were associated with global recessions or slowdowns. The global recession and oil price slump of 1975 followed the shock to world oil prices from the OPEC price hike and the Arab oil embargo initiated in October 1973 (chapter 1). The sharp decline in oil prices in 1998 was associated mostly with weakening global demand stemming partly from the 1997-98 Asian financial crisis, although continued expansion of OPEC production until mid-1998 may have been another contributing factor (Fattouh 2007). The trough in oil prices in 2001 was triggered by weakening global growth following the bursting of the dot.com bubble, exacerbated by the disruptions and uncertainty set off by the September 11 terrorist attacks in the United States (Baffes et al. 2015; World Bank 2015a). The most recent trough, in April 2020, followed the steepest price collapse on record. Global oil demand dropped because of the deepest global recession since World War II as well as widespread COVID-19-related restrictions on transportation and travel, which account for about two-thirds of global oil demand (Kabundi and Ohnsorge 2020; Wheeler et al. 2020).

OPEC decisions/agreements. The oil price slump in 1986 can mostly be attributed to changing supply conditions as OPEC reverted to a production target of 30 million barrels per day after cutting production significantly in the early 1980s (Baffes et al. 2015; World Bank 2015a). Real oil prices dropped by almost 60 percent from January to July 1986, followed by two decades of low oil prices. Likewise, the slide in oil prices after 2014 was triggered by a change in OPEC's policy objective, from price targeting to preserving market share. Muted demand

BOX 3.1 Evolution of commodity cycles *(continued)*

FIGURE B3.1.1 **Commodity prices and global recessions**

Price troughs are common among major commodities. Crude oil prices have experienced 11 troughs since 1970, aluminum experienced 10, and coal and copper each experienced 8. These troughs have typically been associated with global recessions, although several commodity-specific factors have also played a role. Maize prices experienced 9 troughs and coffee 10. The latter is somewhat less correlated with global recessions, with price swings more closely tied to policy and supply factors.

A. Oil price

B. Coal price

C. Aluminum price

D. Copper price

E. Coffee price

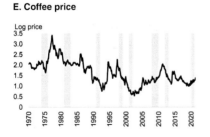

F. Maize price

Sources: Federal Reserve Economic Data (St Louis Fed); World Bank.
Note: Real price of commodities in logs. Shaded areas indicate global recessions as in Kose, Sugawara, and Terrones (2020) and the global recession of 2020. Data from January 1970 to October 2021.

BOX 3.1 Evolution of commodity cycles *(continued)*

and rising oil supply from non-OPEC producers, including U.S. shale oil, Canadian oil sands, and biofuels, also contributed to the decline in prices at that time.

Geopolitical events. Major spikes in oil prices have been associated with geopolitical events affecting supply. For instance, during the 1973 Yom Kippur War, OPEC members cut production, and Arab suppliers imposed an oil embargo against Canada, Japan, the Netherlands, the United Kingdom, and the United States. Average real oil prices in 1974 were more than four times their 1973 level. Subsequent disruptions in oil supplies following the war between Iraq and the Islamic Republic of Iran, and the Iranian revolution caused oil prices to more than double in 1979.

Aluminum

Aluminum prices have undergone 10 troughs since 1970. Price cycles for major industrial metals like aluminum, copper, lead, and zinc generally follow global economic cycles because their demand is closely related to global economic activity, particularly industrial production (chapter 2). These metals are used in a wide range of applications, with changes in usage and related demand occurring only slowly over time. The troughs in real aluminum prices have also been associated with the emergence of new producers and consumers.

Global recessions. Three of the identified troughs in aluminum prices (1982, 2009, 2020) were associated with global recessions. In addition, the global slowdown associated with the 1997-98 Asian financial crisis was accompanied by a sharp decline in aluminum prices. The most recent trough, in April 2020, was associated with the pandemic-related recession, with real aluminum prices falling to their lowest level in over half a century. Prices have since rebounded with the global economic recovery.

Emergence of new producers. In the early 1970s, aluminum production was highly concentrated in a few countries, notably the United States, the former Soviet Union, and Japan. Since then, major shifts have occurred in the geographic location of production with the arrival of new private producers and conglomerates of state-owned enterprises. The collapse in prices in the early 1990s was caused by the breakup of the Soviet Union: countries that had been members of the bloc began participating in the global aluminum market, which resulted in a large increase in supply, especially from the Russian Federation. At the same time, demand for aluminum in these economies declined, adding additional downward pressure. In the 2000s, China emerged as the world's largest aluminum producer, accounting for more than half of global production by 2020 compared to just 1 percent in 1970.

BOX 3.1 Evolution of commodity cycles *(continued)*

Emergence of new sources of demand. Since 2000, the intensity of aluminum use in global gross domestic product has risen, reflecting strong demand from EMDEs, especially China. Between 2000 and 2010, China's share of global aluminum consumption increased threefold. Aluminum consumption has also been driven by its increasing use as a substitute for other metals such as copper in power transmission and steel in the manufacture of automobiles.

Copper

Copper prices experienced eight troughs since 1970. The troughs have been associated with global recessions or slowdowns, technological innovations, shifts in demand away from copper to other materials for some uses, and the emergence of new producers. Additionally, U.S.-China trade tensions contributed to a steep decline in prices in the second half of 2018.

Global recessions. The price troughs of 1999 and 2001 stemmed, respectively, from the global recession associated with the Asian financial crisis and the global slowdown of 2001. Similarly, copper prices fell sharply during (and in some cases after) the global recessions of 1982, 1992, and 2020.

Technological innovations. During the 1980s and 1990s, technological innovations reduced costs of copper production. An important breakthrough was the development of the solvent extraction and electrowinning technology, which extracted copper through dissolution and subsequent electrolysis instead of mining. By 1995, this process accounted for 27 percent of U.S. primary copper output, up from 6 percent in 1980 (Radetzki 2009).

Shifting demand. Over the past half century, copper demand has been dampened by substitutions of aluminum, plastics, and glass fiber. Aluminum has been the predominant substitute, gaining substantial market share and suppressing copper's relative price (Radetzki 2009).

Emergence of new producers. After a decade of largely stagnant mine production, the discovery of new supply sources and new technologies that reduced processing costs played an important role in driving down copper prices from 2011 to 2015. During that period mine supply grew strongly, particularly in the Democratic Republic of Congo, Kazakhstan, Peru, and Zambia.

Coffee

Arabica coffee prices have experience 10 troughs since 1970. The troughs were associated mostly with weather-related supply shocks and the emergence of new producers. In contrast to the troughs for industrial commodities, the troughs had

BOX 3.1 Evolution of commodity cycles *(continued)*

little correlation with global recessions. The prepandemic trough in 2019 was largely caused by overproduction in Brazil, the world's largest coffee producer.

Weather. Following historically low levels in the early 1970s, real coffee (Arabica) prices tripled during 1975-77 and reached a record high in April 1977, following a major frost in Brazil (Akiyama and Varangis 1990). As supplies recovered and producing countries failed to extend the International Coffee Agreement, real coffee prices declined, reaching a trough in late 1992. The agreement operated an export-quota system, first implemented in 1963 and continuing intermittently until 1989. In 2016, the end of a drought supported the coffee harvest in Brazil and resulted in a trough in coffee prices. More recently, a drought hit Brazil in 2021, which once again pushed coffee prices sharply higher (World Bank 2021).

New producer. When adverse weather events in 1994 (frost in Brazil) and 1997 (El Niño in Peru) led to a spike in coffee prices, a new entrant was drawn to the coffee market—Vietnam. Vietnam's emergence as a major Robusta coffee producer not only pushed prices lower but also altered the landscape of the global coffee market for the long term: the country now accounts for nearly 20 percent of global coffee supplies, up from less than 0.1 percent in 1980.

Maize

Maize prices have had nine troughs since 1970. These were associated mostly with commodity-specific supply and policy shocks and less so with aggregate demand shocks, although at times prices were affected by multiple shocks.

Global recessions. Two troughs occurred around global recessions. In both instances, supply-side factors also played a major role. After peaking in 1974, maize prices trended downward for several years, reaching a trough in late 1977. During the 2000s, maize prices followed a pattern similar to other commodity prices: sharp increases during the 2000s leading to a mid-2008 peak, followed by a sharp decline during the global financial crisis.

Technology and policy shocks. Maize prices saw a prolonged downward trend between 1974 and 1987, due to a combination of productivity improvements, falling energy prices, and policy measures (mainly domestic support and export subsidies by Organisation for Economic Co-operation and Development countries). The diversion of maize to the production of biofuels was a key reason behind the price boom in the 2000s (Tyner 2008). The U.S. Energy Policy Act of 2005 mandated strict biofuel requirements in the fuel energy mix, which meant as much as one-third of U.S. maize supply was diverted to the production of biofuels. However, the mandate made the price of maize more closely linked with

BOX 3.1 Evolution of commodity cycles *(continued)*

that of crude oil, and the sharp fall in crude oil prices from 2014 consequently spilled over to maize prices.

Weather shocks. A drought contributed to a price boom during the mid-1990s, with prices peaking in June 1996. This situation was exacerbated by reduced harvests during the transition of the former Soviet Union and policy changes in the European Union (McCalla 1999). As inventories were replenished, prices began falling again, with prices reaching a trough in August 2000 (exacerbated by the Asian financial crisis). In 2012, the United States experienced its worst drought since 1950, sharply reducing U.S. maize production and contributing to the rise of U.S. corn export prices to their highest level since the 1980s (Adonizio, Kook, and Royales 2012; World Bank 2013). However, as weather conditions eased, the United States saw a bumper crop in 2013, triggering a sharp fall in prices and a prolonged period of low and stable prices.

New producers. In contrast to other commodities, maize has been dominated by a single producer since the 1970s—the United States. The United States accounted for between 30 percent and 40 percent of global production over this period, and its output continues to grow steadily because of productivity improvements. However, other major producers have emerged. China's production tripled between 1970 and 1990, increasing its share of global output from 12 percent to 20 percent. Between 2000 and 2020, Brazil and Argentina saw increases in their share of global production, from 7 percent to 9 percent and 3 percent to 5 percent, respectively.

applied to business cycles (Corbae and Ouliaris 2006; Corbae, Ouliaris, and Phillips 2002).[3] The analysis rests on monthly data for 27 commodity price series over the period 1970-2019. It includes 3 energy prices, 6 base metal and 3 precious metal prices, 11 agricultural commodity prices (separated into annual and perennial crops), and 4 fertilizer prices (annex 3A).[4]

The transitory component consists of three components—short-term fluctuations (that unwind in less than 2 years); traditional business cycles with a frequency of 2-8 years, which are typically associated with economic activity (Burns and Mitchell 1946); and

---

[3] This section draws heavily on World Bank (2020a).

[4] The commodity prices analyzed in this chapter were selected by excluding commodities that are close substitutes (for example, selecting only one edible oil), that are no longer economically important (for example, hides and skins), or whose prices are not determined at an exchange (for example, bananas). A few studies that have used both individual commodity price series and indexes used data obtained directly from the International Monetary Fund or World Bank commodity price databases without applying selection criteria (for example, Erten and Ocampo 2013; Jacks 2019; Ojeda-Joya, Jaulin-Mendez, and Bustos-Pelaez 2019).

medium-term cycles with periodicity of 8-20 years, which are often associated with long-term investment trends (Slade 1982). The permanent component captures movements with periodicity of more than 20 years—consistent with super cycles (Cuddington and Jerrett 2008).

The permanent and transitory components account for roughly equal shares. On average across commodities, the permanent component accounted for 47 percent of price variability. Of the remainder (the transitory component), medium-term cycles accounted for 32 percent of price variability and business cycles for 17 percent. Only 4 percent of the price variability is due to the short-term component that is unwound in less than two years. The large role of the permanent component is in line with the findings of research on commodity price super cycles (Erten and Ocampo 2013; Fernández, Schmitt-Grohé, and Uribe 2020). Furthermore, the predominance of the medium-term cycle in the transitory component is in line with recent research that finds a greater role of medium-term cycles than shorter business cycles in output fluctuations or domestic financial cycles (Aldasoro et al. 2020; Cao and L'Huillier 2018).

These averages mask heterogeneity across commodities. The transitory components were more relevant to the variation in prices of industrial commodities, whereas the permanent component mattered most for agricultural commodity price movements (figure 3.2). For annual agricultural commodities, the permanent component accounted for 68 percent of price variability, for metals (including base and precious) it accounted for about 45 percent, and for energy it accounted for less than 30 percent. Precious metals exhibited the largest heterogeneity as a group, with gold prices seeing a larger share accounted for by the permanent component, silver having an equal share accounted for by permanent and transitory components, and platinum exhibiting one of the highest shares of medium-term cyclicality.

The composition of the transitory component differed across commodities. The medium-term component accounted for 55 percent and 27 percent of price variability in energy and metals, respectively, and only 14 percent for agriculture. In contrast, business cycles accounted for 24 percent of price variability for metals. This greater contribution of the business cycle to metal commodity price fluctuations is in line with the strong response of metal consumption to economic activity (chapter 2; Baffes, Kabundi, and Nagle 2022). Indeed, metal prices, especially copper, are often considered leading indicators of global economic activity (Bernanke 2016; Hamilton 2015). Some of the commodities for which the transitory component had the highest contribution to price variability are used mainly in the transportation sector. For example, nearly two-thirds of crude oil is used for transportation, three-quarters of natural rubber goes to tire manufacturing, and half of platinum is used to produce catalytic converters (World Bank 2020b).

How have the transitory and permanent components evolved?

Almost all commodities have undergone three medium-term cycles since 1970 (figure 3.3). The first medium-term cycle, which involved all commodities, began in the early 1970s, peaked in 1978, and lasted until the mid-1980s. The second, which peaked in

FIGURE 3.2 **Commodity price decomposition**

Across commodities, transitory and permanent shocks are found to be equally important in explaining commodity price cycles. At a group level, however, there is a marked difference. Agricultural prices are dominated by permanent shocks whereas industrial commodities are influenced mostly by transitory shocks.

A. Contribution of shocks, 1970-2019

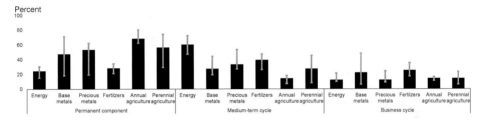

B. Price decomposition, individual commodities, 1970-2020

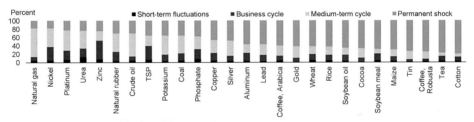

Sources: Baffes and Kabundi 2021; World Bank.
A. Blue bars and orange whiskers denote weighted averages and ranges of each group.
B. TSP = triple superphosphate.

1994, was most pronounced in base metals and agriculture (with similar duration and amplitude to the first cycle) but did not include energy commodities. The third cycle, which again involved all commodities, began in the early 2000s, peaked in 2010, and for some commodities is still under way.

Crude oil's "missing cycle" reflected offsetting oil-specific shocks. Of the 27 commodities, crude oil and natural gas (whose price is highly correlated with that of oil) are the only commodities that had two, instead of three, medium-term cycles. During the period spanning the second medium-term cycle, the oil market saw three shocks:

1. *Unconventional and offshore oil.* New production from unconventional sources of oil came into the market (Alaska, Gulf of Mexico, and North Sea) as a result of innovation and investment in response to the high prices during the 1970s and early 1980s, partly caused by OPEC supply restrictions (chapter 1; World Bank 2020b).[5]

---

[5] The three unconventional sources of oil—U.S. shale oil, Canadian oil sands, and biofuels—are also associated with the third medium-term cycle (Baffes et al. 2015). In the first and third medium-term cycles, these unconventional sources of oil account for about 10 percent of global oil supplies (measured at the end of the cycle).

FIGURE 3.3 Contributions of global shocks to commodity prices

Almost all commodities have undergone three medium-term cycles since 1970, with the exception of energy. Energy did not have a second cycle because of offsetting shocks specific to the crude oil market. The evolution of the permanent component differed markedly across commodity groups. For energy commodities, the permanent component of prices has trended upward, for agricultural and fertilizer prices it has trended downward, and for most base metals it has been largely trendless.

A. Medium-term component, energy and metals

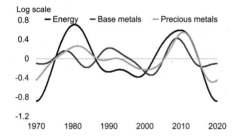

B. Permanent component, energy and metals

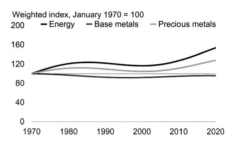

C. Medium-term component, agriculture and fertilizer

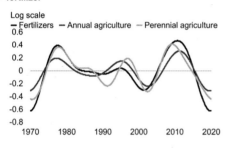

D. Permanent component, agriculture and fertilizer

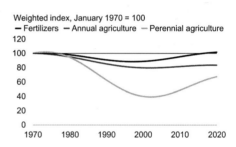

Sources: Baffes and Kabundi 2021; World Bank.
Note: Charts show the medium-term and permanent component of the commodity price indexes, decomposed using a frequency domain approach (see Baffes and Kabundi 2021 for more details). The medium-term component refers to price dynamics with a frequency of 8-20 years; the permanent component covers price movements of greater than 20 years.
C.D. Annual agricultural commodities are produced on an annual basis, which means land use (and other factors of production) can change each crop year, depending on demand and supply conditions. Annual crops include cotton, maize, rice, soybeans, and wheat. Perennial agricultural commodities include cocoa, coffee Arabica, coffee Robusta, natural rubber, and tea.

2. *New spare capacity from the former Soviet Union.* Considerable spare capacity became available in the global oil market following the collapse of the Soviet Union. Before its collapse, the Soviet economy featured both inefficient production and energy-intensive consumption (World Bank 2009).

3. *Substitution and demand contraction.* In response to high oil prices during the late 1970s and early 1980s, electricity generation began to shift from oil to other energy sources (especially coal and nuclear energy). Policy-mandated efficiency standards in many Organisation for Economic Co-operation and Development countries lowered global demand for energy (Baffes, Kabundi, and Nagle 2022).

The evolution of the permanent component differed markedly across commodity groups. For energy commodities, the permanent component of prices has trended

BOX 3.2 Commodity price comovement and the impact of COVID-19

Commodity prices frequently move in tandem, especially during periods of major economic upheaval. Considering all commodity prices, there is evidence of a global common factor, and that factor has become increasingly important over time. The COVID-19-driven global recession of 2020 is the latest example of a common global shock to commodity markets. When compared with previous recessions, the rebound in prices in 2020-21 was faster and steeper for almost all major commodity groups, which reflected the extraordinarily strong economic rebound from the pandemic-induced global recession, along with difficulties in quickly restoring commodity supply.

Introduction

Commodity prices have historically seen periods of comovement and have become increasingly synchronized over time (World Bank 2022). They share common drivers, such as global economic activity, and so tend to be positively correlated with global business cycles. Furthermore, several sets of commodities are close substitutes in demand, so demand surges or supply disruptions in one commodity market affect the prices of similar commodities. For annual agriculture commodities, prices may be synchronized because of the substitutability of inputs to production, including land, labor, and machinery. Energy is a key input in the production of some metals (such as aluminum) and an important cost component for most grains and oilseed crops. Thus, increases in energy prices will tend to put upward pressure on the costs of production (and thus the prices) of these commodities (Baffes 2007).

The COVID-19 pandemic, and subsequent economic recession, is the latest common global shock to affect commodity markets. Against that background, this box first empirically assesses how closely commodity prices comove and the role played by global factors in driving this comovement. It then conducts an event study to compare how commodity prices behaved during the COVID-19 pandemic with their behavior in previous global recessions and recoveries. Specifically, it answers the following questions:

- How has commodity price comovement evolved over the past five decades?

- How does the recent recovery in commodity prices compare with such episodes after previous global recessions and downturns?

Global commodity price comovement

Data and methodology. Global commodity prices are defined as the common factor among 39 monthly commodity prices, estimated from a dynamic factor model as in Kose, Otrok, and Whiteman (2003).[a] The commodity price data are

---

a. Numerous other studies use a similar framework to examine determinants of commonalities in commodity prices (for example, Byrne, Fazio, and Fiess 2013; Lombardi, Osbat, and Schnatz 2010; Poncela, Senra, and Sierra 2014; Vansteenkiste 2009). However, they focus on a subset of commodities.

BOX 3.2 Commodity price comovement and the impact of COVID-19 (continued)

obtained from the World Bank Commodities (Pink Sheet) database, which covers more than 70 commodity prices and indexes. The prices, which are reported in nominal U.S. dollar terms, were deflated with the U.S. Consumer Price Index (taken from the St. Louis Federal Reserve Bank). Series that are either averages or close substitutes of other series are excluded to avoid introducing price comovement by construction. This exclusion leaves 39 commodity prices. The resulting common factor is a standardized (demeaned with unit standard deviation) representation of global commodity price growth.

Main components of global commodity prices. The global factor has played an important role in driving fluctuations in industrial commodity prices (figure B3.2.1). During 1970-2021, it accounted for 18 percent of the variation in energy prices, on average, and 22-37 percent of the variation in the prices of base metals, rubber (used in tires and tubes), and platinum (used in catalytic converters). It accounted for only 2-14 percent of the variation in agricultural commodity prices (excluding natural rubber), precious metal, and fertilizer prices. The larger contribution of the global factor in explaining the variation in industrial commodity prices reflects the strong response of metal and energy consumption to industrial activity. By contrast, in agriculture, supply shocks (primarily driven by weather conditions and policies) dwarf demand shocks.

Changes over time. In recent decades, the contribution of the global factor to industrial commodity prices has increased considerably: it doubled for energy prices and nearly doubled for base metal and platinum prices during 1996-2021 compared to the full data period, which spans 1970-2021. This increased comovement in global commodity prices from the mid-1990s was part of a broader trend toward greater comovement in macroeconomic variables such as inflation and output (Eickmeier and Kühnlenz 2018; Ha, Kose, and Ohnsorge 2019). Trade liberalization and the financialization of commodity markets have also contributed to the increased synchronization of commodity prices.

Recent commodity price movements compared with historical experience

Event study. An event study is used to compare the behavior of commodity prices during the 2020 global recession with price movements around global recessions and slowdowns over the past 50 years.[b] For brevity, the results are presented for three major World Bank commodity indexes—energy, metals, and agriculture. During the 2020 global recession, the troughs in commodity prices generally

---

b. Before 2020, there were four global recessions (1975, 1982, 1991, and 2009) and three global slowdowns (1998, 2001, and 2012). See Kose, Sugawara, and Terrones (2020).

BOX 3.2 Commodity price comovement and the impact of COVID-19 *(continued)*

FIGURE B3.2.1 Global commodity prices

Movements in global commodity prices have often been associated with global business cycles as well as developments specific to commodity markets. Industrial commodity prices, such as those of energy and metals and minerals, have been largely driven by global commodity price movements. Industrial commodity prices have become more synchronized since the mid-1990s.

A. Commodity price variations due to the global factor (indexes)

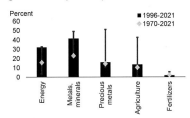

B. Commodity price variations due to the global factor (individual commodities)

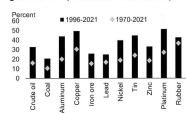

Sources: Baumeister and Hamilton 2019; Ha, Kose, and Ohnsorge 2021; World Bank.
Note: Share of variation in montlhy growth of 39 commodity prices (3 energy commodities, 7 metal and mineral commodities, 3 precious metals, 5 fertilizers, and 21 agricultural commodities) accounted for by the global factor and derived from a one-factor dynamic factor model as in Kose, Otrok, and Whiteman (2003). Bars show consumption-weighted averages. In panel A, whiskers indicate range from minimum to maximum during 1996-2021.

coincided with those in global economic activity. This relationship contrasts sharply with previous, more prolonged recessions, in which commodity prices continued to decline for several months after the trough in economic activity.

Energy and metal prices. The collapse in the energy price index in early 2020 was the steepest of any during global recessions in the past five decades, and the subsequent recovery was likewise the steepest (figure B3.2.2). The fall in energy prices in 2020 was driven by oil, which experienced its largest one-month decline in prices on record in April 2020. Oil demand plummeted by about 8 percent in 2020 because of the twin effects of travel disruptions and the global recession. Energy prices rebounded by about 50 percent within three months of their early 2020 trough, however, and surpassed their precrisis peak in about a year. In comparison, the median recovery after previous recessions was less than 5 percent in 13 months. In addition to rebounding oil prices, natural gas and coal prices rose to record highs in 2021 amid recovery in demand and supply disruptions (World Bank 2021).

Likewise, for metal and mineral prices, the pandemic-driven decline in 2020 was steeper than that during most of the previous global recessions. The subsequent

BOX 3.2 **Commodity price comovement and the impact of COVID-19**
(continued)

FIGURE B3.2.2 **Commodity prices around global recessions and downturns**

The recovery in commodity prices since the COVID-19 recession is in stark contrast to those following previous recessions. The rebound in prices has been exceptionally fast for most major commodity groups.

A. Energy

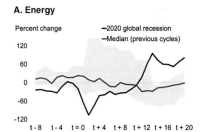

B. Base metals

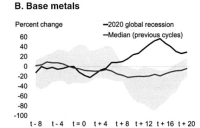

C. Annual agriculture

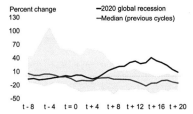

D. Perennial agriculture

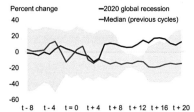

Source: World Bank.
Note: The horizontal axis represents time periods in months, and t = 0 denotes the peak of global industrial production before global recessions and downturns since 1970. The vertical axis measures the percent change in the commodity price series from a year earlier. The blue line shows the trajectory of the current commodity cycle around the COVID-19 recession, and the red line is the median of previous cycles around a global recession or downturn (as in Kose, Sugawara, and Terrones 2020). Gray shaded areas represent the range of observed values in previous cycles. Data from January 1970 to October 2021.

price recovery was also faster than in previous episodes, mostly reflecting the relatively short-lived nature of the pandemic-related recession, a rebound in demand from China due to strong industrial activity, and supply disruptions in Latin America.

Agricultural commodity prices. Prices for annual agricultural commodities declined only slightly during the pandemic but increased sharply in late 2020 and early 2021. This surge in prices was mostly driven by strong demand from China, in part because of the recovery in demand for animal feed after the Africa swine flu outbreak in 2019, and higher energy costs (and, thus, fertilizer costs). For the

BOX 3.2 Commodity price comovement and the impact of COVID-19 (continued)

perennial agricultural price index—which comprises coffee, rubber, and tea—the price decline in 2020 was broadly in line with historical episodes, but the subsequent recovery was faster. Fertilizer prices were relatively unaffected by the recession but rapidly increased in subsequent months as rising energy prices (especially natural gas and coal) drove up the cost to manufacture fertilizers.

upward; for agricultural and fertilizer prices, it has trended downward; and, for most base metals, it has been largely trendless. The upward trend in energy prices may reflect resource depletion and a rising cost of production as well as limited options for substitution, whereas the largely trendless nature of long-term metal price movements may reflect the opposing forces of technological innovation and resource depletion alongside many options for substitution.[6] The downward trend in the permanent component of agricultural prices is consistent with low income elasticities of food commodities and consistent productivity growth in agricultural production (chapter 2; Baffes and Etienne 2016). Commodities with a history of widespread policy interventions (cotton) or subjected to international commodity agreements (cocoa, coffee, crude oil, cotton, natural rubber, and tin) followed a highly nonlinear path (see table 3A.1).

Annual agricultural price trends are highly synchronized and differ from those of other commodity groups. The contribution of the permanent component to annual agricultural price variability (68 percent) is the highest among all six commodity groups, and this component has evolved in a similar manner across annual agricultural prices (figure 3.3).[7] This similarity reflects the diffusion of shocks across commodities due to input substitutability, consumption substitutability, and agricultural policies, which are similar across most crops.

- *Input substitution.* Annual agricultural commodities tend to be farmed using the same land, labor, machinery, and other inputs. As a result, reallocation between different annual crops from one year to another prevents large price fluctuations in individual crops. The impact of China's restriction on soybean imports from the United States in 2018 was short-lived because of land reallocation and trade diversion. Separately, despite a policy-induced increase in demand for maize, sugarcane, and edible oils for use in biofuels over the past two decades, price increases in these three crops were in line with those of other annual crops (for

---

[6] See discussions in Hamilton (2009) and Marañon and Kumral (2019) on oil and metals, respectively.

[7] Permanent shocks to agriculture have lasting effects on economic activity in low-income countries through their impact on labor productivity (Dieppe, Francis, and Kindberg-Hanlon 2020).

example, rice and wheat) as land was reallocated (World Bank 2019). For example, global demand for maize, a key feedstock for ethanol production in the United States, doubled over the past two decades. This jump compares with 26-28 percent increases in global demand for rice and wheat, broadly in line with global population growth.

- *Consumption substitution.* Because annual crops have overlapping uses, substitution in consumption can dampen price fluctuations in any one of them. In the example of import restrictions on soybeans discussed earlier, maize replaced soybean meal for animal use in China and palm oil replaced soybean oil for human consumption (World Bank 2019).[8]

- *Policy synchronization.* Policy interventions for agricultural markets tend to apply to the entire sector and stay in place for several years, even decades, with few or no changes (chapter 1). For example, agricultural policies in the United States and the European Union—the world's largest producers in several agricultural commodity markets—are renewed every few years and apply to the same crops. Indeed, the 1985 Farm Bill reform in the United States and the 1992 Common Agricultural Policy reform in the European Union applied to all commodities of the respective programs (Baffes and de Gorter 2005).

What have been the main drivers of common cycles in commodity prices?

The preceding section focused on statistical properties of commodity prices and their cycles. This section assesses the drivers of commodity prices, particularly the role of global shocks.[9] It uses a factor-augmented vector autoregression (FAVAR) model to empirically estimate the importance of different drivers of commodity prices, particularly the relative role of global demand and supply shocks, and commodity-specific shocks.

Several studies have examined the drivers of common cycles in commodity prices. A popular view in the literature that attempts to provide a macroeconomic explanation for this phenomenon is that a common component of commodity price fluctuations exists and may be captured by measures of the ebbs and flows in global economic activity (Alquist, Bhattarai, and Coibion 2020; Byrne, Sakemoto, and Xu 2020; Chiaie, Ferrara, and Giannone 2017; Marañon and Kumral 2019). However, fluctuations in global economic activity alone do not explain the evolution of commodity prices. Other factors, particularly supply conditions within and across commodity markets, are likely to be key determinants of commodity price cycles (Borensztein and Reinhart 1994; Cashin, McDermott, and Scott 2002).

---

[8] The imposition of tariffs by China on U.S. soybean imports resulted in trade diversion. China began importing less from the United States and more from Brazil whereas the European Union began importing more from the United States and less from Brazil.

[9] This section draws heavily on World Bank (2022).

For example, the 2006-08 spike and the 2014-16 collapse in commodity prices were caused by factors other than global demand. Fluctuations in factor input costs, such as the prices of oil and other energy products, can affect a wide range of commodity markets simultaneously. Energy is both a key input in the production of metals and an important cost component for most grain and oilseed crops, through both direct channels (fuel prices) and indirect channels (chemical and fertilizer prices). Thus, when energy prices increase, the costs of these commodities go up concurrently (Baffes 2007). Similarly, for annual crops, prices could be synchronized because of input substitutability. Often weather patterns (for example, the El Niño or La Niña phenomenon) increase or reduce production across a number of commodities (World Bank 2015b). Yet another strand of the literature has argued that the comovement in commodity prices is partly a response to the financialization of commodity markets, especially following the price boom of the late 2000s (Le Pen and Sévi 2018; Ohashia and Okimoto 2016).

Identifying and measuring shocks

Data and methodology. A FAVAR model is estimated with three variables—global consumer price inflation, global industrial production growth, and global commodity price growth. Each is expressed in month-on-month log changes over 1970-2021, in seasonally adjusted terms, and included with twelve lags. By construction, the methodology is designed to analyze the links between short-term fluctuations in the global economy and global commodity markets, not long-term trends. Global commodity prices are defined as the common factor among 39 commodity prices. Global industrial production is defined as the global economic activity index of Baumeister and Hamilton (2019). Global consumer price inflation is defined as the median headline Consumer Price Index (CPI) inflation for up to 143 economies (taken from Ha, Kose, and Ohnsorge 2021).[10]

Identification of shocks. Although the specific nature of shocks changes over time, they can be grouped into three categories: global demand shocks, global supply shocks, and commodity price shocks. The shocks are identified using a set of sign restrictions on interactions between the three variables in the FAVAR on impact. The restrictions to identify the structural shocks are consistent with theoretical predictions (Fry and Pagan 2011) and follow other empirical studies in the literature (Charnavoki and Dolado 2014; Peersman 2005; Peersman and Straub 2006).

- A positive global demand shock is assumed to increase global industrial production, inflation, and commodity prices.

- A positive global supply shock is assumed to raise global industrial production and reduce global inflation; in commodity markets, it lifts global consumption of commodities and, thus, raises commodity prices.

---

[10] The results remain qualitatively similar when CPI inflation for Organisation for Economic Co-operation and Development countries or the common factor of headline CPI inflation for 143 economies is used as a measure of global inflation.

- A positive commodity-specific shock is defined as raising commodity prices and global inflation but depressing global industrial production. Such shocks could reflect a wide range of commodity market developments that are unrelated to global demand or supply, including geopolitical risks, financialization of commodity markets, and expectations of future demand or supply pressures.

Note that these global demand and supply shocks differ materially from the commodity demand and supply shocks modeled in Kilian and Murphy (2014) and others (Baumeister and Hamilton 2019; Jacks and Stuermer 2020). Here, an increase in both economic activity and commodity prices can reflect either a global demand or a global supply shock—depending on movements in global inflation. Either of these two global shocks drives up commodity demand, consistent with the definition of a commodity demand shock in Kilian and Murphy (2014). But, for commodity shocks, an increase in both economic activity and commodity prices reflects a commodity demand shock, in contrast to a commodity supply shock, which is associated with an increase in commodity prices but a decline in economic activity.

Global demand, supply, and commodity shocks. The model identifies a series of global demand, global supply, and commodity price shocks from 1970 onward. These shocks have often been associated with turning points in the global business cycle and sharp movements in oil prices (figure 3.4). The role of these drivers for individual major commodities is investigated in greater detail in box 3.2.

- *Global demand shocks.* Negative global demand shocks were associated with global recessions (1975, 1982, 1991, 2009, and 2020) and slowdowns (1998, 2001, and 2012). Large positive global demand shocks often occurred in the year before the global economy began to slide into a global recession or slowdown.

- *Global supply shocks.* The widespread rise in inflation amid slow growth during the 1970s and early 1980s has been partly attributed to negative global supply shocks—such as the 1973-74 and 1978-79 oil price shocks and productivity growth slowdowns that reflected expanding government sectors, macroeconomic volatility, and regulatory uncertainty (Bjork 1999; CBO 1981; Charnavoki and Dolado 2014). The global economic recovery starting in the late 1990s, however, has been attributed to positive global supply shocks associated with rising productivity growth linked to advances in information technology, rapidly rising investment, and widespread trade liberalization and global value chain integration in EMDEs, especially China.[11]

- *Commodity-specific shocks.* Positive commodity-specific shocks were associated with the oil price shocks in 1973 and 1979, the Gulf War in 1990, an agreement among major producers to cut aluminum production in 1994, and a general strike in

---

[11] The important role played by supply shocks in the late 1990s is consistent with other studies. See Charnavoki and Dolado (2014); Dieppe (2020); Kabundi and Zahid (forthcoming); Kotwal, Ramaswami, and Wadhwa (2011); Topalova and Khandelwal (2011); World Bank (2020c); and Zhu (2012).

FIGURE 3.4 Contributions of global shocks to commodity prices

Global demand shocks have had smaller and less persistent effects than global supply shocks on global commodity prices. Since the mid-1990s, global demand and supply shocks have accounted for the majority of global commodity price volatility. In the global recession of 2020, both global demand and commodity market shocks depressed commodity prices whereas supply shocks supported commodity prices.

A. Global demand shocks

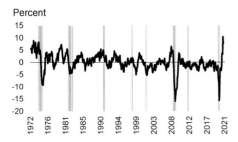

B. Global commodity market shocks

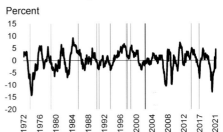

C. Response of global commodity prices to 1 percent increase in global demand

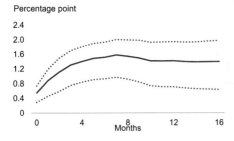

D. Response of global commodity prices to 1 percent increase in global supply

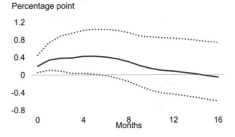

E. Contributions of global shocks to variations in global commodity prices

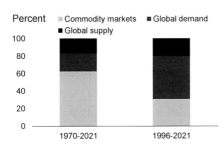

F. Contributions of global shocks to variations in global commodity prices around recessions and slowdowns

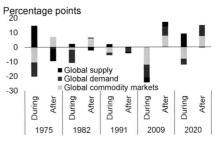

Sources: Baumeister and Hamilton 2019; Ha, Kose, and Ohnsorge 2021; World Bank.

Note: Global demand, supply, and commodity shocks identified using sign restrictions in a factor-augmented vector autoregression of month-on-month seasonally adjusted changes in global inflation, global commodity prices, and global industrial production. All in year-on-year growth rates.

A. Gray shades indicate quarters with global recessions (1975, 1982, 1991, 2009, 2020) and global slowdowns (1998, 2001, 2012), as defined in Kose, Sugawara, and Terrones (2020).

B. Red lines indicate events specific to commodity markets, including the first oil price crisis in October 1973; the Iranian revolution in January 1979; the beginning of the Gulf War in August 1990; the memorandum of understanding between Australia, Canada, the European Union, Norway, the Russian Federation, and the United States to cut aluminum production; Organization of the Petroleum Exporting Countries (OPEC) meetings to ease production quotas (December 1985 and November 2014); and selected OPEC meetings to reestablish production quotas (1998-99 and December 2016).

C. D. Solid line indicates cumulative median response of global commodity price growth to a 1 standard deviation (about 1 percent) increase in global demand (C), or global supply (D). Dotted lines indicate 16th to 84th confidence intervals.

E. Contribution of global demand, supply, and commodity market shocks to variance of month-on-month growth in commodity prices, based on sample covering 1970-2021 and sample covering 1996-2021.

República Bolivariana de Venezuela in 2002-03 that disrupted oil production. OPEC agreements to ease production cuts in December 1985 and November 2014 were associated with negative commodity price shocks. In addition, new producers entered global markets in the 1980s (coal and palm oil), the 1990s (aluminum, coffee, and grains), and in the 2010s (copper, soybeans, and shale oil), which contributed to declining or negative commodity price shocks.

Responses of global commodity prices to global shocks. Since 1970, on average, a 1 percent increase in global demand raised global commodity price growth by up to 0.4 percent over the subsequent 6 months, but the impact dissipated thereafter. In contrast, global supply and commodity market shocks had longer-lasting impacts. A 1 percent increase in global supply raised global commodity prices by 1.6 percentage points over the following 7 months, and the effect remained statistically significant for 18 months. Similarly, a 1 percent global commodity market shock that raised commodity prices was followed by more than 1.1 percent higher commodity prices within 12 months of the shock, and the effect persisted for at least 18 months. The persistence of the response of prices to shocks can partly be attributed to a low elasticity of supply because of long lead times between resource discovery and production (World Bank 2016).

Relative contributions of shocks to global commodity prices. In the full data period since 1970, shocks specific to commodity markets have been the main source of variability in global commodity prices, accounting for more than 60 percent of the variance.[12] These shocks have included major disruptions to oil markets, the collapse of the Soviet Union in the case of agricultural and metals markets, and the emergence of new producers of metals and agricultural commodities in the 1970s, 1980s, and 1990s. Since 1996, however, global macroeconomic shocks have been the main source of commodity price volatility: global demand shocks account for 50 percent and global supply shocks for 20 percent of the variance of global commodity prices.[13]

Interactions between global shocks and commodity prices

The three types of shocks discussed above—global demand shocks, global supply shocks, and commodity price shocks—can occur simultaneously and may influence one another, especially during times of global recession. Commodity prices are generally depressed in recessions because of weak global economic demand. Other forces, however, can occur that either amplify or ease pressure on prices. For example, during the recessions of 1995, 1991, and 2020, weak demand for commodities was amplified by commodity-specific supply pressures. In contrast, in 1975 weak demand for commodities was offset by supply disruptions resulting from trade embargoes, and in 2020 weak demand was

---

[12] The predominant role of commodity-specific shocks in the variability of commodity prices is in line with Charnavoki and Dolado (2014), Ha et al. (2019), and Jacks and Stuermer (2020).

[13] These numbers refer to the variance decompositions for one-year-ahead forecast errors of global commodity price growth. Over a medium- to long-term (5-10 years) forecasting horizon, the variance contribution of global commodity shocks (57 percent) is greater than that of global demand shocks (28 percent) because global commodity shocks are more persistent than demand shocks.

worsened by supply chain disruptions (Mahajan and Tomar 2020). During recoveries, commodity price increases are typically driven by an unwinding of global supply shocks or commodity-specific shocks and, since 2000, by rebounds in global demand. Positive global supply shocks can also depress global commodity prices during nonrecession periods, such as in the 1970s and 1980s. The downward pressure on prices during these periods temporarily reversed between 2000 and 2008 when rapid global value chain integration and productivity growth lifted commodity prices.

Conclusion

This chapter examined the characteristics and drivers of commodity price cycles. The results show that, on average across commodities, the transitory and permanent components account for roughly equal shares of commodity price variability. At a group level, however, agricultural prices are dominated by the permanent component, and the transitory component is more important for industrial commodities. Within the transitory component, the medium-term cycle component (frequency of 8-20 years) accounts for twice the variation of the traditional business cycle component (frequency of 2-8 years), particularly for industrial commodities, in turn highlighting the importance of the investment cycle for commodities.

The chapter also identified three medium-term cycles. Although both the first and third medium-term cycles involved all commodities, the third exhibited higher amplitude and was more synchronized than the first, thus rendering it the largest post-World War II commodity price cycle. The second cycle, which was most relevant to metal commodities, did not involve energy at all. In addition, the permanent component trended upward for most industrial commodities and downward for agriculture.

Considering the drivers of commodity price variability, global macroeconomic shocks have become the main source of fluctuations in commodity prices, accounting for more than two-thirds of the variance of global commodity price growth since the mid-1990s. Global demand shocks, such as recessions, have accounted for the majority of that variance. In contrast, commodity-specific shocks, such as those arising from adjustment to long-term trends in supply and demand, have accounted for just under a third of the variability in global commodity prices since the mid-1990s.

A number of policy implications stem from the analysis. Heterogeneity of shocks across commodities implies that policies should be tailored to the terms of trade faced by each country, rather than applying one-size-fits-all policies. Countries that depend on exports of highly cyclical commodities that experience frequent transitory shocks will need to be more proactive in using fiscal and monetary policy to smooth these shocks and support economic activity. In contrast, countries that rely heavily on commodities that are subject to permanent shocks may need structural policies to facilitate adjustments to new economic environments.

ANNEX 3A Decomposing commodity prices into cycles and long-term trends

Model and data description

The real price of the commodity at time t, p_t, is expressed as the following sum:

$$p_t \equiv PC_t + TC_t^{[20-8]} + TC_t^{[2-8]} + S_t$$

PC_t, which represents the permanent component, can be a linear trend, perhaps subjected to structural breaks. Alternatively, one could include nonlinearities. $TC_t^{[8-20]}$ denotes the medium-term cycle with a periodicity of 8-20 years as proposed by Blanchard (1997) and popularized by Comin and Gertler (2006). $TC_t^{[2-8]}$ represents the business cycle with a periodicity of 2-8 years, following the National Bureau of Economic Research's traditional definition (Burns and Mitchell 1946). Last, S_t captures fluctuations with periodicity of less than 2 years, which may reflect short-term movement in economic activity or other macroeconomic variables (such as exchange rates and interest rates), seasonality or weather patterns (in the case of agriculture), and ad hoc policy shocks. These fluctuations are typically studied within the context of vector autoregression models (Baumeister and Hamilton 2019; Kilian and Murphy 2014) and generalized autoregressive conditional heteroscedasticity models by using high-frequency data, focusing mostly on volatility (Engle 1982). The decomposition is based on the frequency domain methodology developed by Corbae, Ouliaris, and Phillips (2002) and Corbae and Ouliaris (2006).

Price data come from the World Bank's Commodity Markets (Pink Sheet) database. The sample covers 50 years: January 1970 through December 2019 (600 observations). The prices, reported in nominal U.S. dollar terms, were deflated with the U.S. CPI (taken from the St. Louis Federal Reserve Bank). Although the World Bank covers more than 70 commodity price series, this report uses only 27 series. The selection was based on the following criteria:

- *Substitutability.* If two commodities are close substitutes, only one was included. For example, because edible oils are close substitutes, only soybean oil is used in the analysis.

- *Importance.* Commodities whose share in consumption declined throughout the sample (either because of changes in preferences or substitution from synthetic products) were not included in the sample. Notable exclusions include wool, hides and skins, sisal, and tobacco.

- *Price determination process.* Prices are determined by market-based mechanisms, such as on commodity exchanges or at auctions (in the case of tea). Notable exclusions are iron ore (until 2005, its price was the outcome of a negotiation process among key players of the steel industry), bananas (its price reflects quotations from a few large trading companies), sugar (policy interventions reduce the significance of the world price indicator), groundnuts (thinly traded commodity), and tropical timber products (not traded on exchanges).

Following the decomposition analysis, prices were grouped into six broad categories, each of which contained at least three series: energy (coal, crude oil, and natural gas); base metals (aluminum, copper, lead, nickel, tin, and zinc); precious metals (gold, platinum, and silver); fertilizers (phosphate rock, potassium chlorate, triple superphosphate, and urea); annual agriculture (cotton, maize, rice, soybean meal, soybean oil, and wheat); and perennial agriculture (cocoa, coffee Arabica, coffee Robusta, natural rubber, and tea).

Decomposition results are reported in table 3A.1. The numbers in the square brackets of the first column represent weights and add to 100 for each commodity group, subject to rounding. The shares of each component add to 100, subject to rounding. For example, coal's shares are $0.36 + 0.42 + 0.18 + 0.04 = 1$. The penultimate column reports the parameter estimate from the regression of PC_t on a time trend, and the last column reports the root mean square error—a proxy for nonlinearity.

TABLE 3A.1 Real commodity price decomposition

	Share of variance explained by				Number of cycles		Trend	
	PC_t	$TC_t^{[8\text{-}20]}$	$TC_t^{[2\text{-}8]}$	S_t	$TC_t^{[8\text{-}20]}$	$TC_t^{[2\text{-}8]}$	β	RMSE
Energy								
Coal [**4.6**]	0.36	0.42	0.18	0.04	3	11	0.43	5.31
Crude oil [**84.6**]	0.31	0.54	0.11	0.04	2	12	1.02	7.65
Natural gas [**10.8**]	0.19	0.68	0.10	0.03	2	11	0.57	2.50
Average	**0.29**	**0.55**	**0.13**	**0.04**	**2**	**11**	**0.95**	**6.99**
Base metals								
Aluminum [**32.9**]	0.57	0.20	0.20	0.03	4	10	-0.14	0.64
Copper [**47.4**]	0.47	0.30	0.19	0.04	3	9	-0.80	3.31
Lead [**2.2**]	0.57	0.25	0.16	0.02	3	8	-0.54	4.75
Nickel [**9.9**]	0.18	0.44	0.34	0.04	3	11	-0.78	1.63
Tin [**2.6**]	0.74	0.19	0.06	0.01	3	12	0.05	4.38
Zinc [**5.0**]	0.25	0.22	0.46	0.07	3	8	-0.09	2.08
Average	**0.46**	**0.27**	**0.24**	**0.04**	**3**	**10**	**-0.52**	**2.46**
Precious metals								
Gold [**77.8**]	0.62	0.27	0.10	0.01	3	8	1.28	5.38
Platinum [**18.9**]	0.22	0.48	0.23	0.06	3	11	-0.22	1.85
Silver [**3.3**]	0.47	0.36	0.13	0.03	3	11	0.27	13.47
Average	**0.44**	**0.37**	**0.15**	**0.03**	**3**	**10**	**0.96**	**4.98**
Fertilizers								
Phosphate [**16.9**]	0.37	0.30	0.25	0.07	3	9	-0.40	6.48
Potassium [**20.1**]	0.36	0.45	0.16	0.03	3	10	-0.46	3.43
TSP [**21.7**]	0.36	0.24	0.34	0.06	4	9	-0.52	3.91
Urea [**41.3**]	0.24	0.42	0.22	0.12	3	12	-0.02	4.44
Average	**0.33**	**0.35**	**0.24**	**0.07**	**3**	**10**	**-0.28**	**4.47**
Annual agriculture								
Cotton [**8.5**]	0.80	0.07	0.11	0.02	3	13	-0.07	9.00
Maize [**20.5**]	0.70	0.16	0.11	0.03	3	10	-0.50	3.55
Rice [**15.2**]	0.63	0.19	0.14	0.04	3	9	-0.43	3.29
Soybean meal [**29.0**]	0.69	0.10	0.17	0.04	3	10	-0.48	3.48
Soybean oil [**14.3**]	0.66	0.16	0.15	0.03	3	11	-0.72	3.15
Wheat [**12.5**]	0.62	0.18	0.15	0.05	3	9	-0.42	2.60
Average	**0.68**	**0.14**	**0.14**	**0.04**	**3**	**10**	**-0.47**	**3.78**
Perennial agriculture								
Cocoa [**25.6**]	0.67	0.22	0.10	0.01	3	11	0.03	15.41
Coffee Arabica [**15.7**]	0.61	0.24	0.12	0.04	3	14	0.22	10.38
Coffee Robusta [**15.7**]	0.75	0.17	0.06	0.02	3	13	0.42	15.86
Natural rubber [**30.6**]	0.31	0.43	0.23	0.03	3	10	-0.36	17.39
Tea [**12.4**]	0.78	0.07	0.12	0.03	3	13	-0.17	9.47
Average	**0.62**	**0.23**	**0.13**	**0.03**	**3**	**12**	**-0.03**	**14.56**
All average	**0.47**	**0.32**	**0.17**	**0.04**	**3**	**11**	**0.10**	**6.21**

Source: World Bank.

Note: Descriptions of terms appear in the text. Numbers in square brackets indicate weight of the commodity used in constructing weighted indexes. RMSE = root mean square error; TSP = triple superphosphate.

ANNEX 3B FAVAR: Methodology

After estimating a common global factor that affects all commodity prices using a dynamic factor model (World Bank 2022), the drivers underlying the dynamics of the common factor, f_t, are identified using a FAVAR model. The model comprises, in addition to the common factor, a monthly index of world industrial production, q_t, developed by Baumeister and Hamilton (2019), and a measure of global inflation, π_t, proxied by a median inflation rate constructed from the seasonally adjusted consumer price indexes of 143 economies developed by Ha et al. (2019). The data cover the period from January 1970 to September 2021.

The following general form of a structural FAVAR model is employed:

$$B_0 y_t = \sum_{i=1}^{p} B_i y_{t-i} + w_t$$

where y_t is the $K \times 1$ vector that contains the endogenous model variables, w_t is the $K \times 1$ vector of mutually uncorrelated structural shocks, B_0 is the structural impact multiplier matrix that describes the contemporaneous relationships among the model variables, B_i is the matrix of coefficients, and $p = 3$ is the lag length.

The reduced-form representation of the structural FAVAR is given by

$$y_t - \sum_{i=1}^{p} A_i y_{t-i} + u_t$$

$A_i = B_0^{-1} B_i$ and $u_t = B_0^{(-1)} w_t$ are the reduced-form coefficients and errors, respectively, with $K \times K$ variance-covariance matrix $E(u_t u_t') = \Sigma_u$. Thus, given the structural impact multiplier matrix, B_0, the reduced-form innovations can be represented as weighted averages of the mutually uncorrelated structural shocks, w_t. However, because the model is underidentified, further identifying restrictions are required to estimate B_0.

The analysis identifies three shocks—a global demand shock, a global supply shock, and a commodity-specific shock—as underlying drivers of the common global factor of commodity prices. The identification scheme is based on sign restrictions applied to the matrix B_0. Specifically, it uses the following sign restrictions:

$$u_t = \begin{bmatrix} + & + & - \\ + & - & + \\ + & + & + \end{bmatrix} \begin{pmatrix} u_t^{Global\ Demand} \\ u_t^{Global\ Supply} \\ u_t^{Commodity-specific} \end{pmatrix} = B_0^{-1} w_t$$

where signs are imposed on the elements of the inverse of the structural impact multiplier matrix, B_0^{-1}, and all shocks are normalized to increase the commodity price factor.

The impact sign restrictions on B_0 are in line with theoretical predictions and other empirical studies.[14] For example, positive global demand shocks are characterized by positive comovement in the global industrial production index, global inflation, and the common commodity price factor. A positive global supply shock, by contrast, increases global output, decreases global inflation, and increases commodity prices. A positive commodity-specific shock decreases output, increases global inflation, and increases commodity prices. Commodity-specific shocks are designed to account for innovations to commodity prices that are orthogonal to global demand and global supply shocks, such as unexpected shifts in speculative or precautionary demand for commodities (see Charnavoki and Dolado 2014; Kilian and Murphy 2014).

References

Adonizio, W., N. Kook, and S. Royales. 2012. "Impact of the Drought on Corn Exports: Paying the Price." *Beyond the Numbers* 1 (17).

Akiyama, T., and P. Varangis. 1990. "The Impact of the International Coffee Agreement on Producing Countries." *World Bank Economic Review* 4 (2): 157-73.

Aksoy, M. A., and J. Beghin. 2004. *Global Agricultural Trade and Developing Countries.* Washington, DC: World Bank.

Aldasoro, I., S. Avdjiev, C. Borio, and P. Disyatat. 2020. "Global and Domestic Financial Cycles: Variations on a Theme." BIS Working Paper 864, Bank for International Settlements, Basel, Switzerland.

Alquist, R., S. Bhattarai, and O. Coibion. 2020. "Commodity-Price Comovement and Global Economic Activity." *Journal of Monetary Economics* 112 (June): 41-56.

Baffes, J. 2007. "Oil Spills on Other Commodities." *Resources Policy* 32 (3): 126-34.

Baffes, J., and X. Etienne. 2016. "Analyzing Food Price Trends in the Context of Engel's Law and the Prebisch-Singer Hypothesis." *Oxford Economics Papers* 68 (3): 688-713.

Baffes, J., and H. de Gorter. 2005. "Disciplining Agricultural Support Through Decoupling." Policy Research Working Paper 3533, World Bank, Washington, DC.

Baffes, J., and A. Kabundi. 2021. "Commodity Price Shocks: Order within Chaos?" Policy Research Working Paper 9792, World Bank, Washington, DC.

Baffes, J., A. Kabundi, and P. Nagle. 2022. "The Role of Income and Substitution in Commodity Demand." *Oxford Economic Papers* 74(2): 498-522.

---

[14] Charnavoki and Dolado (2014) identify global demand, global supply, and commodity market shocks to examine their effects on macroeconomic aggregates for a small commodity-exporting economy. Ha, Kose, and Ohnsorge (2019) employ a similar identification scheme to investigate the drivers of global inflation.

Baffes, J., M. A. Kose, F. Ohnsorge, and M. Stocker. 2015. "The Great Plunge in Oil Prices: Causes, Consequences, and Policy Responses." Policy Research Note 01, World Bank, Washington, DC.

Baumeister, C., and J. D. Hamilton. 2019. "Structural Interpretation of Vector Autoregressions with Incomplete Identification: Revisiting the Role of Oil Supply and Demand Shocks." *American Economic Review* 109 (5): 1873-910.

Bernanke, B. 2016. "The Relationship between Stocks and Oil Prices." *Brookings* (blog), February 19, 2016. https://www.brookings.edu/blog/benbernanke/2016/02/19/the-relation ship-between-stocks-and-oil-prices/.

Bjork, G. C. 1999. *The Way It Worked and Why It Won't: Structural Change and the Slowdown of U.S. Economic Growth*. Westport, CT: Praeger Publishers.

Blanchard, O. 1997. "The Medium Run." *Brookings Papers on Economic Activity* 2 (1997): 89-158.

Borensztein, E., and C. Reinhart. 1994. "The Macroeconomic Determinants of Commodity Prices." *IMF Staff Papers* 41 (2): 236-61.

Burns, A. F., and W. C. Mitchell. 1946. *Measuring Business Cycles*. New York: National Bureau of Economic Research.

Byrne, J., G. Fazio, and N. Fiess. 2013. "Primary Commodity Prices: Co-movements, Common Factors and Fundamentals." *Journal of Development Economics* 101 (C): 16-26.

Byrne, J., R. Sakemoto, and B. Xu. 2020. "Commodity Price Co-movement: Heterogeneity and the Time Varying Impact of Fundamentals." *European Review of Agricultural Economics* 47 (2): 499-528.

Cao, D., and J-P. L'Huillier. 2018. "Technological Revolutions and the Three Great Slumps: A Medium-Run Analysis." *Journal of Monetary Economics* 96 (June): 93-108.

Cashin, P., C. J. McDermott, and A. Scott. 2002. "Booms and Slumps in World Commodity Prices." *Journal of Development Economics* 69 (1): 277-96.

CBO (Congressional Budget Office). 1981. "The Productivity Slowdown: Causes and Policy Responses." Staff Memorandum, Congressional Budget Office, Congress of the United States, Washington, DC.

Charnavoki, V., and J. Dolado. 2014. "The Effects of Global Shocks on Small Commodity-Exporting Economies: Lessons from Canada." *American Economic Journal: Macroeconomics* (2): 207-37.

Chiaie, S. D., L. Ferrara, and D. Giannone. 2017. "Common Factors of Commodity Prices." Working Papers 645, Banque de France, Paris.

Comin, D., and M. Gertler, 2006. "Medium-Term Business Cycles." *American Economic Review* 96 (3): 523-51.

Corbae, D., and S. Ouliaris. 2006. "Extracting Cycles from Nonstationary Data." In *Econometric Theory and Practice: Frontiers of Analysis and Applied Research,* edited by D. Corbae, S. Durlauf, and B. Hansen. New York: Cambridge University Press.

Corbae, D., S. Ouliaris, and P. C. B. Phillips. 2002. "Band and Spectral Regression with Trending Data." *Econometrica* 70 (3): 1067-109.

Cuddington, J. T., and D. Jerrett. 2008. "Super Cycles in Real Metal Prices?" *IMF Staff Papers* 55 (4): 541-65.

Davutyan, N., and M. C. Roberts. 1994. "Cyclicality in Metal Prices." *Resources Policy* 20 (1): 49-57.

Dieppe, A., ed. 2020. *Global Productivity: Trends, Drivers, and Policies.* Washington, DC: World Bank.

Dieppe, A., N. Francis, and G. Kindberg-Hanlon. 2020. "Productivity: Technology, Demand, and Employment Trade-Offs." In *Global Productivity: Trends, Drivers, and Policies,* edited by A. Dieppe, 361-400. Washington, DC: World Bank.

Eickmeier, S., and M. Kühnlenz. 2018. "China's Role in Global Inflation Dynamics." *Macroeconomic Dynamics* 22 (2): 225-54.

EIA (Energy Information Administration). 2020. *Monthly Energy Review.* April. Washington, DC: U.S. Energy Information Administration.

Engle, R. F. 1982. "Autoregressive Conditional Heteroscedasticity with Estimates of Variance of United Kingdom Inflation." *Econometrica* 50 (4): 987-1008.

Erten, B., and J. A. Ocampo. 2013. "Super Cycles of Commodity Prices since the Mid-nineteenth Century." *World Development* 44 (C): 14-30.

Fattouh, B. 2007. "OPEC Pricing Power: The Need for a New Perspective." Oxford Institute for Energy Studies WPM 31, Oxford, U.K.

Fernández, A., S. Schmitt-Grohé, and M. Uribe. 2020. "Does the Commodity Super Cycle Matter?" NBER Working Paper 27589, National Bureau of Economic Research, Cambridge, MA.

Fry, R., and A. Pagan. 2011. "Sign Restrictions in Structural Vector Autoregressions: A Critical Review." *Journal of Economic Literature* 49 (4): 938-60.

Ha, J., M. A. Kose, and F. Ohnsorge, eds. 2019. *Inflation in Emerging and Developing Economies: Evolution, Drivers, and Policies.* Washington, DC: World Bank.

Ha, J., M. A. Kose, and F. Ohnsorge. 2021. "One-Stop Source: A Global Database of Inflation." Policy Research Working Paper 9737, World Bank, Washington, DC.

Ha, J., M. A. Kose, F. Ohnsorge, and H. Yilmazkuday. 2019. "Sources of Inflation: Global and Domestic Drivers," In *Inflation in Emerging and Developing Economies: Evolution, Drivers, and Policies,* edited by J. Ha, M. A. Kose, and F. Ohnsorge, 143-99. Washington, DC: World Bank.

Hamilton, J. D. 2009. "Understanding Crude Oil Prices." *Energy Journal* 30 (2): 179-206.

Hamilton, J. 2015. "What's Driving the Price of Oil Down?" *Econbrowser; Analysis of Current Economic Conditions and Policy* (blog), January 25, 2015. https://econbrowser.com/archives/2015/01/whats-driving-the-price-of-oil-down-2.

Harding, D., and A. Pagan. 2002. "Dissecting the Cycle: A Methodological Investigation." *Journal of Monetary Economics* 49 (2): 365-81.

Jacks, D. S. 2019. "From Boom to Bust: A Typology of Real Commodity Prices in the Long Term." *Cliometrica* 13: 201-20.

Jacks, D. S., and M. Stuermer. 2020. "What Drives Commodity Price Boom and Busts?" *Energy Economics* 85 (January): 104035.

Kabundi, A., and F. Ohnsorge. 2020. "Implications of Cheap Oil for Emerging Markets." Policy Research Working Paper 9403, World Bank, Washington, DC.

Kabundi, A., and H. Zahid. Forthcoming. "Commodity Price Cycles: Commonalities, Heterogeneities, and Drivers." World Bank, Washington, DC.

Kaufmann, R. K., S. Dees, P. Karadeloglou, and M. Sanchez. 2004. "Does OPEC Matter? An Econometric Analysis of Oil Prices." *Energy Journal* 25 (4): 67-90.

Kilian, L., and D. P. Murphy. 2014. "The Role of Inventories and Speculative Trading in the Global Market for Crude Oil." *Journal of Applied Econometrics* 29 (3): 454-78.

Klümper, W., and M. Qaim. 2014. "A Meta-Analysis of the Impacts of Genetically Modified Crops." *Plos One*, November 3, 2014. https://doi.org/10.1371/journal.pone.0111629.

Kose, M. A, C. Otrok, and C. H. Whiteman. 2003. "International Business Cycles: World, Region, and Country-Specific Factors." *American Economic Review* 93 (4): 1216-39.

Kose, M. A., N. Sugawara, and M. E. Terrones. 2020. "Global Recessions." Policy Research Working Paper 9172, World Bank, Washington, DC.

Kotwal, A., B. Ramaswami, and W. Wadhwa. 2011. "Economic Liberalization and Indian Economic Growth: What's the Evidence?" *Journal of Economic Literature* 49 (4): 1152-99.

Labys, W. C., J. B. Lesourd, and D. Badillo. 1998. "The Existence of Metal Price Cycles." *Resources Policy* 24 (3): 147-55.

Le Pen, Y., and B. Sévi. 2018. "Futures Trading and the Excess Co-movement of Commodity Prices." *Review of Finance* 22 (1): 381-418.

Lombardi, M., C. Osbat, and B. Schnatz. 2010. "Global Commodity Cycles and Linkages: A FAVAR Approach." Working Paper 1170, European Central Bank, Frankfurt.

Mahajan, K., and S. Tomar. 2020. "COVID-19 and Supply Chain Disruption: Evidence from Food Markets in India." *American Journal of Agriculture Economics* 103 (1): 35-52.

Marañon, M., and M. Kumral. 2019. "Dynamics behind Cycles and Co-movements in Metal Prices: An Empirical Study Using Band-Pass Filters." *Natural Resources Research* 29 (3): 1487-519.

McCalla, A. F. 1999. "Prospects for Food Security in the 21st Century with Special Emphasis on Africa." *Agricultural Economics* 20: 95-103.

McGregor, N. F., D. S. Spinola, and B. Verspagen. 2018. "On the Development and Impact of Commodity Prices and Cycles." Inclusive and Sustainable Industrial Development Working Paper 8, Department of Policy, Research and Statistics, United Nations Industrial Development Organization, Vienna.

Ohashia, K., and T. Okimoto. 2016. "Increasing Trends in the Excess Comovement of Commodity Prices." *Journal of Commodity Markets* 1 (1): 48-64.

Ojeda-Joya, J. N., O. Jaulin-Mendes, and J. C. Bustos-Pelaez. 2019. "The Interdependence between Commodity Price and GDP Cycles: A Frequency-Domain Approach." *Atlantic Economic Journal* 47 (3): 275-92.

Peersman, G. 2005. "What Caused the Early Millennium Slowdown? Evidence Based on Vector Autoregressions." *Journal of Applied Econometrics* 20 (2): 185-207.

Peersman, G., and R. Straub. 2006. "Putting the New Keynesian Model to a Test." IMF Working Paper 135, International Monetary Fund, Washington, DC.

Poncela, P., E. Senra, and L. P. Sierra. 2014. "Common Dynamics of Non-energy Commodity Prices and Their Relation to Uncertainty." *Applied Economics* 46 (30): 3724-35.

Radetzki, M. 2009. "Seven Thousand Years in the Service of Humanity: The History of Copper, the Red Metal." *Resources Policy* 34 (4): 176-84.

Roberts, M. C. 2009. "Duration and Characteristics of Metal Price Cycles." *Resources Policy* 34 (3): 87-102.

Rulli, M. C., D. Bellomi, A. Cazzoli, G. De Carolis, and P. D'Odorico. 2016. "The Water-Land-Food Nexus of First-Generation Biofuels." *Scientific Reports* 6 (22521): 1-10.

Slade, M. 1982. "Trends in Natural-Resource Commodity Prices: An Analysis of the Price Domain." *Journal of Environmental Economics and Management* 9 (2): 122-37.

Topalova, P., and A. Khandelwal. 2011. "Trade Liberalization and Firm Productivity: The Case of India." *Review of Economics and Statistics* 93 (3): 995-1009.

Tyner, W. E. 2008. "The U.S. Ethanol and Biofuels Boom: Its Origins, Current Status, and Future Prospects." *Bioscience* 58 (7): 646-53.

Vansteenkiste, I. 2009. "How Important Are Common Factors in Driving Non-fuel Commodity Prices? A Dynamic Factor Analysis." Working Paper 1072, European Central Bank, Frankfurt.

Wheeler, C. M., J. Baffes, A. Kabundi, G. Kindberg-Hanlon, P. S. Nagle, and F. Ohnsorge. 2020. "Adding Fuel to the Fire: Cheap Oil during the COVID-19 Pandemic." Policy Research Working Paper 9320, World Bank, Washington, DC.

World Bank. 2009. *Global Economic Prospects: Commodities at the Crossroads.* Washington, DC: World Bank.

World Bank. 2013. "Commodity Annex: Prospects for Commodity Markets." In *Global Economic Prospects,* 75-89. January. Washington, DC: World Bank.

World Bank. 2015a. *Global Economic Prospects: The Global Economy in Transition.* June. Washington, DC: World Bank.

World Bank. 2015b. "Understanding El Niño: What Does It Mean for Commodity Markets?" In *Commodity Markets Outlook,* 5-10. October. Washington, DC: World Bank.

World Bank 2016. "Resource Development in an Era of Cheap Commodities." In *Commodities Market Outlook,* 11-19. April. Washington, DC: World Bank.

World Bank. 2018. *Commodity Markets Outlook: The Changing of the Guard: Shifts in Commodity Demand.* October. Washington, DC: World Bank.

World Bank. 2019. *Commodity Markets Outlook: The Role of Substitution in Commodity Demand.* October. Washington, DC: World Bank.

World Bank. 2020a. *Commodity Markets Outlook: Persistence of Commodity Shocks.* October. Washington, DC: World Bank.

World Bank. 2020b. *Commodity Markets Outlook: Implications of COVID-19 for Commodities.* April. Washington, DC: World Bank.

World Bank. 2020c. *Global Economic Prospects.* June. Washington, DC: World Bank.

World Bank. 2021. *Commodity Markets Outlook: Urbanization and Commodity Demand.* October. Washington, DC: World Bank.

World Bank. 2022. *Global Economic Prospects.* January. Washington, DC: World Bank.

Zhu, X. 2012. "Understanding China's Growth: Past, Present, and Future." *Journal of Economic Perspectives* 26 (4): 103-24.

CHAPTER 4

Causes and Consequences of Industrial Commodity Price Shocks

Alain Kabundi, Peter Nagle, Franziska Ohnsorge, and Takefumi Yamazaki

The 2020 global recession triggered by the COVID-19 pandemic and the subsequent war in Ukraine in 2022 roiled commodity markets. As demand dropped in the first four months of 2020, global energy prices plunged 61 percent and metal prices fell 16 percent. When global economic activity rebounded and pandemic disruptions to production subsided, energy and metal prices recovered quickly and reached multidecade highs in the wake of the Russian Federation's invasion of Ukraine in 2022. Such large price movements have significant macroeconomic implications for commodity exporters. More than half of emerging market and developing economies rely heavily on industrial commodity sectors for export earnings and fiscal revenues. Energy exporters are particularly reliant on resource sectors. Both oil and metal price shocks have asymmetric effects on economic activity in energy and metal producers: price increases are associated with small, temporary growth accelerations; price declines are associated with pronounced and lasting slowdowns. These effects underscore the importance of robust policy frameworks in energy- and metals-producing countries that can smooth global commodity price shocks. Structural reforms that favor growth and more diversified economic activity would reduce vulnerability to external shocks.

Introduction

Since early 2020, industrial commodity prices have been on a roller-coaster ride. At the start of the COVID-19 pandemic, between January and April 2020, global energy prices dropped 61 percent and base metal prices tumbled 16 percent. Beginning in May 2020, however, they recovered quickly amid rebounding economic activity and an array of supply disruptions (World Bank 2021). Base metal prices regained their prepandemic levels by August 2020, and energy prices fully recovered by February 2021. Energy and metal prices continued to rise through 2021. Base metal prices rose for 19 consecutive months, their longest unbroken increase on record. In 2021, the prices of natural gas, coal, copper, iron ore, and tin reached record highs. The Russian Federation's invasion of Ukraine further lifted the prices of natural gas, coal, wheat, barley, various seed oils, some types of fertilizer, copper, and tin to their highest levels since 1960 and raised other energy and food prices to their highest levels in 15 years.

Global recessions—such as those in 2020 caused by the COVID-19 pandemic and in 2009 caused by the global financial crisis—and subsequent recoveries as well as wars and geopolitical tensions can generate large and synchronized commodity price swings (figure 4.1; see also chapter 3; Bilgin and Ellwanger 2017; Chiaie, Ferrara, and Giannone 2017; Helbling 2012; World Bank 2020a). In addition, less synchronous commodity price swings are often generated by commodity-specific supply disruptions such as those occasionally caused by the pandemic during 2020, policy changes of

FIGURE 4.1 **Oil and base metal prices**

Base metal and oil prices typically move together, although OPEC policy supported the oil price during 2010-14 when metal prices were weakening.

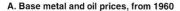

A. Base metal and oil prices, from 1960

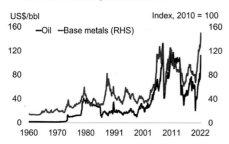

B. Base metal and oil prices, from 2010

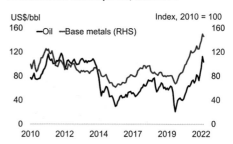

Sources: World Bank Commodity Markets (Pink Sheet) database; World Bank.
Note: Oil price is an average price of Brent, West Texas Intermediate, and Dubai. The base metal index is an export-weighted average of aluminum, copper, lead, nickel, tin, and zinc prices. Last observation is April 2022. bbl = barrel of crude oil; OPEC = Organization of Petroleum Exporting Countries; RHS = right-hand side.

commodity cartels such as those by the Organization of Petroleum-Exporting Countries (OPEC) in 1985 or 2014, or structural changes that shift commodity demand.

In addition to such short-term shocks, medium-term trends are shaping commodity markets. In particular, as global energy consumption transitions away from fossil fuels, metals heavily used in electric vehicles and in renewable electricity generation and storage are expected to become considerably more important (figure 4.2; Boer, Pescatori and Stuermer 2021; World Bank 2020b). This structural shift in output and consumption could have a long-lasting impact on energy- and metal-exporting economies. About a quarter of emerging market and developing economies (EMDEs) rely heavily on oil for export earnings and fiscal revenues, and about a third are similarly dependent on base metals. For these economies, commodity price movements are a key source of macroeconomic volatility (Jacks, O'Rourke, and Williamson 2011). By some estimates, terms-of-trade shocks account for up to half of their business cycle fluctuations (Kose 2002). Because the commodity composition of imports is much more diverse than that of exports, export price shocks generally have a much larger impact on the terms of trade, and the domestic economy, than do import shocks (Di Pace, Juvenal, and Petrella 2021; Richaud et al. 2019). Prospects for these commodity-reliant economies depend significantly on the type of commodity they export.

This chapter analyzes the impact of energy and metal price shocks on energy and metal exporters and importers. It addresses the following questions:

- How important are energy and metals for the global economy and EMDEs?

- What have been the drivers of energy and metal price swings over the past seven decades?

- What are the implications of movements in energy and metal prices for economic activity in EMDEs?

FIGURE 4.2 Copper use

Low-carbon technologies are more metals-intensive than traditional technologies.

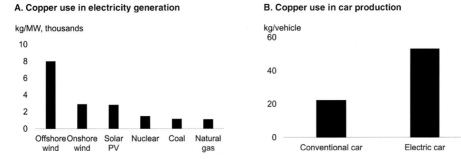

A. Copper use in electricity generation

kg/MW, thousands

B. Copper use in car production

kg/vehicle

Sources: International Energy Agency 2022; World Bank.
Note: kg = kilogram; MW = megawatt; PV = photovoltaic.
B. The values for vehicles are for the entire vehicle including batteries, motors, and glider.

This chapter makes several contributions to the literature. First, it compares the structure of global energy and metal markets, including how much producers in each market rely on commodities for export earnings and fiscal revenues and to generate economic activity. To the authors' knowledge, such a detailed comparison has not been conducted elsewhere.[1] Yet this information is critical to assessing the differential macroeconomic implications of commodity price fluctuations in different regions.

Second, the chapter analyzes energy and metal demand, supply, and price shocks together. Doing so allows a cross-commodity comparison that previous studies have not offered. In particular, it illustrates how different market structures have different implications for the behavior and impact of individual commodity markets.

Third, the chapter is one of a few recent studies to identify econometrically the main drivers of swings in metal prices. It cross-checks the identified drivers against historical narratives.[2] The estimation uses a structural vector autoregression (SVAR) model with sign restrictions. This type of model has often been deployed to decompose oil price swings into those caused by demand, supply, and oil price shocks—using data for oil prices, oil production, economic activity, and, sometimes, inventories.[3] The estimates

---

[1] UNCTAD (2021) provides data on country dependence on commodity exports, but not for fiscal revenue or economic activity.

[2] A separate literature documents commodity price cycles, but not their drivers (for example, Baffes and Kabundi 2021).

[3] Beidas-Strom and Pescatori (2014), Kilian (2009), Kilian and Murphy (2014), and Kilian and Park (2009) decompose monthly oil price swings into demand, supply, and oil price shocks using data on oil prices, oil production, and economic activity (proxied by industrial production or an index largely based on it). Some of these studies also include inventories to identify a speculative demand shock (Beidas-Strom and Pescatori 2014; Kilian and Murphy 2014). Baffes et al. (2015) and Blanchard and Arezki (2014) decompose daily oil price swings into demand and supply shocks using data on stock market indexes (as proxies for economic activity), oil prices, and exchange rates.

typically find that oil prices are driven by demand shocks, stemming either from variations in the level of aggregate output or from short-run speculative activity. SVAR approaches have also been applied to up to a dozen nonenergy commodity prices in three previous studies (Jacks and Stuermer 2020; Stuermer 2017, 2018).[4] These studies, which cover the years 1870–2013, find that global aggregate demand shocks have been the main source of commodity price fluctuations. Although these studies examine a long time frame, they cover only the markets for copper, lead, tin, and zinc. This chapter adds aluminum and nickel to the list and explicitly compares results for metal prices with those for oil prices in a consistent framework.

Fourth, the chapter empirically estimates the response of output in metal exporters and importers to metal price shocks. It does so using the local projections technique, an alternative to the commonly employed SVAR approach for the macroeconomic analysis of oil price changes (Gervais 2019; Sheng, Gupta, and Ji 2020).

The chapter offers the following findings. First, although more than half of EMDEs rely heavily on their resource sectors for export earnings and fiscal revenues, and to generate economic activity, metal exporters are much less dependent on metal sectors than oil exporters are on oil sectors, for now.

Second, global production and consumption are considerably more geographically concentrated for metal than for oil. China, for example, is the single largest consumer and producer of all refined base metals. It accounts for roughly 50 percent of global consumption of metals, but it consumes just 15 percent of global crude oil output.

Third, except for aluminum and tin, demand and supply shocks contributed in almost equal measure to the variability of commodity prices. Demand collapses during global recessions were the main drivers of sharp declines in energy and metal prices. During the global recession of 2009, which was triggered by the global financial crisis, the faster drop in demand relative to production worsened price declines for oil and most metals. In contrast, during the global recession of 2020, which was triggered by the COVID-19 pandemic, initial disruptions in metal production due to the disease, and a limited production cut agreed by OPEC and its partners, temporarily offset some of the downward price pressures caused by the collapse in demand.

Fourth, oil and metal price shocks appear to have asymmetric impacts on output growth in energy and metal exporters. Whereas price increases have been associated with small, temporary accelerations in output growth, price declines have been associated with more pronounced or longer-lasting growth slowdowns. But these results mainly pertain to oil and copper, exporters of which are particularly commodity reliant. Output growth in oil and copper exporters declined significantly several years after oil or copper prices fell. In contrast, there is no evidence of statistically significant output gains (or losses) in

---

[4] Jacks and Stuermer (2020) identify shocks using both short-run and long-run zero restrictions. Stuermer (2017, 2018) identifies shocks using long-run zero restrictions.

aluminum exporters after aluminum price increases (or decreases). Among commodity importers, too, changes in metal or oil prices have had negligible effects on output.

The next section describes the reliance of EMDEs on commodities for export earnings, for fiscal revenues, and to generate economic activity. It identifies which countries are considered commodity exporters for the purposes of this chapter. The third section presents the SVAR analysis of the main drivers of metal prices. The fourth section offers estimates of a local projection model for the response of output growth in metal exporters and importers to metal price shocks. The final section concludes and discusses policy implications.

EMDEs' reliance on commodities

Classification of energy and metal exporters

Commodity exporters are defined as countries in which an individual commodity accounts for 5 percent or more of total goods exports (annex 4A). Metal exports include both industrial ores and refined metals—aluminum, copper, lead, nickel, tin, and zinc. Precious metals (gold and silver) are excluded because they are driven to an unusual extent by special factors in financial markets. Under this construct, 62 EMDEs (out of 153) meet the threshold at which oil accounts for at least 5 percent of goods exports, and 58 EMDEs meet the threshold at which industrial metals (of all types and including iron ore) account for at least 5 percent of goods exports.[5]

With regard to individual metals, there are 14 copper-exporting EMDEs, 10 aluminum exporters, 5 zinc exporters, 3 nickel exporters, and only 1 country classified as a lead exporter and another as a tin exporter (table 4A.1). With the exception of Tajikistan, none of these EMDEs exports more than one metal that exceeds the 5 percent threshold. In Tajikistan, aluminum, copper, lead, and zinc each account for 5 percent or more of total exports.

For four of the six metals, the world's largest exporter of a metal was not classified as a metal exporter, because the largest exporter is a relatively large, diversified economy, and the metal in question amounts to a small share of its total exports. For example, Indonesia accounted for one-third of global tin exports in 2019, but tin made up less than 1 percent of the country's total goods exports that year. Russia exported about one-quarter of the world's nickel in 2019 but that represented just over 1 percent of Russia's total exports. In other metals, the largest exporter is by no means the largest producer. For example, China produces half of the world's lead ore but uses almost all of it in domestic manufacturing. China accounted for only 0.4 percent of global lead ore exports in 2019. The leading exporters of lead ore were Australia and the Republic of Korea.

---

[5] Note that this methodology results in a somewhat larger number of exporters than the definition in World Bank (2022), which sets a threshold of 20 percent of total exports because it refers to broader commodity groups.

The data set used in this chapter includes annual data on consumption and production for 153 EMDEs during the period 1970 to 2020. The UN Comtrade Database and the Observatory of Economic Complexity are the sources for commodity import and export data. Prices for the six metals are drawn from the World Bank's Commodity Markets (Pink Sheet) database.

Commodity reliance of EMDE commodity exporters

As the transition away from fossil fuels progresses, metals are expected to play an increasingly important role in the global economy because they are essential in the production of renewable energy infrastructure and technology, such as solar panels and electric vehicles. This increase in demand for metals will be accompanied by sagging global demand for such fossil fuels as oil, natural gas, and coal. For EMDEs that rely heavily on fossil fuel-based energy commodities and on metals, the energy transition will have significant implications for long-run growth prospects—good for metal exporters and poor for exporters of fossil fuels.

For now, metal exporters tend to be less reliant on metals than oil exporters are on oil (figure 4.3). Metal exports account for 20 percent of total goods exports among metal-reliant exporters; for oil exporters, petroleum accounts for 32 percent of total exports on average. In the 10 most metal-reliant EMDEs, metal exports average 48 percent of their total goods exports. In comparison, oil averages 84 percent of exports for the 10 most oil-reliant EMDEs. Among metal producers, export dependency is particularly high for copper producers, with copper accounting for a median share of 22 percent of their goods exports. In the case of the most copper-reliant economy, Zambia, the metal represents 73 percent of exports. Aluminum is next in export dependency. It has a median share of 15 percent of exports, and in the most dependent economy, Guinea, it accounts for 48 percent of exports.

The contrast between oil and metal exporters is similar for fiscal revenue. Metal exporters are generally less dependent on resource revenues than are oil exporters. On average, resource revenues account for 28 percent of total fiscal revenue in oil-reliant exporters, compared to just over 10 percent in aluminum- and copper-reliant exporters, and less than 4 percent in zinc- and nickel-reliant exporters. Not enough data were available to assess lead and tin exporters. Guinea is the aluminum exporter that relied most on resource revenues, which account for 18 percent of the country's fiscal revenues. Mauritania, a copper exporter, is close, with 16 percent of its revenue stemming from resource sectors. For countries that export both oil and copper, dependence on resource revenues can be very high, reaching 80 percent of fiscal revenue for the Republic of Congo.

The resource sector is also less important to total economic activity for metal-reliant exporters than it is for oil-reliant exporters. Of the countries included in the sample, resource rents (that is, value added in the resource sector) account for 8 percent of gross domestic product (GDP), on average, in oil exporters. By contrast, they account, on average, for 4 percent of GDP in copper-reliant exporters, which are the most resource

FIGURE 4.3 Resource reliance of oil and base metal exporters

Half as many EMDEs rely on a single metal as on oil. Metal exporters depend less than oil exporters on a resource sector for exports, fiscal revenues, and output.

A. Number of base metal and oil exporters

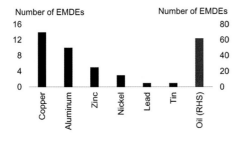

B. Share of oil or metal exports in total exports, oil and metal exporters

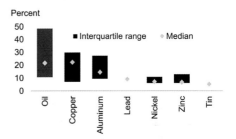

C. Share of resource revenues in total government revenues, oil and metal exporters

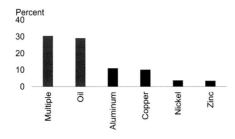

D. Share of commodity resource rents in output, oil and metal exporters

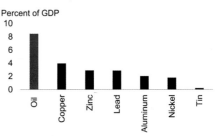

Sources: UN Comtrade; Commodity Markets (Pink Sheet) database; World Bank.

Note: An EMDE is defined as an exporter if exports of a given commodity are 5 percent or more of total exports in a single year between 2018 and 2019. EMDE = emerging market and developing economy; RHS = right-hand side.

B.-D. Charts show the median and interquartile range of the share of exports (B), share of fiscal revenues (C), and share of output (D) accounted for by resource sectors for EMDE exporters of that commodity. Oil includes 62 EMDEs, copper 14, aluminum 10, zinc 5, nickel 3, and lead and tin 1 each.

B. Because of small sample size, lead and tin do not have an interquartile range. Data are from 2019 or 2020, depending on data availability.

C. "Multiple" includes exporters that export both oil and copper. No data are available for lead. Data are from 2018 or 2019, depending on availability.

D. Chart shows natural resource rents from oil for oil exporters and minerals for base metal exporters, in percent of GDP. If a country is an exporter of more than one metal, it is included in each category. Data are from 2018.

reliant of the metal exporters. Once again, there is significant variation within groups. Among oil exporters, resource rents account for more than 40 percent of GDP in the Republic of Congo, Iraq, Kuwait, and Libya. Of the metal exporters, Guinea (an aluminum exporter) is again the most exposed; resource sector rents account for just over 10 percent of GDP in Guinea. Mongolia (a copper exporter) is close behind.

Concentrated location of metal ore reserves

Global ore reserves, ore production, and refined metals production are concentrated in a limited number of countries. For each of the six metals, the top four countries in terms of known reserves account for 50–75 percent of the world total (figure 4.4; U.S. Geological Survey 2022). Chile accounts for 23 percent of known copper reserves, while Australia and Peru have about 10 percent each (U.S. Geological Survey 2022). Guinea has 23 percent of the world's reserves of bauxite, the most common raw material for aluminum. With 22 percent of the total, Indonesia has the world's largest nickel ore reserves. Australia has the world's largest lead ore reserves (41 percent) and zinc ore deposits (27 percent). China has the world's largest tin ore reserves (22 percent).

The discussion thus far has referred to reserves that are economical to extract using current technologies. In general, as reserves that contain a higher concentration of a metal are depleted, production shifts to lower-grade, previously uneconomical reserves. For example, bauxite is the preferred source of alumina, the intermediate product from which aluminum is derived. However, there are vast, currently uneconomic sources of alumina in clay deposits. The U.S. Geological Survey (2021) estimates that the world has an essentially inexhaustible supply of resources of aluminum in materials other than bauxite. For metals more broadly, technological innovations that make it easier to access reserves have dampened price pressures over the past three centuries, despite rapid demand growth (Schwerhoff and Stuermer 2019).

Concentration of crude oil, metal ore, and refined production

Global metal ore production is considerably more concentrated than global crude oil production (figure 4.4).[6] Although it does not have the world's largest ore reserves, China is now the largest producer of lead, tin, and zinc ores, and the second-largest producer of bauxite (figure 4.5). China has only about 3 percent of the world's known reserves of bauxite/aluminum, copper, and nickel; 20 percent of known reserves of lead and zinc; and 22 percent of tin ore reserves. But it mines these ores at a much faster pace than other countries. As a result, it accounts for between 18 percent and 54 percent of global production of bauxite, lead, tin, and zinc ores.

Global refined metal production is also highly concentrated, much more so than global refined oil production. China is the world's largest producer of all refined metals, accounting for between 29 percent and 57 percent of global production, depending upon the metal. Aluminum refining is the most concentrated, with China accounting for 57 percent of global production, even though it has only 3 percent of bauxite reserves and 19 percent of bauxite production. Nickel refining is the least concentrated of metal production. Again, the biggest producer is China, which accounts for 29 percent of global output, followed by Indonesia, which accounts for 25 percent. Metal refining is far more concentrated than oil refining. The United States, as the largest global oil refiner, accounts for just 20 percent of the total.

---

[6] The United States, the world's largest producer of oil, accounts for 18 percent of global crude oil production. If OPEC were counted as a single producer, oil market concentration would increase significantly.

FIGURE 4.4 Geographic concentration of oil and base metal production and consumption

Global metal ore reserves are concentrated geographically and have changed little over the past two decades. In contrast, the concentration of metal production and consumption has risen sharply over the past two decades and is now higher than for crude oil production and consumption.

A. Concentration of metal ore reserves

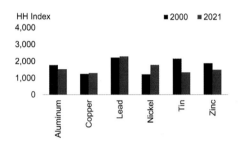

B. Concentration of metal ore and crude oil production

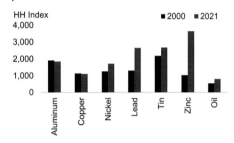

C. Concentration of refined metal and refined oil production

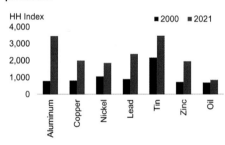

D. Concentration of refined metal and crude oil consumption

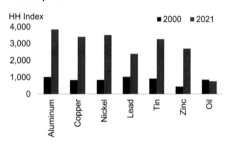

E. Share of top three countries in global ore and crude oil reserves and production

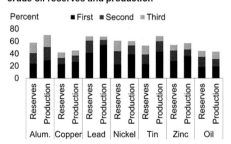

F. Share of top three countries in refined metal and refined oil production and consumption

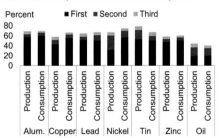

Sources: BP Statistical Review of World Energy 2021; U.S. Geological Survey; World Bank; World Bureau of Metal Statistics.
A.-D. Charts show Herfindahl–Hirschman Index (HH), a measure of market concentration. It is calculated by squaring the market share of each country and then summing the resulting numbers. The HH Index can range in value between zero and 10,000, where a value close to zero would indicate many countries with equal shares, and a value of 10,000 would indicate that a single country accounted for all of global production or consumption. Data are for 2021 for metals and 2020 for oil.

FIGURE 4.5 China's role in oil and base metal markets

After two decades of rapid growth, China is now the single largest consumer and producer of all base metals. Its share of global production and consumption of oil is much lower.

A. China's share of global metal ore and crude oil production and reserves

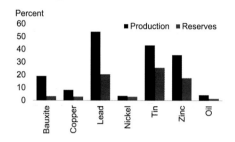

B. China's share of global metal and oil production and consumption

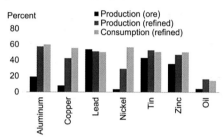

Sources: BP Statistical Review of World Energy; U.S. Geological Survey; World Bank; World Bureau of Metal Statistics.
Note: Data as of 2021 for metals and 2020 for oil.
B. For oil, production (ore) refers to crude oil production; production (refined) refers to refined oil production.

Moreover, with rapid growth in China, the concentration of global production of all refined metals, and some metal ores, has risen sharply over the past two decades. Since 2000, China's share of global production of bauxite and lead has tripled and has nearly doubled for copper and zinc. China's share of global production of refined nickel has risen sixfold, its share of refined copper and aluminum production has risen fivefold, its share of refined lead production has risen threefold, and its share of zinc production has doubled. By 2020, China was the largest producer of all refined metals.

Concentration of global metal consumption

Global consumption of refined metals has also been transformed over the past two decades because of growth in China. In 2000, the United States was the single largest consumer of most metals, accounting for between 15 percent and 25 percent of the world total, depending on the metal. The only exception was zinc, of which China was already the largest consumer. However, China's commodity consumption has risen dramatically since then, and the country is now by far the single largest consumer of all refined metals. At this point, for all the six metals considered here, China accounts for more than half of global refined metal consumption. In contrast, the United States is the largest consumer of oil, but accounts for only 20 percent of global consumption and 12 percent of imports.

For lead and to a lesser extent tin and zinc, China's demand can largely be met by domestic production. For copper and nickel, China relies heavily on imports, accounting for about one-third of global copper imports and one-fifth of nickel imports. China's consumption of aluminum far exceeds what it can produce from its bauxite reserves. As a result, China relies heavily on imported raw materials to produce aluminum, and accounts for about 70 percent of global bauxite imports.

Sources of metal price fluctuations

Global oil and metal markets have frequently been buffeted by demand and supply shocks over the past three decades. This section decomposes the variability of oil and metal prices into contributions from demand and supply shocks. It examines how the impact of these shocks on industrial commodity prices differs with the global market structure. For example, compared to supply shocks for other metals and oil, supply shocks have played a smaller role in the price variability of aluminum, which has by far the most concentrated global production structure.

Methodology and data

For oil and each of the six metals—aluminum, copper, lead, nickel, tin, and zinc—this analysis uses an SVAR, similar to Kilian and Murphy (2014), to model global prices (annex 4B).[7] The SVAR includes three variables: global metal or oil production, real global metal or oil prices, and real global industrial production. All variables are expressed in month-on-month logarithmic changes.

Two shocks—demand and supply—are examined for their impact on each of the three variables. Sign restrictions on the contemporaneous impact of each shock on the three variables help identify the type of shock. Depending on the direction in which each of the three variables moves, a shock is classified as either a demand or supply shock. A *positive demand shock* is defined as a shock that raises global industrial production and at the same time increases both commodity prices and commodity production. A *positive metals supply shock* is defined as a shock that lowers metal prices while raising metal output and global industrial production.

The data set uses monthly data from February 1996 to December 2021. Global industrial production is the production-weighted average of industrial output in 31 advanced economies and 47 EMDEs. Global oil production data come from the International Energy Agency. Real prices for the six metals are derived by deflating their U.S.-dollar prices, as reported by the World Bank's Commodity Markets (Pink Sheet) database, by the U.S. Consumer Price Index.

Demand and supply shocks

The model identifies a series of demand and supply shocks to prices of the six metals and oil from 1996 onward (figure 4.6). These shocks exhibit some clear patterns.

For oil and the six metals, demand shocks were highly synchronized with one other. Large negative demand shocks were associated with global recessions (in 2009 and 2020) and global slowdowns (in 1998, 2001, and 2012). Large positive global demand shocks

---

[7] Similar models have been used by Jacks and Stuermer (2021), Peersman (2005), and Peersman and Straub (2006).

FIGURE 4.6 Shocks to oil and base metal price growth

Demand shocks to oil and base metal price growth are highly synchronized with each other and the global business cycle, such that the price shocks across commodities fall within a narrow band. Metal supply shocks deviate from oil supply shocks and are more dispersed across individual base metals; the wider band suggests that supply shocks are more idiosyncratic.

A. Demand shocks to base metal price growth

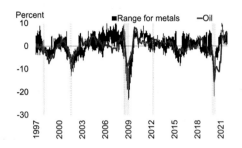

B. Supply shocks to base metal prices

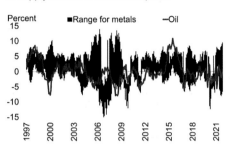

Sources: World Bank Commodity Markets (Pink Sheet) database; World Bank.
Note: Blue areas show the range of demand and supply shocks to year-on-year price growth for six base metals (aluminum, copper, lead, nickel, tin, and zinc). Gray areas indicate global recessions (2009, 2020) and global slowdowns (1998, 2001, 2012), as defined by Kose, Sugawara, and Terrones (2020).

often occurred during the final stage of an expansion—the year before the global economy began to slide into a recession or slowdown.

In contrast to the highly synchronized demand shocks for all six metals and oil, supply shocks varied widely across oil and the different metals, reflecting specific events that had differing effects on individual commodities. For example, nickel supply surged with the opening up of the Russian economy in the 1990s. In recent years there were several episodes of negative supply shocks, relating to extreme weather, government policy, and industrial disputes. These events included the flooding of copper mines in Peru, Indonesia, Mexico, and Mongolia in 2015; and export bans for nickel ore in Indonesia in 2014 and 2019 (U.S. Geological Survey 2014, 2019). In 2020, COVID-19 outbreaks caused supply shocks that helped offset some of the demand collapse, with mine closures and production disruptions in such countries as Bolivia (lead, tin, zinc), Brazil (tin), Indonesia (tin), Kazakhstan (lead), Mexico (lead, zinc), Myanmar (tin), and Peru (copper, lead, tin, zinc). The decision of OPEC and its partners in April 2020 to cut its production quotas also supported oil prices somewhat amid a steep collapse in demand.

Response of oil and metal prices to shocks

The estimated impulse response functions of oil and metal prices to these shocks suggest the following patterns. First, for almost all metals, demand shocks had stronger effects than did similarly sized supply shocks and dissipated sooner. In the oil market, demand and supply shocks had somewhat more symmetric effects on prices but, again, the effects of demand shocks dissipated sooner than those of supply shocks. Second, the effects of demand shocks were broadly comparable for nickel prices and oil prices but were smaller for other metal prices; the effects of supply shocks on all metal prices were smaller than those on oil prices.

A demand shock that increased global economic growth by 1 percentage point raised global oil prices by 11 percentage points and global metal prices by between 4 and 10 percentage points, cumulatively, within about half a year (figure 4.7). The impact was particularly strong on nickel prices, possibly reflecting rapidly growing Chinese demand for stainless steel, an alloy that requires nickel. Conversely, aluminum prices responded the least—with a peak impact about half that of nickel prices—possibly reflecting the relatively limited demand for aluminum in China's rapidly expanding infrastructure investment. The impact peaked about six months after the initial shock for all the metal prices except tin, whose price peaked about a year later. Although larger in magnitude, the price impact for oil shocks peaked earlier (four months after the shock) and receded faster than did similarly sized metal price shocks.

A supply shock that reduced growth in global oil or metals production by 1 percentage point resulted in a 10-percentage-point increase in oil prices and an increase of between 1 and 3 percentage points for metals within six months (figure 4.8). For aluminum and copper prices, responses to supply shocks peaked somewhat earlier than the responses to demand shocks, whereas the reverse was true for lead, nickel, and zinc. Copper prices seemed to be the most responsive to changes in supply conditions. Aluminum prices were the least responsive. The sluggishness of aluminum prices may reflect Chinese policy interventions to smooth prices. China is the predominant actor in all aspects of global aluminum markets, far more important than in other global metal markets. Supply shocks have a smaller impact on global metal prices than they do on global oil prices. One explanation is that metals have no equivalent body to OPEC and its partners whose policy decisions have at times been associated with considerable shifts in production and prices.

Contributions of global shocks to global commodity price variation

Demand and supply shocks make important contributions to the variability of global commodity prices. For oil, copper, nickel, and zinc, demand and supply shocks each account for about half of the price variability, whereas, for aluminum and tin, demand shocks are a larger source of price variation (figure 4.9).[8] Specifically, demand shocks account for 50 percent of the forecast error variance of oil price growth and from 46 percent (nickel, zinc) to 71 percent (aluminum) for metal price growth.[9] The exceptionally small contribution of supply shocks to aluminum price variation may reflect widespread government policies aimed at steering domestic aluminum industries.

---

[8] The predominant role of demand shocks in the variability of commodity prices is in line with Boer, Pescatori, and Stuermer (2021); Jacks and Stuermer (2020); and Kilian and Murphy (2014).

[9] These numbers refer to the variance decompositions for one-year-ahead forecast errors of oil or base metal price growth.

FIGURE 4.7 Impact of demand shocks on oil and base metal prices

Demand shocks lift nickel and, with a delay, tin prices about as much as oil prices, but other metal prices by less.

A. Impact of demand increase on oil price growth

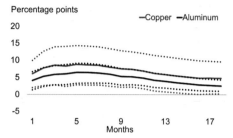

B. Impact of demand increase on aluminum and copper price growth

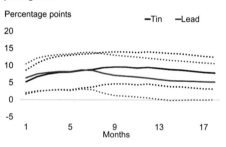

C. Impact of demand increase on nickel and zinc price growth

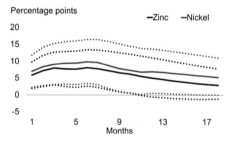

D. Impact of demand increase on tin and lead price growth

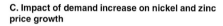

Sources: World Bank Commodity Markets (Pink Sheet) database; World Bank.
Note: Figures show impulse response of log price of six base metals and oil to a positive demand shock equivalent to a 1-percentage-point increase in global industrial production growth, based on a structural vector autoregression model in which sign restrictions identify shocks. A demand shock raises global industrial production, global metal or oil production, and global metal or oil prices. Solid lines indicate median impulse responses; dashed lines indicate 16th to 84th credible intervals.

These include policies aimed at influencing production and investment decisions, notably through government management of input prices and the flow of credit to aluminum producers (OECD 2019). Such policies may act to smooth price fluctuations that would otherwise result from production disruptions.

Global recessions, especially the one in 2020 related to the COVID-19 pandemic, were associated with severe demand weakness, and price collapses for oil and all six metals (figure 4.10). Production cuts, as reflected in negative supply shocks, at most somewhat dampened these steep price declines. However, prices typically rebounded swiftly. In 2009, for example, coordinated G20 policy stimulus, which included large-scale infrastructure investment in China, helped spur a quick recovery in global activity and commodity prices. Similarly, the robust rebound in global economic activity after the pandemic-induced recession of 2020 also supported a bounce back in industrial commodity prices. The more moderate global growth slowdowns (of 1998, 2001, and

FIGURE 4.8 Impact of supply shocks on oil and base metal price growth

Supply shocks have lasting impacts on growth of oil prices and most metal prices, except for aluminum. For all metals, the short-run impact of supply shocks is smaller than that of demand shocks and considerably less than for oil prices. For oil prices, the effects of supply and demand shocks are more symmetric.

A. Impact of a supply decline on oil price growth

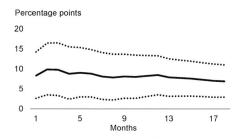

B. Impact of a supply decline on aluminum and copper price growth

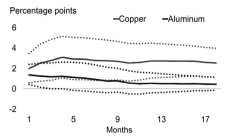

C. Impact of a supply decline on nickel and zinc price growth

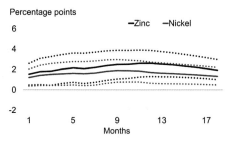

D. Impact of a supply decline on tin and lead price growth

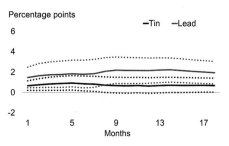

Sources: World Bank Commodity Markets (Pink Sheet) database; World Bank.
Note: Figures show impulse response of log price of six base metals and oil to a positive supply shock equivalent to a 1 percent decline in the respective metal's production growth, based on a structural vector autoregression model in which sign restrictions identify shocks. A supply shock is defined to reduce global industrial production and global metal or oil production but raise global metal or oil prices. Solid lines indicate median impulse responses; dashed lines indicate 16th to 84th credible intervals.

2012) depressed metal prices to a lesser extent, as would be expected from smaller demand shocks. Price increases after a slowdown also tended to be more gradual than after a recession; prices did not fully recover for at least a year.

Robustness

Similar SVAR exercises, using alternative proxies of global economic activity, indicate that the estimates of the model are qualitatively robust to the choice of proxy for global economic activity (annex 4C). These alternatives involved a commodity-specific demand-weighted average of industrial production in the world's 30 largest economies, J.P. Morgan's Global Manufacturing and Composite Purchasing Manager Indexes, and the Global Economic Conditions indicator of Baumeister, Korobilis, and Lee (2020).

FIGURE 4.9 Contribution of shocks to commodity price variability and oil price growth

Oil and base metal price variability was predominantly driven by global demand shocks. These shocks were especially pronounced during global recessions, when demand collapsed. The subsequent unwinding of these demand collapses supported price recoveries.

A. Forecast error variance decomposition of metal and oil price growth

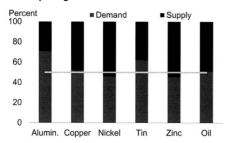

B. Contributions to oil price growth during global recessions and slowdowns

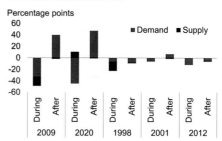

Sources: World Bank Commodity Markets (Pink Sheet) database; World Bank.
A. Variance decomposition of 12-month-ahead forecasts of month-on-month price growth of six base metals and oil based on a structural vector autoregression model of commodity prices, industrial production, commodity production, and commodity inventories. Shocks are identified using sign restrictions as described in annex 4B. Orange line indicates 50 percent.
B. Cumulative historical decomposition of oil price growth into demand and supply shocks between the last month before global recessions (2009, 2020) or global slowdowns (1998, 2001, 2012) and the last month of global recessions or slowdowns ("During") as well as between the last month of the global recession or slowdowns and 12 months later ("After"). Global recessions and slowdowns are defined as in Kose, Sugawara, and Terrones (2020).

Macroeconomic impact of metal price shocks

Commodity price fluctuations have been both symptom and cause of global and national swings in the business cycle. Metal prices, especially of copper, have often been considered barometers and leading indicators of global economic activity (Bernanke 2016; Hamilton 2015). For some commodities, such as crude oil, sharp price movements can cause business cycle fluctuations both globally and at the country level, although the effects have generally been short-lived (Baumeister, Peersman, and Van Robays 2010; Kilian 2009). Other commodities, such as tin, may not cause global business cycle fluctuations but are critical inputs for some sectors—such as the electronics industry—and are important for the small number of countries, such as Rwanda, that produce or export them. This section estimates the impact of commodity price shocks on output growth and identifies asymmetries that are consistent with adverse aggregate growth effects of all types of price shocks.

Methodology and data

To assess the impact of oil or metal price shocks on EMDEs, a local projection model is estimated (annex 4D).[10] The model examines the impact of oil or metal price changes on

---

[10] Other metals are not included in the analysis because of the small number of exporters even at lower thresholds (four for zinc, three for nickel, and one each for lead and tin).

FIGURE 4.10 Contribution of shocks to base metal price growth

Demand shocks were especially pronounced during global recessions, when demand collapsed. The subsequent unwinding of these demand collapses supported price recoveries.

A. Contributions to copper price growth during global recessions and slowdowns

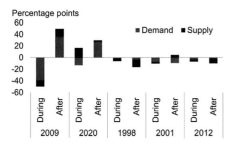

B. Contributions to aluminum price growth during global recessions and slowdowns

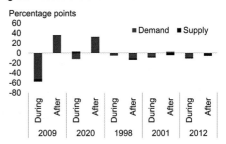

C. Contributions to nickel price growth during global recessions and slowdowns

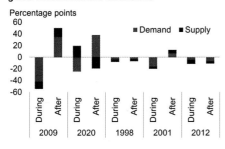

D. Contributions to zinc price growth during global recessions and slowdowns

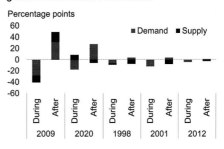

E. Contributions to tin price growth during global recessions and slowdowns

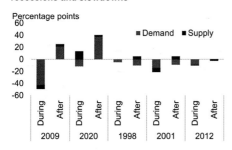

F. Contributions to lead price growth during global recessions and slowdowns

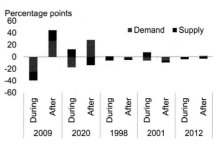

Sources: World Bank Commodity Markets (Pink Sheet) database; World Bank..
Note: "During" refers to the cumulative historical decomposition of base metal price growth into demand and supply shocks between the last month before global recessions (2009, 2020) or global slowdowns (1998, 2001, 2012) and the last month of global recessions or slowdowns. "After" encompasses the last month of a global recession or slowdown and 12 months later. Global recessions and slowdowns are defined as in Kose, Sugawara, and Terrones (2020).

real output over the period 1970–2019 under two different specifications. The first version of the model assumes that the impact is symmetric for price increases and decreases. The second version allows price increases and decreases to have asymmetric impacts. For metals, the estimates provide measures of the impact of shocks to an aggregate index of metal prices on both metal exporters and importers, as well as measures of the impact of shocks to aluminum and copper prices individually. The data sources are described in annex 4D.

Features of large metal price jumps and collapses

The largest jumps and collapses of oil and metal prices—those that exceed 20 percent over a six-month period—were clustered around major economic events. These events include four global recessions (1974–75, 1981–82, 1990–91, and 2008–09) and three global slowdowns (1998, 2001, and 2012) since 1970 (Kose, Sugawara, and Terrones 2020). In general, such large oil and metal price increases occurred in the years just before global recessions and slowdowns (such as 1973, 1980, 2006, and 2018) or in the years when global recoveries were getting under way (such as in 1983, 1999, and 2009). In contrast, large price collapses tended to occur in the midst of global recessions and slowdowns (such as in 1974, 1991, and 2008). For oil, large collapses also occurred after OPEC changed its strategy from targeting a price to targeting market share, such as in 1985 and 2014 (Baffes et al. 2015; Kabundi and Ohnsorge 2020). The clustering of large swings in oil and metal prices around global recessions is consistent with earlier findings about the considerable role of aggregate demand in driving prices.

In general, metal price jumps and collapses were more frequent, but of smaller magnitude, than oil price shocks (figure 4.11). This difference may have contributed to the more muted impact of metal price shocks on metal exporters than the larger effect of oil price shocks on EMDEs that rely heavily on oil exports.

Impact of oil or metal price shocks

For EMDE energy exporters, assuming symmetric impacts, a 10-percentage-point increase in the growth of oil prices was associated with a statistically significant 0.2-percentage-point increase in output growth over the subsequent two years (figure 4.12).[11] The estimated adverse effects from higher oil prices on economic activity in EMDE energy importers were small and built up so gradually that they became statistically significant only after three to four years, perhaps because policy room to buffer higher oil import prices gradually eroded.

For EMDE metal exporters, a 10-percentage-point increase in the growth in metal prices was followed by a gradual rise in output, by a statistically significant 0.1 percentage

---

[11] These results are consistent with the literature on energy-exporting EMDEs (Abeysinghe 2001; Caldara, Cavallo, and Iacoviello 2019; Lippi and Nobili 2012; Mohaddes and Raissi 2017, 2019) or energy-exporting advanced economies (Peersman and Van Robays 2012).

FIGURE 4.11 Oil and metal price shocks

Large oil and metal price jumps often occurred in the years before global recessions and slowdowns, and in the years following them when global recoveries were under way. Metal price shocks were typically more frequent, but smaller, than oil price shocks.

A. Oil price jumps

B. Oil price collapses

C. Metal price jumps

D. Metal price collapses

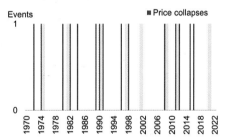

E. Number of metal and oil price shocks

F. Magnitude of metal and oil price shocks

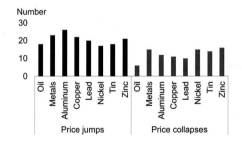

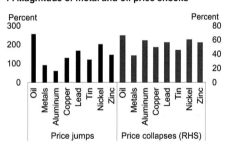

Sources: World Bank Commodity Markets (Pink Sheet) database; World Bank.

Note. A price jump is an increase of one standard deviation over a six-month period; a price collapse is a decline of one standard deviation over a six-month period. Shaded areas indicate period of global recessions (1975, 1982, 1991, 2009, 2020) or slowdowns (1998, 2001, 2012).

F. The bars represent the absolute average trough-to-peak or peak-to-trough price change for price jumps and collapses. Price collapses are shown as absolute averages, so 50 percent indicates a 50 percent fall in prices. RHS = right-hand side.

FIGURE 4.12 Impact of oil price shocks on EMDE output growth

In energy-exporting EMDEs, oil price increases generated short-lived output gains, but oil price declines generated much larger and more lasting output losses. In energy-importing EMDEs, oil price increases were associated with small output losses and oil price declines were associated with statistically insignificant output gains.

A. EMDE energy exporters: Symmetric impact of 10-percentage-point change in oil price growth

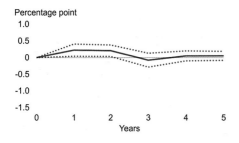

B. EMDE energy importers: Symmetric impact of 10-percentage-point change in oil price growth

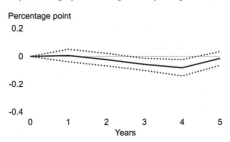

C. EMDE energy exporters: Asymmetric impact of 10-percentage-point higher oil price growth

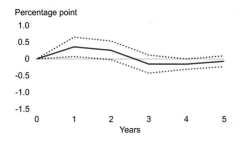

D. EMDE energy exporters: Asymmetric impact of 10-percentage-point lower oil price growth

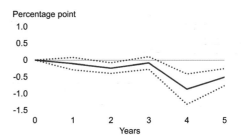

E. EMDE energy importers: Asymmetric impact of 10-percentage-point higher oil price growth

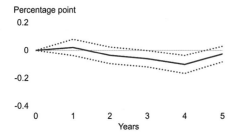

F. EMDE energy importers: Asymmetric impact of 10-percentage-point lower oil price growth

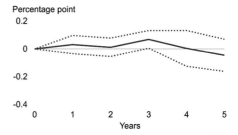

Sources: World Bank.
Note: Cumulative impulse responses of output growth for 153 EMDEs, of which 34 are energy exporters, from a local projection estimation. Dependent variable is output growth after 10-percentage-point change in oil price growth. Solid lines are coefficient estimates and dotted lines are 95 percent confidence bands based on heteroscedasticity consistent standard errors and Driscoll-Kraay standard errors. Panels A and B are estimated assuming symmetric effects of metal price changes; panels C, D, E, and F are estimated accounting for asymmetric effects of price increases and price declines. EMDE = emerging market and developing economy.

point, after two years. But the effect declined gradually, fading to insignificance after three years (figure 4.13). For EMDE metal importers, a price increase had no statistically significant effect, reflecting the small amount of metal they import. On average, metals account for only 5 percent of their total imports.[12] Even for China, the largest consumer of all the six metals in the sample, these metals account for only 4 percent of China's imports. By contrast, oil accounts for about 14 percent of China's imports.

Asymmetric impacts of oil or metal price shocks

The aggregate results mask the asymmetric impacts of oil or metal price increases and declines. For both oil and metal exporters, output gains from price increases were short-lived, whereas output losses after price declines were longer-lasting and larger (although, for energy exporters, these losses were delayed by several years). The impact of a metal price shock remained smaller than that of an oil price shock.

Specifically, a 10-percentage-point increase in the growth of oil prices raised output growth in energy exporters by about 0.3–0.4 percentage point for two years, whereas a similarly sized decline in oil price growth was associated with a statistically insignificant slowdown in output growth for several years. But, four years after the price decline, the slowdown in output growth steepened to 0.9 percentage point and remained statistically significant thereafter.[13] This pronounced and lasting effect of oil price declines in energy-exporting EMDEs is consistent with the damage to potential output growth caused by persistent declines in investment occasioned by the price decline (Aguiar and Gopinath 2007). Meanwhile, energy importers suffered small but delayed output losses several years after an oil price increase but did not benefit from statistically significant output gains after oil price declines.

Similarly, although a 10-percentage-point increase in growth in metal prices was followed by an increase in economic activity in metal exporters, the effects were small and short-lived (an increase in output growth of less than 0.1 percentage point after a couple of years). Price declines had much bigger effects—eight times greater than those from price increases, reaching 0.4 percentage point in the first year and lasting twice as long. In contrast, among metal importers, neither increases nor declines in metal prices were associated with any statistically significant output responses.

This asymmetry for energy and metal exporters may reflect the procyclicality of fiscal policy in EMDEs (Alesina, Campante, and Tabellini 2008; Frankel 2010). Increased fiscal spending during resource booms adds fuel to a domestic economic expansion and

---

[12] These results are consistent with Di Pace, Juvenal, and Petrella (2021) who find evidence of a positive and statistically significant effect of export price shocks on output growth in EMDEs but a smaller impact of import price shocks.

[13] These results are also consistent with Di Pace, Juvenal, and Petrella (2021) who find that positive export price shocks raise domestic output growth in EMDEs, particularly in oil-exporting EMDEs. Mohaddes and Raissi (2017, 2019) also find similar lasting output losses in the Gulf Cooperation Council countries of just over 2 percent from an oil supply shock, equivalent to a 10-12 percent drop in price.

FIGURE 4.13 Impact of metal price shocks on EMDE output growth

Metal price shocks do not have a significant impact on metal-importing EMDEs and have an asymmetric impact on metal-dependent EMDEs. Price increases are associated with higher output in EMDE metal exporters, but the response is modest and short-lived. Output declines after price declines are stronger and last longer.

A. EMDE metal exporters: Symmetric impact of 10-percentage-point change in metal price growth

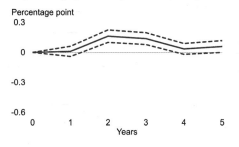

B. EMDE metal importers: Symmetric impact of 10-percentage-point change in metal price growth

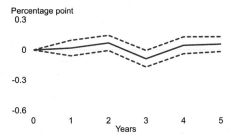

C. EMDE metal exporters: Asymmetric impact of 10-percentage-point higher metal price growth

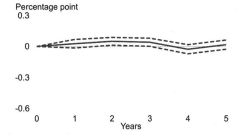

D. EMDE metal exporters: Asymmetric impact of 10-percentage-point lower metal price growth

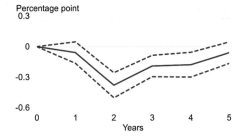

E. EMDE metal importers: Asymmetric impact of 10-percentage-point higher metal price growth

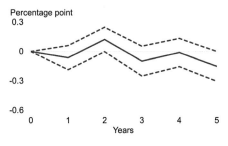

F. EMDE metal importers: Asymmetric impact of 10-percentage-point lower metal price growth

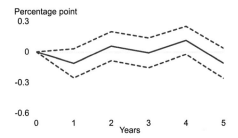

Source: World Bank.
Note: Cumulative impulse responses of output growth in 153 EMDEs, of which 31 are metal exporters, from a local projections model Dependent variable is output growth after 10-percentage-point changes in metal price growth. Solid lines are coefficient estimates, and dotted lines are 95 percent confidence bands. Panels A and B are estimated assuming symmetric effects of metals price changes; panels C, D, E, and F are estimated accounting for asymmetric effects of price increases and price declines. EMDE = emerging market and developing economy.

can go toward less productive purposes, whereas fiscal consolidation during price collapses exacerbates the depth of a recession (Frankel 2011; Medas and Zakharova 2009). Such procyclicality can have lasting negative effects on growth, because public investment, such as infrastructure spending, is typically the first element of public spending to be cut (Richaud et al. 2019). For example, after the 2014–16 commodity price collapses, the sharp decline in fiscal revenues forced abrupt cuts in government spending that exacerbated the economic slowdowns (Stocker et al. 2018).[14]

Impact of copper price shocks

Copper is often regarded as the bellwether metal for the world economy, and copper exporters tend to be considerably more resource-reliant than exporters of other metals. The results from the model for shocks to the price of copper are therefore of special interest.

The effects of copper price shocks are similar to those for the broad group of industrial metals. Copper exporters benefit from short-lived output gains after copper price increases but encounter longer-lasting and larger output losses after price declines (figure 4.14). The effects of copper price declines are somewhat larger than those of general metal price shocks. Among copper importers, neither price declines nor price increases were associated with any statistically significant output gains or losses, as was also the case for metal importers more generally.

Contrast with aluminum price shocks

In contrast to copper, the results suggest that aluminum price shocks are not followed by statistically significant output changes in EMDEs that export or import aluminum.[15] These differences may arise because aluminum exporters rely less on aluminum exports than copper exporters do on copper exports. For the average aluminum exporter in the sample, aluminum accounted for 15 percent of exports, almost one-third less than the 22 percent export share of copper for the average copper exporter. In eight of the copper exporters, copper accounted for 20 percent or more of exports, compared to just three of the aluminum exporters.

Conclusion and policy implications

Many EMDEs rely on energy commodities or metals for a significant share of export earnings and fiscal revenue. This chapter examines the extent to which this reliance makes their macroeconomic stability vulnerable to changes in oil or metal prices on world markets.

---

[14] The asymmetric results are unlikely to simply reflect the nature of commodity price cycles. On average, commodity price increases have tended to be considerably larger and faster, although not much longer, than commodity price decreases (chapter 3).

[15] Because all results are statistically insignificant, they are not separately shown but are available upon request.

FIGURE 4.14 Impact of copper price shocks on EMDE output growth

Copper price shocks have an asymmetric impact on copper-dependent EMDEs. Copper price increases are followed by shorter-lived and more modest output expansions than the output contractions after copper price declines.

A. EMDE copper exporters: Symmetric impact of a 10-percentage-point change in copper price growth

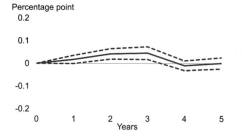

B. EMDE copper importers: Symmetric impact of a 10-percentage-point change in copper price growth

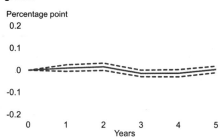

C. EMDE copper exporters: Asymmetric impact of a 10-percentage-point increase in copper price growth

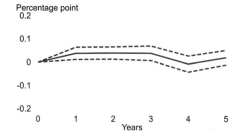

D. EMDE copper exporters: Asymmetric impact of a 10-percentage-point decrease in copper price growth

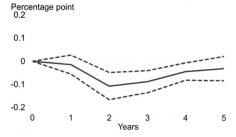

E. EMDE copper importers: Asymmetric impact of a 10-percentage-point increase in copper price growth

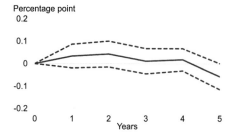

F. EMDE copper importers: Asymmetric impact of a 10-percentage-point decrease in copper price growth

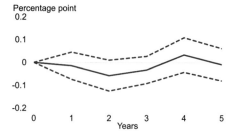

Source: World Bank.

Note: Cumulative impulse responses of output growth in 153 EMDEs, of which 14 are copper exporters, from a local projections model. Dependent variable is output growth after 10-percentage-point changes in copper price growth. Solid lines are coefficient estimates, and dotted lines are 95 percent confidence bands. Panels A and B are estimated assuming symmetric effects of metals price changes; panels C, D, E, and F are estimated accounting for asymmetric effects of price increases and price declines. EMDE = emerging market and developing economy.

It presents econometric analyses showing that global demand and supply shocks have typically contributed about equally to oil and metal price swings. An exception was the price of aluminum. With the most concentrated global market among these commodities and with China having the largest role in both production and consumption, supply shocks were only a minor source of aluminum price volatility. That oil and metal price swings are themselves heavily driven by global demand shocks suggests that, at least in part, oil and metal prices serve as a conduit and amplifier of global business cycles on commodity-exporting EMDEs.

The impact of commodity price volatility has not been symmetric. Increases in oil or metal prices have been associated with short-lived output gains in energy or metal exporters. But declines in oil or metal prices have been associated with longer-lasting and larger (although sometimes delayed) output losses in energy or metal exporters. These effects have been particularly pronounced for copper exporters, which are among the least diversified of EMDE commodity exporters.

For policy makers in metal exporters, these results indicate a need for countercyclical policies to better shield an economy from global commodity price volatility (see also the overview to this volume). The temporary nature of commodity price booms calls for a framework that avoids increasing spending in good times and slashing it when conditions deteriorate. Such a framework would ensure that surplus revenue is saved so that resources are available to support activity when prices collapse. Stronger fiscal frameworks, including fiscal rules, and structural budget rules can help resist pressures to spend revenue windfalls, or reduce nonresource taxes. An independent process for setting the guidelines for such rules—such as determining when to have surpluses and when to run deficits—is critical to successful stabilization policies (Frankel 2011). Sovereign wealth funds can be useful mechanisms to save windfall revenues during price upswings and provide a cushion of assets that can be drawn down during price slumps. Reforms to monetary policy, with flexible exchange rates anchored by credible medium- and long-run inflation targets, could help foster resilience to commodity price fluctuations and ensure smoother adjustment of real exchange rates (Frankel 2018; Torvik 2018). Improved access to international assistance would help provide timely short-term relief to low-income countries suffering from global commodity price declines.

The empirical exercises conducted in this chapter suggest that greater economic diversification could blunt some of the impact of commodity price shocks. Policies to promote raising standards of living in EMDEs—such as investment in human capital, improving institutions, modernizing infrastructure, and promoting higher-value-added activities in resource sectors—would promote diversification of economic activities, even if export diversification per se is unrealistic (World Bank 2015, 2022).

The findings in this chapter point to several avenues for future research. First, the results suggest the presence of important asymmetries in macroeconomic outcomes that depend on the nature of the commodity price shock. Future research could examine other asymmetries, such as what drives price shocks. Second, the analysis used the largest cross-country data set available to derive broadly applicable results, which restricted the analysis to annual data. Future research could examine more granular patterns in responses of macroeconomic outcomes using quarterly data.

ANNEX 4A Stylized facts: Data

The data set includes annual data for 153 EMDEs for 1970–2019. UN Comtrade and the Observatory of Economic Complexity were used as the sources of commodity import and export data. Annual data on real GDP and world per capita GDP are available from the World Bank's World Development Indicators database. Metal prices data are taken from the World Bank's Pink Sheet database. Nominal price indexes are calculated by taking a weighted average of aluminum, copper, lead, nickel, tin, and zinc prices (from the Pink Sheet), and weighting them using EMDE export shares. The real price is obtained by deflating the nominal metal price (in U.S. dollars) with the U.S. Consumer Price Index (CPI). The real metal price was converted into annual growth rates. The control variables are composed of global demand and domestic inflation computed as the annual growth rate of the CPI for each country. Data on the CPI are taken from the International Monetary Fund's World Economic Outlook database.

For the purposes of the stylized facts section, an EMDE is classified as a commodity exporter if its exports of a given commodity represent 5 percent or more of total goods exports. Note that this classification results in a larger number of exporters than would be obtained using the definition in World Bank (2020b), which sets a threshold of 20 percent of total exports because it refers to broader commodity groups. In identifying metal exporters, all exports of industrial metal ores and refined metal exports were included. Exports of precious metals such as gold and silver were not included. This identification provides a total of 58 exporters of industrial metals of all types (including iron ore)—of which 14 are copper exporters and 10 aluminum exporters (table 4A.1).

Similarly, an EMDE is classified as a metal importer if its imports of a metal account for 0.1 percent or more of total imports. This definition resulted in 50 metal importers—including 31 copper and 38 aluminum importers. The average concentration of metal imports as a share of total imports is much smaller than that of exporters.

TABLE 4A.1 Commodity exporters

Oil		Copper	Aluminum	Zinc	Nickel	Lead	Tin
Albania	Libya	Armenia	Bahrain	Bolivia	Madagascar	Tajikistan	Rwanda
Algeria	Malaysia	Bulgaria	Bosnia and Herzegovina	Burkina Faso	Papua New Guinea		
Angola	Maldives	Chile	Guinea	Namibia	Zimbabwe		
Antigua and Barbuda	Mexico	Congo, Rep.	Guyana	Peru			
Azerbaijan	Mongolia	Congo, Dem. Rep.	Jamaica	Tajikistan			
Bahamas	Niger	Kazakhstan	Montenegro				
Bahrain	Nigeria	Lao PDR	Mozambique				
Barbados	Oman	Mauritania	Sierra Leone				
Belarus	Panama	Mongolia	Solomon Islands				
Brazil	Papua New Guinea	Namibia	Tajikistan				
Brunei Darussalam	Peru	Papua New Guinea					
Bulgaria	Qatar	Peru					
Cameroon	Russian Federation	Tajikistan					
Chad	Rwanda	Zambia					
Colombia	Samoa						
Congo, Rep.	São Tomé and Príncipe						
Côte d'Ivoire	Saudi Arabia						
Croatia	Senegal						
Djibouti	Seychelles						
Ecuador	South Sudan						
Egypt, Arab Rep.	St. Lucia						
Equatorial Guinea	Sudan						
Fiji	Syrian Arab Republic						
Gabon	Timor-Leste						
Ghana	Togo						
India	Trinidad and Tobago						
Iraq	Tunisia						
Jamaica	Turkmenistan						
Kazakhstan	United Arab Emirates						
Kuwait	Venezuela, RB						
Liberia	Yemen, Rep.						

Source: World Bank.

ANNEX 4B SVAR: Methodology and data

Econometric model

The SVAR model of the global oil or metal market is written as

$$B_0 Y_t = \sum_{i=1}^{12} B_i Y_{t-i} + \varepsilon_t \tag{4B.1}$$

where Y_t is the vector of endogenous variables, ε_t represents the structural shocks that follow a standard normal distribution. $B_i, i = 0, \ldots, 12$ denotes the coefficient matrices. The structural shocks are composed of supply, demand, and residual shocks. Endogenous variables are $Y_t = [\Delta q_t, \Delta y_t, p_t]'$, where $\Delta q_t, \Delta y_t$, and p_t denote the log-differences of metal production, global economic activity indexes, and metal prices.

Data

Real prices of oil and base metals are drawn from the World Bank's Pink Sheet database deflated by the U.S. CPI from the Federal Reserve Economic Data (FRED) database maintained by the St. Louis Federal Reserve Bank. Global industrial production is the production-weighted average of industrial production in 31 advanced economies and 47 EMDEs (unbalanced sample depending on availability) from Haver Analytics. Production data are from the World Bureau of Metal Statistics. The data set uses monthly data from February 1996 to July 2021.

Identification through sign restrictions

The structural representation (4B.1) can be expressed as the reduced-form representation (4B.2) as follows,

$$Y_t = \sum_{i=1}^{12} A_i Y_{t-i} + e_t, \tag{4B.2}$$

where e_t is errors with mean zero, zero autocorrelation, and variance covariance matrix $\Sigma_e = \mathbb{E}[e_t e_t]$. The identification problem consists of finding a mapping from the errors in the reduced-form representation to its structural counterpart:

$$e_t = B_0^{-1} \varepsilon_t \tag{4B.3}$$

Next, the following relation is exploited:

$$\begin{aligned}
\sum_e &= \mathbb{E}[e_t e_t'] = \mathbb{E}[B_0^{-1}\varepsilon_t (B_0^{-1}\varepsilon_t)'] \\
&= B_0^{-1}\mathbb{E}[\varepsilon_t \varepsilon_t'](B_0^{-1})' = B_0^{-1}\sum_\varepsilon (B_0^{-1})' = B_0^{-1}(B_0^{-1})'
\end{aligned} \tag{4B.4}$$

To explore $\tilde{B}$, the estimate of B_0^{-1}, we generate the random orthogonal matrix $QQ' = I$ and consider Cholesky factor $\Sigma_e = PP'$ as follows:

$$\Sigma_e = PQQ'P' = (PQ)(PQ)' \qquad (4B.5)$$

Relating equation (4B.4) to equation (4B.5), we consider the matrix $\widetilde{B} = PQ$ as a valid candidate. $\widetilde{B}$ should also satisfy the sign restrictions in table 4B.1. A positive demand shock on impact will raise the real price of oil or metals and stimulate oil or metal production, but it will lower global economic activity. A positive supply shock will lower oil or metal production on impact. It also will lower global economic activity while increasing the real price of oil or metals.

Note that these commodity demand and supply shocks differ materially from the global demand and supply shocks modeled in Charnavoki and Dolado (2014) and Ha, Kose, and Ohnsorge (2019). In these approaches, an increase in economic activity and commodity prices can reflect either a global demand or global supply shock, depending on movements in global inflation (table 4B.2). Either of these two global shocks drives up commodity demand, consistent with the definition of a commodity demand shock used here and in Kilian and Murphy (2014). Both here and in Kilian and Murphy (2014), a simultaneous increase in economic activity, commodity production, and prices reflects a commodity demand shock. An oil or metal supply shock is associated with an increase in oil or metal prices and a decline in economic activity and commodity production.

We simulate impulse responses based on a candidate $\widetilde{B}$. The candidate $\widetilde{B}$ is retained if the resulting impulse responses meet the sign restrictions, otherwise it is discarded.

The integrated steps are as follows:

1. Estimate an unrestricted VAR and find $\widetilde{\Sigma}_e$. Implement Cholesky decomposition to extract P.

2. Draw a random orthogonal matrix $\widetilde{Q}$ and compute $\widetilde{B} = PQ$.

3. Compute impulse responses using $\widetilde{B}$ calculated in step 2. If all implied impulse response functions satisfy the sign restrictions, retain $\widetilde{B}$. Otherwise discard $\widetilde{B}$.

4. Repeat the first two steps 50,000 times, recording each $\widetilde{B}$ that satisfies the restrictions, and record the corresponding impulse response functions (table 4B.3). About one-fifth of the draws are discarded.

TABLE 4B.1 Sign restrictions on impulse responses

	Supply shocks	Demand shocks
Oil or metal production	−	+
Global economic activity	−	+
Real price of oil or metals	+	+

Source: World bank.

TABLE 4B.2 Comparison of the estimation framework

Author (year)	Structural shocks	Endogenous variables	Endogenous variables	
World Bank (this study)	Sign restriction	Supply; Demand; Residual	Prices (log level); Economic activity (cycle)	Production (log difference)
Kilian and Murphy (2014)	Sign restriction; Elasticity restriction	Supply; Demand; Speculative demand; Residual	Prices (log level); Economic activity (cycle)	Production (percent change); Inventories (difference)
Jacks and Stuermer (2020)	Zero long-run restrictions	Supply; Demand; Commodity specific demand	Prices (log level); Economic activity (percent change)	Production (percent change)
Stuermer (2018)	Zero long-run restrictions	Commodity common supply; Commodity common demand; Commodity specific demand	Prices (log level); Economic activity (percent change)	Production (percent change)

Source: World Bank.

TABLE 4B.3 Impulse responses

Metals	Shocks	Month 1 (Initial impact)	3	6	9	12
World Bank (this study)	Supply	-2.66	-3.71	-3.85	-3.59	-3.63
Copper	Demand	3.05	4.30	4.35	3.80	3.14
	Supply	-1.92	-1.67	-1.48	-1.11	-0.77
Aluminum	Demand	2.30	3.29	3.63	2.97	2.36
	Supply	-2.90	-3.45	-3.95	-4.71	-4.92
Zinc	Demand	3.40	4.14	4.20	3.43	2.61
	Supply	-3.82	-4.77	-5.00	-5.97	-5.38
Nickel	Demand	3.76	4.90	5.32	4.22	3.72
	Supply	-2.55	-3.23	-3.30	-2.60	-2.45
Tin	Demand	2.80	4.03	4.57	5.13	5.08
	Supply	-3.12	-3.70	-3.80	-4.67	-4.58
Lead	Demand	3.40	4.23	4.63	3.80	3.38
	Supply	-4.03	-4.75	-4.28	-3.93	-4.11
Oil	Demand	4.60	5.10	4.48	3.96	2.88
Kilian and Murphy (2014)	Supply	-2.34	-3.38	-1.71	-0.78	-0.53
Oil	Demand	3.16	6.56	7.25	6.59	7.38
Jacks and Stuermer (2020)	Supply	–		–		-0.088
Copper	Demand	–		–		0.082
Stuermer (2018)	Supply	–		–		-0.041
Copper	Demand	–		–		0.078

Source: World Bank.
Note: The impulse responses values of the preceding studies (listed in table 4B.2 or in table 4B.3) are simulated by their appendix codes. The size of shocks is one standard deviation. – = not available.

ANNEX 4C **SVAR: Robustness tests**

The baseline results are tested for robustness to different proxies of economic activity. They include the following measures:

- The global economic conditions index proposed by Baumeister, Korobilis, and Lee (2020), which is the common factor of many monthly activity indicators

- A commodity consumption-weighted average of industrial production for 48 countries

- J.P. Morgan's global manufacturing Purchasing Managers' Index

- J.P. Morgan's global composite Purchasing Managers' Index

The global composite Purchasing Managers' Index is included to capture the role of the services sector in economic activity.

The baseline results are robust to all four alternative proxies. The results yield qualitatively similar impulse response functions in shape and magnitude (figures 4C.1 and 4C.2 for metal prices; figure 4C.3 for oil prices). They depict small dispersion around the mean for all horizons (that is, on impact, after six months, and over a year). Forecast error variance decompositions also show little dispersion for supply and demand, and across all commodities (figure 4C.4). For supply shocks, the maximum range is 17 percent (copper) and the minimum is 8 percent (aluminum, nickel).

FIGURE 4C.1 IRFs for demand shocks with different proxies of economic activity

A. Aluminum

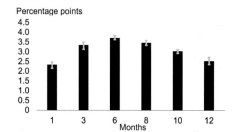

B. Copper

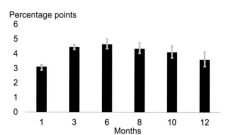

C. Lead

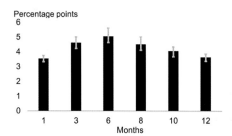

D. Nickel

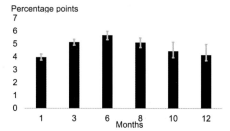

E. Tin

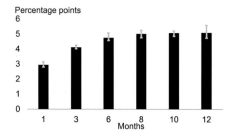

F. Zinc

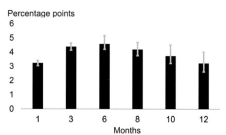

Source: World Bank.
Note: Blue bars show the average impulse responses functions (IRFs) to one-standard-deviation demand shocks at the 1-month, 3-month, 6-month, 8-month, 10-month and 12-month horizons, as estimated from a structural vector autoregression model described in annex 4B using five different proxies for economic activity: global industrial production, the global economic conditions index, commodity-consumption weighted industrial production, the global manufacturing PMI (Purchasing Managers' Index), and the global composite PMI. Yellow whiskers show the range of estimates from the five specifications with the five different proxies for global economic activity.

FIGURE 4C.2 **IRFs for supply shocks with different proxies of economic activity**

A. Aluminum

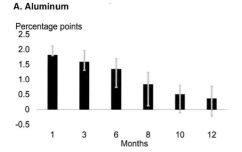

B. Copper

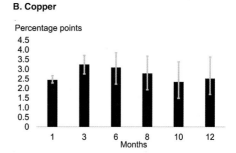

C. Lead

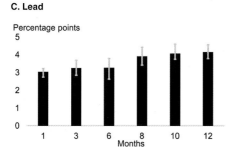

D. Nickel

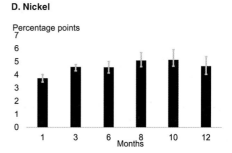

E. Tin

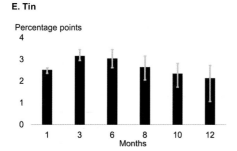

F. Zinc

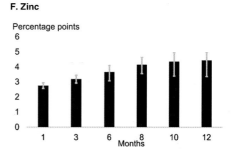

Source: World Bank.
Note: Blue bars show the average impulse responses functions (IRFs) to one-standard-deviation supply shocks at the 1-month, 3-month, 6-month, 8-month, 10-month and 12-month horizons, as estimated from a structural vector autoregression model described in annex 4B using five different proxies for economic activity: global industrial production, the global economic conditions index, commodity-consumption weighted industrial production, the global manufacturing PMI (Purchasing Managers' Index), and the global composite PMI. Yellow whiskers show the range of estimates from the five specifications with the five different proxies for global economic activity.

FIGURE 4C.3 IRFs for demand and supply shocks to economic activity on oil price growth

A. Demand shocks

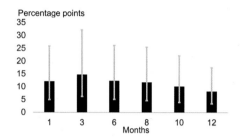

B. Supply shocks

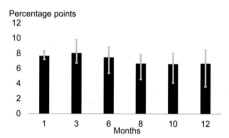

Source: World Bank.
Note: Blue bars show the average contribution of demand and supply shocks to the forecast error variance at the 12-month horizon, as estimated from a structural vector autoregression model described in annex 4B using five different proxies for economic activity: global industrial production, the global economic conditions index, the global manufacturing PMI (Purchasing Managers' Index), and the global composite PMI. Yellow whiskers show the range of estimates from the five specifications with the five different proxies for global economic activity. IRF = impulse response function.

FIGURE 4C.4 FEVDs using different proxies of economic activity

A. Demand shocks

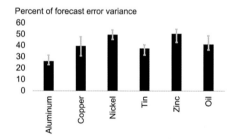

B. Supply shocks

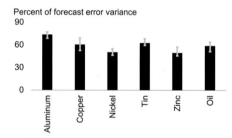

Source: World Bank.
Note: Blue bars show the average contribution of demand and supply shocks to the forecast error variance at the 12-month horizon, as estimated from a structural vector autoregression model described in annex 4B using five different proxies for economic activity: global industrial production, the global economic conditions index, commodity-consumption weighted industrial production (for metals), the global manufacturing PMI (Purchasing Managers' Index), and the global composite PMI. Yellow whiskers show the range of estimates from the five specifications with the five different proxies for global economic activity. FEVD = forecast error variance decomposition.

ANNEX 4D Local projection estimation: Methodology and data

Methodology

The cumulative responses of real output (real GDP) growth at horizon h—denoted by $y_{t+h,j}$—following shocks to oil or metal price growth p_t are estimated using the local projection method of Jordà (2005), with the adjustment developed by Teulings and Zubanov (2014). The increasing popularity of local projection estimations in empirical macroeconomic analysis is mainly due to their simplicity and flexibility. They yield outcomes similar to those of widely used SVAR models (Montiel-Olea and Plagborg-Møller 2021; Plagborg-Møller and Wolf 2021). Local projection estimation is broadly robust to misspecification and nonlinearity, whereas an SVAR produces more efficient estimates (Jordà and Salyer 2003). However, Plagborg-Møller and Wolf (2021) demonstrate that local projection estimations attain efficiency similar to that of the SVAR when p and $T \rightarrow \infty$. Finally, local projection models are not subject to stringent identification schemes, such as the Cholesky zero restriction or similar restrictions used in SVARs.

The model is given by

$$y_{i,t+h} = \alpha_{i,h} + \beta_h p_t + \delta'_h X_{i,t} + \sum_{s=1}^{q} \gamma_{s,h} y_{i,t-s} + \varepsilon_{i,t+h} \tag{4D.1}$$

where $h = 0, 1,..., 4$ is the horizon; $\alpha_{i,h}$ is country i fixed effects; and $\varepsilon_{i,t+h} \sim N(0, \sigma_\varepsilon^2)$ is an independent, identically distributed (idd) error term. The coefficient of interest β_h captures the dynamic multiplier effect (impulse response) of the dependent variable with respect to a shock to oil or metal price growth at time t. Additional control variables, such as global demand (proxied by global industrial production) and domestic consumer price inflation, which are commonly used in SVARs with oil or metal price shocks, are included in an $n \times r$ matrix $X_{i,t}$, while δ_h denotes $n \times r$ matrix parameters. The maximum number of lags for each variable is denoted by $\hat{q}$ and set to 4. The impulse response functions are constructed separately using a sequence of estimates β_h for each horizon based on least-squares technique. Heteroscedasticity- and autocorrelation-consistent standard errors are used to correct for potential effects of heteroscedastic variances and autocorrelation in the error terms. In addition, Driscoll and Kraay (1998) standard errors are used to address cross-sectional and serial correlation.

The local projection estimation allows the investigation of a nonlinear, asymmetric response of domestic economic activity to oil or metal price shocks. Equation (4D.1) is augmented with this nonlinearity:

$$y_{i,t+h} = \alpha_{i,h} + \beta_h^r p_t \times I_t + \beta_h^d p_t \times (1 - I_t) + \delta'_h X_{i,t} + \sum_{s=1}^{q} \gamma_{s,h} y_{i,t-s} + \varepsilon_{i,t+h} \tag{4D.2}$$

where I_t is a dummy variable representing increases in oil or metal prices. Specifically, I_t takes the value of 1 for positive observations of real annual growth rates in metal prices and 0 otherwise. Thus, equation (4D.2) captures an asymmetric response of domestic economic growth (y_t) to rises and declines in oil or metal prices. The output response to oil or metal price increases is captured by β_h^r; the output response to oil or metal price declines is accounted for by β_h^d.

Data

The data set includes annual data for 153 EMDEs for 1970-2019. EMDEs are considered metal exporters if industrial metal exports (in aggregate) account for 5 percent or more of total exports, and the same for copper and aluminum exporters separately. This identification provides 31 industrial metal exporters, of which 14 are copper exporters and 10 aluminum exporters. The sample of industrial metal exporters is smaller than that presented in annex 4A because of data constraints for the regression and the exclusion of iron ore from the aggregate of industrial metal exports. EMDEs are defined as metal importers if their imports of the specific metal account for 0.1 percent or more of total imports. This definition provided 50 metal importers, 31 copper importers, and 38 aluminum importers. Thirty-four EMDEs are considered energy exporting (oil, gas, or coal), as defined in World Bank (2020c); the remainder are considered energy importers. Import and export data come from UN Comtrade and the Observatory of Economic Complexity.

Annual data on real GDP and world per capita GDP are available from the World Bank's World Development Indicators database. Oil and base metal prices data are taken from the World Bank's Pink Sheet database. The oil price is the unweighted average of Dubai, West Texas Intermediate, and Brent prices. Metal prices are calculated by taking a weighted average of aluminum, copper, lead, nickel, tin, and zinc. The real price is obtained by deflating the nominal metal price (in U.S. dollars) with the U.S. CPI from the Federal Reserve Economic Data (FRED) database maintained by the St. Louis Federal Reserve Bank. Real oil and metal prices were transformed into annual growth rates. The control variables comprise global GDP growth and country-specific consumer price inflation. Data on consumer price inflation are taken from the International Monetary Fund's World Economic Outlook database.

Because of limited price data, the estimation of a separate local projections model for metal ore exporters and refined metal exporters is not possible. This is a limitation of the research because metal exporters might specialize in different aspects of exporting metals—as metal ores, as refined metals, or as refined metals embodied in domestic finished goods. A shock affecting the supply of a metal ore could affect metal ore exporters and refined metal exporters differently.

For example, for the Democratic Republic of Congo, exports of refined copper account for more than 50 percent of total exports, whereas exports of copper ore account for about 7 percent. In contrast, for Guinea, exports of bauxite (aluminum ore) account for nearly 50 percent of total exports, but exports of alumina (an intermediate product in the refining process) account for just under 2 percent of exports and exports of refined aluminum are negligible. Finally, China's production of lead ore accounts for nearly half of global lead ore production, but most of this ore is used domestically and embodied in exports of manufactured goods.

References

Abeysinghe, T. 2001. "Estimation of Direct and Indirect Impact of Oil Price on Growth." *Economics Letters* 73 (2): 147-53.

Aguiar, M., and G. Gopinath. 2007. "Emerging Market Business Cycles: The Cycle Is the Trend." *Journal of Political Economy* 115 (1): 69-102.

Alesina A., F. Campante, and G. Tabellini. 2008. "Why Is Fiscal Policy Often Procyclical." *Journal of the European Economic Association* 6 (5): 1006-36.

Baffes, J., and A. Kabundi. 2021. "Commodity Price Shocks: Order within Chaos." Policy Research Working 9792, World Bank, Washington, DC.

Baffes, J., M. A. Kose, F. Ohnsorge, and M. Stocker. 2015. "The Great Plunge in Oil Prices: Causes, Consequences, and Policy Responses." Policy Research Note 1, World Bank, Washington, DC.

Baumeister, C., D. Korobilis, and T. K. Lee. 2022. "Energy Markets and Global Economic Conditions." *Review of Economics and Statistics* 104 (4) 828-44.

Baumeister, C., G. Peersman, and I. Van Robays. 2010. "The Economic Consequences of Oil Shocks: Differences across Countries and Time." In *Inflation in an Era of Relative Price Shocks*, edited by R. Fry, C. Jones, and C. Kent, 91-128. Sydney, Australia: Reserve Bank of Australia and Centre for Macroeconomic Analysis.

Beidas-Strom, S., and A. Pescatori. 2014. "What Has Contributed to Oil Price Volatility?" VoxEU.org, CEPR Policy Portal, December 20, 2014. http://www.voxeu.org/article/oil-price-volatility-and-speculation.

Bernanke, B. 2016. "The Relationship between Stocks and Oil Prices." *Brookings* (blog), February 19, 2016. https://www.brook ings.edu/blog/benbernanke/2016/02/19/the-relationship-between-stocks-and-oil-prices.

Bilgin, D., and R. Ellwanger. 2017. "A Dynamic Factor Model for Commodity Prices." Staff Analytical Notes 17-12, Bank of Canada.

Blanchard, O., and R. Arezki. 2014. "Seven Questions about the Recent Oil Price Slump." *IMFBlog*, December 22, 2014. https://blogs.imf.org/2014/12/22/seven-questions-about-the-recent-oil-price-slump/.

Boer, L., A. Pescatori, and M. Stuermer. 2021. "Energy Transition Metals." IMF Working Paper 243, International Monetary Fund, Washington, DC.

Caldara, D., M. Cavallo, and M. Iacoviello. 2019. "Oil Price Elasticities and Oil Price Fluctuations." *Journal of Monetary Economics* 103 (5): 1-20.

Charnavoki, V., and J. Dolado. 2014. "The Effects of Global Shocks on Small Commodity-Exporting Economies: Lessons from Canada." *American Economic Journal: Macroeconomics* 6 (2): 207-37.

Chiaie, S. D., L. Ferrara, and D. Giannone. 2017. "Common Factors of Commodity Prices." Working Paper 645, Banque de France.

Di Pace, F., L. Juvenal, and I. Petrella. 2021. "Terms-of-Trade Shocks Are Not All Alike." Bank of England Working Paper 901, London.

Driscoll, J., and A. Kraay. 1998. "Consistent Covariance Matrix Estimation with Spatially Dependent Panel Data." *Review of Economics and Statistics* 80 (4): 549-60.

Frankel, J. 2010. "The Natural Resource Curse: A Survey." NBER Working Paper 15836, National Bureau of Economic Research, Cambridge, MA.

Frankel, J. 2011. "How Can Commodity Exporters Make Fiscal and Monetary Policy Less Procyclical? HKS Faculty Research Working Paper 11-015, John F. Kennedy School of Government, Harvard University.

Frankel, J. 2018. "Monetary Regimes to Cope with Volatile Commodity Export Prices: Two Proposals." In *Rethinking the Macroeconomics of Resource-Rich Countries,* edited by A. Arezki, R. Boucekkine, J. Frankel, M. Laksaci, and R. van der Ploeg, 45-54. Vox eBooks. https://cepr.org/publications/books-and-reports/rethinking-macroeconomics-resource-rich-countries.

Gervais, O. 2019. "How Oil Supply Shocks Affect the Global Economy: Evidence from Local Projections." Bank of Canada Staff Discussion Paper 6, Ottawa, Canada.

Ha, J., M. A. Kose, and F. Ohnsorge, eds. 2019. *Inflation in Emerging and Developing Economies: Evolution, Drivers, and Policies.* Washington, DC: World Bank.

Hamilton, J. 2015. "What's Driving the Price of Oil Down?" *Econbrowser* (blog), January 15, 2015. https://econbrowser.com/archives/2015/01/whats-driving-the-price-of-oil-down-2.

Helbling, T. 2012. "Commodities in Boom." In *Finance and Development.* June. Washington, DC: International Monetary Fund.

Jacks, D., K. O'Rourke, and J. Williamson. 2011. "Commodity Price Volatility and World Market Integration since 1700." *Review of Economics and Statistics* 93 (3): 800-13.

Jacks, D., and M. Stuermer. 2020. "What Drives Commodity Price Booms and Busts?" *Energy Economics* 85: 104035.

Jacks, D., and M. Stuermer. 2021. "Dry Bulk Shipping and the Evolution of Maritime Transport Costs, 1850–2020." *Australian Economic History Review* 61 (2): 204-22.

Jordà, Ò. 2005. "Estimation and Inference of Impulse Responses by Local Projections." *American Economic Review* 95 (1): 161-82.

Jordà, Ò., and K. D. Salyer. 2003. "The Response of Term Rates to Monetary Policy Uncertainty." *Review of Economic Dynamics* 6 (4): 941-62.

Kabundi, A. N., and F. Ohnsorge. 2020. "Implications of Cheap Oil for Emerging Markets." Policy Research Working Paper 9403, World Bank, Washington, DC.

Kilian, L. 2009. "Not All Oil Price Shocks Are Alike: Disentangling Demand and Supply Shocks in the Crude Oil Market." *American Economic Review* 99 (3): 1053-69.

Kilian, L., and D. P. Murphy. 2014. "The Role of Inventories and Speculative Trading in the Global Market for Crude Oil." *Journal of Applied Econometrics* 29 (3): 454-78.

Kilian, L., and C. Park. 2009. "The Impact of Oil Price Shocks on the U.S. Stock Market." *International Economic Review* 59 (2): 1267-89.

Kose, M. A. 2002. "Explaining Business Cycles in Small Open Economies: How Much Do World Prices Matter?" *Journal of International Economics* 56 (2): 299–327.

Kose, M. A., S. Sugawara, and M. Terrones. 2020. "Global Recessions." Policy Research Working Paper 9172, World Bank, Washington, DC.

Lippi, F., and A. Nobili. 2012. "Oil and the Macroeconomy: A Quantitative Structural Analysis." *Journal of the European Economic Association* 10 (5): 1059-83.

Medas, P., and D. Zakharova. 2009. "Primer on Fiscal Analysis in Oil-Producing Countries." IMF Working Paper 56, International Monetary Fund, Washington, DC.

Mohaddes, K., and M. Raissi. 2017. "Oil Prices and the Global Economy: Is It Different This Time Around?" *Energy Economics* 65 (June): 315-25.

Mohaddes, K., and M. Raissi. 2019. "The U.S. Oil Supply Revolution and the Global Economy." *Empirical Economics* 57 (5): 1515-46.

Montiel-Olea, J. L., and M. Plagborg-Møller. 2021. "Local Projection Inference Is Simpler and More Robust Than You Think." *Econometrica* 89 (4): 1789-823.

OECD (Organisation for Economic Co-operation and Development). 2019. "Measuring Distortions in International Markets: The Aluminum Value Chain." Trade Policy Paper 218, OECD Publishing, Paris.

Peersman, G. 2005. "What Caused the Early Millennium Slowdown? Evidence Based on Vector Autoregressions." *Journal of Applied Econometrics* 20 (2): 185-207.

Peersman, G., and R. Straub. 2006. "Putting the New Keynesian Model to a Test." IMF Working Paper 135, International Monetary Fund, Washington, DC.

Peersman, G., and I. Van Robays. 2012. "Cross-Country Differences in the Effects of Oil Shocks." *Energy Economics* 34 (5): 1532-47.

Plagborg-Møller, M., and C. K. Wolf. 2021. "Local Projections and VARs Estimate the Same Impulse Responses." *Econometrica* 89 (2): 955-80.

Richaud, C., A. Mendes Galego, F. Ayivodji, S. Matta, and S. Essl. 2019. "Fiscal Vulnerabilities in Commodity Exporting Countries and the Role of Fiscal Policy." MTI Discussion Paper 15, World Bank, Washington, DC.

Schwerhoff, G., and M. Stuermer. 2019. "Non-Renewable Resources, Extraction Technology and Endogenous Growth." Working Paper 1506, Federal Reserve Bank of Dallas.

Sheng, X., R. Gupta, and Q. Ji. 2020. "The Impacts of Structural Oil Shocks on Macroeconomic Uncertainty: Evidence from a Large Panel of 45 Countries." *Energy Economics* 91 (1): 104940.

Stocker, M., J. Baffes, M. Some, D. Vorisek, and C. Wheeler. 2018. "The 2014-16 Oil Price Collapse in Retrospect. Sources and Implications." Policy Research Working Paper 8419, World Bank, Washington, DC.

Stuermer, M. 2017. "Industrialization and the Demand for Mineral Commodities." *Journal of International Money and Finance* 76 (September): 16-27.

Stuermer, M. 2018. "150 Years of Boom and Bust: What Drives Mineral Commodity Prices?" *Macroeconomic Dynamics* 22 (3): 702-17.

Torvik, R. 2018. "Oil Prices and Exchange Rate: Optimal Monetary Policy for Oil-Exporting Countries." In *Rethinking the Macroeconomics of Resource-Rich Countries,* edited by A. Arezki, R. Boucekkine, J. Frankel, M. Laksaci, and R. van der Ploeg, 65-74. Vox eBooks. https://cepr.org/publications/books-and-reports/rethinking-macroeconomics-resource-rich-countries.

Teulings, C., and N. Zubanov. 2014. "Is Economic Recovery a Myth? Robust Estimation of Impulse Responses." *Journal of Applied Econometrics* 29 (3): 497-514.

UNCTAD (United Nations Conference on Trade and Development). 2021. *State of Commodity Dependence.* Geneva: UNCTAD.

U.S. Geological Survey. 2014. "Mineral Commodity Summaries 2014." United States Geological Survey, Reston, VA.

U.S. Geological Survey. 2019. "Mineral Commodity Summaries 2019." United States Geological Survey, Reston, VA.

U.S. Geological Survey. 2021. "Mineral Commodity Summaries 2021." United States Geological Survey, Reston, VA.

U.S. Geological Survey. 2022. "Mineral Commodity Summaries 2022." United States Geological Survey, Reston, VA.

World Bank. 2015. *Global Economic Prospects: The Global Economy in Transition.* June. Washington, DC: World Bank.

World Bank. 2020a. *Commodities Market Outlook: Persistence of Commodity Shocks.* October. Washington, DC: World Bank.

World Bank. 2020b. *Commodities Market Outlook: Implications of COVID-19 for Commodities.* April. Washington, DC: World Bank.

World Bank. 2020c. *Global Economic Prospects.* June. Washington, DC: World Bank.

World Bank. 2021. *Commodities Market Outlook: Urbanization and Commodity Demand.* October. Washington, DC: World Bank.

World Bank. 2022. *Global Economic Prospects.* January. Washington, DC: World Bank.